# Searching for the Self

# Searching for the Self

Classic Stories, Christian Scripture, and the Quest for Personal Identity

ADRIAN T. SMITH

WIPF & STOCK · Eugene, Oregon

SEARCHING FOR THE SELF
Classic Stories, Christian Scripture, and the Quest for Personal Identity

Copyright © 2018 Adrian T. Smith. All rights reserved. Except for brief quotations in critical publications or reviews, no part of this book may be reproduced in any manner without prior written permission from the publisher. Write: Permissions, Wipf and Stock Publishers, 199 W. 8th Ave., Suite 3, Eugene, OR 97401.

Wipf & Stock
An Imprint of Wipf and Stock Publishers
199 W. 8th Ave., Suite 3
Eugene, OR 97401

www.wipfandstock.com

PAPERBACK ISBN: 978-1-4982-9835-3
HARDCOVER ISBN: 978-1-4982-4887-7
EBOOK ISBN: 978-1-4982-9836-0

Manufactured in the U.S.A.　　　　　　　　　　　　　　　　　　　　　　JANUARY 9, 2018

To Avery ("Li'l Monk")

# Contents

*List of Illustrations* | ix
*Preface* | xi

Part 1: In the Beginning Was the Story

    Spoiler Alert 1 (Overview of Part 1) | 3

    1    Spin the Bottle | 5

    2    A Graveyard Shift | 11

    3    Reinventing the Wheel | 18

    4    Cattle Prods | 33

    5    Identity Theft | 51

    6    Sleeping Beauty Awakes | 68

Part 2: Stories Are . . . and Stories Do . . .

    Spoiler Alert 2 (Overview of Part 2) | 77

    7    Somebody Wanted Because But So | 78

    8    The Seven Pillars of Wisdom | 92

    9    Alpha and Omega | 104

    10    Finding Neverland | 114

    11    The Purple Rose of Cairo | 126

    12    End-User Responsibility | 145

Part 3: How Stories Change Lives

    Spoiler Alert 3 (Overview of Part 3) | 159

    13    Don Quixote Rides Again | 161

    14    A Self-Image Problem | 180

    15    According to Script | 193

    16    A Better Life | 206

## Contents

17  American Graffiti | 210
18  Selves under Construction (1): Losing the Plot | 224
19  Selves under Construction (2): Healing Plots | 233
20  Selves under Construction (3): A Work in Progress | 240
21  Twelfth Night | 254

Part 4: The World is a Dark Place—Stories Bring Light

Spoiler Alert 4: (Overview of Part 4) | 271
22  A Clean Slate (John 13) | 274
23  Redefining Your Personal Space (Hebrews) | 279
24  The Men Who Would Be King (Mark's Gospel) | 287
25  Out-of-Body Experiences (Ezekiel 1) | 295

Part 5: Sequels and Backstory

Spoiler Alert 5 (Overview of Part 5) | 305
26  Artists Don't Borrow—They Steal (a select annotated bibliography) | 306
27  From Seed to Tree | 314

*Bibliography* | 325

# List of Illustrations

Figure 1. Plot Structure | 82
Figure 2. Jewish Eschatology | 115
Figure 3. Christian Eschatology | 115

# Preface

## TWO DISCLAIMERS

Disclaimers. Who needs them? Certainly not you, the generous-spirited reader. Sadly, some read with a spirit of fear, which hinders generosity of spirit. This preface briefly addresses two fears some (Christian) readers may have.

*First*, throughout my book, I interweave real-life stories, fictional stories, and biblical stories. Does my emphasis on "story" negate the historical quality of biblical narrative?

The short answer is no. Fiction writers and historians both use the same formal techniques in plotting events. Both tell stories. The difference: historians have real events behind their text.[1]

I love to recite the Apostles' Creed; here are some key lines: "Born of the Virgin Mary; suffered under Pontius Pilate, was crucified, died and was buried . . . The third day he rose again from the dead." This creed tells a story—of real historical events.

*Second*, throughout my book, I interact positively with the emerging discipline of narrative psychology. Some (Christian) readers may wonder if any good can come from any branch of "secular psychology."[2]

I am not a psychologist; I am an ordained minister of the gospel. Accordingly, I believe that the Good Shepherd has more wisdom for healing the soul (*psyche* in Greek) than secular psychology possesses.

The gospel is "good news"—a story that reshapes our misshapen stories. To understand story, I utilize the wisdom of literary critics.

As a gospel minister, I want to know what kinds of stories my parishioners are living. If narrative psychology can help me inventory the stories people live by, I will gladly (yet critically) make cautious use of its "data."[3]

---

1. For discussion of how biblical narrative is both artistic and historical, see Long, *Art of Biblical History*.

2. For what it's worth, narrative psychology tends to view itself as in revolt against mainstream secular psychology. See McLeod, "Storytelling in Postpsychological Counseling," 11–27.

3. For an example of such descriptive "data," see McAdams, *Redemptive Self*.

## TWO PARADOXES

When you are finished reading this book, you may well have a couple of good questions. *First*, you might perhaps ask, *if story is as essential to humanity as this author claims, why are so many folk ignorant of the role played by narrative in shaping their identity*? Good question! My short answer would be the analogy from field workers in linguistics. When linguists write a grammar of a particular language, they are often tempted to ask a native speaker to explain the meaning and usage of a particular grammatical idiom. The linguist is almost invariably disappointed. They find the native speaker unable to explain their own language use! In other words, one can be a competent user of language, and virtually unaware of how language works! Likewise, one can be profoundly shaped by stories, and virtually unaware of their shaping power. For such readers, my book may function as "story grammar."

*Second*, you may perhaps ask, *If narrative is as fundamental as this author claims, why doesn't he merely tell stories, and abandon expository discourse entirely*? Again, good question! Actually, my book does include a fair number of stories. But I also interact with those stories using expository discourse. Allow me to explain why.

In my seminary classes, I use the mantra, "Everything is narrative, but narrative isn't everything." Everything in life has a narrative dimension, but not everything reduces to narrative. Even stories include non-narrative dimensions. Think of a story's setting. The setting often includes much material of a purely descriptive nature, where nothing actually happens.

In our late modern context, many people still process using discourse forms other than narrative. To illustrate: "narrative preachers" like to present their sermons as pure storytelling. But their congregations typically respond with: "Please will you *explain* your stories?"

In my book, I accuse modern Western thought of downplaying stories in favor of more abstract, analytical thinking. However, in pushing back against modernity, I don't wish to throw out the baby with the bathwater. I believe that critical and analytical faculties, honed by modernity, can be useful in reflecting on what narrative is and what it does. I don't wish to discard the tools bequeathed by five hundred years of Western science and philosophy. Rather, I wish to repurpose them as servants for understanding story.

Stephen Crites observes that thought and imagination find outlets other than narrative, and for a good reason.[4] The human mind needs rest from the unceasing temporal flow inherent to story. Non-narrative forms of expression—painting and sculpture, philosophical analysis and abstraction—offer us rest from the stream of time into which narrative plunges us. Crites goes on to argue that Western culture ran into problems when we made resting from narrative permanent—by trying to remain at rest, in abstract analysis, on the riverbank of narrative time.

I agree with Crites. Our culture needs a healthy re-integration of narrative and non-narrative modes of thinking. My book attempts to embody such integration.

---

4. Crites, "Narrative Quality of Experience," 84–88.

## NOTES OF THANKS

- To editors Sue Lutz and Barbara Juliani, for extensive critical feedback on earlier versions of this work. Although the final product is not the book they hoped for, my book is immensely better because of their input.
- To publisher Karen Teears, for graciously releasing me from my earlier contract—and thereby enabling me to pursue my own vision for this book.
- To Wipf and Stock Publishers, for their philosophy of publishing "based on the merits of content rather than marketability."
- To Matt Wimer and Brian Palmer (of Wipf and Stock), for their management of the production of this book.
- To my copy editor at Wipf and Stock, Caleb Shupe, for his diligent interaction with my manuscript. (Any errors that remain are, of course, my responsibility.)
- To my wife Dawn, for imagining a "book that must be written," and for patiently awaiting its birth.

## NOTES ON TRANSLATIONS

Throughout this book, the author's own translations (from the original Hebrew, Aramaic, and Greek) have been used whenever material from the Old Testament, New Testament, or Apocrypha is quoted.

\* \* \* \* \*

# PART 1

In the Beginning Was the Story

# Spoiler Alert 1
(Overview of Part 1)

*Seeing our lives as stories is more than a powerful metaphor.*
*It is how experience presents itself to us.*
*By better understanding story, and our role as characters,*
*we can live more purposefully the kind of life that will give our own story meaning.*[1]

*If our society as a whole is directionless,*
*it is because we have abandoned many of the defining stories of our past*
*without finding adequate replacements.*[2]

THESE QUOTES CONVENIENTLY SUMMARIZE two of the big concerns introduced in Part 1 of this book.

We begin with two chapters of narrative vignettes, of ordinary people trying to make sense of their lives in terms of story. Chapter 1 features five of my friends, telling stories that express who they are. Personal identity is shaped by story. Chapter 2 narrates a key episode from my own story—my "call" to write this book.

Chapter 3 offers the reader a "starter-kit" for constructing their own personal life narrative. Chapter 4 develops this, in the form of structured diagnostic questions designed to surface one's personal story.

Chapter 5 changes gears. We connect the loss of personal identity in (post)modern life with the loss of adequate stories to live out of. In broad strokes, we sketch out the causes behind the demise of grand narratives in postmodern society.

Chapter 6 offers a real glimmer of hope in this darkness. We briefly retell the story of the rebirth of narrative interpretations of Christianity. Reclaiming the Bible as God's "metanarrative" offers us a big umbrella to shelter us from the chilling winds of postmodernity.

---

1. Taylor, *Healing Power of Stories*, 4.
2. Ibid., 3.

Part 1: In the Beginning Was the Story

\* \* \* \* \*

In terms of "story logic," we might say that Part 1 of my book situates the reader in act one of a story (i.e., a *call*, received in a *setting*, using the terms of classical story design).

The "call" invites the reader to search for meaning and purpose via finding the story of your life. The call comes through the vignettes of chapters 1–2, the tool-kit of chapter 3, and the diagnostic questions of chapter 4.

Our discussion of "setting" exposes the antagonist—the rejection of metanarratives in postmodernity (chapter 5). Our "setting" also introduces an ally, in the form of the recent recovery of narrative understandings of the Christian faith (chapter 6).

\* \* \* \* \*

My basic thesis in this book: story is more basic than we realize.

"In the beginning, God created the heavens and the earth" (Gen 1:1). "In the beginning was the Word [*logos* in Greek]" (John 1:1). With a little poetic license, one might say, "In the beginning was the *story*."

Not literally, of course (although the Greek word *logos* can refer to narrative, e.g., Acts 1:1). Rather, God's wisdom, the agent of creation, embeds stories in the world.[3] In Genesis 1, creation results from a story: God overcoming and ordering chaos, through the divine word.

John's Gospel reveals creation as a *cosmic parable*, telling the story of the incarnate wisdom. Vine branches producing fruit, telling the story of Jesus and the church (John 15:1–10). Grains of wheat, buried in the ground, telling the story of the life-giving death of Christ (John 12:23–26).

\* \* \* \* \*

---

3. On *logos* meaning divine wisdom (and other connotations of the term), see Beasley-Murray, *John*, 6–10.

# 1

# Spin the Bottle

**YOU CAN'T MAKE THIS STUFF UP**

"Who will go first?" Following dinner, five close friends sat in comfortable chairs in my den. Refilling everyone's wine glass, I had thrown out a question: "Can any of you name the story that tells who you are?" One or two blank looks. "Do you mean a book or a film, or do you mean the story of my life?" Actually, either or both were fine by me.[1]

"Okay, then, I'll go first." Narrator #1 paused to compose her thoughts. She had been noticing the distinctively different behaviors of the two family dogs, Dreyfus and CP. Dreyfus, our "first-born son," was manifesting a strong sense of entitlement as he protected his space on top of the ottoman. CP, by contrast, was honoring her daddy by nuzzling down next to me on the sofa. Dreyfus had cost us seven hundred and fifty dollars from the breeder as a puppy. We had rescued CP from the animal shelter.

"I'm like CP," said Narrator #1. "I'm a rescued dog. I don't even want to imagine what kind of life I would now be living if someone hadn't rescued me. Viewing my life in terms of rescue makes me grateful. I'm thankful for every day I live. CP is grateful; Dreyfus isn't."

A noise outside the front door startled CP, so she jumped down from the sofa and started circling nervously on the floor. "Why is CP going around and round in tiny circles?" asked Narrator #2. "CP was a breeder dog in a puppy mill. She spent her first four years confined inside a four-foot-by-six-foot crate. Whenever she got nervous, all she could do was circle and circle inside the crate."

"I can relate to CP," said Narrator #2. "My childhood story still shapes how I live. When I was young, my parents were always fighting late into the night. I used to cower upstairs with my older sister, listening to our parents yelling. Once, in the middle of a fight, Mom and Dad *both* left the house in a whirlwind of rage. Two little girls were abandoned—terrified of an impending divorce."

"As I grew older, my life became a search for security. To feel secure, I need to be in control. To be honest, sometimes I think my need for control has started to control me!

---

1. For a popular introduction to the benefits of viewing your life as a story, see Kamps, "Story That Can Change Your Life."

## Part 1: In the Beginning Was the Story

Like, every day, I religiously pack a healthy lunch for my husband to take to work. He was recently diagnosed as pre-diabetic. If I don't pack him lunch, I worry he will eat at Burger King, get diabetes, and die young, leaving me alone with four kids."

"My story is a bit more complex," said Narrator #3. "It's not easy for me to tell." We refilled the wine glasses, while she rehearsed the story in her mind. "I grew up in the mid-West, you know, a typical Christian upbringing. But when I went away to college, I started dating this guy who said he was an agnostic. Anyway . . . at the end of the first semester, he date-raped me. I blamed myself for it, and self-loathing sent me spiraling. Hell, since I couldn't be the Christian I was raised to be, why not p-a-r-t-y!"

"But towards the end of my freshman year, someone gave me one of Hannah Hurnard's book, which is sort of an allegory of the Good Shepherd. Anyway, there is a character called Much-Afraid, and there is an episode where the Good Shepherd shows her this ugly barren mountainside, all scorched and blackened by fire. Then he tells her, 'I let this happen; but I will make it beautiful.' That image re-awakened hope for me."

"The book that changed your life," said Narrator #4, "I can so relate to that. When I was nine years old, I started reading folktales by the Brothers Grimm. A lot of gore and violence—a window into a world I had never experienced. But it was safe—contained between two covers, and I could always close the book."

"Soon after, my dad started physically abusing my mum. Three years later, my mother took a shotgun and killed herself. The Brothers Grimm had prepared me to cope with the reality of violence."

Everyone in the room already knew about the suicide, but the wisdom of folktales came as a revelation.

"Is it cheating to pick more than one book?" asked Narrator #5. No one objected. "I have to pick two very different books, because there are two forces pulling me in opposite directions."

"When I was a teenager, my sister was diagnosed with terminal cancer. Eventually, she became bedridden. So, our family got into this ritual of spending every evening in her room, reading stories aloud together. Near the end of her life, we were reading this diary of a guy who hiked the Appalachian trail—kind of a spiritual journey, really. His only companion on the journey was his dog. Anyway, we were getting close to finishing the book, when one evening my dad read the scene where the dog dies. I rushed out of the room and wept uncontrollably. My sister was soon to die, and that book opened the door so I could let out my grief."

"A month later, my sister passed away. I started reading this collection of biographies of great leaders—guys like Roosevelt and Churchill. There was this common thread to their lives: young boys endure extreme hardship, yet resolve to overcome by sheer force of will. The death of my sister was followed by my father's own battle with cancer. And then his sudden financial catastrophe, due to the collapse of the Dallas real estate market. I resolved to overcome—by sheer force of will. In high school, I over-achieved. I won academic decathlon, and was champion of the debate team."

"But you know what? I'm beginning to realize this whole Roosevelt/Churchill thing has been really unhealthy for me. Ever since high school, I've been using achievement to mask my grief."

The room had one of those silences you want to fill, but lack the right words. Narrator #5 concluded, "It can take a long time to figure out why a particular story so grabs your heart."

\* \* \* \* \*

All these conversations with the five narrators really happened one evening in my house. Like I said, you can't make this stuff up. Let's press the pause button here, and reflect on these five personal narratives.

Several Christmases ago, Starbucks put a "proverb" on their (recyclable) cardboard sleeves that absorb the heat from their coffee cups. The proverb read, "Stories are gifts. Share." As the scribe of the five stories, I was overwhelmed by the gifts my friends gave me that evening. Their candid autobiographical snapshots have given me much wisdom that I have attempted to use in the writing of this book.

As you continue through this book, I hope you will have "déjà vu" moments, as many of the themes from Narrators #1–5 get recycled in my exploration of how stories change lives. By way of a sneak preview, I will mention the following dimensions of the five thumbnail autobiographies:

- Personal *identity* has a dense narrative texture.
- *Inciting incidents* (abandonment; abuse; bereavement; etc.) often set the trajectory for our life.[2]
- *Archetypal* plotlines and images (deliverance; search; renewal; etc.) can provide handy summaries of our biographies.
- *Literature* (not to mention film) exposes us to the archetypes, and allows us to explore unfamiliar worlds of human experience.
- Different and conflicting stories may compete to shape us, in a *clash of narratives*.[3]

Simplifying in the extreme, this book explores this equation: *life = story*.

\* \* \* \* \*

Have you ever considered the *benefits* of viewing your life as story? Allow me to inventory some of these benefits, as we round out this chapter.

---

[2]. The term "inciting incident," used by students of narrative, refers to that event which disturbs the earlier equilibrium of the protagonist, propelling them into a new storyline. See McKee, *Story*, 181–207.

[3]. For the metaphor of clashing or colliding narratives, I am indebted to Stroup, *Promise of Narrative Theology*, 170–75. Cf. the discussion of "battling narratives" in Abbott, *Introduction to Narrative*, 152–53.

Part 1: In the Beginning Was the Story

**BUFFALO SOLDIERS**

If you can own and articulate your personal life story, you may gain multiple dimensions of psychological health. Some of these boons were implicit in the testimonies of Narrators #1–5 retold above. Here is a fuller list:

### A Sense of Order and Stability

Victory over the chaos of random experience. This, most basically, is the gift conferred by stories. In the 2013 film *Saving Mr. Banks*, Walt Disney (played by Tom Hanks) says, "This is what we storytellers do: we restore order with imagination."

### Strong Personal Identity

The Bob Marley reggae classic "Buffalo Soldier" eloquently testifies to the power of story to define who you are. The song's title references the regiments of African-American soldiers formed in the nineteenth century. Marley celebrates their courageous ascendency over racial prejudice as a pointer to a positive contemporary black identity. "If you know your history," the message goes, you would not have to question your identity.

Story preserves the "I," whatever upheavals the past, present, and future may bring. Story integrates the "Yin and Yang" (shade and sunlight) of our personalities, explaining how opposite elements unite in one self. Story supplies our self-image by crystallizing our role in a plotline.

### Guidance

Our self-image (role in a plotline) impacts the decisions we take. Would the character that I say I am choose X or Y in a given situation?

Plotline metaphors also constrain choices. We speak of our life story in terms of roots, paths or journeys, and destinies. Roots tether us. Paths have boundaries on their left and right. Destinies invite an important question—will decision X or Y most likely lead me to my goal?

### Self-Understanding

Life stories locate recurrent problems and weaknesses, as a first step toward healing and change. Specialists in trauma-care advise us to stop asking victims, "What is wrong with you?" and start asking, "What happened to you?"

## Hope

By exploring the many narrative layers of our past, we can find life-affirming wisdom amidst experiences of death (figurative or literal). Finding a positive ending to our story can defang the negativity of previous scenes.

## Health

Alternative medicine (don't let the phrase spook you!) affirms the multiple health benefits of owning and telling your life story.[4] Here are a few of the benefits:

- *Medical Health:* When we hold our story tightly inside us (for reasons of fear or shame), we increase the physical symptoms of stress in our body. When we let our story out, we experience relief—emotionally, and even at the cellular level.[5]
- *Social Health:* Sharing your story with others builds relationships and community. Our listeners can empathize with our struggles and find common ground in the scenes and storylines of our personal narrative. The act of storytelling itself creates bonds between teller and listeners.
- *Psychological Health:* "Children . . . are more resilient and happy and rebound faster from stress when they know their family stories. They know that they're part of something that's bigger than themselves that people in their family have kept going."[6]

## Dignifying the Mundane

Viewing our trivial moments as scenes in a classic story brings meaning and purpose to our daily routine. The glory belonging to epic narratives can shine on our dullest experiences, if only we have eyes to see.

Allow me to offer an illustration (forgive the allegorical quaintness). Washing dishes by hand—a task still undertaken by those who cannot afford a dishwasher. A tedious and meaningless job, right? Well, I had a seminary professor who, at one phase of his life, had to wash dishes by hand. (Junior professors don't make a ton of money.) He once wrote a book on the rituals of the priesthood in ancient Israel. The priests were key players in an epic drama to preserve purity against the entropy of impurity. For ancient Israel, purity symbolized life and order, impurity symbolized death and chaos.

One evening, at the kitchen sink, washing dishes by hand, my professor had an epiphany: "I am separating the clean from the unclean! So," he asked himself, "does my dishwashing train me in maintaining order? Does it prepare me for a bigger part in a struggle against disorder in the world?"

---

4. Fertig, "Healing Power of Story," 18–20.
5. Ibid., 18.
6. Kim Weitkamp, quoted in ibid., 20.

Part 1: In the Beginning Was the Story

## Transcendence

If we can find a universal plotline that meshes with our personal narrative, we may gain access to the transcendent, and deliverance from the prison-house of individual isolation. We can find meaning and purpose, and a home in the cosmos, by locating ourselves within a bigger story.

\* \* \* \* \*

As you journey through this book, I hope to unfold the benefits of owning your life story. The next chapter opens by illustrating the healing power of narrative, via a transformative episode from my own life story. The chapter will also outline more of the working assumptions behind this book.

# 2

# A Graveyard Shift

## ST. ANDREW'S CHURCHYARD

"Adrian, your father passed away this evening. The ambulance came and took him from the nursing home to the hospital, but he never woke up." A quavering message from my mother on the voicemail. By pressing the button marked *play*, I had entered the irreversible. Not that I really believed he was dead, even though I knew it was true.

"Flight BA192, Dallas to Heathrow, is now boarding. Please make sure your baggage fits in the overhead bin, or under the seat in front of you." My transatlantic flight granted me nine hours of headspace, as I returned to my homeland for my father's funeral. "Black Dog" was the name Winston Churchill gave to depression. Lurking, self-sustaining, ready to pounce. Shoving my suitcase into the overhead bin, I thought I heard the Black Dog growl.

The logistics of funerals kept him in the background. So much to prepare, so little time for pondering. Find a cleric to conduct the funeral. Book the church for Thursday afternoon. Put the obituary in the paper.

"I am the resurrection and the life," said Jesus. "Whoever believes in me—even though he has died, he will live."[1] Using the funeral liturgy of the Book of Common Prayer, we buried my father in the churchyard of St. Andrew's Minster. Father had worshipped there, until the progress of his Parkinson's disease made the walk up the hill impossible, and the words of the Book of Common Prayer unintelligible.

The next day, I ascended the hilltop and sat in the graveyard of St. Andrew's Minster. The church had thoughtfully provided a bench for quiet reflection. From the bench, your panoramic gaze takes in the gravestones, and then the steep hill that sweeps down to farmers' fields. Upon these fields, almost one thousand years ago, the Danish army of King Canute slaughtered the Saxon army. The Danish king immediately built a church on the site of the battle, so that prayers might be offered for the souls of the slain.

Sitting in the churchyard, my gaze moved like a camera over the gravestones, over the battlefield, as if drawn by the sun's brilliant reflection bouncing off the surface of the river at the foot of the valley. Bright sky; Black Dog. With no more busyness to keep me

---

1. John 11:25–26.

busy, depression came so close I could smell its dank breath. Where was the prayer for the slain when you needed one for your own soul?

"Why art thou pressed down, O my soul?"[2] A good question. "You say you believe in the healing power of narrative? Physician, heal thyself (Luke 4:23)!" How? "Can you dig down into why you are slipping into depression?"

Was it really that I missed my father? With illnesses like Parkinson's or Alzheimer's, the patient "goes away" long before they die. On my last visit to his care home, the nurse had propped him up in the bed—but did he know it was me, his son, who was talking to him and praying for him?

"Why are you slipping into depression?" I missed my father, but not for the dynamics of the relationship. What I missed went something like this: As long as Father was alive, I could pretend I was a young man. Even though I was in my late forties, if I had a father, then I (by definition) was a son; and if my father was of "the older generation," then I (by definition) must belong to "the younger generation." As my swirling thoughts crystallized in my brain, their musical accompaniment became the words of a well-known generational anthem by The Who.

My father belonged to Tom Brokaw's "greatest generation"—those who fought in the Second World War, and thereafter rebuilt their nations. Father was duty and responsibility personified. For many years, I never had to fill out a tax form; I just handed it to Dad. His Parkinson's had changed my relationship to the taxman, but not my sense of belonging to the younger generation.

The message on my father's gravestone read: "Your protracted adolescence has ended and must end!" How much I had loved being a grad student! How long I prolonged my PhD program! But now I was a professor, in my late forties. The death of my father was the death of my youth.

"You say you believe in the healing power of narrative? Physician, heal thyself!" Sitting on the bench in the graveyard of St. Andrew's Minster, I prayed a prayer for my own dead soul. Scanning inside my head, I searched for a story outside myself to make sense of myself.

Memory retrieval resembles lowering a bucket on a long rope into a deep well, believing (but not knowing) that there is water at the bottom. Then the metal bucket pierces a pool of water, and you begin to pull. Here is the story that surfaced.

In my late twenties, I had read a book on biblical symbolism by a scholar named James Jordan. From the back of his book, Jordan stared out from his photograph. His full-length, raven-black beard made him look like a young Orthodox patriarch. Twenty years later, one month before my father's death, Jordan came to speak at my seminary. His beard had turned white.

"We tend to think of the Bible as a story of redemption," said Jordan.[3] "But that is only one of the plotlines. Within the Old and New Testaments, we may read a story of victory over evil. We may also read a storyline that revolves around growth into maturity."

The speaker had my attention. He continued, "In the Old Testament storyline, the phases of Israel's leadership develop from priesthood, to royal sage, to prophet. The story

---

2. Ps 42:5.

3. This and subsequent quotes from Jordan are my paraphrases based on my memory of his lecture.

arc, from phase to phase, involves increasing freedom and responsibility for the leader. Priests—their responsibility is limited. They must concentrate on strict conformity to the Levitical code. The priesthood symbolizes the childhood phase of Israel's story.

"Kings—these royal sages must exercise their discretion. They need wisdom to extend the Law of Moses to cases not spelt out in the Pentateuch. The monarchy symbolizes the young-adult phase of Israel's story.

"Finally, the Prophets. Rooted in the strict conformity of the priesthood, and the maturing wisdom of the monarchy, the prophet nevertheless transcends these earlier phases. The prophet develops his own God-given vision. The prophetic era symbolizes the mature-adult phase of Israel's story."

Now, I happen to be a New Testament scholar by trade. But, listening to Jordan, I immediately thought of the plotlines of maturation articulated in 1 Corinthians 12:8–13 or Galatians 4:1–7 or Ephesians 4:11–16.

Jordan's lecture moved toward his conclusion. "The coming-of-age storyline of the Old Testament's institutional leadership may offer guidance to those of us whose vocation is teaching.

"The three phases of Israel's story may be taken to symbolize three phases of our personal growth into our teaching vocation. As children and adolescents, our task is assimilation of instruction, and accurate reproduction of the material. As college and graduate students, our task involves extending the insights of our instructors. Finally, if we eventually become pastors or professors, we must search for a distinctive, God-given vision of our own."

Back on my churchyard bench, I emerged from the trance of memory retrieval, and scanned the hillside. At the foot of the valley, the sun reflected off the surface of the river. A proverb I had once heard (from a venerable African-American preacher) resurfaced in my brain: "Your thirties are the adolescence of adulthood; your fifties are the youth of old age."

My vision for my "youthful old age"? This book. (My graveyard shift was a pivotal moment, triggering the composition of this book; but its composition has a lengthier backstory, which I tell in chapter 27, "From Seed to Tree.")

\* \* \* \* \*

My book rests on three interlocking convictions. Here would be a good place for me to spell them out:

- *I am a story. So are you.* Our personal identities are narratives. Roots that entwine us in families, institutions, nations. Destinies that lure us. Settings that color our experience. Our lives are complex plots, in which we struggle against forces external and internal. Our life-plot unfolds as we wrestle to re-shape our worlds, to bring reality into harmony with our most deeply-held values. As our story develops, we may adopt a dominant image for the role we play: "victim"; "survivor"; "rugged individualist"; "bridge-builder"; "nurturer"—endless variations on archetypal themes.

Part 1: In the Beginning Was the Story

- *The Christian message is a story.* From Genesis to Revelation, the plot may be retold in a kaleidoscope of images: paradise lost and restored;[4] triumph of good over evil; death conquered by resurrection; folly overcome by wisdom—again, endless variations on archetypal themes.

- *When our stories collide with Christ's story, transformation occurs.* Jesus' narrative unsettles, rearranges, and heals our own incoherent scripts. Our identity renews in Christ. New metaphors, derived from Jesus' story, redefine our roles. Christian faith, Christian confession, means *owning Jesus' story*.

\* \* \* \* \*

To wrap up this chapter, let me illustrate this third important concept—the clash of narratives.

Episodes of transition in life are moments when we naturally become conscious of our personal narrative. In some transitions, our past and present seem to flow like river rapids, rushing toward the waterfall of the future.

In academia (the domain I inhabit), one such transition is graduation—or, as Americans like to call it, commencement. That idiom certainly captures the "new chapter" feeling, experienced by many newly-minted graduates, lined up in their caps and gowns in a ceremonial procession.

At the commencement exercises of my seminary, I sometimes got invited to deliver the charge to the graduates. The material below is adapted from my May 2014 commencement address. As you read it, I invite you to contemplate the clash of narratives in action. Notice how the frustration of one storyline gives us an opportunity to embrace a bigger and better story.

## GOBLET OF FIRE

I ascended the huge wooden pulpit of the auditorium, to begin my charge to the seminary's class of 2014. My students sat in the front two rows, garbed in a variety of hoods, trimmed (per degree) with crimson fabric or white.

As a visual emblem, I removed my black mortar board, and invited the graduates to focus on the gold tassels, from which dangled a metal emblem, the numeral "2006," denoting the year I received my doctoral diploma (PhD).

> "Today, I can truly identify with the happiest among you graduates. I understand the source of the joy you are feeling. Without exaggeration, my own graduation ceremony was right up there in the pantheon of joyful life events—ranking even close to my wedding day, or the birth of my daughter."
>
> "Back in 2006, my graduation seemed like a portal, a gateway into a better story. Perhaps many of you graduates, already now, are starting to imagine your better future, for which this ceremony is a gateway."

---

4. I develop this storyline in Smith, "Fifth Gospel."

I had no desire to diminish my students' joy. With sincerity, later that evening, I gladly joined them (in a local tavern) to celebrate their solid accomplishments. Nevertheless, my charge began to sound a warning note.

> "As you, the class of 2014, venture out from our seminary, like Hobbits leaving the Shire, I would like to give you a cloak of armor, spun from elfin silver. You won't need it now. But, maybe one day, the cloak will prove useful."
>
> "Graduation—a portal to a better story. Or so I had hoped. In truth, I have never regained the euphoric joy that accompanied my graduation."
>
> "Looking back, I suspect the problem was the plotline I embarked upon. As you leave the Shire, there will be many apparently good—but ultimately dangerous—storylines that may entice you."
>
> "For me, the 2006 photo (clutching my hard-earned diploma) eventually turned into the scene from Harry Potter, book four. The scene where Harry grasps the trophy called the Goblet of Fire. Supposedly an award for superior wizardry, and thus a portal into a better story, the Goblet became—via dark magic—a portal to a graveyard. And the very bad things that happen in graveyards."

Then I summarized how my PhD diploma became a portal to a graveyard:

- In academia, the setting of the professor's story often shapes the outcome in regrettable ways.
- The academic setting can bias the professor toward a storyline that I typify as *ascent through external accomplishments*.
- Schools have ranks: assistant, associate, and full professor. To ascend the ranks (and the pay scale!), you need external accomplishments, like publishing books.
- Now, the seduction happens because publishing and promotion are not intrinsically evil. They are at worst ethically neutral (and may even be good).
- But, in the imperfections of the human heart, these pursuits can become a portal to a spiritual graveyard, strewn with dead bones such as envy, pride, and discontent.

Turning the focus back to my students, I looked for points of contact with their own narratives.

> "Think of some other spheres where such tragedies unfold. Suppose you are called to be a church planter. Nothing intrinsically evil there. Potentially very good, even. But how easily the role of church planter can morph into the plotline of *ascent through external accomplishments*. The people who fund your church plant want results. So you start obsessing with numbers. The graph of average weekly church attendance (and giving!) becomes your icon of success. And, slowly, this plotline of ascent leads you to a spiritual graveyard."

[Time for the clash of narratives.]

> "As you sit here, resplendent in your new wizards' robes, I would like to offer you an alternative story of ascent. The script is found in the first chapter of the second

letter of Peter. I invite you to tuck this chapter away in your back pocket, for a time when you may need it."

Then I read my own translation of 2 Pet 1:2–11:

> Grace to you and peace be multiplied, in knowing God and our Lord Jesus, just as his divine power has given us everything we need for life and godliness, through knowing the one who called us to his own glory and virtue.
>
> Through these channels, great and precious promises have been given to us, so that, through them, we might become participants in the divine nature, and escape the corruption that is in the world through desire.
>
> For this reason, make every effort to produce, by means of your faith, virtue; and by means of virtue, wisdom; and by means of wisdom, self-control; and by means of self-control, patience; and by means of patience, godliness; and by means of godliness, love—for those inside the church, and for those outside the church.
>
> For, if you have these qualities in abundance, they prevent you from being unproductive or fruitless in knowing our Lord Jesus Christ.
>
> But, the person who lacks these qualities is myopically blind, having forgotten the cleansing of their former sins.
>
> Therefore, instead, my brothers and sisters, make every effort to confirm your calling and election. For, if you do this, you will never stumble. And, in this way, there will be provided for you a rich entryway into the aeonic kingdom of our Lord and Savior Jesus Christ.

My charge then continued:

> "Peter invites you into a story. Truly, a story of ascent—but one that leads you, not into a graveyard, but into the aeonic kingdom of Christ. Instead of ascent through external accomplishment, you are invited into a plotline of ascent through *internal transformation*."

Then I summarized briefly for the audience the narrative elements of the Petrine passage:

- There is a *call*: "to God's own glory and virtue."
- There is a decisive *break* with the past: a "cleansing of former sins" (probably an allusion to baptism).
- There is an *exodus*: "escaping the corruption that is in the world."
- There is a *destiny*: the paradise restored, of Christ's aeonic kingdom.
- There is, between these endpoints of exodus and destiny, a *journey* or an *ascent*: "to become participants in the divine nature."

At this point in my charge, I had to pause and delve into the Protestant discomfort over that last phrase, "become participants in the divine nature." (Our Eastern Orthodox brethren—by contrast—embrace this verse as central to their understanding of Christian discipleship.) We Protestants squirm needlessly. In context, the verse refers to ethical participation in God's eternal virtues—patience, self-control, love, etc. Then I wrapped up my charge:

"Some of you graduating students are already, now, living this glorious narrative of inward transformation according to the virtues of God. To you, I can say nothing further. I simply bless you in the name of Jesus."

"Others, like me in 2006, may find yourselves grasping a Goblet of Fire. I pray not. But, if you ever wander into the spiritual graveyard, I pray that the script of Peter's second letter, chapter one, may redirect your feet into the paths of righteousness."

\* \* \* \* \*

In the first two chapters, I have retold portions of my own story, and the stories of five of my close friends. In the next two chapters, I reflect on *how* we can piece together a coherent personal narrative from the episodes of our lives.

# 3

# Reinventing the Wheel

**THE LONG HAUL**

In our first two chapters, we eavesdropped on a random cast of characters (my friends and I), all struggling to make sense of their lives in terms of story. They were, one might say, on a quest for wisdom, seeking narrative answers to profound questions of personal identity. The sought-after treasure: an individualized *life story*, a unique personal narrative that fits who I am. That integrates my past, present, and future. That makes sense out of suffering, and offers hope for change. That explains the contradictory dimensions of one's personality.

Since you are reading this book, you have probably felt a summons to seek the narrative that will give your life meaning. This chapter offers some footholds for the upward climb.

But first, a prediction: whether you are beginning your search, or are further down the path, I expect you will eventually encounter frustration or exasperation, as you gaze at scattered, fragmented scenes from your past which stubbornly refuse to align in a neat narrative arc.

But why did we think the quest would be easy? The gold at the end of the rainbow is nothing less than your purpose and significance. Your unique identity. Your redemption. Your wisdom. Your gift to the world. Your glory, honor and beauty. Your immortality and transcendence.

If stories teach us anything, they underscore that such a prize cannot be won without agonizing. We don't get to put a quarter in a slot machine, turn the handle, and receive a candy bar.

Discouraged? Don't be. Others have traveled the path, overcome the obstacles, reached their destination—and returned, with at least a pencil-drawn map sketched on a scrunched-up piece of paper.

In this chapter, I will share some of their wisdom (reinvent the wheel). In particular, I will cull insights from the growing literature on how to write your memoir. But first, let's briefly list some of the obstacles in the path of discerning one's life story.

## ROADBLOCKS

Look around at your family, friends, colleagues, and neighbors. How many are living a worthwhile story? How many can articulate the story of their life? If you answered, "Not many," what could explain the lack of clear and compelling life stories? Answer that question, and you have a realistic vision of the barriers between you and the narrative that you seek. Here is my list of the obstacles, clustered into seven areas (for convenience, not to imply completeness).

### Intangibility of Narrative

Let's begin with a paradox. Narrative is universal. Intuitive. Child-friendly. But narrative is also *intangible*, and defining it "is like trying to get your hands around a ghost shape."[1] Narrative fits the ancient Indian proverb: "A sea in which a gnat may drink, and an elephant may bathe."[2] The apparent simplicity of narrative leads us into labyrinths of astounding complexity.[3]

When we begin to reflect on life as narrative, the simple wisdom enshrined in story can become obscured by stories' latent complexities. To compound the problem, I sense a widespread loss of competence in using narrative as a critical tool. You can even study for a PhD in literature, and never learn the basics of story structure![4]

### Loss of Oral Storytelling

How many really good storytellers do you know? Not very many, right? *Loss of oral storytelling*, in family and community, tracks with the growth of modern industrial society.[5] Instead of telling one another our stories, we absorb stories in multiple media (TV, cinema, novels, etc.).

This apparently innocuous shift in media loosens our grip on our personal narratives. In first-person oral storytelling, we are the hero, an active agent, with clear goals and motives. By contrast, modern media tend to position us as passive spectators or consumers of stories.[6]

Does loss of oral storytelling lead to thinning of personal identity? Maybe. According to therapist Dan B. Allender, an invitation to "tell me your life story" begets blank stares from many of his counselees. Typically, counselees lack any cogent personal narrative that could guide decisions about their future.[7]

---

1. Rainer, *Your Life as Story*, 37.
2. Applied originally to the game of chess, and much later to John's Gospel.
3. Cobley, *Narrative*, 2.
4. This literally happened to Tristine Rainer (*Your Life as Story*, 65).
5. McLeod, "Storytelling in Postpsychological Counseling," 16.
6. Ibid., 17, 19.
7. Allender, *To Be Told*, 1–2, 5.

## Loss of Grand Narratives

Furthermore, in the "postmodern condition," we are *deprived of grand narratives* that could guide our autobiographical quest. This umbrella narrative (about the loss of umbrella narratives!) will be discussed in chapter 5. For now, consider this observation by Joseph Campbell, on the cultural consequences of losing our overarching script: "It is possible that the *failure of mythology and ritual* to function effectively in our civilization may account for the high incidence among us of the malaise that has led to the characterization of our time as 'The Age of Anxiety.'"[8] Loss of big stories dilutes the value of our personal narratives. Sadly, the emaciation of values gets institutionalized by late modern approaches to literature and psychology. Daniel Taylor highlights the reduction of "heroes" to "protagonists," and the replacement of "character" by the value-neutral category of "personality."[9] Our quest for an autobiography takes a detour through the maze of moral relativism.

## Gap Between Story and "Reality"

If we feel seasick with the value-relativity of postmodernity, many of us (especially conservative Christians) grab onto the railings of objective truth. Understandable. But, ironically, this move can also paralyze our quest for autobiography. We become terrified lest we "impose a story upon the facts." Our *fear that story distorts reality* stillbirths any "personal myth" that would give meaning to our life.

Sure, the relationship between story and life is subtle (and gets a fuller discussion in chapter 11). However, according to the discipline known as "New Autobiography," only the poetic truth inherent in narrative can disclose the unique purpose of our individual lives.[10]

## Tyranny of the Urgent

There is nothing philosophical about our next obstacle: the *tyranny of the urgent*. Overscheduled, always interrupted or distracted by modern communications media—we lack the time and focus needed to patiently unearth our life narrative. We've come a long way from Socrates's dictum: "The unexamined life is not worth living." Autobiography entails study and writing.[11] Writing—not for Pulitzer prizes, but to consolidate your own point of view about your past.

---

8. Quoted in Taylor, *Healing Power of Stories*, 140 (italics mine).
9. Ibid., 52–53, 167–68.
10. For discussion of New Autobiography, see Rainer, *Your Life as Story*, chapters 2 and 11.
11. Allender, *To Be Told*, 1–3, 21, 128–30.

## Fear

"In the cave you fear to enter, lies the treasure that you seek."[12] In the pursuit of your life narrative, you will have to overcome the *many-headed hydra of fear*.

We've already mentioned the (ultra-modern) fear of "imposing" a story that distorts the facts. In tying your life together with a thematic thread, you select key events. And so you discard other events, relegating them to the background of subplots. This can feel like throwing part of your self into the trashcan.[13] (The author of the fourth Gospel shared a similar struggle: John 20:30–31; 21:25.)

Other fears will multiply, as quickly as you lop off their predecessors' heads.[14] Perhaps the biggest: facing the depths of our uniquely painful and shameful experiences.[15]

## No Magic Formula

Lastly, the quest for a life narrative resolves via *faith, not formula*. You dig up dozens of memories, lay them out on the table, and stare at one of those infuriating thousand-piece jigsaw puzzles of grey birds dotted on a grey sky over a grey sea. Where is your narrative arc?

Foggy confusion is normal at this stage.[16] You are rearranging the letters of an anagram to form a word, or scanning "a child's puzzle for the figure hidden in the trees."[17] Discovering your life's theme is not "about fitting your life into . . . a mathematical equation."[18] Rather, the discovery usually occurs via epiphany, the unexpected *aha!* moment.[19] Just like in most good stories.

You need to trust that intuition, if you want your story to guide you into the future. And, just as "faith without works is dead" (James 2:17), you will need to project your provisional story into the unknown future. Take the risk of becoming the character you've been writing about.[20] New experiences may force you to re-draft your narrative version of yourself.[21] But, unless you act, you will never know.

\* \* \* \* \*

If seven (at least!) roadblocks obstruct the discovery of your life story, what makes the quest worth the effort? Listen to the wisdom of a memoir-writing coach: "Turning one's life into memoir is inherently comic in the classic definition of comedy; it

---

12. Joseph Campbell, quoted in Winkler, "What Makes a Hero?"
13. Rainer, *Your Life as Story*, 212–13.
14. Ibid., 184–91.
15. Ibid., 151; Allender, *To Be Told*, 128–29.
16. Ibid., 94, 103.
17. Rainer, *Your Life as Story*, 37, 82.
18. Ibid., 229.
19. Balzer, *Writing & Selling Your Memoir*, 38–39.
20. Allender, *To Be Told*, 140.
21. McAdams, "Personal Narratives," 246.

is redemptive. Memoir triumphs over the view that, because it ends in death, life is tragic."[22] In hunting for a plotline that unifies your past and guides your future, it helps to have a clear idea of what your quarry looks like. You need to overcome roadblock number one (discussed above).

Despite being a published author, Donald Miller admits he lacked a clear grasp of Story 101.[23] That changed when he encountered scriptwriting guru Robert McKee.[24] After attending McKee's thirty-six-hour seminar, Miller distilled story as, "*A character who wants something and overcomes conflict to get it.*"[25] Miller used this insight to turn his life into a meaningful narrative.

In our next section, we will look at similar "starter-kits" on how to think of your life as narrative.

## STARTER-KITS

If existential motives impelled you to pick up this book, and if you've begun to wrestle with the seven roadblocks discussed above, then you already have one working template for how to structure your life as narrative! You are in a classic quest for wisdom. As your quest develops, it will likely take on the classic five act structure (think Shakespeare plays):

| Act 1 | "Call" to seek your life story; overcoming initial resistance |
| Act 2 | Optimism: hopeful gathering of memories |
| Act 3 | Frustration: inability to see a pattern in the memories |
| Act 4 | Despair: temptation to give up the quest |
| Act 5 | Breakthrough: the epiphanic *aha!* moment of intuitive insight |

Lump three of these acts together, and you get the minimalist Aristotelian definition of drama. Beginning-middle-end (or complication-crisis-denouement). This three-act model generates a couple of starter-kits, to help you figure out your life story. The first starter-kit begins at the beginning; the second reverse engineers your life story, by starting at the end.

### Begin at the Beginning

Allender's starter-kit recognizes that, in life, "Tragedy . . . is the rule rather than the exception. There is not a person on earth who has escaped life's pivotal, inciting incidents—incidents that are full of sadness, injustice, failure, and cruelty."[26] This is where literature intersects life; so this is where literature can guide us. "The wound is the place where the myth and the real life meet."[27]

22. Rainer, *Your Life as Story*, 289.
23. Miller, *Million Miles*, 19.
24. Ibid., 39–48.
25. Ibid., 48 (italics mine).
26. Allender, *To Be Told*, 75.
27. James Hillman, quoted in Rainer, *Your Life as Story*, 196.

Accordingly, Allender invites us to begin with our expulsion from paradise. The trigger incident that breached our peace, and drove us on a quest to restore our lost equilibrium. This archetypal plotline condenses to three phases:

*shalom + shattering → search → satisfaction* (temporary).[28]

Allow me to illustrate with a trivial vignette. So trivial, that its very survival in my memory bank probably reflects its perfect realization of the "paradise restored" archetype.

> North West London, 1979. I have graduated from schoolboy to college student. One morning, I take the one-and-a-half-mile walk from my dorm to the nearest post office, new checkbook in hand. In my pocket, my old-fashioned fountain pen. Its stem held an ink reservoir, and its gold-tipped, rounded nib guaranteed a beautiful hand-written script.
>
> My errand complete, I walk back to my dormitory. In my room—*shalom shattered!* Where is my fountain pen? Why was my soul so downcast at the loss? It's "only a pen!" But the pen I used for my last seven years as a schoolboy. A symbol of continuity with my childhood. The pen I used for my college entrance exams.
>
> So, prayerfully (!) I began my *search*. I retraced my steps, head bowed to the sidewalk. One-and-a-half miles later, on the concrete outside the post office, *satisfaction*. My fountain pen restored!

Okay, as we all know, on the grand stage of life, paradise doesn't usually get restored so neatly. Many losses cannot be restored. Our search for equilibrium initiates us into plotlines of escalating complexity. In terms of metaphor, the cult movie *The Big Lebowski* gets closer to reality. The main character (Jeff Bridges) experiences a simple disruption: burglars break into his apartment, and urinate on his rug. In response to this inciting incident, Bridges wants to replace the rug, because "it really tied the room together" (metaphor of equilibrium). However, his search for a replacement rug propels him into an increasingly complex plotline, in which he becomes a courier for ransom money for the (allegedly) kidnapped wife of a billionaire.

Likewise, our attempts to heal the breaches in our lives propel us toward unexpected destinations. Allender invites us to consider three kinds of "shattering," using biblical social images. Cruel and unexpected events give birth to images/experiences like these:[29]

| biblical social image | experience |
|---|---|
| the orphan | abandonment |
| the stranger | betrayal |
| the widow | shame |

Allender, in a bold summons to faith, encourages us to start with our shattered identities, and allow them to guide our search and fuel our dreams (in a positive manner). As a result of your shattering, "What *wrongs* do you dream of *righting*? What *good* do you dream of *growing*?"[30]

28. Allender, *To Be Told*, 41–52.
29. Ibid., 77–87.
30. Ibid., 105, 113–4 (italics mine).

This is one way to figure out your life trajectory. The "shattering → search" plotline can be a good fit for autobiographies initiated by major disruptive pivotal events.

On the other hand, for many people, a life story may emerge from reflecting on endings. Let's turn to this approach.

## Reverse Engineering

Rainer recommends, as our trigger for reflection, a final realization (epiphany). The lasting wisdom, the life lesson, which our struggles have eventually produced.[31] Specifically, "*Is there a turning point . . . where something in me died so something could live or be born?*"[32] The life-giving "death" may center on relinquishing "a belief, a need, a feeling, or a person."[33]

In sketching the meaning of life as a wisdom-epiphany gained via (metaphorical) death and rebirth, Rainer taps into the work of Joseph Campbell.[34] As we will see (in chapter 7 below), Campbell argued that a single "monomyth" plotline underlies all the great stories of world culture. The pervasiveness of this storyline explains its utility as an autobiographical template.

To help locate the wisdom life has taught you, Rainer suggests penning a letter to a grandchild (real or imagined), in which you crystallize "the most important insight, vision of reality, or wisdom you have learned and wish to pass on."[35]

Once you have located the turning point that produced your life-transforming insight, you can begin to reverse engineer your story.[36] What *conflict of values* did the epiphanic pivot resolve? Can you now see this conflict of values as a theme that ties together the episodes of your life? When did the conflict first arise? Was the conflict generated by a specific "inciting incident?"

By answering such questions, you can surface the "desire line" that unifies your personal narrative.[37] Unified by the desire line, your biography coalesces into the classic three-act shape:[38]

| beginning | desire |
| --- | --- |
| middle | struggle |
| end | realization |

Perhaps, as your story unfolded, the desire line intensified and transformed. Perhaps, at the end, in the moment of realization, your initial desire had to die in order to be reborn

---

31. See Rainer, *Your Life as Story*, 72–78, 264–66, for discussion of how such epiphanies fit into the archetypal narrative phases.
32. Ibid., 79 (italics in original).
33. Ibid., 81.
34. Ibid., 41–42, 65–66.
35. Ibid., 43.
36. Ibid., 79–82.
37. See ibid., 15, 51–52, 54, 68–70, for discussion of the "desire line."
38. Ibid., 38–39, 43–46.

in a new, life-giving form. Rainer has a witty device for summarizing this character arc. She references the well-known Rolling Stones lyric about how, over time, you just might get what you need (instead of what you initially wanted).

Now that we have examined a couple of starter-kit plotlines for constructing your autobiography, let's look at some real-life examples of how these (and similar) plots map onto the lives of actual people.

## ROLE MODELS

Disclaimer: I'm not evaluating the "quality of life" of these role models (even if I happen to admire at least one of them). No, they only model the starter-kits for constructing a personal memoir. My first two examples worked *forwards* from an early experience to a coherent life story, and my next two worked *backwards* from a culminating realization.

### Dan Allender

Allender offered us a "shattering → search" template for finding our life story. He invited us to ponder: was there, perhaps, an early trigger event—disrupting the peaceful world of our childhood? And, if so, did the disruption trigger a search? Maybe a quest for answers to "*Why*??" Maybe a desire to combat evil. Maybe a hunt for something to replace what we lost. Maybe a desire to fulfill an aborted trajectory.

In Allender's story, abuse shattered his childhood. This triggered his search—for purpose and hope. His search culminated in his long and fruitful ministry of counseling and writing, sharing with others the hope and purpose he eventually found. In his own words, summarizing the "theme statement" of his life: "My story reveals a surprising and unpredictable God who transforms shame through foolishness, violence through kindness, and arrogance through weakness."[39] Allender's childhood abuse eventually led him to profound wisdom on how to overcome evil. In condensing his story, we have fast-forwarded from beginning to end, skipping the middle. In our next example, we will include the intermediate struggle.

### Frank Schaeffer

Trigger events aren't always *negative*, like painful encounters with suffering. An epiphany, experienced when young, and tilting the rudder for our life, can be a *positive* inbreaking of joy and awe. Like this emotionally-charged event from Frank Schaeffer's time as a precocious teenage painter:

> Of all my shows, the one at the Chante Pierre Gallery was the best. It was a serious gallery, and my work was shown alongside paintings by Miro and Picasso. At the well-attended opening, I almost threw up with nervousness and was also thrilled. It was a wonderful and terrible thing to see my paintings hanging in a real gallery . . . As if by some miracle, several little red dots appeared on

---

39. Allender, *To Be Told*, 121.

> the catalog price list, indicating sales. The feeling I got was like looking over a precipice, thrilled and frightened. And somewhere in my brain, a little explosion went off. It was as if I had just heard a whispered message: "You can escape the madness!" It was the first time I felt I might have a future . . . the message of freedom-through-art stuck in my brain someplace. And years later, when I hit rock bottom, that voice reminded me that there are possibilities beyond one's background. When I would feel most trapped, it would "speak" of freedom.[40]

Here we have the trigger event of a classic coming-of-age plotline, in which the protagonist struggles to become their true self, to realize their potential, to transcend the limitations of their family background.

But what was the "madness" Frank wished to escape? He grew up in a small village in the Swiss Alps. His American parents (Francis and Edith) had moved there as missionaries. Over time, their missionary outpost (L'Abri, "The Shelter") became a magnet for spiritual seekers from all over the globe. L'Abri became an unrelenting, twenty-four/seven center for gospel ministry. Raised in this evangelistic hot-house, Frank rebelled (like many an "MK" or "Missionary Kid"). Summing up his childhood, from his own point of view: "The super-spiritual pietistic grid through which Mom saw life was a heavy load for her children to bear . . . The implication was that whatever you were doing for the Lord, more was required. Normal life was just a series of interludes between bouts of evangelical zeal."[41] Into this oppressive (for him) setting, came the call: "freedom-through-art." But where was the pathway to freedom? How could Frank fulfill his artistic potential? Enter the middle of his story, a struggle lasting for over twenty years.

The next turning point, the event that triggered his middle phase, was sheer opportunism. Billy Zeoli, a Christian film producer from America, showed up in Switzerland, wanting to make a documentary. The topic: a preliminary skirmish in the "culture wars," the evangelical critique of "secular humanism" being articulated by Frank's dad.[42]

In addition to painting, Frank also dabbled in amateur film. "And I was ambitious. I wanted to make films, real movies, movies like my idol Fellini was making. But how could I get from here to there? Billy offered me what seemed like a way."[43]

Light appeared to blaze upon the path. Frank began to glimpse his "long-term exit strategy from the evangelical subculture." "My plan was to jump from making evangelical documentaries to directing Hollywood features."[44]

So Frank signed up, and became director of his father's evangelistic films. Highly successful films, that kick-started the rise of the religious Right in American politics. Films that catapulted a reluctant Francis Schaeffer onto the evangelical superstar circuit. With a massive ironic consequence for his son, Frank:

> The fact that I became my father's sidekick was the self-perpetuation of a nightmare. Like most children, I wanted to be independent of my parents and then found myself exacerbating my dependence. Not only was I drawn into my

---

40. Schaeffer, *Crazy for God*, 219.
41. Ibid., 113.
42. Ibid., 253–61.
43. Ibid., 258.
44. Ibid., 271, 327.

parents' ministry, I was the prime mover and shaker when it came to making sure that Dad got truly famous within the evangelical subculture.[45]

Frank's movement, on his freedom-through-art pathway, was becoming obstructed by obstacles. Antagonistic forces, frustrating the hero's "desire line." Inevitably encountered in the middle phase of a story, antagonists are either external or internal—forces outside the protagonist, or forces within.[46]

In Frank's story, the external antagonist was obvious: deeper entanglement in the evangelistic subculture he yearned to escape!

Subtler, and therefore deadlier, were forces inside Frank which hindered the realization of his goal. If we look back on his jump into directing evangelical documentaries, we see the small and subtle seed of compromise. A utilitarian, exploitative tendency; viewing projects as mere stepping-stones to something better. Loss of moral and artistic integrity inevitably followed.

Lest you think I am harshly accusing Frank, listen to his own testimony on how his story played out. First, his career as director meant abandonment of painting. He speaks of this as "treason": "I knew I had betrayed something important."[47] Second, despite his growing cynicism about the religious Right, he continued to be part of their circus: he "played the game," because he "couldn't figure out any way to earn as good a living anywhere else."[48] Third, once he did finally break into Hollywood as a director, his films belied his original high artistic vision. B-movies, one of which was "a horror film (in every sense of the word)."[49] The contrast with his teenage artwork was painful: "Where, as a painter, doing anything but my best had once been unthinkable . . . all I was intersted in on the movies I directed was to get the job done and move on to something better."[50] Finally, he reached a moral nadir as his film career nosedived and he ran out of money. To feed himself, he "shoplifted pork chops form Ralph's grocery," by stuffing them down his underpants ("the cold meat made my testicles ache.")[51]

Rewind to Frank's initial epiphany ("freedom-through-art"). Almost twenty years later, he is "lost in the middle."[52] The freedom (from evangelicalism) part of the script has been accomplished—but the artist remains unfulfilled. A lapsed painter, making lousy films. The end of act two of his life feels just as restrictive as act one, which turns out to be a common pattern in drama and in biography.

Eventually, Frank emerges into act three. The trigger? Another epiphany. This time, the still, small voice of his wife, Genie. Many years earlier, when Frank was becoming utterly disillusioned with his role as a "celebrity" of the religious Right, Genie had asked him: "Why don't you just quit and write a novel . . . tell all those stories you tell the

---

45. Ibid., 323.
46. See Rainer, *Your Life as Story*, 69, 152–57, 217–19, 224–25.
47. Schaeffer, *Crazy for God*, 402, 259.
48. Ibid., 357, 328.
49. Ibid., 364.
50. Ibid.
51. Ibid., 374, 376.
52. Borrowing a phrase from Tripp, *Lost in the Middle*.

children about your vacation in Italy?"[53] Towards the end of his fruitless season in Hollywood, Frank finally had the sense to heed his wife's wisdom. He began scribbling a novel "on the back of an airline ticket envelope."[54] He submitted a draft to Macmillan—and they published the novel during his phase as a pork-chop thief.[55]

The modest success of his novel persuaded him to exit Hollywood.[56] Finally, he was an artist with integrity, working patiently at his craft, like his old teenage painter self back in Switzerland.[57] His son John could take pride in his dad—a man "who deeply wanted to create something that was artistically valid and that would outlast him."[58]

Frank's transition, from film director to novelist, embodies the death/rebirth metaphor so typical of turning points. In his own words, "Fail as a movie director . . . resurrect as a writer."[59] Furthermore, his story also embodies the morphing of the "desire line": painter → film director → novelist.

\* \* \* \* \*

Our first two role models, Allender and Schaeffer, orientated their life stories around an early trigger-incident. An intensely emotional experience, driving a consistent plotline, producing a clear "genre" of life story.

Our next two memoirists work backwards from a climactic realization at the end of their stories, a hard-won, vivid insight which clarified the beginning and middle of their personal narratives.

## Marlena Fortenay

Marlena was an unforgettable participant in one of Rainer's classes on autobiography.[60] Lived in real time, the beginning of Marlena's story must have felt (to her) like the initiation of a classic rags-to-riches plotline of ascent. However, a devastating realization, crystallizing toward the end of her story, caused her to drastically reinterpret the "genre" of her life.

Marlena worked as a waitress in Los Angeles, but aspired to a musical career as a singer. Her story centers on "her mutually exploitative relationship with Harry, a Hollywood hanger-on."[61] Harry promises to win her a recording contract—in exchange for certain favors.[62]

---

53. Schaeffer, *Crazy for God*, 329.
54. Ibid., 373.
55. Ibid., 376.
56. Ibid., 383.
57. Ibid., 382.
58. Ibid., 385.
59. Ibid., 406.
60. Rainer, *Your Life as Story*, 83–84, 187–90.
61. Ibid., 83.
62. Ibid., 187–89.

Marlena eventually realized that "Harry had been sucking away her life spirit."[63] Her realization forced her to a crisis decision: allow the record deal to die, in order to renew her personal integrity. In her own words:

> I took the contract. Tore it up into little pieces, and sent them floating out over the edge of the terrace. I stood there and watched them fall. Like bits of confetti. Shimmering white in the moonlight . . . The night air was sweet with the smell of lilacs. My granny had a big white lilac bush in her garden and I used to sit under it when I was little and pretend that nobody would ever find me. Now, when I smell lilacs, it makes me cry. And that night, when the tears came, I cried for what I had let Harry do to me. I cried out all the sadness . . . I cried until I felt clean inside.[64]

Her growing realization, culminating in this decision, allowed her to work backwards and reinterpret her personal narrative. Instead of rags-to-riches, with Harry as an ally, she could now see herself as the heroine of a vampire story. Metaphorically, her relationship with Harry featured all the classic elements of the genre: "The initial attraction, the first "kiss," illness and fear, the encounter with death, the final struggle to escape the vampire's control, and ultimately the need to put a stake through his heart."[65] Ends clarify beginnings.

## Tristine Rainer

Ends can also clarify the murky middles of our stories. Rainer's own story illustrates this resolution of experiences which, in real time, felt incoherent.

In mid-life, she plunged into a quest for her true identity. "I wanted to recognize my *daemon*, that unique but continuous spirit which, according to psychoanalyst James Hillman, gazes from the eyes of the little boy and old man unchanged."[66] Let's fast-forward to the satisfying end of her search, a realization that resolved contradictions:

> With that breakthrough, the two irreconcilable images of me—the English lit. instructor and the TV movie honcha—converged, and my wayward life began to make sense . . . I realized I'd *had* to leave academia in order to learn hands-on about writing contemporary true life stories. Only when I'd mastered in the field what no one I'd known in the university understood—story structure—could I couple it with what I knew [from the university] about first person writing. The product of that coupling is this book on seeing and writing your life as story.[67]

This epiphany involved a kind of death. Relinquishing the shame she felt over her earlier career as a TV producer, when the pressure to maintain network ratings lowered her to the level of an "ambulance chaser."[68]

63. Ibid., 83.
64. Quoted in ibid., 84.
65. Ibid., 83.
66. Ibid., 5 (italics in original).
67. Ibid., 8 (italics in original).
68. Ibid., 4.

Her epiphany resolved a conflicted middle phase of her story, where she struggled to find a coherent sense of self. This struggle rooted in the "inciting incident" of her biography.[69]

As a TV producer, she was pressured into making movies about real-life tragedies. The low point arrived when she offered money for film rights to the mother of a fifteen-year-old girl murdered by a jealous classmate. The mother's resolute refusal to sell her grief drove Rainer to quit her job.

Provoked into self-reflection, Rainer began the search for her true identity. Working as an autobiographic writing coach, she attempted to apply her narrative wisdom to herself.[70]

Her search soon appeared to dead-end. The riddle appeared insoluble. Her "antagonists" were legion. Her "episodic life"—a "kind of desperate improvisation"—had fractured her identity.[71] The one "thread of continuity"—her "fascination with people's stories"—provided pattern without plotline.[72] Two of her main jobs had generated morally conflicting self-images: university lecturer (evaluated as honest) versus TV producer (evaluated as dishonest).[73]

The low point of her middle phase arrived in the UCLA Research Library, where she had studied before abandoning academia for the world of television. Rainer noticed, with dismay, that her old academic field—autobiography—"had become a hot interdisciplinary topic" during her absence from the university.[74] She despaired—at the sense of a lost career opportunity, and at her "haphazard, unstructured" life.[75]

And then her epiphany occurred, resolving her contradictory self-images, and restoring a clear sense of purpose and direction to her life. Act three finally made sense of acts one and two. At the satisfying end of her search, she could articulate a personal narrative that explained her identity.

According to McAdams, this is one of the greatest benefits of constructing our life story: to integrate the numerous "contradictories" of our lives and selves: "People's stories about themselves may bring together different self-ascribed tendencies, roles, goals, and remembered events into a synchronic pattern that expresses how the individual person, who seems to encompass so many different things . . . is, at the same time, one (complex and even contradictory) thing as well."[76]

\* \* \* \* \*

69. Ibid., 3–5.
70. Ibid., 5–7.
71. Ibid., 5.
72. Ibid., 5–6.
73. Ibid., 3.
74. Ibid., 7.
75. Ibid.
76. McAdams, "Personal Narratives," 244.

We have surveyed four role models in the art of autobiography. I hope that you, like me, appreciate such writers for their honest exposure of themselves. In our search for our own personal narratives, memoir writers can guide us along the path.

Let us crystallize some insights we can distill from the four writers. First, we are reminded of the substantial rewards of the hard labor of autobiographical reflection. (Recall the list of benefits of owning your life story, summarized in chapter 1 of this book.) Here is my sense of what each writer gained by looking back on their life:

| Writer | Benefit they gained from owning their life story |
|---|---|
| Dan Allender | A sense of hope through "redeeming the past"; discerning how his suffering led to his empathy and wisdom, and his vocation as a counselor. |
| Frank Schaeffer | A rudder for the present and future; reminding him of the priority of personal and artistic integrity (through tracing the cost of abandoning integrity). |
| Marlena Fortenay | The self-respect belonging to a strong personal identity; validating a difficult decision (sacrificing her recording contract) by recounting the events that led up to it. |
| Tristine Rainer | The self-acceptance of a complex personal identity; resolving the apparent incoherence of conflicting and fragmented self-images, by discerning how they all come together in her present vocation. |

Second, observe how each of these four autobiographical sketches may be viewed as particular expressions of broad narrative genres:

| Writer | Genre |
|---|---|
| Dan Allender | overcoming evil |
| Frank Schaeffer | coming-of-age |
| Marlena Fortenay | rebirth |
| Tristine Rainer | quest |

We will discuss these and other genres in chapter 8 of this book. For now, I simply observe that most memoirs fall into a recognized genre. Memoir editor Paula Balzer confirms this observation.[77] My paraphrased selection of some of her more common genres of memoir:

- spiritual quests (often part of a geographical journey);
- adventures (bracketed by entry into, and exit from, a strange "world");
- investigations (riddle-solving);
- surviving tragedy;
- love/relationship stories (classic comedic).

77. Balzer, *Writing & Selling Your Memoir*, 33–38.

PART 1: IN THE BEGINNING WAS THE STORY

Memoir writing is a massive growth industry.[78] Why? I think the growth in memoir publishing meets our inbuilt need to make sense of life in terms of narrative. Balzer's fascination with memoir seems rooted in this need. On moving to New York City as a young single woman, she happened upon Mary Cantwell's *Manhattan, When I Was Young*. Balzer reveals, "I felt an instant kinship with her narrative."[79]

According to Rainer, the "New Autobiography" taps into the synergy between story and life:

> The New Autobiography . . . written as self-discovery . . . beholds the individual's life . . . through the cohesion of literature and myth.
>
> New Autobiography . . . shapes life into story, into personal myth.
>
> Through New Autobiography you may begin to see yourself as the hero of your own story, even as it is happening.[80]

\* \* \* \* \*

In this chapter, we have offered some starter-kits for constructing your unique personal narrative. In the next chapter, I will offer some goads in the form of diagnostic questions designed to bring your personal story to the surface.

But I would like to end this chapter with some questions for reflection. We looked at thumbnail sketches of four autobiographies (Allender; Schaeffer; Fortenay; Rainer). All four authors recognized that story gives *internal coherence* to their life. All four produced an individual life story. But do their stories have any *external coherence*? Do their personal stories intersect any bigger stories, or is their significance purely private?

The very act of autobiography often says that the author sees a wider meaning to their life. But what kind of wider meaning? How do individual autobiographies intersect bigger stories?

- Are autobiographies *embedded*, like scenes or episodes, in some bigger drama that precedes or follows? (For example, was the abuse suffered by Allender a pattern of generational evil, passed down from father to son?)
- If an autobiography seems embedded in a broader narrative, how does the autobiography unfold the plot? How is the life a *reflex* of earlier events? Or, how does the life *generate* later events?
- If "before" and "after" questions don't yield answers, then does the autobiography *symbolize* a bigger story? How is the individual life a *microcosm* of a larger (or even a universal) pattern? (For example, is the trajectory of Schaeffer's life a commentary on the [un]sustainability of ultra-conservative evangelical religion?)

\* \* \* \* \*

78. Ibid., 6; Rainer, *Your Life as Story*, 10.
79. Balzer, *Writing & Selling Your Memoir*, 1.
80. Rainer, *Your Life as Story*, 10, 14, 17.

# 4

# Cattle Prods

### INTRODUCTION

SOMETIMES, EVEN WHEN WE really want something, we still need some prodding to get there. In this chapter, I offer you a structured list of questions, hoping they can guide your path toward owning the narrative of your life.

I usually recycle my Starbucks cardboard sleeve, but not this one: "*Stories are gifts. Share.*" The sleeve, with its invitation, got transferred to the pen-and-pencil holder on my office desk. It became my mantra during the early days of struggling to write this book.

We all share sound bites of our life story on a daily basis. But have you ever taken a "sabbatical" from Twitter and Facebook, and pondered your autobiography as a whole? Where and how would you even begin?

Thankfully, we don't need to reinvent the wheel. Standard checklists of questions can help focus and organize our reflection as we struggle to piece together the narrative of our life. I keep a manila folder whose tab is titled, *"Diagnostic Questions for Detecting Personal Narratives."* These questions helped me piece together my own life story.

In this chapter, I have combined my diagnostics with other questions culled from several helpful sources: the Foley Center for the Study of Lives;[1] memoir editor Paula Balzer;[2] autobiography coach Tristine Rainer;[3] counselor Dan B. Allender.[4]

As indicated in the previous chapter, such questions stimulate and focus reflection, and suggest possible resolutions of your search for a personal narrative. They don't provide a quick-fix answer. They are not the quarter into the slot machine that magically releases a candy bar.

I have tried to cluster the questions into a helpful progression. So I organize them under these headers:

---

1. Foley Center, "Life Story Interview."
2. Balzer, *Writing & Selling Your Memoir*.
3. Rainer, *Your Life as Story*.
4. Allender, *To Be Told*.

Part 1: In the Beginning Was the Story

- The Art of Remembering
- Dimensions of Time
- Dimensions of Plot
- Stories that Shape Me
- Stories in Seed Form

I hope the logic becomes apparent as you work your way down the list. Since narrative threads all weave into one tapestry, you could actually begin anywhere on the list, grab onto a thread, and follow its lead into the narrative whole that patterns your life.

Nevertheless, a reasoned inductive search strategy may help. So, my list of diagnostic questions will unfold with this progression:

- Begin by getting a handle on your memories—the preliminary *raw materials* of your life story. Generate a list of *major events and experiences*. Use standard techniques to jog your memory. See if any provisional patterns emerge from these raw materials.

- Our lives unfold in time, and our timeline has many *dimensions*: past, present, and future; change and constancy; foreground and background; repetitions; seasons; etc. Begin to explore these dimensions, looking for ways to *cluster*, *contour* and *connect* your experiences. The questions in this section will increase your autobiographical raw materials, augmenting past with present and future. The questions also give shape and structure to your raw experiences of time. And when we shape and structure time, we are on the pathway to narration itself, since narrative organizes time.

- Our next section takes our previous work to a deeper narrative level, by exploring *dimensions of plot* in the events of our life. We ask questions designed to surface *narrative arcs* that connect the major "acts" of your personal "drama." The questions focus on: your life setting; trigger incidents; escalations; crises; and resolutions.

- The stories that we live depend upon the stories that we consume. This section tries to detect *the stories that shape me*. Have I (consciously or unconsciously) lived a narrative based on stories I have absorbed from my culture? What novels, films, historical narratives, etc., function as *metaphors of my life*?

- Lastly, particular *episodes* from our own past can also function as metaphors of our entire life. Do any salient episodes from your past seem to *symbolize* your life? In what ways are these episodes *microcosms* of your whole life? How do they *foreshadow* your later trajectories? Our final section illustrates these concepts.

With this tour guide in our back pocket, let us now turn to the *diagnostic questions* themselves. Some of these are presented as direct questions; others are implied by the discussions found in each section.

## THE ART OF REMEMBERING

Autobiography is like a sculptor's studio. We begin by quarrying stone in bulk, and then chip away at the blocks until a pattern emerges. If we "don't know where to start," then we can borrow some helpful recall techniques from the how-to guides.[5] The following exercise concentrates the mind on what matters most to you:

- Suppose you were told that all your memories will evaporate in thirty minutes unless you name them in writing. What memories would you want to preserve? Start writing—not detailed stories, but concrete labels sufficient to identify the event or experience or conversation or person or place, etc.

Now expand your written list of memories by using external triggers:

- *Personal literary artifacts*: letters; diaries and journals; substantive emails; etc.
- *Family photos*; your hoarded objects that "hold the energy of the past."[6]
- *Muscle memory*: physically reproduce body movements, e.g., distinctive motions performed in a previous job.
- *Physically revisit geographical locations* (or use Google Maps/Images!)
- *Draw the floor plan of your childhood home.* "The house we were born in is physically inscribed in us. It is a group of organic habits."[7]
- *Research cultural artifacts of the time period*: popular music and films and TV shows; period documentaries; old newspapers and magazines (kept by libraries); etc.

At the end of these exercises, you will have a random-looking and disorganized list of events, experiences, conversations, people, places, etc. Scenes from your life story (even if it doesn't yet look like a story).

Now scroll down your written list of memories, and highlight any that provoke "pauses for reflection" or "emotional jolts." Your deep and intensified responses to a subset of memories may guide you to the center of your narrative:

> Key memory pieces are those surprising little sections that cause you to pause and actually reflect on a memory for a moment or two.

> Those unexpected emotional jolts often hold hidden keys to parts of your story that need to be highlighted.[8]

Emotional epiphanies offer clues to our life story, because they allow us to reverse engineer the following chain: story → values → emotions. Here I am piggybacking on philosopher Martha C. Nussbaum, who theorizes:

---

5. E.g., Rainer, *Your Life as Story*, chapter 7 (utilized for several of my suggestions below).
6. Ibid., 116.
7. Gaston Bachelard, quoted in ibid., 117.
8. Balzer, *Writing & Selling Your Memoir*, 40.

> Emotions are appraisals or *value* judgments, which ascribe to things and persons outside the person's own control great importance for that person's own flourishing.
>
> Emotions... have a complicated cognitive structure that is part *narrative* in form, involving a *story* of our reaction to cherished objects that extends over time.[9]

By concentrating on the subset of memories with maximum emotional resonance, you reduce and simplify the grab bag of impressions you scribbled down from your past. The result: a manageable set of key memory pieces, capable of coalescing into the plotline of your life.

To illustrate the movement from memories to narrative, let us turn to Paula Balzer's own example. Her key memory pieces included the following list of must-be-included items:[10]

> 1970s
> classic rock
> *Stephen*
>
> . . .
>
> Mrs. Laubenheimer
> bullies
>
> . . .
>
> The Greendale Public Library
>
> . . .
>
> walking to school through the woods
>
> . . .
>
> playing outside
> not fitting in
> reading
> grandma's house

How could this random-looking list possibly generate a story? Pondering the list, Balzer suddenly perceived the figure in the marble. The list pointed to a "memoir focusing on *the friendship of two unlikely best friends and the unusual strength of their relationship*."[11] The key turned out to be *Stephen*. Balzer had taken for granted a surprising thread. She'd had the same best friend since she was four years old. Looking over her list of key memories, she "realized that he was with me when I experienced almost every single thing on that list."[12]

In seeking a thread to tie her memories into a tapestry, Balzer (we might say) got lucky. Maybe your list of key memories still looks chaotic. Don't be discouraged. Further disciplines can prompt the *aha!* moment.

---

9. Nussbaum, *Upheavals of Thought*, 4, 2 (italics mine).
10. Balzer, *Writing & Selling Your Memoir*, 74 (italics mine).
11. Ibid., 81 (italics mine).
12. Ibid., 77.

Stories unfold in time, and time has many dimensions. Furthermore, we construct many of these dimensions, by using time schemes to differentiate and cluster our moments. So, if we begin to explore the temporal dimensions of our biography, the scenes played out in our personal "theater" may begin to cluster into meaningful "acts."

## DIMENSIONS OF TIME

Past, present, future. Changes and constants. Without these basic temporal dimensions, meaningful storytelling would be impossible. Furthermore, reflecting on our *timelines* can birth our *plotlines*.

Time is objective (we measure it with a clock). However, as autobiographers, we can and do view time through our personal, subjective lenses. Let's reflect on some of the objective dimensions of time, and then consider how we each have unique experiences of the same objective reality.

The duration of time ("how long") is a given fact for everyone. Usain Bolt is the fastest human in the world, because his Olympic one-hundred-meter sprint can be timed with precision instruments to within one-hundredth of a second. And here's another objective quality of time, true for me and true for you: the past is fixed, but the future is malleable. In addition, certain turning points are undeniably objective—such as dates of births, and dates of deaths.

However, we *experience* time subjectively. Einstein observed that a man would experience two minutes sat on a hot stove as an eternity, but two minutes in the presence of a pretty girl as an instant.

Likewise, the way we *slice* and *batch* undifferentiated past time employs subjective divisions and clusters (even if these overlap with objective dimensions of time). Let's take a look at some of the temporal frameworks that might generate your life story.[13]

### Decades

Perhaps your personal story intersects strong generational and socio-cultural trends. If so, slicing your past into decades may crystallize your life story.

For example, a participant in the Woodstock music festival (1969) may be able to plot their overall mood changes across the decades. Their American experience might go something like this:

| 1950s | dull conformity; frustration |
|---|---|
| 1960s | ecstatic optimism; radicalism |
| 1970s/1980s | disappointment; conformity (*The Big Chill*)* |
| * The title of a 1983 movie that explored the latter phase of this generational cycle. ||

---

13. My discussion utilizes categories from Rainer, *Your Life as Story*, chapter 4.

## Seasons

Shakespeare's famous "All the world's a stage" speech proposed "seven ages" that males of his era experienced.[14] Each age or season has its own dominant goal and role. His consecutive seasons of life: infant; schoolboy; lover; soldier; judge; (with retirement and senility rounding out the pessimistic ending).

The "seasons" metaphor invites us to think of natural phases that overlap biological changes. Each season has its own distinct feel (the chill of winter versus the scorching summer). But seasons also connect through a common "theme" (the rise and fall of temperature; presence or absence of rain; etc.)

- How many seasons make up your past?
- What initiated and terminated each season?
- What makes each of your seasons distinct?
- Does anything remain constant across your seasons?
- How would you label each season?
- Do you see any kind of progression from your initial season to your current season?

## Single Slices

Perhaps your life is dominated by a single defining season. If so, you can readily explore your life story with a simple three act structure: before, during, and after the particular season (prologue, season, epilogue).

For example: an inner-city youth brought up in gangs (act one); imprisoned long-term as an eighteen-year-old (act two); currently out on parole, as a middle-aged man (act three). Here, the long-term imprisonment of act two probably constitutes the single, life-defining slice. With such clear-cut structures, obvious questions concern one's changes in outlook and behavior in the movement from prologue to epilogue.

## Patchwork Quilts

At the opposite end of the spectrum from the "single slice," Rainer highlights a curveball thrown at many of us, hindering the construction of our life story as a clear and simple trajectory. "Women's lives, especially, are *fragmented by constant interruptions*."[15] Career may be interrupted by child-rearing. A second career may be interrupted by caregiving for an elderly relative.

Such lives may feel more like a "quilt" (comprising disconnected episodes) than a "quest" (integrated by a single dominating goal).

---

14. *As You Like It* 2.7.
15. Rainer, *Your Life as Story*, 60 (italics mine).

Nevertheless, if you lay out before you the "patches" (episodes) of your life, can you see any narrative "threads" that might tie them together? For example, a recurrent problem, or a repeated pattern of behavior?

Pivots

A list of turning points offers another way to structure past time. Seasons and slices focus on experiences lived *between* two endpoints. But for some of us, the sequence of transition-points themselves may offer our clearest narrative thread. Pivots can be major ("after X, nothing was ever the same") or minor (stepping-stones toward irreversible changes).

- Write down all the events *you* consider turning points in your life: high-points, low-points, and *irreversible* changes. (Be honest about what matters to you. Don't rely on conventional social markers; maybe high-school graduation meant nothing to you!)
- Organize these events into chronological sequence.
- Label them as relatively major or minor.
- Looking over your list, do any of the pivots *cluster* into phases?
- Looking at your list from start to finish, do you see any *progression* (e.g., intensification of a problem; proximity to a goal; etc.)?

According to screenwriting guru Robert McKee, a *scene* in a film terminates with an upbeat or a downbeat.[16] "Up" and "down" concern the dominant *value* embraced by the protagonist. At the turning-points, is the value affirmed or denied by events? Is the embodiment or realization of the value developed or hindered? McKee gives these examples of values (and their binary opposites): "Alive/Dead; Love/Hate; Freedom/Slavery; Truth/Lie; Courage/Cowardice; Loyalty/Betrayal; Wisdom/Stupidity; Strength/Weakness; Excitement/Boredom; etc."[17] Looking back over your list of your pivotal events, do they reveal any *dominant value* that you struggle to embody in your world? Any growing insight into what really matters most?

Tristine Rainer shares the upbeats and downbeats of two of her *relationships* (with her mother and her husband).[18] Looking over her list, clear narrative arcs emerge. In her disposition toward her mother, over the course of a lifetime Rainer moved from adoration, to contempt, to profound sympathy. In her marriage, she experienced initial unity, growing disunity, a temporary recovery of unity, and ultimately a cool, distant coexistence.

* * * * *

16. McKee, *Story*, 33–37.
17. Ibid., 34.
18. Rainer, *Your Life as Story*, 57–59, 153–54.

Hopefully, by now you have some angles on how you might fruitfully structure your past, and some insight on how slicing and clustering time can lead you into story. Regardless of how you phase your past, the following exercise can help consolidate your reflection:[19]

- Try to think of your past life as a *novel*, with the different phases as *chapters*. How many chapters would your unfinished life story contain? Try to give an apt *title* to each chapter of your story.
- How would you title the *"next chapter"* of your life?

So far, our questions have concerned the overall *structure* of our *past*. But time has many other dimensions, and exploring these can move us closer to our personal narrative. Let's move onto some more diagnostic questions, beginning with some particular textures of our past not covered in the above discussion.

## My Past

In constructing our life story, we are most interested in the past in terms of *how it bears upon our present and future*.

- What is the single biggest *challenge* you have faced? How are you now different as a result of that experience?
- Describe any *health crisis* you (or a family member) may have faced. What is the lasting impact of this?
- Describe any major *losses* you have experienced, such as bereavement. (See my autobiographical material in chapter 2 of this book.) How did the event change you?
- Have there been any major *failures* or *regrets* in your life?
- Do you have an "if only" episode from your past ("*If only* X not Y had happened back then, everything would now be okay . . .")?
- Is there anything from your *childhood* that you would like to *regain*, or replicate in the present? Is there anything in your childhood that you are trying to *avoid* in your present?
- If you could *re-experience* any *one day* in your life, which day would it be, and why?
- Can you recall a *wisdom event* (when you acted wisely; gave wise counsel; made a wise decision)? How does that story shape your sense of personal identity?
- Can you recall a *religious* (or spiritual or mystical) event—e.g., a powerful sense of transcendence? How does that event shape your present life?
- What impact have *"chance"* events had on your life?
- What are some of the *subplots* (digressions) and *loose ends* of your story?

---

19. Borrowed from Foley Center, "Life Story Interview."

## My Present

Problems and tensions, struggles and conflicts, are the essence of story; use these to focus on your current situation:

- What is the biggest *challenge* you are currently facing?
- What *outcome* do you most desire (or fear) from this situation?
- What are you *doing* toward resolution of your difficulty?
- What (if any) *risks* are you currently taking? What *reward* do you hope to obtain by taking these risks?
- Do you identify with any current social/cultural/religious *movements*? If so, in what direction do you think your movement is heading? What challenges does your movement currently face?

## My Future

"The end of the story changes how we see each part of it."[20] Our projected future constrains many of the decisions we make in the present. Our projected self-image potentially alters how we act in the present. Donald Miller experienced this, when film-makers invited him to turn his autobiography into a movie: "In creating the fictional Don[ald], I was creating the person I wanted to be, the person worth telling stories about . . . in an evolution I had moved toward a better me. I was creating someone I could live through, the person I'd be if I redrew the world, a character that was me but . . . flesh and soul better."[21] Accordingly, Allender invites us to contemplate this possibility: What is your *ideal name* for your *future* self, in life roles such as worker, friend, parent, spouse, child, citizen, believer?[22] Here are some further questions directed at our projected self:

- What are your *long-term* dreams, hopes, plans?
- Do you have a *single-focus* "life project" that organizes your narrative?
- What do you *daydream* about? In your daydreams, what is the basic plot, and what role does your character play? Do you ever attempt to act out your daydreams (at least partially)?
- Do you have a "someday" fantasy ("*Someday*, when X happens, everything will be okay . . . ")?
- What is your biggest *fear*? How does this fear constrain your present behavior?
- What *legacy* do you hope to leave to future generations? What do you hope will be "inscribed on your tombstone"?

---

20. Rainer, *Your Life as Story*, 195–96.
21. Miller, *Million Miles*, 29.
22. Allender, *To Be Told*, 71.

One master plot that transcends particular cultures is the quest for paradise. This plot is a metaphor for many of our strivings and ambitions. The quest for *place* often intersects a storyline of ascent: our desire for personal *flourishing* (fulfillment of potential; attainment of happiness). Looking back on my own life story dug up these two related questions:

- Do I believe that finding "the right *place*" will allow me to flourish? Is my focus on finding a particular geographical location, or the right community, or the right institution to belong to?

- Or, do I believe that, once I have "*flourished*," I will gain access to a better place?

## Changes

Changes we strive for, changes we never asked for. Without change, story doesn't exist. Our assumptions about change (and constancy) are windows to our personal narrative.

- What do you hope *remains constant* as your life unfolds over time?
- If you could change *one thing* about yourself or your circumstances, what would it be?
- In terms of the changes you hope will happen, what do you expect will *cause* them? Your own efforts? Chance/luck? God/prayer? Other agents (family; church; government; etc.)?

## Habitual Scripts

Over time, we develop habitual responses ("scripts") in response to recurrent "scenes." These scripts operate at micro and macro levels of our story.

- In your story, are there any *scenarios* that keep playing themselves out, like a broken record? Are your own behavior patterns contributing to this "Groundhog Day" storyline?[23]

- Whenever you *fail* at something, do you have a standard *response*? For example, do you tend to give up? Try harder (repeating the same strategy, with added resolve)? Think outside the box (search for a new strategy)? Switch goals?

Allender gives a couple of examples, both pertaining to leadership, of how our current scripts may root in earlier experiences.[24]

- *Avoiding Leadership*: Allender describes four decades of his life as "a flight from leadership." He chose this pattern of avoidance in reaction against his early boyhood experience of being thrust unwillingly into leadership. His father died when Allender was young, and his mother remarried. His stepfather was passive and

---

23. See the 1993 movie *Groundhog Day*, in which the protagonist (Bill Murray) is compelled to relive the same day over and over and over again.

24. Allender, *To Be Told*, 65, 124, 132.

uncommunicative. So, the young Allender became the mediator between step-dad and mom. Furthermore, his mother doted on him, and deferred significant family decisions to her eight-year-old son! The burden of responsibility became oppressive to the child, who consequently fled from leadership as an adult.

- *Assuming Leadership:* Not everyone responds in the same way to the burden of being a childhood leader. Allender tells the story of Judi, whose single mom was highly irresponsible as a parent. As the oldest child, Judi became the functioning "parent" of her younger siblings. In her twenties, Judi overachieved as a church leader and as a salesperson. The early leadership role became her life script.

\* \* \* \* \*

Our diagnostic questions about temporal dimensions of life were all designed to move us toward reflection upon the plotline of our life. Accordingly, our next sections batch questions under the classic elements of plot.

## DIMENSIONS OF PLOT

The next batch of questions covers different *phases* of classic literary plot structure. The questions reflect our instinctive (and often unconscious) tendency to organize our life using narrative structure.

### Setting

Any story begins with establishing the "rules of the game." These basic assumptions constrain the protagonist and the outcome.

- What seems fixed or "given" in your personal situation?
- How do these "givens" constrain your choices? How do they limit potential outcomes to your story?
- Do you or feel the world is (or is not) a safe place for you to flourish? Why or why not?

### Trigger Incident

For a story to actually get going, something must disrupt the routine of the protagonist. For some of us, the disruption was big and dramatic and obvious. Balzer calls these events "cornerstone days"[25] (using an architectural metaphor; the cornerstone *aligns* all the other stones in a building).

For others, their life trajectory was set by something apparently very trivial, which somehow triggered a different way of thinking. For food journalist Anthony Bourdain,

---

25. Balzer, *Writing & Selling Your Memoir*, 52–54.

he was traveling through France with his parents. Despite the gourmet foods available, all he ever insisted upon eating was hamburgers and soda. One evening, his parents wearied of this monotonous diet, and left Bourdain and his brother in the car for three hours, while they themselves dined in a five-star restaurant. Left to ponder, Bourdain's curiosity was awakened. What culinary experience was available behind those walls?[26]

If you struggle to find a pivotal beginning to your story, Rainer suggests this exercise (as a way of tapping into our subconscious awareness of story archetypes):

- Imagine your life as a *fairy tale*; complete the following sentence: "Once upon a time, there was a boy/girl who . . ."[27]

Here are some more diagnostics related to the narrative inception of your life story:

- If you feel you are on some sort of trajectory, reflect upon the initial trigger that put you into motion. What caused a change of direction? Was the change irreversible? What problem arose, or what new horizon opened up?
- Looking back to that moment, what expectations did you have about your destination?
- How does the present compare with those initial projections?

## Escalations

In one sentence, story = "a character who wants something and overcomes conflict to get it."[28] Our next diagnostics all focus on desire and conflict.

You've heard it said, "He/she is his/her own worst enemy." Often, the conflict we must overcome resides within ourselves. Frequently, this conflict is a clash of *opposite values*. The values may be good, bad, or relative. Rainer's own life story oscillated around "professional self-fulfillment versus family commitment."[29]

Sometimes, a superficial conflict can offer a window into deeper struggles. For Rainer's student Cheryl, *diet versus eat-what-I-want* offered a window into challenges Cheryl faced in her marriage. She was a problem-avoider, who nevertheless wanted to please her husband, who was a problem-confronter![30]

- If your life has a clear goal, what are some of your internal values that may *hinder* that goal?
- *When* has your internal-value conflict been most acute?

Rainer speaks of your *desire line* as "the engine of your story," and observes that your desire line may "bend or intensify" over time.[31]

---

26. Ibid., 56–57.
27. Rainer, *Your Life as Story*, 42–43.
28. Miller, *Million Miles*, 48.
29. Rainer, *Your Life as Story*, 155.
30. Ibid., 224–26.
31. Ibid., 68, 80.

To illustrate the morphing of desire, she mentions her student Liesal, who resided in Washington, DC. Tired of fast-paced urban life, Liesal and her husband developed a pivotal desire for *more time with their children*. So they sought a *place* away from the bustle of the capitol. They chose Costa Rica. But then their desire shifted toward finding a suitable *house*. Once they located their new house, they had to face the problem of *making a living* in that location.[32]

- Make a chronological list of the *strongest desires* operating over the course of your life.
- Do you see any pattern of *intensification* of desire? Any pattern of *morphing* of desire? If your desires have morphed, is there a *plotline thread* that ties them together?

Another lens for viewing our plotline comes through consideration of *antagonists* and *allies*.

- In your struggles, what *external* forces and powers align against you and your goals?
- Name some *people* who have *helped* or *hindered* you along your path. How did they help or hinder?
- Do you have any *weakness* or *disability* that makes your goals harder to accomplish?

## Crises

At various points in our story, we reach crossroads, points of no return. "The Chinese ideogram for Crisis is two terms: Danger/Opportunity."[33] Often, the crisis involves choosing between competing goods, or between the lesser of two evils. Our decision may involve personal sacrifice.

- When have you been forced to choose between competing goods? Or between the lesser of two evils? What decision did you make, and why? Do you ever regret your choice?
- When have you made a costly personal sacrifice? Why? Do you ever regret the cost?
- "Was there a point where something in you *died* so something else could be *born*? Was it a belief, a need, a feeling, or a person that died in you?"[34]

## Resolutions

Maybe some of your plotlines have resolved, and your sense of endings can help crystallize your personal narrative. As Allender observes, positive endings naturally lead to *celebrations*.[35] Accordingly, what we choose to celebrate offers clues to our personal story.

---

32. Ibid., 237–38.
33. McKee, *Story*, 303.
34. Rainer, *Your Life as Story*, 81 (italics mine).
35. Allender, *To Be Told*, 23.

Part 1: In the Beginning Was the Story

- What *milestones* have you celebrated?
- Does your list of milestone celebrations give insight into your personal values and goals?

Resolved narratives give us perspective for looking back on events and on ourselves. The context of a finished story can make sense of puzzling episodes. Our character arc can redefine who we are.

Look back on some of the finished stories of your life. Goals achieved; problems resolved; etc. And reflect on some of the ways you are now a different person as a result of living those stories:

- At the end of those stories, did you experience any *aha!* moments? Any *life lessons* that now guide you?
- Did your *values change* as you lived the story from beginning to end?
- Was there *moral improvement* within you, or in your behavior, as a result of your struggles?
- Looking back on the story as a whole, can you see how your particular life has manifested *transcendent meaning*? How you have uniquely embodied some *universal* human value? How your story reveals some truth about *God*?

Most of our stories involve *suffering* at some point. And suffering can seem pointless. And yet, the passage of time offers the perspectives of narrative, perspectives that may perhaps make sense out of the senseless. Our suffering connects us to transcendent narratives. As Jungian psychologists say, "The wound is the place where the myth and the real life meet."[36]

- Has your story revealed how *good* can emerge from *evil*?
- Did any surprisingly positive *doors* open up in connection with a *loss* experience?[37]
- What *wisdom* can you pass on to people whose *suffering* mirrors your own experience?

## STORIES THAT SHAPE ME

In chapter 1 of this book, Narrator #5 made a profound statement: "It can take a long time to figure out why a particular story so grabs your heart." Following this trail, some basic questions about *novels* and *films* may help:

- Do you have a film you've watched more than twice, or a novel you've read more than once? What compels your revisits?
- Is there any film that made you *weep*? Why?

---

36. James Hillman, quoted in Rainer, *Your Life as Story*, 196.
37. See Balzer, *Writing & Selling Your Memoir*, 61.

- Is there a novel that you "couldn't put down"? Was it a plotline you are currently in, or would like to be in?
- "The book that changed my life is ___." Fill in the blank. How did it change your life?
- Is there a *character* in a play, novel, or film, with whom you most strongly *identify*? Why?

We not only encounter stories in fictional form, but also in *historical narratives*. Let's explore how these may have influenced us:

- Do you have a favorite narrative book (or episode) in the Bible? What has that story done for your life?
- Do you look back longingly at a *golden age* in history? What, exactly, about that era kindles your longing? Which elements from that era do you attempt to *replicate* in your present?

Culture, religion, and history are not the only sources of stories that shape us. Most of us grew up hearing *oral* narratives from family, neighbors, teachers, and friends.

- Try to recall some word-of-mouth stories and anecdotes you heard growing up. Did any of these have lasting impact upon you? How?

We can dig from many other angles to surface the stories that have shaped us. For an additional list of diagnostic questions (under headings like "family stories," "school stories," etc.), one might consult Daniel Taylor's helpful work.[38]

## STORIES IN SEED FORM (MICROCOSMS AND FORESHADOWINGS)

Culture, religion, history, and oral anecdotes have supplied us with stories that shape us. Oftentimes, these stories shape us as *metaphors of our own life*. However, particular *episodes* from *our own past* can also function as metaphors of our entire life.

- Do any salient episodes from your past seem to *symbolize* your life?
- In what ways are these episodes *microcosms* of your whole life?
- How do the episodes *foreshadow* your later trajectories?

To wrap up this chapter, let's illustrate the workings of this "microcosm" concept, using one example from the Gospels, and a couple more from my own life.

### Dewdrops and Rainbows

Almost one hundred years ago, a New Testament scholar suggested a brilliant analogy. His proposal: each episode in the Gospels is like a drop of dew on a field in the morning sunlight. As it catches the sunlight, the tiny pearl of water hosts a miniature rainbow.

---

38. Taylor, *Healing Power of Stories*, 159–65.

Inside the dewdrop, the full spectrum of the seven colors of the rainbow. Likewise, each episode in the Gospels is a microcosm of the entire story of Jesus.

Let's pick a random illustration of the analogy. In the episode of Luke 8:42b–48, Jesus is on the way to the house of a religious leader. As usual, Jesus is mobbed by big crowds. In the crowd, a woman, suffering from chronic internal bleeding that has persisted for twelve years.

Weird though it may seem to us, in her ancient society, a culture obsessed with symbolic purity, her affliction made her something of an outcast, which explains her secrecy. Hidden in the crowd, she sneaks up behind Jesus, and touches the edge of his robe. Immediately, her internal bleeding ceases. She is healed.

Jesus asks, "Who touched me?" Others in the crowd reply, "Not me!" Peter (trying to be helpful) states the obvious: with all the jostling people, it could have been anyone! But Jesus reaffirms, "Someone did touch me." And so the woman, trembling, comes forward and publicly tells her story of medical problems, ostracism, and now healing. Jesus had persisted with his inquiry because he wanted her to experience public removal of her shame, and social restoration.

According to the ancient cultural symbolism, Jesus would have contracted impurity through physical contact with the impure. Hence the episode becomes a *microcosm* of the entire story of Jesus, who bears our shame, and restores us to a full relationship with God.

As literary works, the Gospels don't waste any episodes, and contour each episode to highlight its symbolic expression of the entire story of Jesus. In our humdrum existence, not every scene signifies that much. But, if we have eyes to see, from time to time a microcosmic episode rises from the mundane, and represents a life story. Here are some examples.

## Escapade in the Rio Grande

In the summer of 2013, my wife and I chaperoned a dozen Hispanic teenagers on a church retreat. We stayed in a cabin in the mountains of New Mexico. Somewhat reluctantly, the teens participated in our carefully-scheduled morning devotions and afternoon Bible studies. By the end of the week, you could say that cabin fever had set in.

So, as a highlight of the trip, we ended the week with a visit to the Rio Grande River Gorge out in the semi-desert. Think Grand Canyon, on a smaller (but still massively impressive) scale.

As soon as we reached the Rio Grande, the teenage boys (not the girls) emptied out of the SUVs, and headed for the perimeter of the gorge. "Be careful, wait for a grown-up!" we yelled (with futility).

My wife and I tried to keep up, as the boys raced into the distance. Soon, they were half a mile ahead of us, pinpricks in the desert sunlight. And then they disappeared. Not just from sight, but down the steep rocky sides of the gorge. A vertical plunge of several hundred feet. Briar and cactus lined the sides of the canyon. If you slipped, nothing but rocks to break your fall.

By the time we reached the edge, the boys had clambered to the bottom of the gorge and back up again. With only a few scratches.

Later that summer, I used this episode in one of my youth group talks. I asked the boys to volunteer an explanation of their escapade in the gorge. Reluctantly, they agreed to the following motives: freedom from chaperones; competition in bravery with other males; testing oneself against physical danger.

This episode, I suggested, is a *microcosm* of the young Hispanic male quest to establish a personal identity, complete with an appropriate amount of machismo.

## Fireworks and Foresters

When I was five years old, I lived in what Americans would call a row-home in Cambridge, England. We had a narrow backyard, with a long flagstone path.

Each year, on the Fifth of November, my family celebrated the English equivalent of the Fourth of July—well, at least as far as the fireworks are concerned. Unlike America, the norm was for each family to have a private firework display in their own backyard. (Something about an Englishman's home being his castle, perhaps.)

As a four-year-old, I had accompanied my father to the local store that sold fireworks. Dad allowed me to pick out fifty different fireworks from under the protective glass case. Roman Candles. Pinwheels. Banshees. Screech Owls. Rockets.

Later that evening, my mother, my younger sister and I stood (at a safe distance) on our back porch, while Dad walked down the flagstone path, and lit the fireworks one by one.

The next year, I turned five. We purchased the fireworks a week early, and kept them in a square tin box with a lid. Each day, leading up to the celebration, I took them out of the box, and lined them up on the floor, to determine the "best" sequence in which to light them. Start with a Rocket. Then a Roman Candle. Next a Firefly, or maybe a Burning Bush. (Don't try this at home, kids.)

Like a good narrative, or a classical music symphony, the firework display needed a proper sequence. Moments of intensified drama, followed by moments of relative calm. That evening, my father "conducted" my pyrotechnic symphony, lighting the fifty fireworks in the sequence I had selected.

When I turned six, my father got a new job. So we moved away from Cambridge, to a rural village in the county of Essex. I was enrolled at the local elementary school. Back then, English elementary schools only had four grades. First grade was like entering Hogwarts for Harry Potter. My school had four "houses." The houses competed against one another for intermural sports trophies—especially soccer (or football, as we called it). In a big ceremony, each child was randomly placed in a particular house.

There were four houses, each with their own color for the soccer uniform, and each with names evoking English history. Vikings (wearing blue); Crusaders (red); Templars (yellow). Any first-grade boy would be proud to compete under any of those heroic-sounding banners!

And then there was Foresters (wearing green). Foresters! What were they, a bunch of tree-huggers?

At the "sorting ceremony," the (non-magical) equivalent of Hogwarts' sorting-hat assigned boy after boy to different houses. We all wanted to be in Templars, because

Part 1: In the Beginning Was the Story

senior boy Kevin Ingold was captain of Templars soccer team. Every first-grade boy had a man-crush on Kevin Ingold. But Vikings or Crusaders would do. Anything but Foresters, who had not won the school soccer trophy for as long as anyone could remember.

Foresters. The green soccer jersey. I cried that night. My soccer career was ruined.

My father persuaded me to keep practicing soccer (even if he acknowledged that the school trophy seemed out of the reach of Foresters). Second grade turned into third and then fourth. I was a senior boy, and elected captain of the Foresters soccer team.

One morning, in the school library, I found a book on "advanced football tactics," written by Alan Ball (who had helped England win their only world cup when I was a five-year-old). Opening the pages, I entered a new world.

Up until then, I had believed (like every boy in my school) that soccer was about individual brilliance. Dribbling and scoring goals. That was how we played on the field at every recess.

But the book-of-tactics shared a different wisdom. "Let the ball do the work. Pass, don't dribble. Keep the ball on the ground. Look for the teammate located in the most open space."

At that moment, I knew my "calling." As captain, I assembled my fellow Foresters at the next recess. From now on, I told them, no more dribbling. No more aimless punting the ball long and high. We will practice passing the football. Short passes, keeping the ball on the ground.

That year, for the first time that anyone could remember, the green shirts of Foresters had a winning season (five wins and only one loss). We topped the intramural league table. As captain, I got to raise the trophy at graduation in May.

\* \* \* \* \*

When I did the *memory-joggers* recommended at the start of this chapter, "Fireworks" and "Foresters" were two of the first episodes I wrote down. I wasn't sure why. But from my vantage-point as a fifty-five-year-old teacher, storyteller, and writer, the episodes do resemble child-like analogues of what I now consider my vocation. The child is the father of the man.

# 5

# Identity Theft

IDENTITY THEFT. TERRIFYING WORDS. Loss of money. Loss of credit. Loss of privacy. We instinctively guard our passwords and social security numbers, to protect our identity.

Meanwhile, a subtler, ultimately more-devastating loss of identity has consumed two generations of Americans. The loss of identity that occurs when you lose your story (capital S). Without an overarching story, we lose our roots, our roles, our destiny. Without these, our identity evaporates.

Generations X and Y have lost their story. The postmodern collapse of the "grand narrative" reduces life to a succession of trivial, disconnected moments. These husks of hollowed-out stories cannot feed the soul. Without a bigger story, the big questions (Who am I? How should I live? Why should I live?) go unanswered.

I am writing this book partly in response to this cultural moment.

Zero Story = Zero Identity.

To grasp this equation, consider patients suffering *memory loss* (caused by accidents or medical problems). The patient does not know who they are, because they have literally lost their story—the narrative of their personal history and experiences. It's like their personal GPS malfunctioned.

More broadly, we speak of a *confused* person as someone who "has *lost the plot.*" And this popular idiom is not merely a figure of speech.

In earlier times and places, the dominant culture provided an overarching "myth," a big umbrella narrative that shaped the personal narrative of the individual. And, functionally speaking, this situation had a lot of positives. If your personal story fits under your culture's big umbrella narrative, here are some of the payoffs:

- *Plausibility.* Rooted in tradition, affirmed in community. "When all around take fundamental ideas for granted, these must be the truth. For most minds there is no comfort like it."[1] The ancient mind nestled secure under the big umbrella of its tribal myth.

- *Inheritance.* Born into such a community of tradition, your umbrella narrative comes with your birth certificate, so to speak. You inherit a narrative that makes

---

1. Barzun, *Dawn to Decadence*, 23.

Part 1: In the Beginning Was the Story

sense of yourself and the world. No angst-ridden existentialist struggle to "create" your own meaning. No burden to perpetually "re-invent" yourself.

- *Transcendence.* When a Big Story embraces you, it offers you a privileged role in an epic, like being a character in Tolkien's *Lord of the Rings.* Inside such an epic, even mundane actions have transcendent dignity and purpose.

- *Answers.* Umbrella narratives answer our basic human questions. What is valuable (worth struggling for)? What is virtuous (worth becoming)? What is wrong with us, and what can make it right? Such basic questions have components of narrative (struggle, becoming, change) at their core. So, we can only answer them by appealing to an overarching narrative.

In this chapter, we will explore the contemporary experience of losing our big stories. What stole them away? As an on-ramp, our next section sharpens the contrast between ancients and moderns.

## NATIVE AMERICANS VERSUS CARTESIANS

Who am I? How do I *know* who I am? Ancient traditions answer these questions one way; modern Western philosophy has chosen a very different pathway. To illustrate, let's turn to a poignant Native American myth.

Kiowa author N. Scott Momaday won a Pulitzer Prize (1969) for his novel *House Made of Dawn.* The author explains the origins of his Kiowa name, Tsoai-talee = Rock-Tree Boy. The Kiowa tell an etiological tale, to explain the origins of a remarkable rock-formation. The rock looms upwards into the sky, and its sides are scarred with vertical lines.

According to Kiowa narrative, a boy was playing with his seven sisters. Suddenly, the boy became a bear, and chased his sisters. They fled to a tree stump, which spoke and invited them to safety. As they climbed the tree stump, it stretched upward to the heavens. The pursuing bear scratched the tree with its sharp claws, creating the vertical lines of the rock formation. The sisters were changed into the star formation commonly called the Big Dipper.[2]

> Momaday claims this . . . tribal story helped shape his understanding of himself and his place in the world. It tells him who he is. "My name is Tsoai-talee. I am, therefore, Tsoai-talee; therefore I am." The echo of Descartes's famous "I think, therefore I am" is undoubtedly intentional. Descartes said his awareness of himself thinking proved he existed; Momaday knows he exists because he is part of a story that has given him a name. He *is* the boy in the story—they share the same name—and therefore the stars of the constellations are his sisters. He is connected to the universe. No matter where he is, he can look into the sky and feel at home.[3]

---

2. Cited in Taylor, *Healing Power of Stories*, 23–24.
3. Ibid., 24–25 (italics in original).

Contrast this with Descartes, one of the fathers of modern Western philosophy. In the 1630s, Descartes wrestled with a widespread loss of certainty (resulting from the Protestant Reformation's overturning of the consensus of medieval Catholicism). Descartes sought a new certainty. His method: critical doubt. Sift and reject all your beliefs, until you find "a clear and distinct idea," which you cannot doubt.[4] The result: a philosophical abstraction, "I think, therefore I am."

Henceforth, abstract philosophical logic would usurp the place traditionally occupied by religious narratives. Philosophy joined forces with science, whose mathematical description of the cosmos replaces the narrative depictions offered by traditional religions.

Jean-François Lyotard accurately describes modern Western skepticism toward narrative ways of knowing:

> The scientist questions the validity of narrative statements and concludes that they are never subject to argument or proof. He classifies them as belonging to a different mentality: savage, primitive, underdeveloped, backward, alienated, composed of opinions, customs, authority, prejudice, ignorance, ideology. Narratives are fables, myths, legends, fit only for women and children.[5]

Western philosophy's downgrading of traditional narratives has very deep roots: Plato himself, the fountainhead of Western philosophy. In his famous allegory of the Cave, Plato depicts the unenlightened human condition.[6]

Those untrained in philosophy are, says Plato, like individuals perpetually inhabiting a cave whose entrance opens to the sunlight. Deep inside the cave, the inhabitants are chained with their backs to the entrance, and their heads immobile, so they can only see the back wall of the cave. Behind the prisoners, there burns a fire, illuminating the back wall. A parade of objects passes behind the cave-dwellers, and these objects cast shadows onto the back wall.

Under these conditions, asks Plato, wouldn't the cave-dwellers mistake the shadows of the objects for their reality? Wouldn't they be oblivious to the true light of the sun that enables perception of reality?

Plato's allegory depicts traditional knowledge as several steps removed from reality. Traditional knowledge uses secondary light (fire), not the primary light of the sun. Furthermore, traditional knowledge only sees the shadows of objects, not the reality.

What is the traditional knowledge which non-philosophers confuse with reality? Plato answers this in his (in)famous attack on "poetry"—by which he means epic narrative (Homer) and Greek drama. These traditional narratives, says Plato, are several steps removed from reality (just like the knowledge of the cave-dwellers in the allegory). In attacking Greek epic and tragedy, Plato also attacks the traditional mythology of the gods (woven into the fabric of epic and tragedy).[7]

---

4. Barzun, *Dawn to Decadence*, 200.
5. Lyotard, *Postmodern Condition*, 27.
6. Plato, *Republic* 7.
7. Plato, *Republic* 10.

How, asks Plato, can the mind be weaned away from defective knowledge, and enlightened toward real knowledge? By studying the abstract sciences of arithmetic and geometry![8]

At this point, it's hard not to fast-forward to Descartes—who not only helped kick-start modern philosophy, but also gave us the Cartesian geometry of the x, y, and z axes.

Many have noted a certain irony in Plato's dismissal of narrative knowledge: he relies on narrative (the allegory of the cave) in order to downgrade narrative. "Knowledge is thus founded on the narrative of its own martyrdom."[9] As we will discuss below, the same irony gets recycled through Western thought down to the present.

* * * * *

If the modern world—roughly the last five hundred years of Western history—has been unfriendly toward traditional religious metanarratives, the postmodern world is unfriendly toward *all* metanarratives. In Lyotard's famous expression, "Simplifying in the extreme, I define *postmodern* as incredulity toward metanarratives."[10]

## THE POSTMODERN CONDITION

Geologists speak of "tectonic shifts," or global and irreversible movements of the earth's "plates," creating a new and distinct land mass, where new forms of life emerge. (Think of marsupials in Australia.) By analogy, the emergence of the postmodern world is a socio-cultural tectonic shift (or maybe a "*tech*-tonic" shift).

Like Australia, the vast terrain of the postmodern is hard to circumnavigate. "Postmodernism is a slippery concept which evades definition."[11] So, instead of attempting to bottle quicksilver, I will merely register some social and cultural forces which have pushed the big stories off the postmodern stage. (My approach also avoids chicken-and-egg discussions [of what caused what]. Likewise, I'll avoid debating whether some socio-cultural forces are best viewed as "late modern" or "hypermodern" rather than distinctively *post*modern.[12])

Immersed in my present context—America in the new millennium—I feel the tug of many undercurrents, all pulling me from the safe harbor of my traditional narrative. Some currents feel impersonal and objective, technological and economic forces. Other currents feel more personal and subjective; a cultural style, a critical stance. Some currents seem unavoidable (digital media; market forces); others (relativity of moral and religious truth) seem more like personal choices.

In any case, the two types of current flow together. The material conditions of Western technology and economy provide a fertile womb for the growth of postmodern

---

8. Plato, *Republic* 7.
9. Lyotard, *Postmodern Condition*, 29.
10. Ibid., xxiv (italics in original).
11. Cobley, *Narrative*, 183.
12. Cf. Middleton and Walsh, *Truth Is Stranger*, 41, 54.

values. Postmodernism has been dubbed "the cultural logic of late capitalism."[13] (Scholarly aside: some commentators reserve the label "postmodern*ity*" for the technological and economic context, and use the label "postmodern*ism*" to refer to a set of beliefs and/or a value system espoused by postmodern people. I don't promise to be so consistent in my usage!)

In the subsections below, I register some of the forces behind the emergence of the postmodern condition. These forces are cumulative, overlapping, mutually reinforcing. Their vortex plunges us into a strange new world. Like Dorothy in the film *The Wizard of Oz*, "We're not in Kansas anymore."

If I were producing a pop-culture documentary on postmodernity, I would probably use the title, "*Banishing the Big Stories: Seven Deadly Forces*." And the forces I would depict are these:

- media and technocracy
- post-industrial consumerism
- (post)modern art
- liberal democracy
- post-colonialism
- the "linguistic turn"
- philosophy and science

Now here's the kicker: not all the forces discussed in my subsections are bad! For instance, few would choose to live outside a democracy. Few would forego the convenience of electronic communications.

Regardless of how we evaluate the forces, my focus remains simple: how the postmodern has disempowered our big stories.

Now let us briefly annotate each of these seven forces, and sketch their negative, vitality-sapping impact upon our traditional "grand narratives."

## Media and Technocracy

| Spheres of Impact | daily life; pop culture; commerce and government |
|---|---|
| Results of Impact | proliferation of narratives (pluralism); the triumph of means (efficiency) over ends.* |
| * Lyotard, *Postmodern Condition*, 37, 46–49, 51. ||

People need stories as guideposts, but late modernity struggles to provide us with a story we can inhabit. Or maybe it provides too many stories. The twentieth century *proliferation of media* (radio; cinema; TV; internet) has led to a proliferation of narratives,[14] mu-

---

13. Frederic Jameson, quoted in Cobley, *Narrative*, 183.
14. Cobley, *Narrative*, 189, 193, 197, 200, 212.

tually canceling each others' authority. Choosing one story as your basic guide becomes as near-impossible as choosing one breakfast cereal from the hundreds of brands in the supermarket aisle.

Hence the commonplace observation that postmodern life resembles a *carnival*, which "offers only the clamor of multifarious sideshow hawkers calling out for our momentary attention."[15]

Maybe if we had a proliferation of great stories—an embarrassment of riches—this would be okay. Just pick one; they're all good. Sadly, the verdict of scriptwriting guru Robert McKee seems to sum up the reality of narrative proliferation:

> Each year, Hollywood produces and/or distributes four hundred to five hundred films, virtually a film a day. A few are excellent, but the majority are mediocre or worse . . . Despite . . . the exhaustive efforts of development personnel, Hollywood cannot find better material than it produces. The hard-to-believe truth is that what we see on the screen each year is a reasonable reflection of the best writing of the last few years.[16]

Proliferation of media belongs to a bigger technological revolution—the transformation of society into a *technocracy*.

Have you ever been perfectly content with version 1.0 of some digital device, only to be forced by its producer to "upgrade" (to something with more bells and whistles)? Welcome to the world of technocracy, where means eclipse ends. Efficiency eclipses eschatology. Being faster or flashier becomes its own end. Think of "special effects" in the cinema, dominating many films to the detriment of the traditional elements of plot and character. The "tail" (medium) wags the "dog" (message).

The older grand narratives answered the question "Why?" Daily choices contributed to the realization of a big, noble, long-term goal. The technocratic imperative saps the urgency of the "Why" question, by focusing all our energies onto a reductionist "How." How can daily life operate more efficiently?

Lyotard aptly describes the citizens of a technocracy, seeking to harness the complex "machinery" available to them: "They have at their disposal no metalanguage or metanarrative in which to formulate the final goal and correct use of that machinery. But they do have brainstorming to improve its performance."[17] Technocracy and multi-media; discussion of these forces leads naturally into our next category, and a focus on the distinctive *economy* that emerged in the West in the second half of the twentieth century.

---

15. Middleton and Walsh, *Truth is Stranger*, 42.
16. McKee, *Story*, 13–14.
17. Lyotard, *Postmodern Condition*, 52.

## Post-Industrial Consumerism

| Sphere of Impact | marketplace |
|---|---|
| Results of Impact | exaltation of *individual* narratives (of enjoyment of goods and services);* loss of commonly-shared economic tasks |
| * Lyotard, "Postmodern Condition," 38. ||

The twentieth century witnessed the emergence of *post-industrial economies*.[18] We shifted from the machine age of mass production of material goods, into a highly-diversified economy based on services, information, and consumption.

This shift has fed the postmodern decline of the grand narrative. An economy driven by consumer sovereignty fits hand-in-glove with sovereign individual choice of one's own personal life-narrative. Peter Berger explains how our consumer economy contributes to the demise of traditional religious narratives:

> The religious tradition, which previously could be authoritatively imposed, now has to be *marketed*. It must be "sold" to a clientele that is no longer constrained to "buy." The pluralist situation is, above all, a *market situation*. In it, the religious institutions become the marketing agencies and the religious traditions become consumer commodities.[19]

Furthermore, in the post-industrial economy, our ultra-diversified job descriptions dilute our ability to connect to the homogenous narrative of any broad community.[20] Many of us spend our working hours inside task-narratives that few others can relate to.

By contrast, the older agrarian economies at least provided common tasks and shared symbols to unite large communities. (Think of the communal importance of the harvest, and its frequent "mythic" connection to transcendent narratives.) Similarly, the machine age united large numbers of workers in factories, and this often gave the workers a shared narrative (such as "class struggle").

## (Post)Modern Art

| Spheres of Impact | advertising; pop culture; architecture |
|---|---|
| Results of Impact | *abstract* art challenges power of narrative to represent reality; *abstract* art → viewer creates meaning; *eclectic* art → pluralism of values |

---

18. Many of the implications of this shift are discussed in the works of Alvin Toffler. Toffler posits three socio-economic "waves" in history, differentiated according to their means of production: agrarian; industrial; post-industrial. See Toffler, *Third Wave*.

19. Quoted in Middleton and Walsh, *Truth is Stranger*, 43 (italics in original).

20. Sociologists speak of our (post)industrial society as "low context," in contrast to the "high context" societies of agrarian antiquity. People in "high context" societies have many more commonly-held narratives. See Malina and Pilch, *Social-Science Commentary*, 19–21.

Why would art impact the stories we live? Humans use arts—such as painting and sculpture—to freeze the experience of time encountered in narrative and in life:

> Experience is molded . . . by narrative forms, and its narrative quality is altogether primitive . . . [But] there seems to be a powerful inner drive of thought and imagination to overcome the relentless temporality of experience . . . The kind of pure spatial articulation we find in painting and sculpture, with all movement suspended, gratifies this deep need.[21]

Perhaps this is one reason why traditional painting frequently depicted scenes from biblical and classical narratives, as well as scenes from everyday life.

But when we turn to modern art, scenes from life and from traditional narratives disappear. In their place, the abstract geometry of Mondrian, or the paint-thrown-randomly-onto-canvas of Jackson Pollock. Implication: traditional narrative scenes cannot truly represent reality.

Most of us don't visit modern art galleries. But we are all exposed to advertising. A few years ago, a well-known shampoo manufacturer designed their bottles to resemble a Mondrian painting. Art critic H. R. Rookmaaker describes his style: "Pictorial elements were reduced to their simplest and most rigid terms: black horizontal and vertical lines, white, red, yellow and blue colour[sic]—and nothing else."[22] What drove the abstractness of modern art? A quest for the transcendent, the universal, the absolute.[23] However, previous generations of artists had abandoned the themes and subject-matter of classical narrative—the traditional house of the transcendent.[24] Accordingly, twentieth-century artists turned to ever-increasing compositional abstraction as a gateway to the transcendent. Unsurprisingly, their quest failed, and their work degenerated into ever-increasing assertions of the absence of meaning.[25]

The abstract tendencies of modern art had another implication for narrative. Meaning was no longer "given" in a painting, but the viewer had to figure out what the splashes of color might mean: "In all this type of art the onlooker is asked to be active. He has to "go into the picture," and in a kind of irrational, completely free action get his own meaning out of it."[26] Analogous to "reader-response" approaches to studies of literary texts, such art enthrones the autonomous self over against external authorities (such as traditional narratives).

If modern abstract art exhibited an austere consistency, postmodern art revels in the playfulness of the eclectic. Postmodern art celebrates a mishmash of styles, fusing symbols which previous generations considered contradictory.[27] Pop culture mass-markets these hybrid art forms. Like avatars of the "*coexist*" bumper sticker, celebrities

---

21. Crites, "Narrative Quality of Experience," 84.

22. Rookmaaker, *Modern Art*, 123.

23. Ibid., 102–22.

24. Ibid., 57–61.

25. Ibid., 119–22. Cf. Lyotard's analysis of modern art's nostalgia for the unattainable sublime (*Postmodern Condition*, 78–81).

26. Rookmaaker, *Modern Art*, 168.

27. For brief analysis of the alliance of eclectic art and postmodern philosophy, see Kimball, *Emerging Church*, 51–54.

decorate themselves with symbols of syncretized religion. Crucifixes, crescents, and tattooed symbols of Eastern religions crowd onto one body.

These art forms contribute to the demise of grand narratives, by relativizing their claims. In Lyotard's expression, postmodern art and literature "wage a war on totality."[28]

## Liberal Democracy

| Spheres of Impact | politics; legislation |
|---|---|
| Results of Impact | curtailing "heroic" impulse of epics; relativizing of values (pluralism) |

Some readers might wonder why this category appears as a "foe" of big stories. Isn't the rise of liberal democracy the stuff of epics? (The American Revolution, for example.) Heroic struggles to establish individual rights, and ensure government of the people for the people by the people. What's not to like?

Yes, many nations proudly recount their struggle toward liberal democracy. But then the irony kicks in. Once achieved, free and democratic societies tend to curtail the heroic impulse which birthed them.

Francis Fukuyama explains the inner logic of this ironic development.[29] Liberal democracies arose, he argues, to restrain the human *desire for recognition*, to encourage contentment with equal recognition in the eyes of others.

What's so bad about desire for recognition? Doesn't it beget greatness in the arts, for example? Yes. But it also begets war and tyranny, valorized in heroic narratives of conquest (Homer's *Iliad*; Virgil's *Aeneid*).

Desire for recognition has a dark side, and modern Western democracy arose to restrain it. Foundational thinkers like Thomas Hobbes (1588-1679) and John Locke (1632-1704) sought a social system that would restrain the pride and vainglory that begets tyranny:

> Fundamental to Hobbes's social contract is an agreement that in return for the preservation of their physical existences, men will give up their unjust pride and vanity. Hobbes demands . . . that men give up their struggle to be recognized, in particular, their struggle to be recognized as superior on the basis of their willingness to risk their lives in a prestige battle. The side of man that seeks to show himself superior to other men, to dominate them on the basis of superior virtue, the noble character who struggles against his . . . limitations, is to be persuaded of the folly of his pride.[30]

The result: "Democratic societies are dedicated to the proposition that all men are created equal, and their predominant ethos is one of equality. While nobody is legally prevented

---

28. Lyotard, *Postmodern Condition*, 82.
29. Fukuyama, *End of History*.
30. Ibid., 156-7.

from wanting to be recognized as superior, nobody is encouraged to do so."[31] And, since the heroic impulse intersects desire for superior recognition, heroic narratives often lack the requisite "political correctness." In place of such narratives, little-league soccer that awards trophies to all the losing teams.[32]

If offered an alternative (such as the Hindu caste system), most of us would unhesitatingly opt for the principle of equal recognition for all. But this noble principle can, unqualified, erode all others (and even itself!). "Democratic societies constantly tend to move from simple tolerance of all alternative ways of life, to an assertion of their essential equality."[33]

Thomas S. Hibbs discusses the fate of narrative in such cultures. He detects a profound nihilism in popular TV shows like *Seinfeld*. These "shows about nothing" feature story lines and characters that deny any possibility of making a "right" decision.[34]

Hibbs cites a diverse range of philosophers who say, what did you expect? Nihilism, they argue, is the fruit that tends to grow on the tree of liberal democracy. Nihilism is the denial of all values. America increasingly values individual autonomy and pluralism. But, pushed to the max, these two values undermine all other values. If all views are equal, they cancel each other's validity or value. In film and literature, values constrain the protagonist; he or she makes sacrifices to uphold a value. But, if personal freedom is the absolute, what value could constrain the individual, or compel them to sacrifice anything?[35] Cue the demise of the grand narratives (which tend to demand loyalty and sacrifice from those who would participate in them). Taylor sums it up well:

> One of the enemies of story and of a healthy society is an uncritical relativism that says that truth and goodness are entirely subjective opinions, that everyone's stories (and values) are radically different and incommensurable, and that affirming some stories and rejecting others is by definition intolerant. Such knee-jerk relativism pervades our society and is the often-unacknowledged basis for the fatalistic shrug of passivity, paralysis, and cynicism.[36]

## Post-Colonialism

| | |
|---|---|
| *Spheres of Impact* | politics; education |
| *Results of Impact* | metanarratives seen as legitimizing violence and oppression |

1992. The five-hundred-year anniversary of Columbus's "discovery" of America. Flag-waving or funeral? The muted celebrations of Columbus's half-millennium crystallized

---

31. Ibid., 321.

32. Foer, *How Soccer Explains the World*, 238.

33. Fukuyama, *End of History*, 324. For a detailed discussion of the degeneration of democracy into relativism, see Bloom, *Closing of the American Mind*.

34. Hibbs, *Shows About Nothing*.

35. For more analysis of the linkage of liberal democracy and nihilism, see ibid., 6–38.

36. Taylor, *Healing Power of Stories*, 2–3.

the postmodern demise of the grand narrative. A previously unproblematic script about a New World and a City on a Hill was deconstructed, exposed as concealing abuses of the aboriginal peoples.[37]

More generally, the second half of the twentieth century witnessed the former European empires ceding control of their colonized territories. With the dawning of the post-colonial world, proud imperial myths were revisited. Revisionist history impacted pop culture. Circa 1980, pop musicians UB40 penned this guilt-ridden lyric about the British Empire: "I'm a British subject, not proud of it / While I carry a burden of shame."

Here's the sharp end of the postmodern resistance to totalizing narratives: such scripts tend to legitimize violence and oppression against the "other."[38] Richard Bauckham offers a succinct summary of postmodern convictions:

> Postmodernism . . . is rejection of all metanarratives, because, as attempts to universalize one's own values or culture, they are necessarily authoritarian and oppressive . . . Postmodernism exposes metanarratives as projects of power and domination. In place of such universal pretensions postmodernism opts for particularity, diversity, localism, relativism.[39]

In the interests of full disclosure, my book (cautiously!) advocates on behalf of Christianity as a metanarrative. Since this present chapter merely itemizes and expounds the forces that have eroded the plausibility of metanarratives, it is not the place to offer a lengthy response to the postmodern indictment of (traditional) Christianity. (Bauckham's *Bible and Mission* would be a good read for anyone interested in such a response.) I hope that, as you continue reading my book, you will encounter expressions of Christianity that highlight the *non*-oppressive quality of the biblical story. For now, let me simply quote from a review of Bauckham's book:

> Bauckham owns the sense that the Bible presents a metanarrative of sorts. But, he contends, it is one that privileges the poor and the "least" and expects multicultural expressions to thrive—working against the grain, therefore, of the socially and culturally coercive and oppressive effects observable in other metanarratives.[40]

## The "Linguistic Turn"

| | |
|---|---|
| *Spheres of Impact* | universities; literature |
| *Results of Impact* | exposes narratives as "constructs"; drives a wedge between narrative and reality |

---

37. Middleton and Walsh, *Truth is Stranger*, 9–13.
38. Ibid., 69–75.
39. Bauckham, *Bible and Mission*, 88.
40. Hunsberger, "Missional Hermeneutic," 312.

Part 1: In the Beginning Was the Story

Philosophers have always reflected upon language. But in late modernity, the reflection became obsessive, and the obsession fed the postmodern condition. Here's a summary of the linguistic turn:

> In the latter half of the twentieth century, the focus in philosophy generally shifted from history to language. Human beings are now thought of not so much as creatures of the past as creatures of language. As a result . . . interest has shifted . . . toward questioning how a text as a piece of language determines who we are and how we think.[41]

In Derrida's aphorism, "*Il n'y a pas de hors-texte*" ("Nothing exists outside of text").[42] Furthermore, language is no longer seen as a neutral tool for innocently describing the world. Instead, language profoundly conditions how we actually see the world. What is more, language is no longer seen as value-free, but it is a social construction. (Hence the interminable and torturous political-correctness debates about how to properly "label" minorities.) In the pithy statement by two famous sociologists, "The sociology of knowledge understands human reality as a *socially constructed* reality."[43]

The postmodern turn radically extends this insight on the sociology of language. To illustrate, an oft-repeated joke:

> [There were] three umpires having a beer after a baseball game.
> One says, "There's balls and there's strikes and I call 'em the way they are."
> Another responds, "There's balls and there's strikes and I call 'em the way I see 'em."
> The third says, "There's balls and there's strikes, and they ain't *nothin'* until I call 'em."[44]

The first umpire represents a naïve or "common-sense" realism. He uncritically considers his language a direct, one-to-one map to reality. The second umpire represents a "chastened modernism," his confidence tempered by the lengthy Western tradition of critical doubt. The third umpire represents full-blown postmodernism: his vocabulary of balls/strikes, for all practical purposes, *creates* the "reality" of baseball.

The linguistic turn encourages a hermeneutic of suspicion toward metanarratives (and thus reinforces the post-colonial turn discussed above). Metanarratives can no longer be trusted as innocent reflections of reality. They must be deconstructed, their ideological biases and internal contradictions exposed.[45]

---

41. McCartney and Clayton, *Let the Reader Understand*, 111.
42. Derrida, *Of Grammatology*, 158.
43. Berger and Luckmann, *Social Construction of Reality*, 189 (italics mine).
44. Walter Truett Anderson, quoted in Middleton and Walsh, *Truth is Stranger*, 31.
45. Cf. Cobley, *Narrative*, chapter 5 ("Beyond Realism").

## Philosophy and Science

| Sphere of Impact | universities |
|---|---|
| Results of Impact | ancient narratives dismissed ("myths"); modern "grand narratives" unable to legitimize themselves |

Under these categories (philosophy and science), our discussion of the banishment of the big story comes full circle. Let's briefly revisit the eight-hundred-pound philosophical gorilla in the room. The modern western intellectual project labeled "the Enlightenment," aptly described as "the story that kills stories."[46]

During the last three to four hundred years, enlightened western thought increasingly sustained itself via a myth of progress, of the triumph of science and reason over religion and superstition, leading to the liberation of humanity from the bondage of ignorance, poverty, and disease. The myth posits the following three-act drama:

> First came religion in the form of stories, then philosophy in the form of metaphysical analysis, and then science with its exact methods . . . each of these ages supplanted the other as a refinement in the progressive development of reason. So stories are pre-scientific.[47]

Each of the three "ages"—religion, philosophy, science—privileged a distinctive mode of discourse for the expression of ultimate truth:[48]

| age of religion | truth expressed in drama, metaphor, symbol, poetry |
|---|---|
| age of philosophy | truth expressed in rhetorical and deductive reasoning |
| age of science | truth expressed in realistic, inductive description |

Unfortunately for Christianity, its roots belong to the biblical world of story and symbol. In the age of philosophical and scientific rationality, modern Christianity behaved like an adolescent embarrassed by the clothes received from their parents, and eager to dress in the more fashionable garb of the times. Whether in "liberal" or "conservative" form, modern western Christianity largely abandoned storytelling in favor of rational propositions.[49]

The irony, of course, is that the Enlightenment relied on its own story (the myth of progress) in legitimating its claim to eliminate stories as vehicles of truth. And so, with remorseless logic, the Enlightenment eventually fell victim to its own lofty demands for proof. The Age of Reason experienced "a process of *delegitimation* fueled by the demands

---

46. Tilley, *Story Theology*, 35.
47. Hauerwas and Burrell, "From System to Story," 174–75.
48. Frye, *Great Code*, 3–30.
49. Walter Brueggemann describes how both "liberal" and "conservative" Protestants, in different ways, danced to the same rationalist tune of the Enlightenment: *Texts Under Negotiation*, 65–67; *Cadences of Home*, 39–40.

for legitimation itself."⁵⁰ By the late twentieth century, the myth of progress had lost its credibility, buried under the postmodern incredulity toward all metanarratives.

In a further irony, "Postmodernism is itself a grand narrative, announcing the death of another grand narrative in its rearview mirror."⁵¹ (I suspect many postmodern folk will happily shrug off this ironic critique.)

If I wanted to "tweet" the last couple of pages, it would go like this: "The Enlightenment killed off the older Christian narrative, and postmodernism killed off the Enlightenment, leaving a vacuum of grand narratives."

\* \* \* \* \*

Let's wrap up this chapter with a narrative crystallization of the contemporary loss of grand narratives. To feel the pulse of postmodern life, we can scarcely do better than re-visit Douglas Coupland's epochal novel *Generation X*.

Through the prism of this novel, we may perceive the wider fate of cultural scripts in America at the tail end of the millennium. In my judgment, the generation that came of age circa 1985 was the first to fully feel the impact of the postmodern earthquake discussed in this chapter.⁵²

## GENERATION X

Coupland probably wouldn't appreciate me using literary archetypes to classify his novel, but I'm now the one sitting at the keyboard, so here goes. As I read the *plot*, the protagonists undertake a variant of the classic quest. What are they searching for? Stories. Very early in the novel, Claire makes an assertion that gains the assent of the other two *protagonists* (Andy, the first-person narrator, and Dag):

> Claire . . . breaks the silence by saying that it's not healthy to live life as a series of isolated little cool moments. "Either our lives become stories, or there's just no way to get through them." I agree. Dag agrees. We know that this is why the three of us left our lives behind and came to the desert—to tell stories and to make our own lives worthwhile tales in the process.⁵³

---

50. Lyotard, *Postmodern Condition*, 39 (italics mine).

51. Klaus Bruhn Jensen, quoted in Cobley, *Narrative*, 189.

52. In my ultra-simplified generational analysis of post-war America, the more idealistic of the "Boomers" of the 1960s could be considered the last-gasp of nineteenth-century romanticism. For romanticism, the emotions, intuition, and the subconscious grant the individual privileged access to reality. By contrast, the earlier generation of "Builders" (Tom Brokaw's "Greatest Generation") may be considered the last-gasp of the eighteenth-century Enlightenment, with its commitments to the rational ordering of life via science and bureaucracy. For the "Builders," reason grants us privileged access to reality. Both generations agreed that reality is accessible; their dispute concerned only the *mode* of access. Generation X, on the other hand, was fully exposed to the postmodern dictum: both emotions and reasons are linguistic-cultural "constructs"; neither give unmediated access to reality.

53. Coupland, *Generation X*, 8.

The novel's "desert" *setting* is actually Palm Springs, California: "The three of us chose to live here, for the town is undoubtedly a quiet sanctuary from the bulk of middle-class life."[54] In this minimalist setting, the three Gen Xers abandon the American dream. Their involvement in work/career extends no further than a "*McJob*: A low-pay, low-prestige, low-dignity, low-benefit, no-future job in the service sector."[55]

The true highlight of their life in Palm Springs: their daily ritual of storytelling. Their stories occupy much of the novel's actual text. In the *middle* of the novel, Dag voices his dream of moving to Mexico to open a rather unusual hotel:

> I'd open up a small place for friends and eccentrics only, and for staff I'd only hire elderly Mexican women and stunningly beautiful surfer and hippie type boys and girls . . . We'd spend nights washing zinc salves from each other's noses, drinking rum drinks, and telling stories. People who told good stories could stay for free.[56]

At the *end* of the novel, the three of them cross the border into Mexico (a journey symbolizing the very antithesis of the American Dream), with the hope of one day starting their hotel for storytellers.[57]

\* \* \* \* \*

Why this desperate search for stories—stories that could make their lives "worthwhile tales"? If we follow up this "why" question with a "what" question, we eventually find ourselves in the labyrinth of postmodernity. What kind of stories do the three protagonists tell each other? In addition to the autobiographical, they tell short fictional tales that they themselves have created ("postmodern parables" is my term for their tales).

For Andy, Claire, and Dag, there is no "Western canon" worth recycling. There are no "off-the-shelf" cultural scripts that they wish to buy into. So, the three of them set out to create their own canon of wisdom, to write their own scripts to guide them.

Why had the available cultural scripts become dead letters for these Gen Xers? An archaeologist can (almost) piece together an entire civilization from scraps of pottery. Likewise, pieces of Coupland's epochal novel allow us to reconstruct a (fragmented) mosaic of late-modern American culture. The Xers' create-your-own-parable quest seems driven by a cultural experience of losses and absences (nature abhors a vacuum). Here is my list of the losses that drove the quest for stories in Coupland's novel.

---

54. Ibid., 10.
55. Ibid., 5 (italics mine).
56. Ibid., 116.
57. Ibid., 170–72.

## Loss of the American Dream

Clearly, the American Dream no longer provided a compelling cultural script for Andy, Clair, and Dag.[58] And who can blame them for rejecting the reductionist consumer version on offer?[59]

## Loss of Family Narratives

The characters in Coupland's novel are alienated from family. Traditionally, families passed down rich, inherited narratives. Andy's parents are a wisdom vacuum. Clair's family members merely dispense shallow sound bites. Reading these sadly realistic accounts of families devoid of narrative inheritance, I thought of the words of an African writer: "It is only the story . . . that saves our progeny from blundering like blind beggars into the spikes of the cactus fence. The story is our escort. Without it we are blind."[60]

## Loss of a Sense of History

Coupland's characters also experience "*historical underdosing*."[61] Situated in middle-class America in the late 1980s, Andy voices his feeling of being disconnected from any big historical narrative: "I get this feeling . . . that our emotions are transpiring in a vacuum, and I think it boils down to the fact that we're middle class . . . when you're middle class, you have to live with the fact that history will ignore you . . . that history will never champion your causes . . . It is the price that is paid for day-to-day comfort."[62] This feeling explains why Andy clings to his childhood memories of seeing the Vietnam War on television: "They were the only times I'll ever get—genuine capital H history times, before history was turned into a press release, a marketing strategy, and a cynical campaign tool. And . . . its not as if I got to see much real history, either—I arrived to see a concert in history's arena just as the final set was finishing."[63] "Historical underdosing" dovetails with 1990s hip-think, in the form of Fukuyama's hypothesis on "The End of History." USSR—dismantled. Berlin Wall—collapsed. Cold War—done and dusted.

---

58. Coupland recognized that many of his X generation were still living by the rejected cultural script, but even they lacked conviction. He skewers this sub-group in the following sidebar: "*Squires*: The most common X generation subgroup and the only subgroup given to breeding. Squires exist almost exclusively in couples and are recognizable by their frantic attempts to recreate a semblance of Eisenhower-era plenitude in their daily lives in the face of exorbitant housing prices and two-job lifestyles. Squires tend to be continually exhausted from their voraciously acquisitive pursuit of furniture and knickknacks" (ibid., 135).

59. I should add that, twenty years after Coupland wrote, James Truslow Adams's original (1931), less materialistic version of the dream—"fulfill your potential"—is still available (on the Disney Channel).

60. Chinua Achebe, *Anthills of the Savannah* (quoted in Hudson, "Bring your Story," 73).

61. "*Historical Underdosing*: To live in a period of time when nothing seems to happen" (Coupland, *Generation X*, 7, italics mine).

62. Ibid., 147.

63. Ibid., 151.

With the supposedly irresistible global triumph of Western-style liberal-capitalist democracy, what grand social epics remained?[64]

## Loss of the Myth of Progress

I get a pervasive sense that Coupland's protagonists are disconnected from the Western myth of progress—the belief that science and technology will liberate humanity. The disconnect from this mega-script surfaces throughout the novel, in the protagonists' perpetual angst over industrial pollution and the potential threat of nuclear war.

## Loss of Judeo-Christian Traditions

Lastly, one doesn't sense that traditional Judeo-Christian narratives are on the radar screen of the protagonists in their search for story. The novel's most sustained discourse on religion occurs in one of Clair's parables, about "New Age" spiritual quests, described as "strange little handcarved religions."[65] Coupland's sidebar on "Me-ism" seems apt.[66]

* * * * *

Piecing this all together, the protagonists of the novel *Generation X* are searching for stories that could make their lives into worthwhile tales. However, they undertake this journey radically disconnected from existing narratives. They are disconnected from family narratives, from the narrative of the dominant culture, from the narrative of modern history, from the narrative of scientific progress, and from traditional Judeo-Christian narratives. Small wonder the stories they seek must be spun from inside their own heads.

Welcome to the postmodern world. Coupland's protagonists are DIY parable makers, because of the absence of a plausible grand narrative for them to shelter under.

* * * * *

Unless you uncritically celebrate the advent of the postmodern era, this will have been a pessimistic chapter. Coupland's novel testifies to an aching loss of plausible narrative foundations for personal identity. Our analysis of "seven deadly forces" cataloged the cultural streams that have swept away the grand narratives.

Don't be discouraged. As in the structure of archetypal stories, it's usually darkest just before the dawn. In my next chapter, I take note of another, more hopeful subcultural trend from the late twentieth century. The rebirth, in some Christian circles, of religion as participation in sacred narratives—and, in some cases, sacred *meta*narratives.

64. Fukuyama, *End of History*.
65. Coupland, *Generation X*, 128.
66. "*Me-ism*: A search by an individual, in the absence of training in traditional religious tenets, to formulate a personally tailored religion by himself. Most frequently a mishmash of reincarnation, personal dialogue with a nebulously defined god figure, naturalism, and karmic eye-for-eye attitudes" (ibid., 126).

# 6

# Sleeping Beauty Awakes

**THE APOSTLES' CREED**

THE PRIMITIVE CHURCH CONFESSED its faith as narrative. Witness the Gospels according to Matthew, Mark, John, and Luke-Acts (originally a single work in two volumes).

Even letters like Hebrews, when you dig down to their deep structure, are narratives. Hebrews imagines the Christian life via the plotline of a pilgrimage through the wilderness, to reach the celestial city.

> I believe in God, the Father Almighty, Creator of heaven and earth
> And in Jesus Christ, His only Son our Lord
> Who was conceived by the Holy Spirit
> Born of the Virgin Mary
> Suffered under Pontius Pilate
> Was crucified, died, and was buried . . .
> The third day he rose again from the dead
> He ascended into heaven, and is seated at the right hand of God . . .
> From thence he will come to judge the living and the dead.

The Apostles' Creed is a plotline summary.

## What Put the Christian Story to Sleep?

Sleep came gradually. Some would even trace the problem back to the first centuries of the church, when adaptations to the Greco-Roman world began to sever the Jewish roots of Christianity. (The Hebrew Bible relies on narrative to confess its faith.)

However, I believe we can fast-forward to around five hundred years ago, the period known as the Renaissance and Reformation—which academic historians now label "early modern."

Modernity, the Enlightenment, science and technology, rationalism.

The belief that story is a primitive, outmoded way of viewing the world. To be replaced initially by logical deductions from "first principles," and later by inductive assembling of hypotheses from atoms of factual data.

Poetry, symbol, imagination—out. Logic, statistics, math—in.

The triumph of the left half of the brain, the suppression of half of our humanity.

## How Did Sleeping Beauty Re-Awake?

Not by one prince, but by many.[1]

In the 1800s, the romantic poets and writers reclaimed story, myth, symbol, intuition, emotion—claiming these accessed deeper truths than those available to logic and science.

Nineteenth-century biblical scholars realized that the Bible didn't drop from the sky, whole and entire, but built up over centuries, as part of a slowly unfolding plotline, an organic growth from seed to tree.

Twentieth-century movements like surrealism, and depth psychology, explored the intersection of mythic narrative structures and the unconscious, the world of dreams. Thus surfaced the "archetypes" of Carl Gustav Jung and Joseph Campbell, informing us of the struggle between light and darkness, and the torturous journey of the self toward enlightenment.

In the 1960s, feminism challenged the stereotypically male ways of knowledge, based on the rational conquest of nature. Also, into the mainstream came the African-American tradition of oral culture, of dramatized narrative preaching, of fusing communal history with biblical stories like the Exodus.

In my own field of New Testament studies, scholars began taking really (really) seriously that fact that Jesus taught in *parables*.

Philosophers like Alasdair MacIntyre began asserting "the narrative quality of human existence."[2] We are born, we mature, we decline, we die. In between these great acts of the human drama, are innumerable tiny scenes, in which we remember, anticipate, suffer, experience conflict, make crucial decisions.

Story resonates with us, because story plucks at the melodic strings that make us human.

In the 1940s, H. Richard Niebuhr's essay, "The Story of our Life," highlighted the power of a shared narrative to create community, to ground identity, and to guide behavior. He alludes to the Gettysburg Address:

> Fourscore and seven years ago,
> 
> *our* fathers brought forth on this continent,
> 
> a new nation, conceived in liberty,
> 
> and dedicated to the proposition that all men are created equal.[3]

---

1. For discussion of some influences behind the revival of narrative interpretations of Christianity, see: Bausch, *Storytelling*, 15–28; Tilley, *Story Theology*, 18–38.

2. MacIntyre, "Virtues," 89–110.

3. Quoted in Niebuhr, "Story of our Life," 30 (italics in original).

Niebuhr highlights the power of the personal pronoun: *our* fathers—meaning their story becomes our story.

* * * * *

With broad brushstrokes, we have sketched the backstory of the emergence of the "narrative theology" movement in the 1970s and beyond. Some of the contributors concentrated on local and personal religious stories. Others were bold enough to confess Christianity as metanarrative.

This recovery, of interpreting Christianity as story, continues to bear fruit in the churches. The seed has been planted and watered. But how abundant is the crop? In the arithmetic of Jesus' parable, has the seed of narrative theology multiplied itself thirty-fold, sixty-fold, or one-hundred-fold? (Mark 4:8).

After much reading and reflection in the standard texts of narrative theology, I've concluded that the movement has not yet realized its full potential.

There are lots of reasons behind this relative failure. But I only wish to highlight one reason.

Surprisingly, narrative theology has (in my judgement) *failed to give sustained attention to the nature of narrative itself.* Perhaps the narrative theologians took narrative for granted. ("Surely, everyone grasps story—it's elementary!") Perhaps twentieth-century thinkers were preoccupied with making a case for narrative, instead of developing narrative as a tool for personal transformation.

Whatever the reason, I sense a gap, which is one reason I am writing this book. I profoundly value narrative as a lens for viewing life. In Part 2 of this book, I hope to begin to polish the lens, to produce a sharper picture of life-as-story.

So, in Part 2, I will reflect on some (deceptively) simple questions. *What is story? What kind of story is Christianity? How is life story-like (and not story-like)? How do people respond to stories, and use stories to shape their lives?*

* * * * *

Before we leave Part 1, let me briefly reflect on why the recovery of the Christian metanarrative matters for our culture. Think back to the contemporary spirit of aimlessness and nihilism that kept asserting itself in our previous chapter ("Identity Theft."). A massive sense of futility needs an equally great (or greater) affirmation of hope and purpose; exactly what the Christian story provides.

## ARCHITECTS OF THE NEW JERUSALEM

The Apostles' Creed is a serviceable summary of the Christian story. Like any good plot (on Aristotle's definition), it has a beginning, middle, and end.

*Beginning*: Creation. *Middle*: triggered by the miraculous birth of Jesus Christ, whose life (according to the Gospel writers) inaugurated a *new creation*. (This is not the place to explore further, but simply note the parallels between Genesis 1:2 and Jesus' baptism [Mark 1:9–11]. In Genesis, the Spirit of God hovers [like a bird] over the primordial waters. At Jesus' baptism in the waters of the River Jordan, the Spirit descends—in the form of a dove. This is perhaps also an echo of the dove motif in the "new creation" story of Noah and the Flood [Gen 8:8–12].)

The middle of the biblical epic continues with the pivotal events of Christ's crucifixion, death, and burial, followed by his resurrection and ascension/enthronement. From there, the Creed fast-forwards to the end of the story. *End*: Jesus "will come *to judge the living and the dead.*"

That last line just quoted sounds scary—but not necessarily so. Think how the second Advent of Jesus gets interpreted in the "Parable of the Minas (Pounds)" in Luke 19:11–27. In this story, a man of noble birth travels to a far country in order to receive a kingdom. Before he departs, he distributes a sum of silver money to his slaves, commanding them, "Do business until I return!" Each slave received a "mina"—which, as the study bibles like to tell us, was about three months' wages for a laborer.

Eventually, the nobleman receives his kingdom, and returns for an accounting with his slaves. The first slave had turned a handy profit on the mina, increasing its value ten-fold. His master rewards him: "Excellent, good slave! *Because you were faithful in the smallest stuff—become one having authority over ten cities!*" (The next slave, having engineered a five-fold profit, gets authority over five cities.)

Does this make the second Advent of Jesus sound a little less scary, and rather something to anticipate eagerly? The "Parable of the Pounds" is traditionally interpreted as an allegory of the time between Christ's ascension and return.

The imagery of the parable connects faithful activities in the mundane stuff of this life to the reward of ruling over "cities" in the next. In literature in general, the "city" symbolizes culture, civilization, and human accomplishment. The symbolism of the city can help weave our stories into the biblical story.

For a point of contact between the biblical narrative and our own, I invite you to reflect on the *impermanence* of even the greatest of cities.

This impermanence is stated, with detached resignation, in the civilization-building ("paradise restored")[4] life story of the Solomonic sage figure in Ecclesiastes. He summarizes his story for us:

> I magnified my works.
> I built for myself houses, and planted for myself vineyards.
> I made for myself gardens and parks ["*paradises*"],[5]
> And I planted in them every kind of fruit-tree.
> I made for myself pools of water, to irrigate . . . the trees. (Eccl 2:4–6)

Quite an accomplishment in the arid Middle East. Lest we missed this, the philosopher-king adds, "I became greater . . . than all who were before me in Jerusalem" (Eccl 2:9).

However, his story ends with a deep sense of futility, because of his realization that death and time erode all accomplishments, even those of the greatest and wisest and

---

4. See: Longman, *Ecclesiastes*, 90; Horne, *Proverbs-Ecclesiastes*, 406.
5. The Hebrew word translated "parks" uses a Persian loan-word, from which we eventually (via Greek) derive our English word "paradise" (ibid., 405).

most powerful of kings: "I turned to all the works which my hands had performed . . . And, look! It was all futile—pursuing wind" (Eccl 2:11).

We can compare this Solomonic figure with Ozymandias, the king in the poem published in 1818, by Percy Bysshe Shelley:

> I met a traveler from an antique land
> Who said: "Two vast and trunkless legs of stone
> Stand in the desert . . . Near them, on the sand,
> Half sunk, a shattered visage lies, whose frown,
> And wrinkled lip, and sneer of cold command,
> Tell that its sculptor well those passions read
> Which yet survive, stamped on those lifeless things,
> The hand that mocked them and the heart that fed:
> And on the pedestal these words appear:
> *'My name is Ozymandias, king of kings:*
> *Look on my works ye Mighty and despair!'*
> No thing beside remains. Round the decay
> Of that colossal wreck, boundless and bare
> The lone and level sands stretch far away."[6]

Reconstruct, in your imagination, the implied scene while King Ozymandias was still alive. His towering statue probably stood at the epicenter of a bustling metropolis. Thousands of merchants, craftsmen, soldiers and princes would pass the imposing statue. To all who could read (or have the inscription read to them), a wounding challenge, belittling their own accomplishments: *"Look on my works, ye Mighty, and despair!"*

Fast forward through the millennia. Ozymandias—no more. His metropolis—nothing remains. The head of his statue—"Half sunk, a shattered visage." Instead of thousands of passersby, viewing his glory—"the lone and level sands stretch far away." With painfully piercing irony, Shelley embeds the works of Ozymandias in a larger, tragic narrative: time itself. Back then, "despair" came to those whose works could not measure up to those of the self-proclaimed "king of kings." Now, a different, more deadly despair confronts the readers of his inscription—the knowledge that our works, however big or small, are destined for erosion into insignificance by the sands of time.

Okay, that's probably enough pessimism for now. But, as they say, "One person's pessimism is another's realism." The impermanence of even the greatest of cities, the greatest civilization, can either drive us to despair, or trigger a "clash of narratives" in which the futilities of our story jostle alongside the hope of the Christian story.

When students graduate from seminary, often young men in their twenties or thirties, I often detect the glint of ambition in their eyes. The quest for "kingdom building," not unlike the Solomon figure of Ecclesiastes, or the Ozymandias of Shelley's poem.

In 2009, the lot fell to me to give the charge to graduating seminary students. As an old (by their measure) greybeard, I felt able both to offer them some Solomonic/Ozymandias wisdom, and—more importantly—a metanarrative that will outlast the tragedy of time.

6. Shelley, "Ozymandias" (italics mine).

## Sleeping Beauty Awakes

What follows is adapted from my charge. (Alert readers may see a flip-side of the "Goblet of Fire" message from chapter 2 of this book.)

That evening, in May 2009, the graduating class was small. The obligatory class photograph did not need a wide-angle camera lens. And I, their professor, looking out over their assembled row, could name off the personal ambitions of each one of them. The church planter; the campus minister; the doctor of philosophy (to name but three).

Accordingly, I began my charge.

"Your post-seminary future is the proverbial blank canvas. But I know that every one of you—perhaps even as you listen to this charge—is eagerly imagining a frame and a thumbnail sketch for your open canvas. Church planter. Campus minister. Doctor of philosophy. And several other worthy pursuits."

"Allow me to offer you a frame of gold for your blank canvas. A job description that will endure into eternity."

"I would invite each one of you to become an *architect* . . . an architect of the New Jerusalem."

Leaving the invitation dangling, I expounded on the symbolic archetypal power of civic imagery.

"If you have ever visited one of the great cities of the world, you will have experienced its power to inspire cultural endeavor. New York. London. Oxford. Cambridge. Paris. Rome."

"And yet, the noblest of cities eventually declines. Decays. Becomes dust."

Here was my connection between the biblical narrative and their personal narratives.

"Your unwritten future narrative will, inexorably, include dust and decay. The church plant that becomes a cemetery. The unpublished dissertation."

Now it was time to zoom out into the epic biblical metanarrative.

"The quest for the imperishable propels the biblical plotline. In terms of sacred space, recall how the tabernacle became the temple. Cloth became stone. The impermanent became the "permanent."

However, the "permanent" temple was destroyed, dismantled brick by brick by Nebuchadnezzar of Babylon.

Yet, so strong was the quest for the imperishable, that the prophet Ezekiel envisaged a perfected, end-time city-temple. A New Jerusalem."

"The good news, the gospel according to the book of Revelation, is the declaration that New Jerusalem is destined to come down out of heaven."

Then I wrapped up my charge by quoting from Revelation 21:24–26, describing the imperishable future city:

And the nations will walk in her light,

And *the kings of the earth bring their glory into her* . . .

And they *will carry the glory and the honor of the nations into her.*

One might even say, Revelation invites us to become architects of the New Jerusalem. In the words of one commentator:

All that is truly good and beautiful in this world will reappear there, purified and enhanced in the perfect setting its Maker intended for it; nothing of real value is lost.[7]

* * * * *

---

7. Wilcock, *Message of Revelation*, 211; cf. Caird, *Revelation of St. John*, 279–80.

# PART 2

Stories Are . . . and Stories Do . . .

# Spoiler Alert 2
(Overview of Part 2)

AT THE END OF Part 1, I celebrated the partial recovery of narrative wisdom in the West at the tail-end of the millennium. I also suggested that further riches of wisdom remain for those willing to dig deeper into the mines of story. As with most wisdom quests, the simplest questions turn out to offer the richest rewards: *What is Story? What kind of Story is Christianity? How is life story-like (and not story-like)? How do people respond to stories, and use stories to shape their lives?* We explore these basic questions in the six chapters that comprise Part 2.

If you are striving to make sense of your life in terms of story, then a map of the dimensions of story may help you toward the wisdom you seek. Accordingly, chapter 7 examines the elements, phases, and plots of typical stories. Chapter 8 continues and refines the work of chapter 7, with a working inventory of basic plots common to literature and to life.

This plot-inventory provides lenses for reading the whole Bible in chapter 9, where I trace several archetypal plotlines from the Old Testament into the New Testament. These plotlines offer the reader a home underneath the big umbrella narratives of Genesis to Revelation. Chapter 10 zooms in on the storylines of the New Testament, along with some snapshots of life lived under the gospel umbrella.

Chapter 11 discusses the "art imitates life"/"life imitates art" proposals. How is life like and unlike stories? Many readers struggle to balance the "life = story" equation, and some thinkers reject the equation entirely. We dig deeper into these concerns in chapter 11.

Chapter 12 offers a panoramic view of how "consumers" of narrative use stories to re-shape their lives. This inventory of "best practices" can help us to evaluate the benefits of whatever story we might indwell (or seek to indwell).

\* \* \* \* \*

# 7

# Somebody Wanted Because But So

### ENG LIT 101

WHAT MAKES A STORY? Westerners like to analyze. Break stuff down into its "component parts." See how each individual part "works." The Western approach has benefits. For instance, the computer software typing my next word (and letting me rephrase it without liquid paper). Software whose code may be broken down into strings of ones and zeros.

Some of you remember Eng Lit 101 from your freshman year in college. Breaking stories down into their component parts. Maybe this generated real insights (depending, I suspect, on the caliber of your professor). But maybe the dissection removed the power and the joy from the stories?

Whatever "elements" stories may have, we experience stories holistically. That's the beauty and power of art. All the elements combine, creating something whose total impact exceeds the sum of its parts.

That said, ever since Aristotle's analysis of six elements of tragedy,[1] literary critics have dissected stories. Whilst dissection can of course kill, it can also reveal the source of life. Speaking for myself, literary criticism helps me tap into the power of story. In order to investigate how stories change lives, I use a rudimentary map to guide me through the maze of narrative.

If you are striving to make sense of your own life in terms of story, a map of the various dimensions of story may help you find the wisdom you are seeking.

To keep my map simple, I view story as five interlocking dimensions: setting; character; plot; point of view; medium.[2] Some critics would expand and nuance my list. For instance, I've left out the *audience*—and stories only change lives when someone interprets and uses them! (Accordingly, I discuss the role of the audience in chapter 12 ("End-User Responsibility") below.) Even if my list is too sparse, all five elements routinely occupy the table of contents of standard guides to literary criticism.[3] Here, then, is my five-dimensional map for exploring narrative:

---

1. Aristotle, *Poetics* 6.
2. Cf. Johnston's analysis (*Reel Spirituality*, 145–49).
3. To pick a totally random example off my shelf: Kennedy and Gioia, *Literature*.

| Setting | Time, place, circumstances; the "givens" (immutable dimensions) of the story-world |
|---|---|
| Character | Especially the protagonist, with whom most readers identify |
| Plot | Arc of tension, completed by crisis leading to resolution of initial problem |
| Point of View | Authorial evaluation of plot/character/setting (expressing the ideology (world and life view) of the author) |
| Medium | Material form of the story (oral, written, film, theater, etc.); style/texture of presentation |

My fifth element, *medium*, recognizes that "the word becomes flesh," so to speak. There are no disembodied stories. We encounter stories through their "incarnations" in diverse media (novels, cartoon strips, video games, conversational anecdotes, etc.) Furthermore, there are no abstract novels, movies, or plays. Each medium offers the storyteller an array of formal devices. Using these formal textures, each storyteller weaves a narrative tapestry with a unique feel, style, and pattern.

My other four elements appear linked to childhood language learning. So strong is the impulse to narrate, that children soon acquire the grammar, vocabulary, and modulation needed to tell stories. These key elements of language overlap my other four elements of story. Here is one cognitive psychologist's summary of early language acquisition:

> It is a "push" to construct narrative that determines the order of priority in which grammatical forms are mastered by the young child. Narrative requires . . . four crucial grammatical constituents . . . It requires, first, a means for emphasizing human action or "agentivity" . . . It requires, secondly, that a sequential order be established and maintained . . . Narrative, thirdly, also requires a sensitivity to what is canonical and what violates canonicality in human interaction. Finally, narrative requires something approximating to a narrator's perspective: it cannot, in the jargon of narrativity, be "voiceless."[4]

Children rapidly develop standard linguistic forms to signal agent, sequence, abnormal events, and voice. These components map neatly onto my scheme. Agent relates to character; sequence relates to plot; abnormality of events relates to setting; and voice relates to point of view.[5]

These four elements (plus medium) will resurface in chapter 12 below, where I discuss how stories change lives. For the remainder of this chapter, however, I will try to provide a sharper understanding of *plot*, since this one element will bind the rest of my book together.

But before we get into plot, let's pause and consider how the other elements of story might factor into the construction of your own personal narrative. The following list of questions is suggestive rather than exhaustive . . .

---

4. Bruner, *Acts of Meaning*, 77.

5. These four elements (character; plot; setting; point of view) also match the four components *journalists* incorporate into real-life stories. According to my student Michel Duarte (a former journalism major), news stories must feature "people, plot, place, and purpose."

| Story Elements | Autobiographical Questions |
|---|---|
| Setting | How does your "world" constrain your possibilities, by operating "to allow certain kinds of experience and to prohibit others"?*<br>Is your world a safe and hopeful place, a dangerous and hopeless place, or somewhere in between?<br>How do social and cultural "backstories" (from previous generations) impact your role in the world? |
| Character | Do you see yourself as the main character in a story?<br>Who are your antagonists and allies?<br>Do you see yourself in terms of a "collective" character, i.e., a member of a group that has a distinctive role in the world?<br>Does your personality have any fixed traits that shape your role in the world?<br>Do you hold to any fixed values that shape your role in the world? |
| Point of View | When you tell anecdotes from your life, what is your stance or tone as a narrator? Self-aggrandizing? Self-effacing? Self-justifying? Ironic? Satirical? Wistful? Thankful? Resentful? (Etc.) |
| Medium | What are the advantages and disadvantages of *writing* your life-experiences (say, in a journal)? Does writing lead to clarity or discovery?<br>What are the advantages and disadvantages of *conversing* about your life-experiences? Does feedback from listeners make you modify your personal narrative? |

\* Tilley, *Introduction to Plot*, 5.

\* \* \* \* \*

## THE PLOT SNAKE

When we strive to make sense of our lives in terms of story, we are seeking meaningful connections between our past, our present, and our future. In other words, we are searching for plot.

Two of the biggest questions we can ask: What *kind* (genre) of plot am I living? What *phase* of the plot am I now in?

In the remainder of this chapter, I will discuss these two topics (genres of plot and phases of plot) in reverse order.

By way of an on-ramp, I invite you to recall our preliminary treatments of plot genres and structures in earlier chapters. In chapter 3 (our discussion of autobiography), we touched on some basic genres of narrative, such as the quest and the coming-of-age. This chapter also introduced a basic five-act structure of plot. This structure resurfaced in chapter 4, in our diagnostic questions (under the headings of "setting," "trigger incident," "escalation," "crises," and "resolution").[6]

I visualize plot as an *arc of tension, completed by a crisis, leading to the resolution of the initial problem*. Let's visualize this in more detail, using a hypothetical real-life narrative as illustration.

---

6. Subsection, "Dimensions of Plot."

*The Interview*

I'm driving north on Interstate 75. Dreadful traffic congestion, as usual. Mustn't be late for my job interview. But it's a red light (with cameras). Better obey.

#$*#! Why did my battery choose to die today? (OK, the little icon on my dashboard had been warning me for weeks.) So I put my car in neutral, get out, and push my vehicle onto the hard shoulder.

Don't panic. My wife works downtown, just a few blocks away. I'll call her cell phone, she'll collect me and drive me to my interview. (We'll deal with the stalled vehicle afterwards.)

She's not answering. Don't panic. This is why we have auto insurance with roadside assistance. I reach into my wallet for the little plastic card with the 800 number. "What do you mean, someone will be with me within the hour? I'll be late for my interview!"

Where's a passing police vehicle when you need one? I look up at the well-maintained cars speeding by. Hitch a ride? Too creepy. Too many of America's Most Wanted on the loose. If only a good Samaritan (with jumper cables) would stop and help.

An enormous black pick-up truck pulls over. I glimpse the confederate flag bumper sticker (not good). A shaven-headed, tattooed Caucasian male gets out (extremely not good). Will he just take my wallet, or will he beat me up first? "Hey, Bubba, looks like your vehicle stalled. Let me get my jumper cables from my truck. Never leave home without them!"

This narrative combines plausible realism with a paragraph structure deliberately designed to highlight the phases of the plot arc. Let's see how the paragraphs work together to increase and resolve the tension.[7]

| Paragraph | Contribution to Narrative Arc |
| --- | --- |
| 1 | *Setting* (story-world). Introduces the "givens" that constrain the plot: shortage of time, plus reliance on an automobile. Also introduces the (first person) protagonist, and their core value or goal (get a job!) |
| 2 | *Inciting Incident.* Dead battery disrupts the story-world, blocking the attainment of the protagonist's core value. This incident triggers an escape-from-predicament storyline. |
| 3–4 | *Progressive Complications.* My initial optimism gives way to despair, as easy solutions (wife; auto insurance) fail to materialize. |
| 5 | *Crisis.* I'm at a point of no return, and start contemplating a riskier solution. |
| 6 | *Climax/Resolution.* My problem can only resolve in two ways: decisive negation of my core value, or surprising turn toward actualization of my core value (thankfully, the latter). |

The story hinges on two decisive turning points (inciting incident and climax). Without such decisive changes, we scarcely have any story. So we can use those two turning points to visualize plot structure:

---

7. Cf. McKee's inventory of the elements of story design (*Story*, 181).

PART 2: STORIES ARE . . . AND STORIES DO . . .

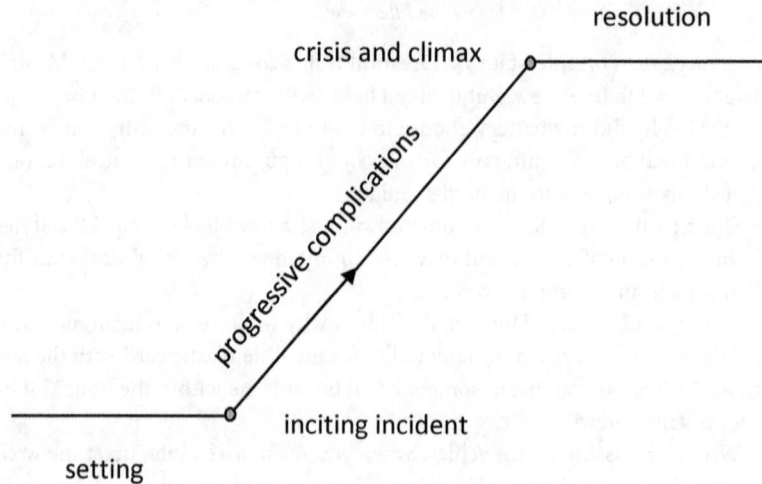

Fig. 1. Plot Structure

Looking at this diagram, we immediately see why so many dramas have three or five acts, right? Well, sort of. Actually, it's a bit subtler. Thankfully, deeper acquaintance with the "plot snake" can open our eyes to the life-changing wisdom embedded in story.

I teach Sunday school to eight and nine-year-olds. Accordingly, I frequent the teachers' supplies stores. On one such visit, I'm browsing the wall-chart section. I find a chart designed to teach plot to kids. A picture of a human hand, with fingers and thumb spread out. Each digit labeled with a single word, in the following order: *Somebody Wanted Because But So.* Writing for grown-ups, Donald Miller summarizes story as, "*A character who wants something and overcomes conflict to get it.*"[8]

Both simplifications make story turn on the goals/values of the protagonist: his or her struggle to realize a goal, to actualize a value; the obstacles in the path, and how they were overcome.

As the plot snake twists and turns, these simplified definitions help us track the story.[9] The acts of drama, the phases of story—these are not arbitrary. In binary fashion, they mirror the progress and retardation of the protagonist's goal, the affirmation or negation of the value that motivates the main character.

The *five-act* story structure, Shakespeare's standard, can be traced back to the comedies of the Roman playwright Terence.[10] The modern literary critic Christopher Booker explains the five-phase dynamic, using the binary metaphor of constriction versus liberation of the hero.[11] Three "constriction" phases alternate with two phases of "liberation," and the constriction progresses (great → greater → greatest). This dynamic generates the following five-phase plotline (using Booker's labels):

---

8. Miller, *Million Miles*, 48.

9. I borrow the expression "plot snake" from Tilley, *Plot Snakes*. His preferred plot-structure (or "snake") is slightly more complex than mine.

10. Baldwin, *Shakespere's* [sic] *Five-Act Structure*, vii.

11. Booker, *Seven Basic Plots*, 227–28.

| Phases of Plot | Constrictions and Liberations |
|---|---|
| 1 (Call) | Initial constriction of hero, and their resolve to escape |
| 2 (Dream) | Optimistic sense of liberation (obstacles/trials/antagonists overcome) |
| 3 (Frustration) | Antagonistic forces push back, revealing their persistence and power, leading to a crisis (point-of-no-return) |
| 4 (Nightmare) | Unequal tension of forces: dominance of antagonism; minor hope for protagonist |
| 5 (Escape or Demise) | Climactic event resolves crisis positively. (Negative resolution for protagonist of a tragedy) |

Here, we may begin to glimpse something of the power of narrative rhetoric. Via this five-phase dynamic, stories engage universal questions of life. What is the *problem*, the lack, the restriction, that plagues the human condition? What's the *solution*? What are the *obstacles*? What prize is so *valuable*, worth undergoing a nightmare ordeal to obtain?

As the audience of a story, we participate (vicariously) in the hero/heroine's quest to make life conform to their central *value*. Natural "breaks" in storyline flow occur with major reversals in the fate of the central value. Is the gap between life-as-is and life-as-desired widening or narrowing? Screenwriting guru McKee argues that great stories demand *three* major reversals in the fate of the central value.[12] (Anything less, and the story fails to plumb the depths of human experience.)

McKee's axiom suggests a *three-act* story structure, with each act terminating with a major reversal (positive or negative) for the central value. He illustrates this using the Oscar-winning 1979 movie *Kramer vs. Kramer*.[13]

Act One contains the inciting incident: Mrs. Kramer (Meryl Streep) walks out on her workaholic husband (Dustin Hoffman), leaving him to juggle career and caring for their young son. Mr. Kramer's central value: love for his son, keeping the father-son relationship intact. Father and son gradually adapt to their new situation, when suddenly Mrs. Kramer returns, demanding custody of the child.

Act Two is the bitter courtroom custody battle, which resolves in favor of *Mrs.* Kramer. This represents the crisis for Mr. Kramer's central value. He could appeal the verdict—but this would force his young son onto the witness stand.

Act Three brings the climax and the resolution. Mr. Kramer decides *not* to appeal the custody verdict, since love for his son precludes forcing the boy to testify in court. The final reversal (spoiler alert!) occurs when Mrs. Kramer decides it is best for the boy to live with his father, and returns their son to Mr. Kramer.

If the five-act structure is old, the three-act structure may be even more venerable, going back to Aristotle's demand that unified stories have a beginning, middle, and end.[14] By "beginning," he actually meant *inciting incident*, not zero time. He labeled the story

---

12. McKee, *Story*, 218.
13. Ibid., 215–16, 221, 307–8.
14. Aristotle, *Poetics* 7 and 23.

span from inciting incident to crisis the "complication," and the span from crisis to resolution the "denouement" (unraveling).[15]

Many literary critics adopt Aristotle's three-act model of plot (act one = complication, act two = crisis, act three = denouement). A comparison with the five-phase model shows that its phases one through three (discussed above) get lumped together into act one of the three-act model. Furthermore, three acts can easily become five by adding an exposition and an ending to each side of the central core of three, generating a concentric or pediment diagram of plot.[16]

Three or five? I'm not sure it matters. I think the difference stems from the fact that stories unfold like a dynamic *wave*. Sure, the crest of a wave differs from the water on either side of it (ask a surfer!), but beyond that, how you "divide" the wave is to some extent a matter of choosing perspectives. Interestingly, in most films, "Crisis and Climax happen in the last minutes and in the *same scene*."[17] Furthermore, advocates of lumping phases one through three into act one generally recognize the progression from phase two ("dream") to phase three ("frustration").[18]

My advice: work with whatever model helps *you* better appreciate the dynamics of plot. In particular, choose the model that secures the tightest link between literature and your own life story.

Before we leave our discussion of plot structure, here's some "streetwise" input for those on the road to figuring out the narrative shape of their life: how a story begins does *not* determine how it ends, and the beginning of a story is *not* an infallible clue to its ending.

If you've ever tried to guess the ending of a book after reading its first chapter, then you know what I'm talking about. As the literary critics inform us, the "inciting incident" (trigger event) merely destroys the equilibrium of the protagonist's world, provoking him or her to struggle to restore order.[19] The outcome of that struggle may have very little to do with the value destabilized by the trigger event. (Recall my own "Graveyard Shift" in chapter 2. The trigger event—bereavement—propelled me into the storyline that led to the writing of this book.)

So—be open to surprising twists, and unexpected resolutions, as your life story unfolds. By way of illustration, Charles D. Drew tells the story of "John," a law student.[20] I rework his story, to highlight the unpredictability of the ending relative to the trigger-incident.

---

15. Aristotle, *Poetics* 18.

16. Amit, *Reading Biblical Narrative*, 47; cf. Longman, *Literary Approaches to Biblical Interpretation*, 92–93, 102–4.

17. McKee, *Story*, 306 (italics mine).

18. E.g., McKee writes, "Generally, progressions run from the Positive to the Contrary in Act One" (ibid., 333).

19. Ibid., 189–97; Miller, *Million Miles*, 100–105; Tilley, *Introduction to Plot*, 5–8.

20. Drew, *Journey Worth Taking*, 256–59.

| Setting | John, a first-year law student, has labored for three hundred hours, typing case notes into his laptop. Case notes which he neglected to "back up" to any external storage device. |
|---|---|
| Trigger | Sitting in class, John powers up his computer, only to see an error message, indicating hard-drive failure. |
| Struggle | His thoughts surge toward terrifying scenes. Failed exams. Poor grades. Stalled legal career. Inside his head, John lashes out in uncontrolled anger at God. Then he goes to phone his mother, who invites him to pray—and receives her son's curses for her spiritual invitation. |
| Ending | Provoked into self-examination by his desperate response, John experiences a spiritual re-awakening. He gains a new insight into the flimsiness of his own faith; and, on the flip-side of that insight, John perceives anew the graciousness of God, who somehow still manages to love someone so weak in faith. |

Zooming out, the computer-crash episode mattered to John because it threatened to derail his chosen life story. A story I would label "ascent" (achieve a status; fulfill a potential). But the end of the episode revealed a different set of values: a new understanding of self and of God. A story of ascent morphed into a story of rebirth.

(*Epilogue:* the campus techie-guy managed to fix the problem with John's hard-drive, and recover his files.)

Now that we have discussed plot structure, let us turn our focus to plot genres.

## THE WORLD IS FULL OF STORIES—BUT HOW MANY?

I well remember two animated films from my childhood: 101 *Dalmatians,* and *The Aristocats.* My friend Paul liked the first, but not the second. "Why?" I asked. "It's just like the first, except with cats instead of dogs." Perhaps a bit unfair, although both stories do feature an evil human antagonist scheming against the welfare of the canine/feline protagonists.

Do the commonalities of stories cluster into big masterplots? If so, how many? Going all the way back to Aristotle, literary critics have wrestled with the question, how many "big umbrella" plots do you need to cover all narratives?

Will three or four suffice? Or maybe seven? Fourteen? Thirty-six? All these have been proposed by one critic or another. Alternatively, is there maybe one mega-plot from which we can derive all the others?

To begin exploring these questions, let me retell a simple anecdote from real life, one often retold on my wife's side of the family. I have two sisters-in-law, Debbie and Deana, and this tale took place forty years ago when they were children in Indiana.

The story will no doubt seem remarkably trivial—but that is my point! The sisters can still remember this narrative vividly after forty years. What made the story so memorable?

> *Setting:* Indianapolis, early 1970s. Mid-December. Nine-year-old Debbie and four-year-old Deana are enjoying the school holidays and getting ready for Christmas.
>
> Debbie is hand-crafting her first-ever Christmas present for her younger sister Deana, who loves the cartoon character Tweetie Pie (the cute little birdie preyed upon by Sylvester, the black-and-white cat with the speech impediment).

So Debbie works secretly on making a Tweetie Pie from scraps of yellow fabric. She wants to hide her unfinished gift from Deana, so Debbie puts the half-made birdie up high on a shelf in the bedroom.

The next morning, Deana is alone in the bedroom. Lifting up her eyes, she spies the unfinished Tweetie Pie sitting on the shelf! Deana pushes a chair over to the shelf, climbs up and claims the birdie.

Taking him to her mother, she says, "Please will you finish stuffing this birdie that *Ms. Cindy, our next-door neighbor*, started making for me!" Mom complies.

On Christmas Eve, Debbie goes to the shelf, but the bird has flown the coop!

Then she finds Deana in the kitchen, playing with Tweetie Pie!

Debbie confronts her sister in anger. Deana confesses, leading to laughter and forgiveness.

What made this story so memorable for both sisters? I would suggest that the sisters remembered and retold this story because it embodies two archetypal, universal plots: the *quest* for something of transcendent value; the *comedy* of restoration of fractured relationships.

From Deana's point of view, the episode was a quest story (with a twist at the end; perhaps a little taste of "forbidden fruit"). Let's analyze the plotline components from Deana's point of view:

- In the archetypal quest, the protagonist perceives something far off, something of life-changing significance. Tweetie Pie, high on the shelf!
- Summoned by the distant object, the heroine journeys toward the prize, showing bravery and resource (climbing up to the high shelf).
- At the threshold of reaching her goal, frustration! Tweetie Pie is *unstuffed*!
- At this crisis moment, extra resourcefulness is needed. Playing the archetypal role of trickster, Deana persuades Mom to finish the birdie.
- Deana's quest resolves in a state of bliss: playing with Tweetie Pie in the kitchen.

This joy soon turns to sorrow, as Deana's narrative segues into Debbie's story. From Debbie's point of view, the story has all the elements of classic comedy. Here are the plotline components from Debbie's point of view:

- She begins working on a gift, to affirm and deepen her relationship with her younger sister.
- On Christmas eve, on the threshold of finishing the gift, frustration and despair! She discovers the loss, and discovers the culprit. The thoughtful Christmas surprise—ruined!
- At the crisis of the narrative, she confronts the culprit in anger.
- The crisis is resolved via an epiphany into the delightful cunning of her sibling.
- The result: a deepened relationship, and a story to last a lifetime.

The quest; the comedy. Let's move out from here and consider some other standard plotlines that transcend cultures.

My current academic research is a quest, a search for wisdom. I am searching for a concise inventory of basic plots that can describe all or most of the stories ever told. I still haven't found what I'm looking for, and probably never will. There are some stories so unique as to defy genre classification. (One sage literary critic warns us that my quest is "a path to madness"!)[21]

However, I do have a working model (which I will describe in my next chapter). As an on-ramp, let me introduce a couple of thinkers and how they have tackled the problem. The most helpful literary critics may give us a tool-box of plots for figuring out the shape and texture of our own life story.

My first thinker is Northrop Frye.[22] His method of investigation seems to fuse three ideas:

- Ancient myth as the root of literature
- Archetypal imagery/symbols (drawn from nature) as the key to myth
- Ancient myth intersects the natural cycle of four seasons

Putting all this together, Frye sees the four seasons as images (metaphors) of four basic plots:

| Season | Plot Genre |
|---|---|
| summer | romance (epic; adventure) |
| autumn (fall) | tragedy |
| spring | comedy |
| winter | irony/satire |

Epic, tragedy, comedy . . . not so different from the three classical Greek genres.[23]

My second thinker is Norman Friedman.[24] In contrast to the historical and image-based approach of Frye, Friedman's method of investigation is purely formal or structural. He begins with the question: Relative to the *protagonist*, what is the major change? Do the circumstances of the protagonist change? Or does his/her behavior change? Or is the change in his/her beliefs?

If the big change is the *circumstances* of the protagonist, this umbrella covers several plot types:

- Successful quests
- Escapes from threats
- Cinderella stories (rags to riches)
- Various kinds of tragedy

---

21. Morrison, *Key Concepts in Creative Writing*, 132.
22. Frye, *Anatomy of Criticism*.
23. See Aristotle, *Poetics* 5.
24. Friedman, *Form and Meaning in Fiction*.

Part 2: Stories Are . . . and Stories Do . . .

If the big change is in the *behavior* of the protagonist, this umbrella also covers several plot types:

- Coming of age
- Reform of character
- Initiation; success under testing
- Moral degeneration

Lastly, if the major change is in the *beliefs* of the protagonist, this third umbrella, too, covers several plot types:

- Education; epiphany
- Disillusionment
- Disposition toward others (a staple of comedy)

Looking back over your own life, have the biggest changes been in your circumstances, your behavior, or your beliefs? With your answer in mind, do any of Friedman's fourteen plots ring any bells in your own life?

Classifying changes in the protagonist (under headings of circumstances, behavior, and beliefs) generates around fourteen basic plots. These include the classical trio of epic, comedy, and tragedy. Furthermore, some of the fourteen plots could perhaps be absorbed into that trio.

It looks like we are dealing with the time-worn dilemma of categorization: lumping or splitting. On the principle of the "golden mean," I wonder if there is some wisdom in taking a middle ground between the four basic plots of Frye and the fourteen of Friedman. My next chapter will explore such middle ground, with an inventory of seven basic plots.

To end this chapter, I would like to take up the possibility that all the world's plots (however many) can be absorbed into one mega-plot. The most persistent claimant is known as the "monomyth."[25] I will describe and illustrate this arch-plot below. But if you would like an animated guide, then YouTube the TED talk by Matthew Winkler ("What Makes a Hero?"). I for one was hooked by Winkler's introduction: "What do Harry Potter, Katniss Everdeen, and Frodo have in common with the heroes of Greek mythology?"[26] (Spoiler: they're one and the same character!)

## THE MONOMYTH

This plot has four distinct phases. 1) The hero undertakes a *journey* (quest). The goal may be positive (wisdom; immortality; the divine; the transcendent; etc.), or negative (the destruction of evil).[27] 2) The hero undergoes a *death* experience of some kind. 3) The

---

25. Campbell, *Hero With A Thousand Faces*.
26. Winkler, "What Makes a Hero?"
27. Frye (*Anatomy of Criticism*, 192) explains why "epic romance" (or quest) is the basis for all other plots.

hero receives *enlightenment*, or attains to a union with the "divine" (ultimate reality). 4) The hero returns to *impart wisdom* to the rest of humanity.

One of the world's oldest stories follows this template perfectly. The *Epic of Gilgamesh* dates back to the third millennium BC. This pessimistic quest for wisdom is known as the "Sumerian Ecclesiastes" (for its parallels to the Old Testament book). Here are the epic's four phases according to the monomyth template:

1. Gilgamesh undertakes a journey to find the secret of immortality.
2. Gilgamesh crosses the "waters of death."[28]
3. Gilgamesh learns the "mystery of the gods"[29]—a plant, with power to grant the restoration of youth. (Gilgamesh obtains the plant, but a serpent steals it.)
4. Gilgamesh returns to his city, and imparts the (pessimistic) wisdom he obtained.

There are screenwriters who see the monomyth as the template for any number of successful films (e.g., *Star Wars*).[30] (Schmidt points out male-centered trait of the classic quest, and proposes modifications of structure to encompass "the female quest.")

With the four phases of the monomyth, throw in a setting and you have a classic five-act stage play, or the three major acts (sandwiched by setting and closure) of most films.

If the monomyth is a template for successful screenwriting, could it also be a template for a truly meaningful life? Think of the story of Saul of Tarsus (Acts 9). His narrative embodies the four-phase scheme rather well:

1. Zeal to destroy evil (as he perceived it) impels Saul on a journey to Damascus.
2. His encounter with the Christ results in Saul's "death" experience (blindness).
3. Saul receives enlightenment (sight + commission).
4. Saul returns to impart his new wisdom (that the Christ is Jesus of Nazareth).

Readers may recall that, in chapter 3 of this book, the monomyth surfaced as the plot advocated for *autobiography* by memoir coach Tristine Rainer.

In my struggle of rewriting the multiple drafts of this book, I derived great comfort and hope from viewing the process through the lens of the monomyth. That primordial plot process, stretching all the way back to Gilgamesh, truly captured my authorial experience. Here are the CliffsNotes, using the classic five-act structure (outlined earlier in this chapter, and applied to a "wisdom quest.")

## Trigger → Call

You may recall, from chapter 2 (above), how reflecting on the death of my father (in 2008) propelled me into the writing of this book.

---

28. Sandars, *Epic of Gilgamesh*, 104.
29. Ibid., 116.
30. McKee, *Story*, 196–97; Schmidt, *45 Master Characters*.

## Journey ("Dream" Phase)

On a sabbatical from my seminary in 2010, I began my search for narrative wisdom. I absorbed many classics of narrative theology, literary criticism, and narrative psychology. I gathered, in manila folders, kept in a cardboard "banker's box" (from Office Depot), a "scrapbook" of anything with narrative potential—from my readings, my lectures, my sermons, and random ruminations.

In 2012, I plunged into writing. Chapter upon chapter spilled out, freeing all the thoughts I had internalized and "marinated."

At the start of 2013, exhausted and relieved, I emailed attachments of version 1.0 to my (original) publisher.[31]

## "Frustration" Phase

I waited. Then, in the summer of 2013, I received my "editorial review." Not encouraging. The publisher wanted me to write more. Much more. I feared my authorial journey was becoming a version of the myth of Sisyphus, in which the protagonist pushes a rock almost to the top of a hill, only for the rock to roll all the way down to the bottom.

Or, to change the metaphor, I felt like someone who had signed up to run a marathon, completed the twenty-six miles, only to be told at the "finish" line: "Well—sorry to inform you—but you are actually in an "iron man" *tri*athalon. So, we need you to get on your bike, and ride a hundred kilometers. Oh, and then we finish with a mile-long swim across the lake."

## Crisis Phase

Generally speaking, you recognize the onset of a crisis when you come to realize, Hey, I'm actually no better off than when my journey began; in fact, I now see massive obstacles I was blissfully ignorant of back then.

And, if you are a typical human being, you respond to the onset of crisis by repeating your "go-to" formula. Trying harder.

So that's what I did, starting in the fall of 2013. More research (which generated chapters 3 and 4 of this book). More writing. Result: version 2.0, emailed to publisher, January 2014.

Generally speaking, you recognize the "jaws" of a crisis when your "just-keep-going" strategy runs into even bigger roadblocks. At this point, the "plot snake" has slithered to its lowest point.

Summer, 2014. I got my second "editorial review." To finish the book, I would need to write more—and not just more in quantity (that I can do), but more in quality. That was the *big*, unmovable roadblock.

---

31. *Not* Wipf & Stock, please note!

In terms of the monomyth—I was thankfully able to remind myself—the road to wisdom travels through the valley of the shadow of "death." In the mantra of Joseph Campbell: "In the cave you fear to enter, lies the treasure that you seek."[32]

## Resolution

The "more" that my publisher was asking me to incorporate: greater sympathy for the experience of the *reader*. Not fair! I'm an academic, by training and by temperament, and all our energy goes into climbing the mountain of knowledge. When we get to the summit, we have no energy left over for the reader.

Nevertheless—impelled by the monomyth—I asked myself, would the "death" of scholarly habits really be such a terrible ordeal? And, even if the process of change proved uncomfortable, might I perhaps emerge with greater wisdom at the end (a kind of rebirth)?

## Epilogue

I chose to follow my editor's advice. I tried to relinquish decades-old scholarly habits, and start paying more attention to the experience of the readers of texts. Version 3.0 (fall, 2014) incorporated my attempts at greater sensitivity toward you, the reader. How well I did—you can be the judge.[33]

However well or poorly I did, there *was* a change in me (my wife will testify). With sincere apologies to those diagnosed with the condition known as Asperger's Syndrome—my wife has long suspected that I suffer from a mild to moderate version of that quasi-autistic condition. (Most academics do; it's how we get our research done.) In other words, reader-awareness never will be my strongest attribute. But, via undergoing the "hero's journey" described by Joseph Campbell, I did "return" from my quest, with a pearl of wisdom distinctly different from what I was originally seeking.[34]

\* \* \* \* \*

---

32. Quoted in Winkler, "What Makes a Hero?"

33. Not well enough for their particular readership, according to my original publisher. Our contract was dissolved by mutual agreement, and version 3.0 (with minor modifications) found a home with Wipf & Stock.

34. Concretely, Buttrick's *Homiletic* helped me to start thinking more about how readers/listeners process discourse.

# 8

# The Seven Pillars of Wisdom

**THIRTY-FOUR YEARS OF SEARCHING**

IN MY LONG SEARCH for masterplots, I am most indebted to Christopher Booker's work, *The Seven Basic Plots: Why We Tell Stories*. Booker's work emerged from thirty-four years of inductive study of plays, novels, and films. (His wife must have loved him.)

I freely admit that the number seven is attractive, suggesting completeness. However, Booker's model grabbed me for three substantial reasons.

*First*, I used to teach a seminary class where students wrote a critical film review. One year, I had forty papers reviewing forty different films. The "seven basic plots" accounted for all forty films. Half the films were "pure types"; half were hybrids (e.g., quests for missing objects lead to comedic reconciliation between fellow-searchers).

*Second*, as I will explain later, the seven plots offer a unified meaning. They reveal seven facets of a single gemstone of wisdom.

*Third*, I also like the way these seven "pillars of wisdom" connect to real life.

Let's briefly identify and illustrate seven of the most common plotlines in narrative. We'll also hint at the roots of these scripts in physical, social, and spiritual realities. For some plots, we will also mention interpretative issues generated by that storyline.

## Quests

Quest stories seem rooted in universal scarcities that provoke a search for abundance, or our sense of finiteness that provokes a search for transcendence, or maybe even our sense of exile that provokes a search for home.

> As Jean-Paul Sartre expressed it, the essence of reality is scarcity, a universal and eternal lacking. There isn't enough of anything in this world to go round. Not enough food, not enough love, not enough justice, and never enough time. Time, as Heidegger observed, is the basic category of existence. We live in its ever-shrinking shadow, and if we are to achieve anything in our brief being that

lets us die without feeling we've wasted our time, we will have to go into heady conflict with the forces of scarcity that deny our desires.[1]

As classic literary exemplars of quests, we need only mention Bunyan's *Pilgrim's Progress*, Virgil's *Aeneid*, and the ancient Mesopotamian *Epic of Gilgamesh*.

## Comedy

Comedic plots seem rooted in our social nature and our need of relationships. This generates narrative tension, since our relationships typically produce confusion and estrangement.

We see this script played out in classics such as many of the plays of Shakespeare, or the novels of Jane Austen. Think of the estrangement of Beatrice and Benedict in *Much Ado About Nothing*, or Elizabeth and Darcy in *Pride and Prejudice*. If you want a pop culture reference, just about any "chick flick" will do.

Comedies often pivot on a moment of *epiphany*, when characters suddenly see others through new eyes.

## Tragedy

Tragedy may be rooted in the reality of death, the nemesis of us all; or in a sense that the cosmos imposes constraints upon us, and those who transgress its boundaries face inevitable demise.

Once again, Shakespeare provides a ready illustration (*Macbeth*). Or to pick a random movie, *Bonnie and Clyde*. This tale of "romantic" bank robbers begins as an adventure, and ends in a rain of bullets killing the protagonists.

## Rebirth

If death is a fundamental reality, so is birth, as evidenced by procreation, and rebirth, as evidenced by spring. These realities undergird classic tales of revitalization (often metaphorical or spiritual).

Fairy tales often feature this plotline: *Sleeping Beauty; Snow White; Beauty and the Beast*. Charles Dickens's *A Christmas Carol* is another abiding example.

## Ascent

The biological accompaniment of birth is maturation, and this reality undergirds another archetypal storyline. Narratives abound which turn on the ascent of the protagonist, often transforming humble origins into glory.[2]

---

1. McKee, *Story*, 211.
2. Booker labels this plotline "Rags to Riches" (*Seven Basic Plots*, 51–68).

How do we reach our full potential? What distinguishes a well-rounded human being? How do we overcome obstacles to growth?

Such questions drive the plot of fairy tales like *Cinderella*, or the narratives of Dickensian orphans. For those of you with memories of the 1970s disco scene, the John Travolta movie *Saturday Night Fever* (famous for the soundtrack by the Bee-Gees) belongs to the same underlying genre.

## Voyage-and-Return

The human condition entails being-in-time. Embedded in history, we cannot avoid experiencing change. Sometimes the change is welcome, sometimes not.

An entire genre exists to explore the effects of change. Booker labels this genre "Voyage-and-Return." The change may involve a drastic geographical relocation, as in adventure stories such as Tolkien's *The Hobbit*, or the visits to *Narnia* in the C. S. Lewis chronicles, or Mr. McGregor's garden in Beatrix Potter's *Peter Rabbit*.

On the other hand, the change may involve social or cultural relocation, as in the novel *Brideshead Revisited* by Evelyn Waugh, whose main character is plunged into the heady world of the aristocracy via Oxford University in the 1920s.

In the movie *It's a Wonderful Life*, the "voyage" takes the main character into an alternative history, namely, the history that would have transpired if the protagonist *had never lived*.

In typical exemplars of this genre, perhaps the major interpretative questions become, Was the protagonist changed by their alien experience? What did they learn? Other questions raised include, Is it ever possible to truly return to "the way things were"?

## Overcoming the Monster

Our final genre roots in the reality of evil, and our seemingly innate sense of justice. Some of the most popular stories involve the conflict between light and dark forces (with the latter often personified in monstrous forms such as dragons). Booker labels such plots "Overcoming the Monster." We need only mention *Harry Potter*, or *Lord of the Rings*.

\* \* \* \* \*

By way of a quick review, we can apply a binary test to determine if these seven plots really are distinct and basic. For a plot to be basic and distinct, it needs an essential feature, and this feature cannot be essential to any other basic plot. Applying this binary test generates the following chart:

# The Seven Pillars of Wisdom

| Plot Archetype | Essential Feature |
|---|---|
| Overcoming the Monster | presence of external enemy |
| Tragedy | destruction of protagonist |
| Rebirth | passivity of protagonist (requires agent of rebirth) |
| Ascent | elevation of protagonist |
| Comedy | ends in social/relational unity or reconciliation |
| Quest | goal-directed journey (literal or metaphorical) |
| Voyage-and-Return | *in*voluntary (non-purposeful or accidental) journey plus return |

(The difference between the last two on the list, quest versus voyage-and-return, may intersect another classification scheme. Some critics believe that the deep structure of any story is either "Someone Leaves Town," or "A Stranger Comes to Town." The latter would overlap the involuntary change feature of voyage-and-return.)

At the start of this chapter, I indicated my preference for lists of plot types that readily overlap our life experiences. As you look over the above list of seven archetypes, do any of them capture your major experiences of life? Would any of them help you articulate the narrative shape and texture of your life story?

The rest of my book will constantly back-reference these seven "pillars of wisdom," exploring their resonance with the lives of individuals and communities. (Chapter 13, "Don Quixote Rides Again," does this in a systematic fashion.)

\* \* \* \* \*

I am drawn to Booker's scheme of seven plots for reasons beyond their value to literary critics. Taken together, the seven plots combine to offer multi-faceted wisdom on the problem of the human condition, and its solution.

Booker himself ties the seven together using a story that I don't buy into, but I will present it anyway, since I think some of it may be salvageable. He argues that the unconscious mind has been hardwired to generate stories expressing archetypal values:

> These values, like the archetypal structures which shape stories, are programmed into our consciousness in a way we cannot modify or control. The essential message implicit in that programming is that the central goal of any human life is to achieve the state of perfect balance which we recognize as maturity; and how the central enemy in reaching that goal is our capacity to be held back by the deforming and ultimately self-destructive power of egocentricity.[3]

In the interests of full disclosure, I should point out Booker's express indebtedness to the psychological theory of Carl Gustav Jung. The skeleton (bare bones) of the theory would go something like this:

1. Animals have a better instinct to preserve their species than humans (when did you last see animals practicing genocide?)

---

3. Ibid., 347.

2. During the course of evolution, humans become self-conscious, aware of our individuality—we developed an *ego*.
3. Nevertheless, the *unconscious* retains knowledge of the more psychologically-integrated and more socially-integrated pre-human condition.

If we interface Jung with the plots, here is what the plots teach:

- *Quest* narratives remind us that something is *lacking*
- Narratives of *ascent* teach us that true *maturity* may be what we lack
- *Comedy* reveals the lack as *alienated relationships*, restored via *epiphany*
- Stories of *voyage-and-return* symbolize the *resources for change in the unconscious*, represented by the unfamiliar world entered by the protagonist
- Stories about *overcoming-the-monster* remind us of the *objectivity of evil*
- *Tragedy* warns us against the *egocentric* pathway
- Stories of *rebirth* hold out *hope for change*

Like I said, I don't buy into all the Jungian story of the subconscious. But, as a Christian thinker, I do wonder: Is there some sort of *theological* explanation for the pervasiveness of these seven basic plots?

Some folk (not me!) believe that God made the *zodiac* constellations in the sky as a celestial mural of the gospel. Virgo = Virgin Mary; Leo = Lion of Judah; Scorpio = Satan; Aquarius = Baptism; etc.

Even if we don't buy this Christian zodiac stuff, it provides an interesting analogy. Instead of a celestial mural of the gospel, did God provide a *narrative grammar* for the gospel? Did God hardwire us to generate seven archetypal plots, because the gospel follows the narrative arcs of these typical plotlines? (In chapters 9 and 10, I will explore the biblical story using the seven basic plots as a starting point.)

Putting it in theological terms, archetypal plots would be "natural revelation," and the gospel would be "special revelation." Through his missionary work, Don Richardson concluded that God has placed "redemptive analogies" in the cultural scripts of every nation, tribe, and tongue on the earth.[4]

In learning the stories of the Sawi people of Indonesia, Richardson was shocked at how they valorized treachery. Their heroes formed relationships in order "to fatten with friendship for the slaughter."[5] On hearing the Gospel narrative for the first time, the Sawi cheered and celebrated Judas's betrayal of Jesus![6]

Obviously, this cultural "value" of treachery posed an acute social problem for the Sawi. If treachery is supreme, how can two villages ever live at peace with one another? The culture provided a remarkable "redemptive analogy": the *peace child*.[7] The two villages exchange an infant, who is adopted by the opposite tribe. The peace child is sacred,

---

4. Richardson, *Peace Child*, 10, 182, 288.
5. Ibid., 8.
6. Ibid., 177.
7. Ibid., 201–6.

and an enduring bond of peace and trust. For the Sawi, "If a man would actually give his own son to his enemies, that man could be trusted."[8]

\* \* \* \* \*

Humans (in contrast to animals) are storytellers. The Creator loves to narrate, and created narrators who instinctively produce stories as explanations of life. If fundamental story types and patterns actually house wisdom implanted by the Creator, then thirty-four years—the time devoted by Booker to uncovering his seven basic plots—would scarcely be too long for such a vital quest.

But did his quest uncover pure gold—or maybe only silver? Is there a "platinum version" of plot archetypes out there—a model that better captures the varied forms in which we tell stories?

Well, we certainly generate his seven plotlines over and over in film, literature, and theater. And they do have a remarkable reach to encompass a large percentage of human narrative products. Especially when you allow hybrid versions, reduced or incomplete versions, and anti-versions.

Booker himself recognizes that many stories are hybrids. Indeed, Tolkien's famous trilogy may incorporate all seven archetypal plots. Three obvious ones spring to mind. Frodo's journey intersects the archetype of the quest. But this quest was itself part of overcoming-the-monster.[9] As a foil for Frodo's quest, the story interweaves the tragedy of Gollum.

However, there are plots that don't fit the scheme so neatly. What about the ancient stories of cosmic creation (Genesis 1, for instance)? Booker concedes that these don't fit under the seven-plot umbrella.[10]

And there are other classification schemes (cf. those of Frye and Friedman, mentioned in our previous chapter). For example, Blake Snyder offers a ten-plot version.[11] Ronald B. Tobias doubles that number.[12] Leland Ryken reduces the number back down to eleven.[13] Allen Tilley further reduces the number to five.[14]

Okay, time to rein in the developing skepticism. Do the multiple classifications of plot mutually cancel their validity? No, and here's why. *First*, there is substantial overlap between the lists. *Second*, many critics merely use different labels for one and the same genre of plot. *Third*, some critics are "lumpers," others "splitters." When plots share some (but not all) key features in common, do you batch them together, or separate? For example, some critics tend to lump anything involving a *journey* under a generic label such as "romance." Others discriminate, according to the purpose of the journey.

---

8. Ibid., 206.

9. Many of the Russian folk tales studied by V. Propp (*Morphology of the Folktale*) combined the journey + overcoming-the-monster motifs.

10. Booker, *Seven Basic Plots*, 215.

11. Snyder, *Save the Cat*, 25–41.

12. Tobias, *20 Master Plots*.

13. Ryken, *Windows to the World*, 43–44.

14. Tilley, *Introduction to Plot*.

Part 2: Stories Are . . . and Stories Do . . .

Is it a search for treasure? An expedition for battle? A departure from home in order to come-of-age? Or merely an unplanned plunge into a strange world? *Fourth*—and most importantly—different critics legitimately use different features of story to generate their own list of plots.

Building on this fourth point, the same story can—quite properly—be classified using more than one plot genre. As readers, "We may have *complementary experiences of a single text*."[15] (And—by implication—there may well be more than one plot that describes the narrative shape of your life story.)

Let's look at three features of story that different critics use to build their inventory of plots. Most readers probably engage a story by identifying with the *protagonist*. Accordingly, many inventories of plot focus on the main character. What were their initial goals, and what transformations emerged in or around them as the story reached its conclusion? (The lists we have cited from Friedman and Booker are protagonist-centered.)

Alternatively, since there is no story without struggle, why not classify plots according to the kind of *antagonism* faced by the main character? Some critics do just that, resulting in plot types such as these:

- man/woman versus nature
- man/woman versus society
- man/woman versus technology
- man/woman versus self
- man/woman versus rival(s)
- man/woman versus monsters
- man/woman versus God(s)
- man/woman versus fate

As we work on constructing our own life story, it's always worth asking, what (or whom) did I struggle against? How did that struggle, that "opponent," shape my narrative?

Lastly, stories deal with cause-and-effect. So, one could itemize plots based on the kind of *causality* which propels the storyline. This is precisely the approach taken by Tilley (who asserts, provocatively, that, "So long as plot is assumed to be a character's story, confusions will multiply.")[16] According to Tilley, all plots are driven by one of five basic types of cause.[17] His five arch-plots do encompass the classic genres from Greek antiquity (epic; comedy; tragedy), but he avoids those labels, since they remove focus from causality.

I paraphrase his scheme below. As you look over the list of causes, I invite you to ponder your own view of life. What kind(s) of causes seem most strongly operative in your own experience? For example, do your own desires/fears best explain your story?

---

15. Ibid., 14 (italics mine). Tilley illustrates this elsewhere (ibid., 23–24, 28–29, 39–42).
16. Tilley, *Plot Snakes*, 38.
17. Tilley, *Introduction to Plot*, 17–20.

Or, does family history seem to determine your fate? Alternatively, does some future destiny seem to exert a mysterious pull on the direction of your life?

Here is a list of causal types (that drive the plot forward):

- ordinary desires and fears in present time
- "fatalistic" influences inherited from previous generation(s)
- "coincidences" that reveal hints of destiny
- meaningless "accidents"; mere contingency of events; futile interruptions (i.e., *absence* of traditional cause-and-effect)
- actions with universal resonance; wholly inter-dependent events

Looking back over this list of plot-driving causes, we may glimpse how certain genres of plot tend to match one of the five basic causal modes.[18]

For example, epic quests tend to have heroes with a strong sense of destiny. By contrast, tragedies often involve protagonists defeated by fatal forces from the past. Then again, anti-plots (postmodern film and fiction; theater-of-the-absurd; irony and satire) utilize the pseudo-causality of futile interruptions. While stories where actions have universal resonance, establishing unchangeable worlds, tend toward the genre of myth.

We may leave this brief analysis (of the intersection of causality and genre) with an interesting question. In your own consumption of fiction and film, do you gravitate toward a storyline governed by one of the five causal modes listed above? For example, do you like heroes with a strong sense of personal destiny, who experience meaningful "coincidences"? (I know I do!) And, what might your genre-preference reveal about your view of life?

\* \* \* \* \*

In the light of the fact we have been considering—that plots can legitimately be approached from multiple complementary angles—here is my advice. Find a model, a rudimentary inventory of plots, which *works for you*. Use it flexibly, not rigidly, as a search strategy for starting conversations with literature and with life. Remain open to additional insights offered by other windows onto the world of story, other inventories of plots.

\* \* \* \* \*

We end this chapter with an example of how a rudimentary grasp of plot can give us a framework for understanding real-life events. Plot makes sense of isolated events, by connecting them to a meaningful storyline.

---

18. For abundant examples from literature and film, see Tilley (*Plot Snakes*; *Introduction to Plot*).

Part 2: Stories Are . . . and Stories Do . . .

## THE BISHOP OF EPHESUS

Protestants have treated "Saint" Paul as the Christian equivalent of the philosopher Plato. An ivory-tower thinker, dedicated to producing an abstract system of "timeless truth." Nothing could be further from the truth. Paul, writing concrete responses to specific circumstances, was a "task" or "occasional" theologian. And a narrative theologian. His letters initiate a flexible dialogue between the story of Jesus and story of a local Christian community.[19]

Paul's letters are usually a *crisis-intervention*. So, to understand a Pauline letter, we need to know its *backstory*. And plot is the lens that brings the story of the letter into focus.

Let me illustrate, with a concise treatment of Paul's shortest letter—to *Philemon*. I invite you to pause and read the letter (if you read quickly, you can do this in a minute or two).

Some readers may wonder how, exactly, this twenty-five-verse "papyrus postcard" ever got into the canon of Scripture, alongside the more august Epistle to the Hebrews.

However, for those who explore the depths of the little letter to Philemon, there is no doubting its value. One commentator remarked, "The single epistle to Philemon very far surpasses all the wisdom of the world."[20] Another writer, Karl J. Ernst, used the letter as the basis of a primer on pastoral counseling.[21]

To scratch the surface of the letter's profound wisdom, I will use the plotline of "classical comedy." Popular parlance notwithstanding, humor is *not* the essence of this genre. Rather, the plotline of comedies moves from social/relational tension and fragmentation to peace and unity (chaos to order), usually via an "epiphanic" moment of recognition, when characters see anew ("blindness" to "sight").

The topic of literary comedies is "us in our public roles."[22] The narrative world of comedy is "haunted by barriers" between people.[23] In exploring how these barriers break down, comedies evince "a yearning for utopia," symbolizing our desire for an ideal society.[24]

In one subgenre of comedy, "Important characters undertake *physical journeys*, hoping to establish a better society."[25] But this attempt is incomplete, and the better society only emerges through *illumination*: "The hero achieves a *vision* of a possible new order."[26]

The letter to Philemon can be read as a comedic story, in which Paul acts as a catalyst for illumination, in the hope of reconciling two estranged characters, and transforming their relationship—"in Christ."

---

19. See Strom, *Reframing Paul*.
20. Frankius, quoted in Bengel, *Gnomon*, 327.
21. Ernst, *Art of Pastoral Counseling*.
22. Tilley, *Introduction to Plot*, 68, 70.
23. Ibid., 69, 71.
24. Ibid., 68, 71.
25. Tilley, *Plot Snake*, 48 (italics mine).
26. Ibid. (italics mine).

As backstory for the letter, we need the *dramatis personae*: the three main players and their inter-relationships. Using details from within the text, we may cautiously sketch the triangular history of relationships between Paul, Philemon, and Onesimus.

Philemon was the host of a first-century house-church, and a respected fellow-worker of Paul (Phlm 1–2). Philemon stood indebted to Paul—verse 19b—for some life-giving benefaction (perhaps Paul led Philemon into relationship with Christ). Philemon also owned a domestic slave, Onesimus (a common nickname for slaves in antiquity (verse 10); the Greek means "useful.")

Sadly, Onesimus had failed to live up to his name, becoming "useless" in the eyes of his master (verse 11). The slave had undertaken a physical journey away from his master (verse 15). Perhaps he fled, maybe even pocketing the first-century equivalent of his master's credit card (verse 18a). Or perhaps—in accordance with Roman custom—Onesimus sought out Paul as third-party mediator of some conflict between master and slave.

Whether by design or accident, Onesimus encounters Paul—and Christ—in Paul's prison cell (verse 10). Now, Onesimus is a new person in Christ (verse 11), capable of gospel ministry alongside Paul (verse 13).

But the problems from Onesimus's past—his estrangement from Philemon—remain. In an attempt to resolve these problems, Paul sends Onesimus back to Philemon (verse 12), bearing the letter designed to reconcile the two men in a radically transformed relationship (verses 16–17).

Significant barriers, however, blocked the path toward reconciliation and domestic transformation. Philemon's natural reluctance would be doubled or tripled by the cultural "scripts" of the Greco-Roman social pyramid in which he lived, moved, and had his being. These cultural scripts worked against any transformation of the social status quo.

The biggest barrier: master and slave occupied different levels of the social pyramid. The institution of slavery went largely unquestioned in the ancient world. Indeed, the Roman economy depended on it. Maintaining the status quo was an imperial priority.

Greco-Roman males (like Philemon) were socialized, from birth, into the supreme value of maintaining your honor and status, your rung on the social ladder. And Onesimus (at least in Philemon's eyes) had dishonored his master. Such debts must be repaid.

The indebtedness of others—according to ancient Mediterranean practice—was something to exploit to your own advantage. Obligations incurred by others increased your power over them. And Onesimus's obligations toward Philemon had increased (verse 18a).

In the ancient Mediterranean social pyramid, power and coercion were exerted downwards with little of the modern concern for "rights." In particular, runaway slaves (who were unable to furnish a valid excuse) were subject to public humiliation (including flogging or branding) at the "discretion" of the master.

You begin to see the problem faced by Paul?

Paul undermines these cultural obstacles to reconciliation, by tapping into the power of the gospel. In his letter to Philemon, the gospel dynamic works like this:

new story → new society → new identity → new scripts

Let's investigate this dynamic . . .

## New Story

Throughout his little letter to Philemon, Paul taps into the transformative power of the gospel meta-narrative. How? Through repetition of the key phrases "in Christ" and "in the Lord" (Phlm 8, 16, 20, 23).

Let's unpack the full resonance of this idiom. In Romans 6, Paul takes for granted that *baptized* individuals understand their baptism as symbolizing participation in the story of Christ—his story of death and resurrection. Participating in Christ entails death to old modes of existence, and liberation into new modes of existence. In a statement regarded by many scholars as a baptismal formula, Paul summarizes the implications of union with Christ for social identity. Galatians 3:27–28 declares, "Everyone baptized into Christ has clothed themselves with Christ. Jew/Greek, slave/free, male/female—[divisions] no longer, for you are all one in Christ Jesus."

Baptism into Christ submerges you into the comedic plotline, in which social barriers (such as Jew versus Gentile) are obliterated, through the creation of a new humanity "in Christ" (e.g., Ephesians 2:14–16).

In Philemon 6 (a tough verse to translate), Paul taps into this meta-narrative, when he prays that, "The mutual-participation [*koinonia*], which characterizes your [Philemon's] faith, might become energized, through recognition, . . . *into Christ*." This last phrase—"into Christ"—functions in Paul as shorthand for the new society emerging in connection with Messiah.[27] And, in verse 17, Paul requests Philemon to welcome Onesimus as a member of this new society (*koinonia*).

## New Society and New Identity

Participation in this new society brings a new social identity. In the letter to Philemon, this new identity expresses itself in the high density of *familial* and *collegial* metaphors.

The letter abounds in sibling designations of the relationship between Christians—"brother" (Phlm 1, 7, 20) and "sister" (verse 2). Paul invites Philemon to re-imagine his relationship with Onesimus in fraternal terms instead of master-slave terms (verse 16). In the ancient Mediterranean world, intra-familial relationships offered respite from the struggle for honor that preoccupied males within the public arena.

Voluntary associations (clubs—*collegia* in Latin, *koinonia* in Greek) also offered males respite from the constant public competition for honor. Paul imagines the church in such terms in the letter to Philemon. He twice refers to the *koinonia* (verses 6 and 17), and also uses collegial terms for his ministry partners: "fellow-worker(s)" (verses 1 and 24); "fellow-soldier" (verse 2); "fellow-prisoner" (verse 23).

The overall effect of this density of sibling and collegial terms: to replace the "tough" master-slave relationship with the "tender" relationship of brotherhood and partnership.

---

27. See Wright, *Climax of the Covenant*, 53–55.

## New Scripts

With this new social identity come new behavioral scripts for how we treat one another. Throughout his letter, Paul models these for Philemon, hinting at how the story of Christ's voluntary self-humiliation (Philippians 2:5–11) was imprinted on Paul's DNA.

These Christ-shaped scripts all subvert the behavioral norms inherited by Philemon from his Greco-Roman milieu. By subverting these scripts, Paul undermines the barriers blocking reconciliation, and points to a pattern of transformed relations.

Paul starts by gently challenging Philemon's assumptions about *status*. Paul identifies himself as a "*prisoner* for Christ"/"*prisoner* for the gospel" (Phlm 1, 9, 13, italics mine). This untypical designation not only identifies with the slave Onesimus in his lack of freedom; it also implies the "downward social mobility" of the gospel. Humility replaces pride; lowliness replaces exaltedness. Paul gently challenges Philemon-the-master: is "mastery" a proper concern for the Christian?

Next, Paul challenges Philemon's assumptions about *power*. In the ancient world, if you had power, you tended to use it. As an apostle, Paul had power—but he prefers not to use it; rather, he appeals to Philemon, on the basis of love (verses 8–9). Instead of coercing a decision from Philemon, he entrusts Philemon with the resolution of the matter concerning Onesimus (verse 14).

Finally, along similar lines, Paul subverts the ancient Mediterranean script for exploiting the indebtedness of others. Philemon owed Paul (verse 19b). The culturally-accepted practice would be for Paul simply to call in the debt. Instead, Paul obligates himself to pay Onesimus's debt to Philemon (verse 18–19a). Martin Luther rightly saw this as an echo of Christ, paying humanity's debt to God.

*Epilogue:* Was Paul's letter successful? Well, if the addressee Philemon had ignored the letter, its preservation would have been unlikely.

Intriguingly, an early church tradition mentions a certain Onesimus as a first-century bishop of Ephesus. Was this the (former) slave of Philemon? The correlation is, of course, unprovable; but as conservative and cautious a scholar as F. F. Bruce gives credence to the tradition.[28]

\* \* \* \* \*

Our next two chapters pick up where this one left off. These chapters offer a more systematic and wide-ranging exploration of how basic plot genres help us understand the literature of the Bible. The chapters also confirm the power of story to bridge the gap between the world of the Bible and the world we live in.

---

28. Bruce, *Epistles*, 202.

# 9

# Alpha and Omega

**INSIDE THE ABBEY**

My wife, daughter, and I were getting ready to welcome a foster-child into our home. We had installed the smoke-detectors ("one per bedroom") required by Texas State Law. We had purchased a sock-monkey stuffed toy for the little girl's bedroom. Materially, we had created as good an environment as middle-class parents, employed by non-profit organizations, can afford.

Still, a sense of under-preparedness prevailed. Imagine, for a moment, you are a seven-year-old child. Without warning, a strange lady (from Child Protective Services) knocks on the door of your apartment (where you live with your single-parent mom). The child hears that she is being removed ("for her own good.") Something—she doesn't really understand—to do with her mom's "drug use." Plus the bruises on mom's arm (from the boyfriend who stays over a few nights each week). The CPS lady tells the child, "You are going to live with another family, while your mom gets her life sorted out."

Imagine how this child would feel, when they arrive at your front door for the first time.

I'm not an expert in social work. Nor in child psychology. But I wanted to give our foster-child a way to feel safe, somehow. And my best resource happens to be stories.

An unplanned visit to my local public library gave me what I was searching for. A classic children's tale, illustrated with exquisitely-detailed color drawings. *A Redwall Winter's Tale*, by Brian Jacques.[1]

The author has skillfully created a warm, beckoning, realistic world, centered on a large abbey (built in red sandstone), populated by animals of the English countryside. As you turn the illustrated pages, and read the well-crafted story, you become transported into the safe "narrative world" conjured up by the text.

My favorite part of the book: an illustrated page showing the youngsters rabbit, hedgehog, and mole, snug asleep under their quilts, within the protective walls of the abbey.

---

1. Illustrated by Christopher Denise.

Here's what I would say to our foster-child: "I know the world does not seem a safe place for you at this moment. Sometimes I do not feel safe either. When I am scared, I like to read the story of Redwall Abbey. I imagine I am one of the creatures—mole, hedgehog, or rabbit—tucked under my quilt blanket, in the ancient chamber of the abbey. Behind the thick stone walls. Inhabiting the world of Redwall, where life has continued, unchanged, for centuries."

\* \* \* \* \*

And here's what I would say to you, the reader of this book. I hope you will find a home in the biblical story.

After the destruction of the Jerusalem temple in 70 CE, the Rabbis must have agonized over the loss of their holy place. Sacred space, evoking the transcendent, enables us to center our lives on something permanent. So, how did the Rabbis respond to the loss of their temple? They came to view the Torah scroll (the five books of Moses) as a "portable temple." Meditation upon the Torah became a portal to sacred space.

A sacred text constructs a narrative world that is a kind of sacred space. Accordingly, our small stories can inhabit or indwell the world of the Bible's big story. Like the walls of an ancient abbey, the story of Scripture gives us a fixed and stable "stage" plus "scenery" for the unfolding of our personal narratives.

\* \* \* \* \*

In this chapter, I offer concise CliffsNotes on the big plotlines of the Bible. We'll zoom the lens out, for a multi-angle view of God's redemptive work in history, an overall sense of what God *has* done in the world. And, by implication, a sense of what God *is* doing in the world, right now (and what he might be doing in your life and in mine).

After sketching seven basic plots found in the Bible, I will zoom the lens in, with a personal illustration of how the macro-story of Scripture can intersect the micro-story of everyday life.

## WHAT KIND OF STORY IS THE BIBLE?

Like Tolkien's trilogy, the biblical story is a thick, multi-layered tapestry of interwoven plotlines. All seven of the basic plots from our previous chapter seem present in Scripture, either as multi-colored threads of the main plot, or as subplots.

Here is a "starter-kit" for retelling the drama of Scripture through a variety of narrative images.[2] My plotline thumbnails below are suggestive not exhaustive. I will tug on several of these threads in later chapters.

---

2. Cf. Buechner (*Telling the Truth*), who views the gospel through the lenses of three genres: tragedy, comedy, and fairy tale.

Part 2: Stories Are . . . and Stories Do . . .

## Tragedy

According to Christopher Booker, this is the plot that most closely mirrors real life.[3] The plotline of human degeneration, begun in Adam,[4] transmitted to his descendants, tending downward into an abyss of violence,[5] encapsulated in Romans 1:18–32, and culminating in the "fallen, fallen" refrain of Revelation 18:2, gives the whole Bible a sadly realistic or tragic texture.

This unflinching realism of scripture, looking evil in the eye and not blinking, invites a question. Does the redemptive counterpoint of Scripture belong to the realm of reality, or to the saccharine optimism of genres screened on the Disney channel?

## Comedy

In the pages of the New Testament, the funeral dirge accompanying the tragic plotline gets drowned out by the music accompanying the comedic plotline of reconciliation on a cosmic scale, celebrated in the hymn of Colossians 1:15–20. As the notes from this hymn ripple throughout the world, a symphony of unity replaces the cacophony of violence of Genesis 4 and 6. Swords get beaten into ploughshares, tribal hostilities cease.[6]

In the pages of the Old Testament, humanity breaks faith with God, but God renews his peace treaty.[7] Using language comfortable to mystics, the Bible imagines the divine-human encounter as a male-female romance.[8] The divorce between us and God ultimately resolves in the wedding celebration of Revelation 21:2 and 9–10.

## Rebirth

The ultimate passivity of the protagonist, and the need for an external agent of renewal, distinguish this plot archetype from the others. Accordingly, scripts of rebirth and renewal are the plotlines of hope for the hopeless.

Pessimism pervades the book of Ecclesiastes; a philosophical quest for meaning, rendered futile by the biography-obliterating fact of death. Romans 8:20 picks up Ecclesiastes's idiom, and extends it to the domain of nature, whose entropic death-ward storyline echoes the futility of death-haunted human existence.

But Rom 8:21–23 rewrites the cosmic music of despair, superimposing earth-mother's cry for deliverance in hope of new birth. God's Spirit, first-fruits of cosmic harvest, echoes the cry of birth-pangs.[9] God's Son, second Adam, first-fruits of a resurrection

---

3. Booker, *Seven Basic Plots*, 577–83.

4. Northrop Frye speaks of "the archetypal tragedy of . . . the loss of innocence of Adam and Eve, who, no matter how heavy a doctrinal load they have to carry, will always remain dramatically in the position of children baffled by their first contact with an adult situation." (Frye, *Anatomy of Criticism*, 220.)

5. Gen 4:1–24; 6:5–6, 11–13.

6. Isa 2:1–4.

7. Gen 8:21—9:17.

8. Jer 2:2; 3:1, 20; Ezek 16:8; Hos 2:16.

9. Rom 8:23 and 26.

harvest of new creation.[10] The New Testament rebirth story, focused as *resurrection*, is not just inward and individual.

The image of resurrection dominates the New Testament's plotline of rebirth. But, as writings like Hebrews show, the image of *purification* also focuses a narrative of rebirth. In the ancient world of the Old Testament and Judaism, purity symbolized order and life, and impurity disorder and death.[11]

Accordingly, the removal of defilement signals a rebirth. The external agent of rebirth? The ritual use of archetypal elements of water and blood, elements highlighted in the narrative of the cross in John 19:34. What the fourth Gospel hints at, Hebrews announces, imaging the cross of Jesus as the definitive purging of defilement, a drama symbolized by water and blood.[12]

## Quest

If rebirth narratives happen to passive protagonists, quests reveal protagonists at their most purposeful, seeking, searching for something life-renewing. Go back beyond Homer, back beyond Moses, and eventually you reach *The Epic of Gilgamesh* from the third millennium before Christ. A search for wisdom in the face of death, goading Gilgamesh on his epic journey, may well be the primordial human narrative.

Curious, then, the comparative neglect of the wisdom-quest plotline by those who avow to retell the biblical narrative. Nevertheless, a strong search-for-wisdom plotline unfolds, moving from the "thesis" of Proverbs, through the "antitheses" of Job and Ecclesiastes, and culminating in John's narrative of wisdom incarnate. Bridging Old and New Testaments, we read of a wisdom-quest that begins with the self-assured proverbs of Solomon, takes a detour through the tortured doubts of Ecclesiastes and the unanswered questions of Job, and resolves with the "one greater than Solomon" (Matt 12:42).

## Ascent

If quests are driven by external objects, then plots of ascent are often driven by character development toward maturity. But this distinction only highlights the inextricably multi-threaded quality of the tapestry of biblical narrative. A major quest within the Bible searches for wisdom; wisdom is a prize for attaining maturity. In the person of Solomon, the Old Testament intertwines wisdom with kingship.

The royal ideal of the king as apex of humanity, the image of God, means that the plot of ascent most naturally focuses on the story of kingship. This story accelerates in the books 1–2 Samuel. An abhorrent leadership-vacuum. No priest who will act

---

10. 1 Cor 15:20–25, 42–49.

11. For sociological discussion, see Neyrey, "Symbolic World of Luke-Acts," 271–304. Neyrey notes that, "The *dead*, who rank among the most *unclean* of all people, were objects of Jesus' touch and that of his disciples" (ibid., 287 [italics mine]).

12. Heb 9:13–14; 10:22.

according to the values of God's heart and mind; no king after God's own heart.[13] Unless we count David. Overlooking his Saul-sized weaknesses, his positives got abstracted into the messianic ideal.

Fast-forward to Mark's Gospel, with its "secretive" (partially-hidden) Messiah, and its anti-triumphalist message of suffering Messiah. Not what the Apostle Peter was expecting (Mark 8:27–33). Reading Mark, we learn that the ideal actualized in Christ was no simple one-to-one map from the Davidic messianic prototype.[14] The ascent to maturity is more complex than we realize.

If the biblical story of kingship interweaves the peaceful, contemplative quest for wisdom, the kingship narrative of the Bible also intersects the "holy warfare" version of the "dragon-slaying" archetype. (Given the military role of kings in the ancient world, this intersection was inevitable.) Classic literature in general tends to intertwine a number of basic plots, perhaps in recognition of the complexity of the human condition. Frye notes that, "The central form of the quest-romance is the dragon-killing theme exemplified in the stories of Saint George and Perseus."[15]

## Slaying of Dragons

We can trace the whole story of the Bible via the "holy warfare" plotline, triggered by Genesis 3:15, with its promise of human offspring to bruise the serpent's head.

And, despite having a serious pacifist substratum, Christendom had a lengthy love-affair with martial imagery. The Salvation Army. The various "crusades" devoted to evangelizing the "heathen." (In the interests of full disclosure, I used to work for a seminary whose logo features a gigantic sword atop a pulpit.)

That said, in the post-9/11 world, a storyline with an eerie resemblance to jihad or the Crusades might not be the most politically-correct way to retell the biblical epic. Furthermore, in a postmodern world, what is the future of narratives with a clean-cut dichotomy between good and evil? In reply, one may mention the outrageous success of the *Harry Potter* series. If fact, this example illustrates the adaptability of the archetype. The evil incarnate that Harry must slay? Intolerance.

As the biblical epic unfolds, its dragon-slaying archetype also morphs. The battle narrative culminates in the disarmament of evil powers—not by greater violence, but by the cross of Christ.[16] Accordingly, the enemy the church battles is not our "flesh and blood" human kindred,[17] but systemic evil of all kinds.[18]

In my previous chapter, I suggested that the essential element of dragon-slaying narratives is the presence of an external entity that threatens the well-being of the

---

13. 1 Sam 2:35 and 13:14.

14. I develop these ideas further in chapter 24, "The Men Who Would Be King".

15. Frye, *Anatomy of Criticism*, 189. V. Propp's *Morphology of the Folktale* derived a plotline abstract from Russian folktales, in which the basic plots of quest, dragon-slaying, and ascent all combine.

16. Longman and Reid, *God is a Warrior*.

17. Eph 6:12.

18. For discussion of systemic evils, see Gombis, *Drama of Ephesians*, 48–57.

protagonist's community. Accordingly, we can discern a number of non-militaristic "warfare" plotlines within the Bible.

For example, ancient Canaanite myths depicted Creation in terms of a *Chaoskampf*, in which an "Apollonian" god (representing order) overcomes the forces of chaos (often depicted as a sea-monster). The authors of Scripture were not shy about incorporating modified versions of this narrative, with Yahweh as the God who brings order out of chaos. Is there, perhaps, a faint echo of this plotline in 1 Corinthians 14:13, where Paul challenges the disorderly worship service with the assertion, "God is not of disorder but of peace"?

Then again, the "battle" fought by a community may be purely defensive and not offensive. If a minority community feels besieged by a culture that threatens to assimilate it, the community may resist this external threat by putting up walls. The walls may be metaphorical (boundary markers), or even literal (as in the storyline of Ezra-Nehemiah).[19] In the New Testament era, a version of this storyline undergirds the Pastoral Epistles (1–2 Timothy, Titus). When the post-apostolic church approached the second century, as a tiny sect in the Roman empire, she took care to barricade the walls of her "household" (the dominant image for the church in these Epistles, which also employ "soldier" imagery for the pastoral ministry).[20]

## Voyage-and-Return

This plot type differs from the quest (which also involves a journey) chiefly with regard to the absence of inner direction in the protagonist. The journey may be casual, accidental, or entirely involuntary.

Accordingly, the Old Testament subplot of Israel's Babylonian captivity belongs to this genre. Key questions addressed in such plotlines concern the means of return, and the lessons learned from the alien environment.

Both of the following questions receive clear answers in Israel's captivity narrative.[21] How did a small remnant of deportees manage to return to Jerusalem? By the power of Yahweh, who thereby revealed his supremacy over the Mesopotamian "gods." What did Israel learn from the seventy years in Babylon? The necessity of strict monotheism.

In terms of the panorama of the entire Bible, the narrative sequence Eden to Exile to New Eden could also be studied as a large-scale instance of *voyage-and-return*,[22] especially if one emphasizes how the wanderer gets home (and what the wanderer learns from the experience).

---

19. The physical wall built by Nehemiah has a corresponding spiritual wall (the Law) reinforced by Ezra. See Green, "Ezra-Nehemiah," 206–15.

20. 1 Tim 3:15 makes the "church = household" equation explicit; the same notion is implicit in the household codes (e.g., Titus 2:2–10). Pastoral ministry is equated with military service explicitly in 1 Tim 2:3–4, and implicitly in the injunction to "fight the good fight" (1 Tim 1:18; 6:12; 2 Tim 4:7).

21. Isa 43:1–13.

22. See also Frye's description of this plot (*Anatomy of Criticism*, 191), although he doesn't use the particular plot-label that I have borrowed from Booker (*Seven Basic Plots*).

In this story of paradise lost, wilderness wanderings, and exile, the turning point is Jesus' voluntary exile on the cross, and his words to an exiled thief: "Today you will be with me in paradise" (Luke 23:43).

Equally, one can view this story (of paradise lost and regained) through the lens of the quest plotline: the post-Eden journey to a glorious garden-city, initiated by the call to Abram, continued in the pilgrimage of Hebrews, and culminating in the transformed Eden at the end of Revelation.

The quest plotline underscores active seeking by the protagonist, emphasizes the supreme value of the end goal, and highlights the ordeals encountered along the journey. Exactly the "narrative rhetoric" employed by the Epistle to the Hebrews, as the author persuades weary Christian readers to persevere on the pathway of faith.

\* \* \* \* \*

Our whistle-stop tour through seven plots of Scripture has glimpsed a vital lesson that needs to be spelled out. The *one* story of the Bible can—and must—be told in *many* ways. One gospel, told as four canonical Gospels. One history of monarchy and temple, told from divergent viewpoints for distinctive audiences.[23]

This reader-oriented flexibility of the biblical narrative, patient to multiple retellings, explains the uncanny power of Scripture to engage our personal stories. Whatever your story, there is a version of the biblical meta-narrative that is sure to grip you.

Speaking personally, my own experience of "exile" makes me resonate with the biblical story of land.[24] Land gives us our home, our roots, our boundaries, and our identity. Lose our land, and we risk losing all of these. For the past twenty-five years, I have been a "resident alien" in the USA, "exiled" from my homeland in England. In response, I have explored the themes of land and exile in the Bible.[25]

If we sketch out some key phases of the biblical story of land, we can see how Genesis to Revelation really does have the narrative ebb and flow of a master plotline.

| | |
|---|---|
| *Bookends* | Imagine these verses as pictures on the front and back covers of a book: Genesis 2:10–12; 3:22 . . . Revelation 21:18–21; 22:1–2. What do you see? Rivers, trees, minerals and gemstones. Does the repetition of images imply the storyline inside the book? |
| *Disruption* | We speak of Gen 3 as "the Fall" (a spatial metaphor of descent), but *exile* would be a more literal reading of the narrative (verses 23–24). Notice also the cursing of the ground (verses 17–18) as emblematic of the loss of paradise. |
| *Search* | Quests arise from felt absence. Noah's father names him using the Hebrew word for *rest*—seeking rest from the cursed-ground, post-paradise existence (Gen 5:28–29). |

---

23. See the brief discussion of the different narratives of Kings and Chronicles in Dillard and Longman, *Introduction to the Old Testament*, 173.

24. In chapter 23 ("Redefining Your Personal Space"), I dovetail elements of my own life story with the treatment of sacred space in Hebrews.

25. Smith, "Fifth Gospel," 77–91.

| "Success" (increasing) | The call of Abram initiates a *journey*, whose destiny promises blessing to "all the families of the *ground*" (Gen 12:3)—the ground cursed in chapter 3 of Genesis.<br>Exodus 3:16–17 promises Abraham's descendants a "land flowing with milk and honey" (echoing ancient imagery of paradise).<br>Joshua 11:23 celebrates "*rest*" in the land of promise.<br>At the center of this new paradise, Solomon builds a temple decorated with tapestries of palm *trees* and "cherubim" (1 Kings 6:29)—the latter a reminder of the mysterious guardians of Eden (Gen 3:24). |
|---|---|
| Reversal | Israel undergoes a new *exile* from "paradise" (2 Chronicles 36:11–21). |
| New Hope | Isaiah 51:3 offers hope of *paradise restored.*<br>"For Yahweh will comfort Zion,<br>he will comfort all her waste places,<br>He will make her wilderness like *Eden*,<br>and her desert like the *garden* of Yahweh."<br>(Despite the trickle-back of a remnant from Babylonian exile, Israel continued to sense her story was one of *ongoing exile.**) |
| Resolution (partial) | Jesus recapitulates Israel's history, inaugurating a *new "exodus"*** with his *journey* to Jerusalem, where his cross, denoting exile from God, becomes a gateway to *paradise* (Luke 23:43).<br>Jesus' *journey* to the true epicenter of sacred space (Hebrews 6:17–20) paves the way for the Christian *pilgrimage* into "rest" (Heb 4:9–11) and into the "heavenly Jerusalem" (Heb 12:22–24). |
| Resolution (complete) | The final chapters of the Bible depict the destiny of a transformed Eden, in which the river, trees, minerals and gemstones of paradise are transfigured into a higher glory (Revelation 21:18–21; 22:1–2). |

\* Ezra 9:7–9 gives poignant expression to this sense of ongoing exile. This feeling persisted up to the time of Jesus; see Evans, "Jesus & Exile," 77–100.
\*\* "Exodus" is the literal Greek of Luke 9:31.

Notice that the New Testament depicts the *resolution* of the search for paradise as occurring in two phases: "partial" and "complete." This two-phase resolution of the biblical narrative is the key to unlocking the meaning of the New Testament. Without this two-phase perspective, "the entire New Testament is a book with seven seals," tight-wrapped in riddles that block our attempts to understand it.[26] Accordingly, my next chapter unwraps the seals.

To end this chapter, a personal illustration of how the macro-story of Scripture can intersect the micro-story of everyday life. For the macro-story, I will take the paradise-quest plotline which we thumbnailed above. For the micro-story, I will resume my family's foster-care story which introduced this chapter.

## SONGS OF ASCENT

The imminent arrival of our foster-child compelled us to re-evaluate our home environment. And not just the safety-issues (like smoke detectors and fire extinguishers) required by state law. I started pondering our domestic culture (for want of a better

26. Cullmann, *Christ and Time*, 145.

term). What *ethos* prevails within our home? And (being the narrative thinker that I am), what *story* feeds that ethos? Finally—is there a better story, nourishing a better domestic environment?

The answer to that last concern (better story → better culture) came to me while sitting in the pew at church. My pastor was preaching on Psalm 127. My wife was sitting next to me; we had our Bibles open to the right page of the Psalter. As the pastor was speaking, my wife grabbed her pen, and waved it (like a wand) over the page of the open Psalter. Without words, the direction of her gesture spelled out a link between Psalm 127 and the psalm immediately before it.

That afternoon, I got out my Hebrew Bible, and started tracing the links. Starting in Psalm 127, I found echoes of Psalm 126, *and* anticipations of Psalm 128. (This should not surprise us; the editor(s) of the Psalter often clustered psalms together, when they discerned hook-words, parallel images, and overlapping motifs.)

Indeed, Psalms 120–34 are almost the equivalent of an ancient "concept album" (to borrow a term from the popular music of the 1970s). All the psalms of this cluster have the same superscription, "A Song of Ascents." They were sung by *pilgrims*, making their way up to Jerusalem on Mount Zion. A pilgrimage into sacred space ... We are certainly within the ballpark of the plotline of paradise-renewed.

The Psalms are poems (maybe not the kind of rhyming poetry familiar to Western ears; but instantly recognizable as poetry to ancient Semitic ears, trained in hearing the echoes of the parallel lines). Poetry *can* be the vehicle for direct narration of a story. But, more often, poems *freeze-frame* a storyline. Poems press the pause button, creating time and space for *experiential descriptions* of life lived within the story. Poetry accesses these experiences via *imagery*—images evoking "universal" experiences, and threading the poem into the plotlines of archetypal narratives.

Let's identify some of the hook-words and images which weave our cluster of three psalms together, and thread the cluster into a larger narrative tapestry. I invite you to take a minute and read through the three psalms (Pss 126–28), and then reflect on the following observations.

## Imagery

The core imagery of our three psalms intertwines the spheres of architecture, agriculture, and domestic culture. Architecturally, we hear repeated mention of "Zion," "the city," "Jerusalem," and the "house" (Pss 126:1; 127:1; 128:3, 5). Agricultural references abound: sowing and reaping (Ps 126:5–6); produce (Ps 128:2). Agricultural imagery also provides metaphors of domestic culture: wife as "fruitful vine"; children as "olive shoots" (Ps 128:3). More allusively, does the "seed" reference (Ps 126:5–6) possibly echo the promise to Abraham, of innumerable descendants (Gen 12:1–3)? Also worth a mention: the equating of children with an "inheritance" from God (Ps 127:3)—vocabulary used elsewhere in the Old Testament to reference the land of Israel.

## Sequence

Next, imagine our psalm-cluster as a sequence of scenes in a film. As the "camera" moves through the verses, notice the spatial plot dynamic. In Psalm 126, the camera glimpses a return to Zion, irrigation of the Negeb (dry southern region of Israel), and a field of grain. Psalm 127 starts in the house, and moves to the city, ending up in the "gates" of the city (the place for legal proceedings). Psalm 128 has a similar spatial trajectory—from the house, to Zion/Jerusalem.

All these movements capture a key dimension of *culture-building*, namely, the "definition" of space, by designating spaces for specific purposes.

## Plot

The scenes of our psalm-cluster also hint at a temporal plot dynamic. In Psalm 126:5–6, those who scatter seed begin with weeping, but harvest with rejoicing. In Psalm 128:5–6, the blessed live to see the prospering of Jerusalem, and their own grandchildren. Most interestingly, Psalm 126:1 speaks of the reversal of Zion's captivity/exile as a *past* event, but Paslm 126:4 uses the same language to speak of a *future* deliverance.

## Metanarrative

This motif, of reversing captivity/exile, offers us the overarching *metanarrative* alluded to in our cluster of psalms, namely, the *re-inauguration of paradise*. This storyline is also echoed in the references to children as "*fruit* of the womb," and wife as "*fruitful* vine" (Pss 127:3; 128:3). These phrases employ the same Hebrew root used in the primordial mandate of Genesis 1:28, "Be *fruitful* and multiply!" Furthermore, in another allusion to the Eden narrative, Psalm 127:2 contrasts "eating the bread of the *toilers*" with the peaceful sleep God gives to those he loves. The "*toil*" idiom echoes the primordial cursing-of-the-ground in Genesis 3:17 (using the same Hebrew root).

In conclusion, Psalms 126–28 offers us the possibility of locating our mundane domestic micro-stories inside a macro-story of the re-inauguration of paradise. (Lest this claim sound ludicrously utopian, Psalm 126:4 witnesses to the ongoing incompleteness of the story!) The paradise-renewal storyline involves the growth of civilization and culture, building an environment fit for human flourishing.

The primordial paradise described in Genesis 1–3 was perfect, yet incomplete. Very good, but not yet glorified. The gold and gemstones (Gen 2:11–12) remained under the rocks, symbolizing the unrealized potential of the world—potential to bring forth even greater beauty.

In our domestic environments, we have the opportunity to designate space as an environment for human flourishing, a place where beauty can emerge. One household a civilization does not make—but we may as well begin somewhere.

\* \* \* \* \*

# 10

# Finding Neverland

IN OUR PREVIOUS CHAPTER, we traced the big plotlines of the whole Bible, from Genesis to Revelation. In this chapter, we zoom our lens in for a closer look at the New Testament. I will explain the special structure of the story found in the various books of the New Testament. Along the way, I will comment on the Christian experience of indwelling the story of the New Testament.

## NEW TESTAMENT STORYLINES

"The Bible is a strange story, because it ends in the middle."[1] To explain this aphorism, we need another. "[Apocalyptic is] the mother of Christian Theology."[2] To explain *this* aphorism, we need a backstory. Nowadays, scholars refer to the backstory of the New Testament as "Second Temple Judaism."

Narrative analysis sheds interesting light on this "Second Temple" phase of Israel's story. For a birds-eye overview of Israel's story, I would refer you back to my discussion of the *land-narrative* found in the previous chapter.

In the phase structure typical of narrative, Israel's call (to a *paradise-quest*) led to a phase of optimism, followed by a phase of frustration leading to crisis. In our sketch of this plot, we depicted the frustration/crisis phase as the exile, and its lack of satisfactory resolution.

Out of this crisis came an abundance of *apocalyptic* literature. The apocalyptic mindset sees resolution of Israel's crisis in a colossal act of divine intervention. An intervention comparable to a new exodus (dragon-slaying and quest-initiating archetypes), or even to a new creation (rebirth archetype). This momentous epiphany, "The Day of Yahweh," cleaves history into two discrete eras (as displayed in the diagram on the next page, where X denotes "The Day of Yahweh.")

---

1. I am paraphrasing John Dominic Crossan (a lecture given on November 19, 2011, at the Annual Meeting of the Society of Biblical Literature, San Francisco).

2. Ernst Käsemann, quoted in Beker, *Paul the Apostle*, 17.

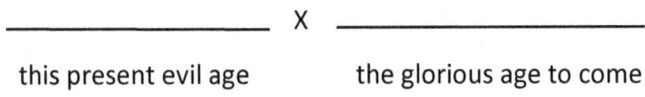

**Fig. 2. Jewish Eschatology**

This plotline gives the CliffsNotes to apocalyptic visions like Daniel, in which a succession of bestial pagan empires gives way to the everlasting empire of the Son of Man (Dan 7:1–14). This *"time of the end"* (Dan 12:9) features *resurrection* (Dan 12:2), and the bestowing of celestial *glory* upon the wise and righteous (Dan 12:3; cf. Philippians 2:15).

In the perspective of the New Testament writers, *the end-times began two thousand years ago!* Hebrews 1:2 declares that God spoke to us by his Son "at the end of these days [of the prophets and patriarchs]." The incarnation, death, and especially the resurrection/ascension of God's Son—this was the apocalyptic event-complex that triggered the dawn of the end-times two thousand years ago. As one theologian has put it: "The significance of Jesus' resurrection, for Saul of Tarsus as he lay blinded . . . on the road to Damascus, was this. *The one true God had done for Jesus of Nazareth, in the middle of time, what Saul had thought he was going to do for Israel at the end of time.*"[3] This, one might say, flips the script. The CliffsNotes diagram for the New Testament storyline piggybacks on Jewish apocalyptic, but now looks like this (where X-1 denotes the first advent of Christ, and X-2 the second advent):

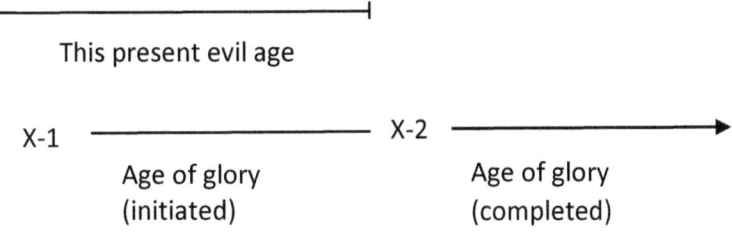

**Fig. 3. Christian Eschatology**

Notice how, in contrast to the plot-diagram of Jewish apocalyptic, the "present evil age" *co-exists* in tension with the inaugurated age of glory (until the second Advent of Christ).

Theologians have scratched their heads over how to explain such a story—*It is finished / No it isn't*. Some explained it by analogy with the Second World War: D-day and V-day. The decisive battle in a war may occur long before the war itself is finally over.[4]

This analogy works quite well for those of us whose parents fought in the Second World War. I use it all the time in my classroom teaching. However, in one of those "so this is what growing old feels like" moments, I am now finding that the analogy is meaningless to the younger generation.

---

3. Wright, *What Saint Paul Really Said*, 36 (italics in original).
4. Cullmann, *Christ and Time*, 84.

So I invited my students to update it. One student compared the "present evil age" to the grating discordant sounds of cacophonous music, and the inaugurated age of glory to the beautiful symphony that competes for airtime with the cacophony, but gradually overwhelms it.[5]

Another illustration came from the 2004 film *Finding Neverland*.[6] The film tells the story of how playwright J. M. Barrie created *Peter Pan*. As a young boy, Barrie suffered bereavement, losing his brother. That loss killed Barrie's childhood. The boy in him disappeared, or "went to Neverland." Neverland symbolizes the lost paradise of joy, innocence, and everlasting youth.

As an adult, the successful playwright Barrie suffered his first failure on the London stage, as audience and critics dismissed his play. Searching for a new and better play, Barrie befriends a widow and her young boys, a family grieving the loss of a husband and a father.

Barrie and the boys spend hours playing make-believe, imagining themselves into a world of cowboys and Indians, or pirates and treasure ships. Via the technical resources of modern cinematography, we the audience witness a miracle. Games that start in a back garden in London end up in the world of Neverland. By faith, Barrie experiences the inbreaking of moments of paradise.

These experiences were the genesis of the stage play *Peter Pan*. Towards the end of *Finding Neverland*, the widow Barrie befriended is dying of incurable chest problems. Barrie brings the cast and set of his stage play into the widow's home, and she witnesses a performance of the play. We witness her rising from her deathbed and entering the world of Neverland.

No analogy is perfect. But the film captures the notion of an alternative world, a restored paradise, which hovers over the "real world" of death and sorrow, and occasionally breaks in bringing joy and hope.

Likewise, in the Christian life, there are moments when the age of glory breaks in, bringing joy, hope, and a preliminary experience of the end of the story.

Let's pause here, and briefly consider some implications for those who indwell the strange plotline of the New Testament.

Inside this paradoxical plot, the paradise-renewal of the ending has been planted, in seed form, in the middle of history. The pivotal event: the resurrection plus ascension/glorification of Jesus, which inaugurates the age-to-come (even while the present age endures).

This paradoxical plot has paradoxical consequences. The importance of the present time is relativized, and also dignified beyond measure. The end is better than the now, but the now is the beginning of the end!

In terms of the venerable life-as-theater analogy, our earthly lives are not the entire play, nor even a dress rehearsal. However (switching from theater to cinema), our present lives can be a *trailer* for God's movie—the movie of eternity.[7]

---

5. Joel St. Clair, currently a church planter in Washington, DC, gets credit for this one.

6. My student James Madden wrote a term paper on the movie, and gave me the analogy below.

7. I am indebted to Brian Sorgenfrei for this movie-trailer analogy, which he used in his sermon series "Hope in a Hopeless Age" (RYM Colorado Summer Conference, June 2014).

For instance, the book of Revelation (7:9–17) depicts the end of God's movie as an ecstatic *multi-ethnic celebration* of the redemption wrought by Christ. What a contrast with our typical Sunday-morning church services (aptly described by Dr. King as "The most [racially] segregated hour of Christian America.") Multi-ethnic church can be messy—but what a movie trailer it can be, when members of diverse "tribes" imagine into present reality the future scene from Revelation 7.

The paradoxical plotline of the New Testament generates a *tension* between present and future—a tension with numerous implications for those who indwell this story. The list below is far from exhaustive. It paraphrases a discussion by John Stott.[8] The storyline of paradise-renewed has both present (now) and future (not yet) dimensions. These twin realities contour the Christian life in all its realms. I invite you to ponder this list, and feel the tension of the twin realities:

| *Dimension of Life* | *Impact of New Testament Storyline* |
| --- | --- |
| Creeds and Confessions of Faith | The *now* encourages *certainty* in central truths; <br> The *not yet* encourages *humility* in lesser matters |
| Church Purity and Discipline | The *now* encourages the gracious use of *discipline* to maintain the peace and purity of the church; <br> The *not yet* encourages us to remain as members of *imperfect* churches. |
| Holiness | The *now* enables us to fight our personal sins from a *position of strength*; <br> The *not yet* guards against *perfectionist delusions* |
| Physical Suffering | The *now* encourages us to *pray for healing*; <br> The *not yet* encourages *patient endurance* |
| Social Transformation | The *now* encourages us to work for the *improvement of society*; <br> The *not yet* guards against *utopian delusions* |

\* \* \* \* \*

Regardless of how we illustrate the "now" and the "not yet" of the New Testament, all of its authors tell the same paradoxical story: *It is finished / No, it isn't.*

Furthermore, they tell this story using a rich variety of master metaphors, archetypal images that crystallize the plotline. In the table below, I offer suggestions on how this narrative crystallization happens in some of the major segments of the New Testament canon. (Inevitably, such simplifications entail loss of complexity, but hopefully with gain of clarity).

---

8. Stott, *Contemporary Christian*, 375–92, 431–32.

| Canonical Unit | Image for Plotline of "Finished but Unfinished" | Narrative Archetype |
|---|---|---|
| Synoptic Gospels | Kingdom | Dragon Slaying; Ascent |
| John's Gospel | ("Eternal") Life | Rebirth |
| Paul | Resurrection | Rebirth |
| Hebrews | Sacred Space | Quest |
| James | Harvest | Ascent |
| Revelation | Victory in Holy War | Dragon Slaying |

Some elements of this table will (hopefully) seem obvious to readers, but other elements will need a little unpacking. So I will go through the table row by row, explaining briefly how each image crystallizes a finished-but-unfinished storyline, and how each storyline is drawn from an archetypal plot.

## Synoptic Gospels

Matthew, Mark, and Luke all share (in varying degrees) an emphasis upon "the kingdom of God/Heaven."[9] When Jesus opens his mouth to speak in parables, the kingdom is the default topic. The Synoptic Gospels starkly assert the paradox of a kingdom that has already arrived (but not yet). Jesus announces the present reality of the kingdom, as well as its future manifestation. Compare, for instance, Matthew 12:28 and 26:29.

This kingdom narrative seems to borrow from two archetypal plots, namely, "dragon slaying" and "ascent." The former, because the arrival of the kingdom of God undermines the *realpolitik* of the existing world order. The latter, because the kingdom requires the comprehensive cultivation of a new order.

The Synoptic Gospels narrate a rather distinctive version of "dragon slaying," since Jesus spends so much time subverting first-century (militaristic) expectations about the Kingdom of God.

Luke construes Jesus' ministry as liberation, a kind of *Jubilee* (see Luke 4:16–21). This metaphor activates the Old Testament ideal involving freeing of slaves, cancellation of debts, and restoration of land to the homeless. The story of liberation intersects those "dragon-slaying" plots where the "dragon" acts as a "holdfast," imprisoning its victims.[10]

## John's Gospel

When we turn from the three Synoptics to the Gospel of John, the absence of "kingdom" vocabulary slaps us in the face. In John, Jesus barely mentions the kingdom—mostly in one verse, during his trial before Pilate (John 18:36). Linguists will remind us that

---

9. Matthew prefers "Heaven," as a pious Jewish circumlocution to avoid mentioning the ineffable name of God.

10. See Booker (*Seven Basic Plots*, 32), who classifies the archetypal roles of the "monster" as "predator," "holdfast," and "avenger."

the concept can exist apart from the term, but the demise of the idiom in John remains striking. What could explain this?

Even conservative scholars recognize that John "translated" the kingdom vocabulary of Jesus into a different idiom, namely, "[eternal] life."[11] (The Greek term *aeonic*, which we render "eternal," denotes the age-of-glory; the focus is therefore more on quality of life and less on temporal duration.) When John wants to summarize the purpose of Jesus, and the purpose of the Fourth Gospel, he relies on the image of "life" (John 3:16; 20:31). This is clearly a rebirth archetype. Both the future and the present dimensions of this new life find expression in the refrain, "The hour is coming and now is." (E.g., John 4:23; 5:25.)

What can we learn from John's radical vocabulary shift from "kingdom" to "life"? The shift (away from the more political metaphor of kingdom) involved some adaptation to his audience and setting.[12] I believe we can emulate this. Consider the following anecdote.

Several years ago, at the annual general assembly of a rather conservative American Presbyterian denomination, the assembly invited a representative non-Christian to address the floor. The non-Christian told the assembly, "If you want outsiders to listen to your message, you need to stop saying *kingdom* every time you open your mouths. When you use that term, all that unbelievers hear is the agenda of the religious Right."

## Paul

When we turn to the letters of Paul, we find that he, like John, employs a rebirth archetype in his narrative of the gospel. Specifically, Paul uses the category of resurrection to express both the present and the future dimensions of Christian experience (Romans 6:1–10 and 8:18–25).[13]

Whilst resurrection obviously belongs to the rebirth archetype, it is striking that Paul virtually eschews the vocabulary of rebirth, even when explaining (Rom 6) the *spiritual* renewal of believers.[14] Rather, Paul insists on speaking of renewal in terms of resurrection.

There are several reasons why. Using resurrection underscores participation in the story of Jesus. Using resurrection emphasizes the holistic character of redemption, encompassing the material realm. Using resurrection hooks the reader into the story of the age-of-glory (resurrection being a key dimension of that apocalyptic vision).

## Hebrews

Despite being traditionally (and wrongly) attributed to Paul, the anonymous letter to the Hebrews occupies a relatively unique place in the canon. The writer pays more attention

---

11. Carson and Moo, *Introduction to the New Testament*, 251–53.
12. Köstenberger, *Theology of John's Gospel*, 286.
13. For discussion of resurrection as the key to Paul's gospel in Romans, see Kirk, *Unlocking Romans*.
14. Schweitzer, *Mysticism of Paul*, 13–15; Gaffin, *Resurrection and Redemption*, 140–41.

to sacred space than any of his colleagues.[15] He views the Christian life as a pilgrimage, a quest to reach holy ground. He depicts the object of the quest as a future goal, commanding the reader to strive to enter the promised rest (Heb 4:11). At the same time, he declares that we already enjoy access to the inmost sanctuary (Heb 10:19). This paradox, whereby we do and do not occupy sacred space, finds expression in Heb 12:22–24, which locates the Christian in the suburbs of the heavenly city, so to speak.

## James

Turning to the step-child of the Protestant canon,[16] the letter of James actually shares the same narrative DNA as his colleagues. James's pervasive concern with wisdom suggests the archetypal plotline of ascent, given wisdom literature's goal of producing maturity in the reader. Indeed, the Greek word *teleios* ("mature"; "perfect") and its cognates occur eight times in the letter.[17] The term connotes the proper destiny of humanity.

James uses the agrarian image of the harvest to focus this plotline of ascent. His first agrarian metaphor is a negative counterpoint to his message, as he compares transient riches with the grass withered by the sun (Jas 1:11).

By contrast, the Christian, birthed by the seed of the implanted word of truth, is a first-fruit of new creation (1:18, 21), a tree bearing appropriate fruit (3:12), a sower of the good fruit of peace (3:17–18). The Christian awaits the second advent, like a farmer awaiting the harvest (5:7; cf. 5:17–18).

By this cluster of agrarian metaphors, James is able to tell his story of ascent toward wisdom. The flexible metaphors allow him to express the finished/unfinished paradox: the first-fruits of wisdom are already here now, but the full harvest awaits.

## Revelation

The last book of the canon has all the "final conflict" imagery of a graphic novel, complete with a fiery red dragon (Rev 12:3). No prizes for guessing which plot archetype we are dealing with here.

Popular expositions of Revelation locate the victory over the dragon entirely in the *future*. However, a closer reading of the book suggests that Revelation shares the narrative DNA of the rest of the New Testament. Paradoxically, the victory has already occurred in the past, despite being delayed into the future!

The "not yet" dimension of victory is obvious in the struggles of the seven churches addressed in chapters 2–3 of the book. However, chapter 1 establishes the tone for the whole by hinting that "D-day" has already happened!

---

15. Isaacs (*Sacred Space*, 60–61, 67) speaks of the "preoccupation with sacred space" in Hebrews.

16. For a Protestant exposition of James that respects his distinctive contribution, see McCartney, *James*.

17. Five occurrences of the adjectival form *teleios* (Jas 1:2 [twice]; 1:17; 1:25; 3:2); two occurrences of its verbal cognate (2:8; 2:22); one occurrence of the cognate noun *telos* (5:11).

The present dimension of victory is the resurrection of Jesus Christ, "the firstborn from the dead, and the ruler over the kings of the earth" (1:5). The next verse describes the Christian reader using the language of Exodus 19:6 ("kingdom, priests"), thereby implying a victorious status akin to Israel after the demise of Pharaoh's army. And the chapter ends (Rev 1:12–20) with a vision of the Son of Man, who—unlike in Daniel 7—is here in the present, instead of being a future expectation.

## FOUR FEATURES OF MY NARRATIVE THEOLOGY

This book takes its place among a multitude of contemporary writings that emphasize the primacy of narrative for doing theology. My book taps into this *Zeitgeist*, this "narrative turn" in contemporary culture.[18] Accordingly, my work intersects that of other narrative theologians at many points.

Nevertheless, my deep roots in the "biblical theology" of Vos and Clowney give my overall package a somewhat distinctive feel.[19] Here are the four main components of my package.

### Unity of the Story

Our confidence in the organic unity of Scripture emboldens us as we trace plotlines from Genesis to Revelation. No matter how many twists and turns, no matter how many retellings, the tale ultimately soars above the seas of chaos and confusion.

### Diversity of the Stories

The coherence of Scripture is not a flat, one-dimensional unity. As I have attempted to show, the reader who would travel from Genesis to Revelation needs (at least) seven distinctive road-maps, seven basic plots, each with their own set of values. The plots intertwine, but they do not cancel each other. Accordingly, different individuals and communities may take shelter under one or more of the plot umbrellas.

If plot analysis confirms the diversity of Scripture, then metaphor analysis compounds the diversity. In my discussion of the blocks of the New Testament canon, I tried to show how they articulate the same paradoxical finished-yet-unfinished narrative. However, that unifying storyline finds expression via a rich diversity of master metaphors. And metaphors tend to have a life of their own. They offer fresh visions of the world, and resist reduction to a single point of view.

So, like the Trinitarian theologian that I am, I celebrate both the unity and the diversity of Scripture, and celebrate them equally.[20] I resist the temptation from the left

---

18. The last quarter of the twentieth century saw the emergence of the "narrative theology" movement, whose early contributions are reviewed in Fackre, "Narrative Theology," 340–52.

19. For discussion of Vos and Clowney, see chapter 27 ("From Seed to Tree").

20. For a concise statement of how Trinitarianism demands a "multi-perspectival" approach to knowledge, see Poythress, *Symphonic Theology*, 50–51. For a more extensive treatment of "multi-perspectival"

wing of theologians (who undermine the unity of Scripture), and from the right wing of theologians (who flatten the diversity of Scripture).

Accordingly, I feel the angst of a postmodern theologian like Walter Brueggemann, who fears that focus on the big story of Scripture marginalizes the little stories of Scripture.[21] Says Brueggemann, "Our lives are not lived in a single, large, unified drama. In fact, we are party to many little dramas."[22]

His solution: give up on the big story. My solution: emphasize the rich diversity of expressions of the one big story (and the cultural diversity this produces in our churches).[23]

### Stories that Focus on Christ

All the Old Testament plotlines converge in Christ, and radiate out from him to the ends of the earth. Christ is the main protagonist in the drama of Scripture.

Furthermore, Christ is the main protagonist in the ongoing drama of history. All stories have power to change lives. Some stories transform us by the inspirational example of the protagonist; others by opening the doors of perception onto a new way of seeing the world. The gospel can and does affect readers in these ways. But the gospel does more. The water of baptism, the bread and wine of the Lord's Supper, these "performative" signs superimpose the story of Jesus' death and resurrection onto our personal and communal stories. In every other story, the protagonist is either fictional, dead, or soon to be dead. The gospel story is unique; the protagonist lives. We can participate in his narrative, not merely by imitation of an example, but by a real, dynamic relationship with him.

### Closed and Open-Ended Stories

Through the resurrection (glorification) of Christ, the final chapter of the story has begun to imprint its glory on life in the middle of the story. Accordingly, the Christian life is lived in acute tension between the "already-now" and the "not yet" of the semi-finished narrative.[24]

This semi-finished quality of the Christian story finds literary expression in the carefully-crafted open-endedness of Matthew, Mark, Luke, Acts, and John: "All five of the books . . . have . . . "suspended endings." Like some modern playwrights, each of our

---

approaches, see Frame, *Doctrine of the Knowledge of God*.

21. Brueggemann, *Texts Under Negotiation*, 57–58.

22. Ibid., 70.

23. Cf. Bauckham, *Bible and Mission*, 90–94. Readers interested in fleshing out the diversity-in-unity of the New Testament may wish to consult: Burridge, *Four Gospels*; Hays, *Moral Vision of the New Testament*.

24. For a classic exposition of inaugurated eschatology, see Vos, *Pauline Eschatology*.

authors invites the members of his audience to take up the story and write the final scene of the drama for themselves."[25]

\* \* \* \* \*

An invitation to take up the story where it breaks off, and write the final scenes of the drama ... You can see how the New Testament narrators are the inspiration behind my book.

Let's sketch a rough outline of life shaped by the unfinished New Testament story, using the *Acts of the Apostles* as our template.

When you read the final sentence of Acts 28, it's easy to feel robbed by the narrator. "Yes, but what happened *next*?" we instinctively inquire. The previous chapters have built tension around the Apostle Paul's upcoming trial before Caesar. But the book ends without the anticipated trial scene!

Furthermore, the journey-based plotline of Acts terminates in Rome—capital of the Empire, yes ... but hardly "the ends of the earth" destiny demanded of the protagonists at the beginning of the narrative (Acts 1:8). Especially given Paul's desire (stated elsewhere) to bring the gospel to Spain (Rom 15:24, 28).

The unfinished story of Acts ends with Paul (under house arrest in Rome) continuing to "herald the *kingdom of God*" (Acts 28:30–31, italics mine). This parallels the beginning of Acts, where we find Jesus instructing the Apostles "about the *kingdom of God*" (1:3, italics mine). These opening and closing "frames" suggest a theme for the story—the ongoing action of declaring the existence of an alternative kingdom, an alternative culture or civilization.

This thematic frame fits neatly around the "call" of the apostolic protagonists—to be *witnesses* of Jesus in Jerusalem, Judea, Samaria, and to the *ends of the earth* (Acts 1:8).[26] This plot summary—*journey* + *testimony*—highlights the *epic* quality of the story of Acts.[27]

Ancient epics (like Virgil's *Aeneid*) typically use the plotline of journey + battle. Acts replaces the "battle" component with *testimony* by witnesses of Jesus' resurrection and ascension. But, as we shall see, these testimonial speech-acts do entail a battle of sorts—a *clash of narratives*.

The Apostles are called into a journey-to-witness (Acts 1:8), and the verses that follow (1:9–11) drop a massive hint about the *content* of their testimony. These verses repeatedly mention *visual* activity by the Apostles ("looking"; "eyes"; "gazing"; "looking"; "seeing"). What did they see? The *ascension* of Jesus into heaven. Specifically, the ascension into a *cloud*.

Our modern western scientific context predisposes us to ask "meteorological" questions about such verses. But, to the ancient reader, symbolic dimensions loomed

---

25. Hooker, *Endings*, 82.

26. This call picks up the global role assigned to Israel in Isaiah's prophecy (Isa 43:10, 12; 44:8; 49:6).

27. For a list of the literary parallels between Luke and Acts, and ancient epics (especially Virgil's *Aeneid*), see Bonz, *Past as Legacy*. Bonz ascribes considerably less "historicity" to Acts than I do—but her *literary* analysis of the epic features of Acts remains helpful.

larger. Specifically, Daniel 7:13 associates "the clouds of heaven" with a character "like a son of man"—which happened to be Jesus' self-identification in the Gospels. In Dan 7:14, the son-of-man character receives an *everlasting kingdom*. This kingdom replaces the bestial empires grotesquely caricatured in Dan 7:1–12 (the Mesopotamian, Greek and Roman empires which had oppressed Israel). In this context, "son of man" may be typifying the ruler of God's kingdom as *truly human or humane* (in contrast with the predatory beast-like imperial powers that ruled the ancient world).

If this narrative—the Daniel 7 storyline—shapes the apostolic witness, then we would expect an epic clash-of-narratives as the book of Acts unfolds. And we would not be disappointed! The apostolic church expresses its counter-narrative in word and in lifestyle. This counter-narrative challenged all the alternative big stories on offer in the ancient Mediterranean world. The counter-kingdom, inaugurated by the ascension of Jesus, competed in the market-place of ideas, challenging the prevailing ideologies. The ideology of Roman imperialism. Jewish nationalism. Greek philosophy. Pagan religion. Magic and superstition.

In this battle of world-and-life-views, whenever and wherever the apostolic testimony prevailed, humane and liberational consequences followed. Poverty was overcome by communal sharing of resources (Acts 2:44–45; 4:32–37). Tribal divisions were overcome by unity combined with respect for diversity (6:1–6; 15:1–29).

Sadly, humane and liberational consequences did not always follow the post-apostolic growth of the church down the centuries. Sometimes, when the church became a dominant force in society, it began to resemble the oppressive empires depicted in Daniel 7. Whenever the church becomes imperialist, it betrays its own metanarrative.

The unfinished metanarrative of Acts readily provides a thumbnail plot for those who would remain true to its trajectory. The epic structure of Acts, the inauguration of the humane kingdom of the ascended Son of Man, imprints itself upon the individual episodes of the book. In story after story, we see the epic script imprinted in miniature upon the work of individual witnesses. Many episodes in Acts follow this narrative template:

Call

Journey

Testimony (clash of narratives)

Resistance (from entrenched ideologies)

Transformation (of responsive hearers)

A couple of brief comments on the "resistance" phase may be in order. First, I get that the church in America has gotten embroiled in some very questionable "culture wars," and one can even sympathize with some of the resistance to Christianity. And, for some of us peace-loving Christians, there may be a temptation to avoid any testimony that could possibly lead to a clash of narratives. But—would that be faithful to the script of Acts?

Second, notice how the apostolic church overcame resistance. Not by coercion, but by reliance upon the Spirit of God (a gift from the ascended Jesus—Acts 2:32–33), and by willingness to endure suffering and humiliation. It's no coincidence that the Greek word for "witness" is "martyr."

To finish my brief engagement with the unfinished script of Acts, I will focus on the *journey* dimension of the story. In Acts, the journey is not an end in itself, but a means to an end. The end: a localized telling and embodying of the story of the Ascension of Jesus.

But the journey theme does have implications for those who would continue the story of Acts. For one, the journey has metaphorical dimensions. It expresses a willingness to enter a local culture, and understand its idioms, in order to re-tell the Ascension of Jesus in the most compelling manner. And whenever we immerse ourselves in another culture, we make a sacrifice. We forego old habits and customs, and even risk losing our roots.

Mention of roots brings us to additional *geographical metaphors* in Acts. The book has been described as "a tale of two cities";[28] namely, Jerusalem and Rome.

The geographical movement of Acts has a strongly centripetal feel, moving outward in ever-expanding circles. And the final quarter of the story is dominated by Paul's journey to Rome. Nevertheless, despite this outward trajectory, the story begins in Jerusalem, and participants constantly circle back to Jerusalem.

These two cites have symbolic significance in Acts. Jerusalem represents the roots of the Jesus movement in Judaism. Rome, the imperial capital, represents the religious aspirations of the non-Jewish world.

Accordingly, the concern of Acts with Jerusalem and Rome expresses the *universality* of the Jesus movement, and its self-understanding as a world religion.

Further, the two cities express a *tension* within the early church—the pull and tug of *roots versus destiny*. Throughout the story, the church strives both to preserve its Jewish heritage, and to adapt its idioms and practices in order to commend its faith to Greeks and Romans.

This story of pull-and-tug, roots versus destiny, reverberates down the centuries of church history. In ever-changing contexts, the church struggles to maintain continuity with the past, while adapting to present needs.

In the twenty-first century, the Western church faces an especially intriguing version of this challenge: how to respond to the rapidly-shifting cultural landscape of postmodernity.

\* \* \* \* \*

So far, Part 2 of this book has involved a search for story-genres that can make sense of life. We've been assuming (somewhat uncritically) that story and life overlap substantially, and the overlap is a good and natural fit.

In the next chapter, we wrestle with some of the *challenges* we encounter when we try and fit our lives into a narrative framework.

---

28. Scobie, "Journey Motif," 341.

# 11

## The Purple Rose of Cairo

FACT OR FICTION? REALITY versus fantasy. Dichotomies enshrined in the shelving system of any public library. This dualism is explored in Woody Allen's film *The Purple Rose of Cairo* (1985).

A plot synopsis will highlight the film's thematic tension: conflict of characters who want life to mirror a Hollywood movie, and characters who stubbornly assert the disconnect between movies and "real life."

Act 1: Depression-era New Jersey. Cecelia (played by Mia Farrow), a waitress—with an unemployed, drunk, abusive, philandering husband. Black-and-white movies are her escape—disdained by her husband, who refuses to "sit through that junk."

At her work in the local diner, Cecelia constantly gossips about movies, earning rebukes from her boss. One dropped plate too many leads to loss of her job.

Cecelia escapes to the local cinema. For the fifth time, she sits through "The Purple Rose of Cairo." A romantic comedy—debonair aristocrats in dinner jackets, cocktails at the Copacabana night club.

Act 2: Suddenly, a breach in the wall between theater and life! A character from the film, Tom Baxter (archaeologist in pith helmet), steps out from the screen and into the audience—"I'm free!"

Baxter wants to explore the "real world," to be unscripted, "free to make my own choices." He declares his love for Cecelia, and the two enjoy a romantic dinner-date. But Baxter is still scripted by the movie; his real-world activities are shaped by the conventions of his black-and-white film. As Baxter and Cecelia kiss, he stops and asks, "Where's the fade-out?" (Referencing the screen convention, from the golden age of cinema, of cutting a kissing scene after the first few seconds.)

Meanwhile, news of Baxter's escape has reached the Hollywood producers of his film. Gil Shepherd—the real-life actor who portrays Tom Baxter on screen—shows up at the New Jersey movie theater where Baxter escaped, and engages in dialogue with the characters on the screen. Listening to their dialogue, someone from the film's production company comments, "The real ones want their lives fictional, and the fictional ones want their lives real!"

Act 3: The conflict (between story and reality) intensifies, personified in Cecelia's blossoming romances with both the screen character (Tom Baxter) and the actor (Gil Shepherd) who portrays him.

Alone with Baxter in an empty church, Cecelia asks him if he believes in God. Baxter doesn't understand the question, so she replies, "God is the reason for everything—otherwise, life would be a movie without a point, without a happy ending!" Baxter sees the parallel between God and the scriptwriter of his film.

Alone with Shepherd in a music store, Cecelia joins him in song as he plays the ukulele—enacting a scene from one of Shepherd's movies. They kiss—but Cecelia backs out, because she remembers she had agreed to meet Baxter.

Act 4: Back at the movie theater, Baxter and Cecelia dialogue with the black-and-white characters on the screen. In a reversal of Act 2, Baxter steps into the screen and into "The Purple Rose of Cairo," taking Cecelia with him.

The couple arrive at the Copacabana night club in time for Baxter's familiar scene—but the black-and-white characters stand perplexed at Cecelia's presence in their script. Eventually, Arturo (maître of the club) draws an existentialist conclusion: "We're chucking out the plot!" Baxter replies, "Every man for himself!"

Meanwhile, Shepherd returns to the movie theater, and engages in debate with Baxter and the other black-and-white characters. Whom should Cecelia choose—the real Shepherd or the fictional Baxter? Finally, Cecelia chooses Shepherd, telling Baxter: "In your world, things always work out; I am real, so I must choose the real world."

Act 5: Her mind made up, Cecelia returns home to inform her husband that she is leaving him. His retort: "Out there it's real life; it ain't the movies!"

Heading out of their apartment, Cecelia is passing the movie theater. The theater's owner meets her and informs her that Shepherd has returned to Hollywood. There will be no real-life romance for Cecelia.

In response to her disappointment, the theater owner encourages her to step inside, and see the new release starring Ginger Rogers and Fred Astaire.

Woody Allen's film ends with Cecelia back in her regular movie seat. Cecelia is shedding tears (over Gil Shepherd), but, as she watches Fred and Ginger dancing on screen, her tears are replaced by a smile.

* * * * *

Is life a story? Is life story-*like*? Or is life "a tale told by an idiot, full of sound and fury, signifying nothing"?[1] Does history have genuine plot-lines, or is history "just one effing thing after another"[2]?

I got to discuss these questions a while back with teenagers from my church youth group. "Your life—is it like a film or a novel?"

Paulina's answer represents the "thesis": "Many films are about suffering, and suffering is part of life. Two years ago, I experienced a painful betrayal. I remember thinking,

---

1. *Macbeth* 5.5.
2. Bennett, *History Boys*, 85, 106 (expletive modified).

## Part 2: Stories Are . . . and Stories Do . . .

'No, this cannot be happening to me—it's the kind of thing that happens in movies!' But it was real."

Betti (whose mother abandoned her when she was twelve) stated the "antithesis": "Most films have positive, upbeat endings—but I'm not so convinced that my life is going to be OK. It could turn out bad."

These two perceptive teenagers set up the "plot" of this chapter: does art imitate life (does life imitate art)?

As we work toward narrating our own life story (or "personal myth," some say), these questions always butt in. We use story to make sense of experience—but does story falsify experience? This challenge looms larger in our postmodern context (discussed in chapter 5).

So, this chapter explores the overlap between narrative and reality. Gaining clarity on this relationship equips us for a wiser use of narrative as a tool for understanding our lives.

## ALL THE WORLD'S A STAGE

> All the world's a stage
> And all the men and women merely players:
> They have their exits and their entrances;
> And one man in his time plays many parts,
> His acts being seven ages . . .[3]

Easy for Shakespeare's rhythmic cadences to trip off the tongue as a cliché. But the "life as theater" metaphor confronts us as a vital and persistent image of existence. From the sages of antiquity to the postmodern theologian Walter Brueggemann,[4] "taking" reality as *drama* spotlights the universal tensions experienced by every human.

My family has, over the years, belonged to shakespearedallas.org; we regularly watch live plays. Maybe you don't, and maybe this life-as-theater stuff confirms your sense that artificial dramas are poor mirrors of reality.

But ponder this for a moment: why do we refer to a theatrical production as a *"play"*? Play is a natural, fundamental activity of children. If we dig beneath the stories told by young children, we find their play activities at the root. Chases, fights, games with winners—these play activities generate corresponding plotlines.[5] Along similar lines, Aristotle saw the genesis of drama in children's natural capacity for imitation.[6] Children imitate what they see and hear, and what they see and hear is reality.

Sophisticated drama merely refines children's native use of play and imitation to explore their world and their possibilities within it. Accordingly, classical thinkers felt

---

3. *As You Like It* 2.7.
4. Brueggemann, *Texts Under Negotiation*, 65–70.
5. Cobley, *Narrative*, 22.
6. Aristotle, *Poetics* 4.

compelled to explain life in terms of theater.[7] For example, the Stoic philosopher Epictetus (first century AD) advises us:

> Regard yourself as an actor in a play. The poet gives you your part and you must play it, whether it is short or long. If he wants you to play a beggar, act the part skillfully. Do the same if you are to play a cripple, a ruler or a private person. Your task is only to play well the part you have been given; the choosing of it belongs to someone else.[8]

Shakespeare's famous "All the world's a stage" monologue clearly follows in this classical tradition. The monologue traces seven "acts" of life's drama, corresponding to seven "ages," in which the individual plays seven "parts." Here (partly paraphrased) are the phases of life according to Shakespeare:

1. Infant
2. Schoolboy ("creeping like snail unwillingly to school")
3. Lover
4. Soldier ("seeking the bubble reputation even in the cannon's mouth")
5. Judge ("full of wise saws and modern instances")
6. Retirement
7. Senility/Dementia ("second childishness and mere oblivion")

Obviously, certain elements of this list reflect a male point of view (not to mention a sixteenth-century European context). Nevertheless, the middle three (lover, soldier, judge) can, perhaps, provoke useful reflection on our own biography. Looking back over your life, were there phases dominated by an overriding concern? (Romance? Accomplishment? Passing on wisdom?) What marked the transition from one phase to another? Are the phases isolated, or do later ones build on earlier ones?

\* \* \* \* \*

Performed in real time, by actors distinct from (yet merged with) their parts, scripted-yet-freely-interpreted—the theatrical performance embodies three tensions felt by every individual. We can bullet-point these intersections of theater with the tensions of life, using the elements of story discussed in chapter 7.[9]

- The *plot-line* device reminds us: "ultimate meaning must wait." Ends clarify middles and beginnings. Every tick of the clock awaits a "tock." Individual threads make sense in the finished tapestry.

---

7. Balthasar, *Prolegomena*, 135–51.
8. Quoted in ibid., 140–41.
9. For my discussion of three tensions intrinsic to life, I am indebted to Balthasar (ibid., 249–57).

- The *characters* onstage embody the tension "I am (not) my role." The prince may be disguised as a beggar. My social role may change, and the change changes me; but my sense of identity endures "unchanged."
- The *setting* of the drama constrains the action; through the *medium* of the script, the playwright's *point of view* circumscribes the actors. Balancing out these determinisms, the freedom of actors to interpret their roles. Theater symbolizes the inexplicable mystery, the existential tension: "I am (not) free."

When I discuss life-as-theater with family and friends, my wife voices a bottom-line conviction. In the drama of scripture, God writes a story into the lives of real, historical people. This affirms a story-shaped view of the world. (Recall our discussion of the *Acts of the Apostles* at the end of the last chapter. The epic journey of the Apostles was triggered by divine interventions into history—the resurrection/ascension of Jesus, and the outpouring at Pentecost of the Holy Spirit. As you read the story of Acts, you sense a narrative strongly shaped by providential patterns.)

When, however, Western culture loses any sense of providence (whether classical or Christian), the world-as-theater metaphor breaks down into "a tale told by an idiot, full of sound and fury, signifying nothing."[10]

## THERE ARE NO MORE COFFINS

Ironically, the resultant radical skepticism, canceling the "life = theater" equation, finds expression in the theater. In 1921, Luigi Pirandello wrote a play (*Six Characters in Search of an Author*) about the impossibility of performing a play. This meta-play informs the audience of the absurdity of any attempt to mirror reality in story. Theater is an illusion that falsifies reality.[11]

In perpetrating this illusion, this falsification, traditional theater uses one magic trick above all. Closure, resolution, unknotting—the end. The archetypal storyline leads to "a closed ending of absolute, irreversible change"; "all questions raised by the story are answered; all emotions evoked are satisfied."[12]

But does life itself resolve so neatly and meaningfully? No, said the Theatre of the Absurd, and wrote plays to embody this negation. Samuel Beckett's *Endgame* expresses the creed in a snippet of dialogue:

> "Put me in my coffin."
> "There are no more coffins."[13]

Closed endings imply fixed meanings for their stories, and by extension for life itself. The postmodern turn—in film, theater, and the novel—overturns this stability, declaring the

---

10. *Macbeth* 5.5.
11. See Balthasar's discussion of Pirandello (*Prolegomena*, 244–48).
12. McKee, *Story*, 45, 47.
13. See the analysis of Beckett in Brooks, *Reading for the Plot*, 313.

end of the ending. The only kind of story that truly mirrors reality is the tale-told-by-an-idiot variety.[14]

For the romantics of the nineteenth century, narrative was *the* primary mode for comprehending the world.[15] The twentieth century came out counter-punching: our traditional narrative configurations of life are mere wish-fulfillments, arbitrary attempts at imposing order upon an underlying chaos. Against the view that narrative (whether historical or fictional) can be true-to-life, a "strong coalition of philosophers, literary theorists, and historians" rails against our naïve error: "Real events simply do not hang together in a narrative way, and if we treat them as if they did we are being *un*true to life. Thus . . . in virtue of its very form, any narrative account will present us with a distorted picture of the events it relates."[16]

## IT'S IN OUR GENES

Despite the twentieth-century philosophical onslaught against the credibility of story-shaped accounts of life, human beings struggle to heed the counsel of the philosophers: "We dream in narrative, daydream in narrative, remember, anticipate, hope, despair, believe, doubt, plan, revise, criticize, construct, gossip, learn, hate and love by narrative. In order to really live, we make up stories about ourselves and others, about the personal as well as the social past and future."[17] The default setting of human beings views life through narrative lenses. Is this mass delusion? Or is human existence "an implicit story," "pre-plotted" in particular ways, so that "every human existence is a life in search of a narrative"?[18]

We are born, we mature, we decline, we die. Biological realities give life a rudimentary narrative arc. Indeed, Tilley argues for the origins of theatrical five-act drama in the five-phase life cycle: "birth, puberty, parenthood, menopause, and death."[19]

If biological phases give life an overall narrative shape, then so do social and psychological realities.

Take conversation, for instance. Nothing is more basic to our social existence. Whenever you participate in a conversation, you are a player in a miniature drama. Formal cues open and close the conversational "theater" like curtains on the stage (from "What have you been up to lately?" to "It's been great catching up with you"). If you are in an argument, your conversation builds tension, seeks resolution, and may feature the "reversals and recognitions" of classic comedy. Because conversation has these narrative

---

14. See the discussions of "antiplot" films in McKee, *Story*, 44–66; of "absurd literature" in Morrison, *Key Concepts in Creative Writing*, 1–2; and of "irony" in Tilley, *Plot Snakes*, 101–14, and in Tilley, *Introduction to Plot*, 83–88.

15. Brooks, *Reading for the Plot*, xi–xii.

16. Carr, "Narrative and the Real World," 117.

17. Barbara Hardy, quoted in Long, "Out of the Loop," 120.

18. Kearney, *On Stories*, 129.

19. Tilley, *Plot Snakes*, 12–14, 80; Tilley, *Introduction to Plot*, 10–12.

properties, we need narrative genre-labels to evaluate our conversations ("tragic misunderstanding; farcical misunderstanding"; etc.)[20]

Turning inward, from sociology to psychology, we once again find an irreducible narrative core at the bedrock of human experiences.[21] Consider the passive experience of an event in the present moment. I'm typing this sentence, and accidentally knock my coffee cup with my elbow, so it falls and shatters on the floor. Let's ponder what my brain must assume, for me to conceptualize this as an "event." My brain must recognize a past time, in which my elbow is uninvolved with my cup (rather than a timeless state in which my elbow is perpetually in contact with my cup). By analogy, my brain must recognize a future time, in which my cup is no longer on the floor (rather than a timeless state in which the cup remains forever frozen to the floor). Unless my brain recognizes past (cup on table) and future (cup no longer on floor), it cannot conceptualize the accidental elbow nudge as an event in the present moment. In terms of the Gestalt psychology of visual perception, the "foreground" of the present event cannot even be perceived as an event apart from the "background" of past and future. In other words, elementary temporal sequence belongs both to narrative and to passive experiences in the real world.

Turning from passive experience to active agency, "Whatever we encounter . . . functions as an instrument or obstacle to our plans."[22] As goal-oriented creatures, we constantly strive to get from A to B, to connect ends with means, to resolve the tension of our incomplete purposes. Going back to my broken coffee cup illustration, the broken cup represents a disordering of my world, a "crisis" I can resolve by a) sweeping it up, b) waiting for my housekeeper to do it, or c) adapting to a new world of permanent disorder. Either way, the illustration shows that the most mundane human actions are miniature narratives, with inbuilt storylines (problems → solutions).

In sum, "Narratives must be regarded not as a departure from the structure of the events they depict . . . but as an extension of their primary features."[23] Returning to the life-as-theater metaphor, we can affirm that, "The drama of experience is the crude original of all high drama."[24]

Zooming out from micro-experiences, to the panorama of human life-spans, can we identify the "genre" of the story mapped out by our biological constraints? Consider these CliffsNotes offered by Donald Miller:

> Humans are alive for the purpose of journey, a three-act structure. They are born and spend several years discovering themselves and the world, then plod through a long middle in which they are compelled to search for a mate and reproduce and also create stability out of natural instability, and then they find themselves at an ending that seems to be designed for reflection.[25]

20. See MacIntyre, "Virtues," 96.
21. In the following paragraphs of this subsection, I rely on the work of two thinkers in particular: Carr, "Narrative and the Real World," 121–22; Crites, "Narrative Quality of Experience," 72–79.
22. Carr, "Narrative and the Real World," 122.
23. Ibid., 131.
24. Crites, "Narrative Quality of Experience," 79.
25. Miller, *Million Miles*, 69.

Poetic license? Maybe. Maybe not.

## REALITY CHECK

But what about artifice? Isn't *medium* integral to story (film; literature; theater; etc.)? And doesn't medium entail style, form, artifice? And if artificial, then surely unreal? We might say that stories (in any medium) are more or less like real life. In fact, stories appear both more and less when measured against reality.

Stories give *less* than the full quota of reality, since stories tend to omit events extraneous to their plot. In composing a literary symphony, an author omits any "noise" that doesn't contribute to the pattern being unfolded.[26] To paraphrase Donald Miller, story is life with the boring parts edited out.[27]

On the other side of the same "editorial" coin, stories appear to give us *more* than real life. Stories add *patterns*, particularly through the device of plotting. Some of these patterns can seem contrived. Take the ubiquitous pattern of threes. The how-to guides for budding novelists instruct us: make sure your hero fails twice before he succeeds at the third attempt.[28] (Hold this thought; we will revisit it later.)

Stories—we maintain—are more-or-less like real life. Mapping out both the more and the less will give us much-needed wisdom in using narrative to understand our lives.

Let's focus on the crucial question: Is literary contrivance and convention automatically unreal? Here's a specific example. In fiction, "The number five crops up in many . . . narrative templates."[29] Think of the classic five-act drama, and the five-phase model of plot that we discussed in chapter 7. Convention? Not entirely.

Christopher Booker notes that one particular version of tragedy gets replayed in real life only too often.[30] He refers to real protagonists gripped by delusional fantasies that lead to transgression of boundaries. Their storylines tend to unfold exactly according to Booker's five phases: 1) transgression; 2) "getting away with it"; 3) real life pushes back; 4) crisis; 5) demise.

Of all his basic plots, Booker only regards this form of tragedy as an exact mirror of life.[31] However, others see five-phase storylines unfolding in multiple real-life settings. As an experiment, I invite you to google "The Five Stages of . . . " and read the numerous Wikipedia entries that come up.

"The Five Stages of Culture Shock" intrigued me. Not just because I've experienced them, but because living in a strange culture obviously resembles a version of Booker's "voyage-and-return" template. With minor reworking, Booker's five phases map quite well onto the classic five-stage model of culture shock:

---

26. Carr, "Narrative and the Real World," 119, 123.
27. Miller, *Million Miles*, 25, 39.
28. Tobias, *20 Master Plots*, 51.
29. Morrison, *Key Concepts in Creative Writing*, 131.
30. Booker, *Seven Basic Plots*, 577–81.
31. Ibid., 583.

## Part 2: Stories Are ... and Stories Do ...

| Act/Stage | Booker's "Voyage-and-Return" Plot | Five Stages of Culture Shock |
|---|---|---|
| 1 | Plunge into new world | (Presupposed) |
| 2 | Dream | Honeymoon |
| 3 | Frustration | Distress |
| 4 | Nightmare | Crisis: desire to return home → decision to remain |
| 5 | Escape *or* adjustment | Realistic embrace of new home |

Like many immigrants, I deliberately chose to live in the USA. For folk like me, there are built-in factors that generate the culture-shock plotline outlined above. Since the USA was an attractive lure, our early experience tends to accent the positive (the honeymoon phase). But, as they say, the novelty wears off. Roots exert a deep pull. A negative phase seems inevitable once the honeymoon is over. Then, if you have the freedom to return home, you face a crisis decision: should I stay or should I go? In order to stay, you must count the cost, leading to a realistic embrace of your new home.

A more controversial model is "The Five Stages of Grief". Known as the Kübler-Ross model, the alleged plotline even gets boiled down to an acronym. DABDA stands for: Denial, Anger, Bargaining, Depression, Acceptance.

This plotline resembles the "rebirth" archetype we mentioned in chapters 8–10. In a classic rebirth narrative, the trigger incident is some kind of "curse" that threatens to consume the life of the main character. In the DABDA model, grief is triggered by an awareness of imminent *loss*. You, or a loved one, gets diagnosed with an incurable illness. Your spouse announces they intend to leave you. An employer gives notice that your services are no longer required. The subsequent storyline (with a little tweaking) maps fairly well onto the rebirth archetype:

| Acts/Stages | Rebirth Plotline | "Five Stages of Grief" |
|---|---|---|
| 1 | "Curse" | Loss (presupposed) |
| 2 | Dream (threat seems unreal) | Denial |
| 3 | Frustration (threat seems real) | Anger |
| 4 | Nightmare | a) Bargaining b) Depression |
| 5 | "Rebirth" | Acceptance |

Stage four of the rebirth archetype, the "nightmare," is the crisis. The threat is all too real, the protagonist may summon all resources to resist, but "death" triumphs. The crisis phase combines desperate resistance and eventual defeat, analogous to the grief cycle of desperate bargaining ("I'll do anything provided you don't leave me") followed by depression when the bargaining fails.

So much for the narrative coherence of DABDA. But what of its correspondence to real life? Empirical studies (as they say) have shown mixed results. Some "patients" experience grief according to the "prescribed" pattern. But others skip phases, or experience them "out of sequence."

Despite these cautions, the model thrives, not only in popular thinking, but also in clinical practice. But what if the square peg of my grief doesn't fit in the round hole of DABDA? And what if my grief counselor and my family adhere dogmatically to the model? Their counsel won't help me, and may even harm me. They may "demand" an anger from me (phase three!) that I simply cannot produce. "Your inability to express anger shows that you are still in denial!" No place for Job's stoic response, "The Lord gives, and the Lord takes; may the name of the Lord be blessed" (Job 1:21).

May I invite you to pause here for reflection? Perhaps your own story has been overshadowed by a difficult loss. My own story includes bereavement (chapter 2 above) as an episode of deep significance. If so inclined, perhaps you may wish to revisit the unfolding of your own loss and grief. (If not, feel free to read on.)

More generally, what does this example teach us about life-as-story? Is the problem with DABDA the assumption of a one-size-fits-all storyline? Or does the problem expose a broader and deeper difficulty; namely, what exactly *is* the relationship between story and reality?

This broader question has a long history of discussion in the field of literary criticism, usually under the rubric of *realism*. By venturing briefly into Engish Literature 101, we will glean insights to resolve (or at least reduce) the conflict-of-ideas played out in this chapter. And so we can grow—both in confidence and in prudence—as narrators who construct our own life stories.

Realism was the holy grail of much nineteenth-century literature. From Jane Austen to Thomas Hardy, nineteenth-century novelists abandoned the epic heroes of the mythical past, and narrated the ordinary lives of real people in the present. Realist novels demanded objective correspondence between story and reality. (No surprise to learn that the ascendancy of realism coincided with the development of photography.[32]) As close observers of the massive social changes of the industrial revolution, realist authors saw themselves as "secretaries to the nineteenth century."[33]

Given these lofty ambitions, we may be surprised to discover that "Realism is, in fact, a highly formalized literary convention which demands the selection of particular elements and their arrangement within a clear narrative shape."[34] The selectivity and shaping generates the illusion of a clear-eyed view of life. Reinforcing this illusion of objectivity is another key convention: the omniscient, third-person narrator. Furthermore, the preference for direct-over-indirect speech seems to allow the characters "to speak for themselves," without narrator interference (whilst in fact the narrator remains discreetly in control of everything they say).

---

32. Morrison, *Key Concepts in Creative Writing*, 113.

33. Balzac, quoted in Cobley, *Narrative*, 89.

34. Morrison, *Key Concepts in Creative Writing*, 112. For inventories of the literary techniques of realism, see: Cobley, *Narrative*, 88–116; Wood, *How Fiction Works*, 223–32.

Unmasking the ideological biases of "objective" realist narrators became an easy way to earn a PhD in literary criticism. An American subgenre of realism, the "hard-boiled" detective story, may serve as witness for the prosecution in the deconstruction of realism's objectivity: "Those who populate and pollute the universe of the hard-boiled detective story are described in terms of excess: excess smell (stink), excess bodily fluids (sweat, urine, tears, vomit), and/or excess desire (sexual proclivity, sexual perversion, greed, cunning and so forth)."[35] We could easily conclude that narrative simply cannot represent the world truly, because narrative cannot eliminate artificial convention or narrator viewpoint. But this would be knee-jerk reaction. First, all discourse uses convention (language itself is artificial), and all observers view from an angle. Second, these limitations do not automatically sever all links between reality and the perspectives/conventions used to describe it.[36]

So, in place of skepticism over narrative, we need to refine our understanding of the subtle link between story and reality. Thankfully, good discussions of this topic are not hard to find (and Aristotle may have been right all along). Accordingly, I will merely offer a cluster of conclusions (with footnotes for those interested).

As you read these conclusions, I invite you to ponder your own attempts to find a story that "fits" your life. Stories inevitably simplify existence. Are our narrative simplifications of life helpful clarifications—or harmful reductions?

## Mind the Gap

These words are familiar to passengers on London's underground trains. As the train doors open, a gap appears between the safety of the train and the safety of the platform. The gap may not be vast, but you ignore it at your own risk. Similarly, there is a gap between life story and life itself.[37]

The realist author George Eliot observed, "Art is the *nearest thing* to life; it is a mode of amplifying experience and extending our contact with our fellow-men beyond the bounds of our personal lot."[38] Any representation of life *re*-presents life. "A depiction can *never be* that which it depicts"; "The rendering of an object can never be the object itself."[39]

There will always be a gap between your life-narrative and the events you narrate. Instead of fretting about the gap, perhaps we can ask about its depth. Is your life story merely a useful abstraction from events, allowing you to see meaningful connections? Or is your "personal myth" profoundly disconnected from reality? Do you need to keep affirming your narrative self because of persistent evidence that undermines your construction?

---

35. B. Ogdon, quoted in Cobley, *Narrative*, 115.
36. See the succinct discussion of convention in Wood, *How Fiction Works*, 233–35.
37. "The act of *mimesis* which enables us to pass from life to life story introduces a 'gap' (however minimal) between living and recounting." (Kearney, *On Stories*, 132.)
38. Quoted in Wood, *How Fiction Works*, 241 (italics mine).
39. Cobley, *Narrative*, 82 (italics in original), 93.

## Metaphorical Truth

The negative statement of the gap between story and life leads to a positive statement: "Story is metaphor for life"; "A great work is a living metaphor that says, 'Life is like *this*.'"[40] Elizabeth Ellis uses a powerful metaphor to convey this truth about metaphor:

> Everyone must take a trip to the underworld . . . Making those painful journeys is part of the price we pay for being human. When we return . . . we tell the story of our journey as a way of saying to others, "Look, *I drew you a map*. This might be useful to you on your journey. You're going to need a coin for the boatman. You will want to take some bread to throw to the three-headed dog. And safe travels, friend."[41]

I love metaphor. It has a unique, paradoxical power. Metaphor preserves the gap between sign and signified, and also bridges the gap! "God is a rock," declares the psalmist. Obviously, he isn't; but in another way (e.g., stability), he is!

Applying this to narrative, one might say, "As plot is a trope [figure of speech] for human experience, character is a trope for human identity."[42] More poetically, Johann Gottfried Herder expressed the like/unlike relationship between Shakespeare's dramas and reality:

> When I read him . . . the theatre, actors, and scenery disappear! I see only separate leaves from the book of events, of Providence, of the world, blown by the storm of history; individual impressions of peoples, estates, souls, all the most various and independently acting machines . . . which come together to form a single, whole dramatic image, an event of singular grandeur that only the poet can survey . . . Step before his stage as before an ocean of events, where wave crashes into wave. Scenes from Nature come and go, each affecting the other, however disparate they appear to be; they are mutually creative and destructive, so that the intention of the creator, who seems to have combined them all according to a wanton and disordered plan, may be realized—dark little symbols forming the silhouette of a divine theodicy.[43]

What figures of speech do you employ to describe your own character, your own role in life? How do these images of yourself benefit you—and might there be detriments to the self-images you employ?

## Poetic License and Rhetoric

The quote we just read (from Herder) implies that the gap between story and life can actually work to our advantage. Paradoxically, the storyteller "shortchanges" life in order

---

40. McKee, *Story*, 25, 122 (italics in original).
41. Ellis, *From Plot to Narrative*, 65–66 (italics mine).
42. Leitch, *What Stories Are*, 148.
43. Herder, *Shakespeare*, 32–33.

to enrich life. Narrative form obscures some dimensions of life in order to reveal other, deeper dimensions. Imaginative literature is "the 'lie' that tells the truth."[44]

Beyond viewing the contrivance of story as poetic license, we can view narrative artifice as a form of rhetoric.[45] Rather than passively photograph the real world, narrative seeks to *persuade* us to embrace a way of looking at the world. This rhetorical function of narrative was recognized by Aristotle.[46] He used the Greek term *mimesis* (poorly translated as "imitation" or "representation") to describe the relationship between story and life. One commentator explains the term admirably:

> *Mimesis* may be seen . . . as an imaginative redescription which captures what Aristotle called the "essence" . . . of our lives. *Mimesis* is not about idealist escapism or servile realism. It is a pathway to the disclosure of the inherent "universals" of existence that makes up human truth . . . Far from being a passive copy of reality, *mimesis* re-enacts the real world of action by magnifying its essential traits . . . It remakes the world . . . in the light of its potential truths.[47]

This quote suggests a good question about personal narratives: does the story I tell about myself give me (and others) access to the essential me?

\* \* \* \* \*

To round off our discussion of story as metaphor (or poetic license, or rhetoric), let us revisit a common instance of literary contrivance mentioned above, namely the convention that requires the hero to fail twice and succeed at the third attempt.

Obviously, this pattern of three isn't a literal transcript of universal experience. With some of my personal goals, I have triumphed at the first attempt; with others, I have lost count of the number of failures. So then, if not literal truth, what truth does the classic pattern-of three express?

Indulge me in a little mathematical illustration. Identify the next number N in the following sequence: 2, 4, N. Could N = 6? Maybe. Or could N = 8? Possibly. Both answers could be correct, and it all depends upon the kind of *pattern* underlying the sequence. If the pattern is addition, then N = 6; if the pattern is multiplication, then N = 8. Here is the punchline: the number three seems to be the minimum required to establish a clear pattern.

Applied to literature, the pattern of success at the third attempt can teach several truths. For example, if the first two failed attempts involve trying opposite extremes, the successful third attempt may reinforce the value of the "golden mean."[48] Alternatively, two failures underscore the difficulty of success (failure is twice as likely), and invite us to ask what the hero did differently at the third try.

---

44. Ryken, *Windows to the World*, 35–62.
45. Abbott, *Introduction to Narrative*, 162.
46. Aristotle, *Poetics* 8.36–9.31; cf. Wood, *How Fiction Works*, 237–39.
47. Kearney, *On Stories*, 131 (emphasis his). Cf. Aristotle, *Poetics* 2; 9.5–9.
48. See Booker's discussion of the symbolic functions of "three" in narrative (*Seven Basic Plots*, 230–33).

* * * * *

Stories, especially classical narratives, can enshrine centuries of wisdom. Accordingly, good stories have great power to change lives. This transformative power plugs into the narrative shape of life itself. Story offers me a new story for the story of my life.

However, as our discussion in this chapter has shown, the map from story to life isn't one-to-one, isn't simple. Rather, story = metaphor for life. Story employs poetic license to persuade us to see life through new eyes.

Given the subtle relationship between story and life, using story to reshape your story will demand some wisdom from you, some critical thinking. When you emerge from the cinema or the theater, or put down a novel, how does the story you have just experienced plug into your life? How does the story enter into genuine dialogue with your life?

These questions are an on-ramp into our next chapter. But first, we can both wrap up this chapter, and head for the on-ramp, by shifting from "English Literature 101" to sociology.

## DON'T SLEEP, THERE ARE SNAKES

So far, we have mapped out a spectrum of three answers to the question, How is life a story? The spectrum has thesis and antithesis as contrasting extremes, and synthesis to moderate the extremes:

| *Thesis* | a literal reading of Shakespeare's "All the World's a Stage"; life imitates narrative art very closely. |
|---|---|
| *Antithesis* | life is a "tale told by an idiot"; narrative falsifies the random chaos and banality of real life. |
| *Synthesis* | life is like and unlike narrative; narrative = metaphor for life. |

This spectrum maps out actual options for navigating life taken by real people. I will discus these options in the following order: antithesis, thesis, and synthesis.

## Antithesis

Arguably, no one has done more to shatter the link between narrative and life than the existentialist philosopher Jean-Paul Sartre. He started out "imprisoned by the illusion that one could actually live one's life in conformity to some noble type playing the leading role in a masterplot."[49] His novel *Nausea* (1938) expresses the radical shift in his thinking. Sartre's protagonist attempts to write a biography of an historical character, but the project runs aground on the chaotic and contradictory nature of real life. Sartre

---

49. Abbott, *Introduction to Narrative*, 132.

argued that there are no true stories, that narrative imposes false order upon the mystery and flux of existence.[50]

This philosophy offers you a stark choice of lifestyles: live inside an illusory narrative, or live "existentially" in the moment, disconnected from anything that precedes or follows that moment.

Many Westerners are content with living "episodically" rather than "diachronically," satisfied with the pleasures of present-tense existence, freed from the burdensome need to construct a personal narrative.[51]

Furthermore, there is at least one non-Western indigenous tribe (which certainly never read Sartre) who share the bliss of episodic living. Daniel L. Everett (author of *Don't Sleep, There are Snakes*) lived among such a tribe. (The title of his book is a piece of practical advice commonly uttered within the community.[52])

Unusually, the Pirahãs (Amazonian Indians) have no Creation story, and no interest in their roots or their destiny.[53] Their culture and existence reflect the supreme value of "the immediacy of experience."[54] The western author came to envy the simplicity of their episodic, present-tense lifestyle.[55]

## Thesis

At the other extreme, late-twentieth-century America witnessed the potential for a total, seamless fusion of story with life. In our media-saturated existence, fantasy is the new reality. Neal Gabler charts this cultural shift in his book *Life: The Movie: How Entertainment Conquered Reality*. The crucial players in this drama are the celebrities.[56] Like the heroes and heroines of classic narratives, celebrities have no trivial moments. Every episode in the life of the celebrity furthers the archetypal plotline of their existence (as mediated to us by the media). Think of the "tragedy" of Princess Diana, whose funeral was "the saddest day in their life" for thousands who never knew her.[57]

Or think of the stereotypical movie star career, as thumbnailed by actor Bruce Willis: "There's only four basic stories they can write about you One: You hit the scene. Two: You peak. Three: you bomb. And four: You come back."[58] Gabler notes the overlap between this script and the four phases of Joseph Campbell's monomyth (discussed in chapter 7 of my book).[59] Accordingly, the celebrity life story affirms that ordinary Americans, too, may emerge from hardship to find their true self.

---

50. Ibid., 19–20, 128–29.
51. Long, "Out of the Loop," 120–26.
52. Everett, *Don't Sleep, There are Snakes*, xvii.
53. Ibid., 133.
54. Ibid., 129–31.
55. Ibid., 273.
56. Gabler, *Life: The Movie*, 7.
57. Ibid.
58. Quoted in ibid., 170.
59. Ibid., 168–73.

## Synthesis

Between the extremes of *Don't Sleep, There are Snakes* and *Life: The Movie*, we find a solid middle ground, where folk use the wisdom of story to interpret and guide their lives. Summing up the function of theater, Balthasar writes, "Theatre intends to be an interpretation of the world, in its 'unreality' shining a ray of light into the confusion of reality."[60]

For all the reasons discussed in this chapter, I occupy this middle ground. In theory. In practice, some people tell me I tend toward the naïve end of the spectrum (life = theater).

I suspect it is easier to occupy one of the extremes of the spectrum. It certainly requires less input of critical, dialectical thinking. To conclude this chapter, I will offer some reflections from the middle of the spectrum.

## IN AND OUT OF FOCUS

In addition to the argument of this chapter, I have another reason for occupying the middle of the spectrum. The foundational story of my creed (discussed in the previous chapter) implies that history is a story-in-the-making, a complete embryo with all the narrative DNA needed to realize an archetypal plotline, yet struggling painfully toward maturity. (Life is perpetual adolescence.) In the words of Saint Paul, living in the midst of the Christian epic entails seeing reality through "indistinct images in a [smudgy] mirror" (1 Cor 13:12).

For those of us who self-consciously rely on narrative to guide us through life, our archetypal plotlines offer us real, but finite, wisdom. Through narrative lenses, we see truly but dimly.

This awareness suggests that our use of narrative as life-lens should be flexible, adjustable, in constant conversation with our experiences. Plot types and character types both reveal and conceal. Their double-edged quality is aptly captured by Abbott:

> It may be that characterization and thinking in types is part of our mental equipment, and it may also be that the rich complexity and constantly changing nature of human beings can never be adequately captured by this narrative equipment. But this is not the same thing as saying that character is inevitably deceptive and that narrative can only deal in illusions because of this.[61]

Indeed, the discerning use of a "masterplot" can focus the true meaning of an individual's life. Think of Augustine's *Confessions*, an autobiography structured around the conversion masterplot.[62]

On the other hand, inappropriate use of a masterplot can have comic or tragic consequences. Jane Austen's novel *Emma* pivots on the regrettable consequences of the misuse of a masterplot as a life-lens:

---

60. Balthasar, *Prolegomena*, 10.
61. Abbott, *Introduction to Narrative*, 130.
62. Ibid., 132–33.

> Emma insists on viewing her protégée, Harriet, as a character in an eighteenth-century romance. She endows her, deceiving both herself and Harriet, with the conventional qualities of the heroine of such a romance. Harriet's parentage is not known; Emma converts her into the foundling heroine of aristocratic birth so common in such romances. And she designs for Harriet precisely the happy ending of such a romance, marriage to a superior being. By the end of *Emma* Jane Austen has provided Emma with some understanding of what it was in herself that had led her not to perceive the untruthfulness of her interpretation of the world in terms of romance. *Emma* has become a narrative about narrative.[63]

In Greek mythology, Procrustes would invite travelers to sleep in a particular bed. He wanted the bed to be a precise fit for each guest. So, he ensured the proper fit by either stretching or amputating his guests! The "Procrustean bed" can be a metaphor of our tendency to force the world to fit our story, rather than revising our story in the face of new evidence.

My friend Shannon used to work as a journalist on a small-town newspaper. She quit, largely because her quest for the true story was hindered by editors who demanded that she "boil it down" to narrative categories the readers could easily digest. A story involving a Caucasian and an African-American "had" to be about racial tension.

Abbott sees the same, potentially problematic use of masterplots in the courtroom. He argues that the O. J. Simpson trial was a battle of narratives. Black victim of institutionalized racism? The wife-beater who escalates to murder? The celebrity afforded unjust privileges?[64]

I suppose one "solution" would be to ban narratives from the courtroom—at the cost of ever being able to make sense of any crime in terms of cause, effect, and responsible agency.

Skepticism about one-size-fits-all plotlines is, of course, a defining trait of postmodernism. Hence the radical individualism of the postmodern interest in life stories:

> What makes people despair is that they try to find a universal meaning to the whole of life, and then end up by saying it is absurd, illogical, empty of meaning. There is not one big cosmic meaning for all, there is only the meaning we each give to our life, an individual meaning, an individual plot, like an individual novel, a book for each person.[65]

Since she buys into this philosophy, autobiography coach Tristine Rainer offers her students the following disclaimer:

> A lot of people think I mean that they should choose a fairy tale or a myth that already exists and try to fit their life into its template, but this isn't what I mean at all . . . I feel a mission to teach the *underlying structure of story* and not the application of preexisting myths as the key to finding meaning within each person's contemporary life.[66]

---

63. MacIntyre, "Epistemological Crises," 141.
64. Abbott, *Introduction to Narrative*, 42–46.
65. Anaïs Nin, quoted in Rainer, *Your Life as Story*, 1.
66. Ibid., 40–41 (italics mine).

Interestingly, when she exposits "the underlying structure of stories," Rainer uses a component that seems to borrow the *content* of "preexisting myths." She finds the key to personal narrative meaning in a death + rebirth pattern: "a turning point . . . where something in me died so something could live or be born."[67] Perhaps universal archetypes have more to teach us than postmoderns like Rainer are willing to concede.

\* \* \* \* \*

Viewing life in terms of story has immense promise and huge pitfalls. In the martial arts TV series from the seventies, *Kung Fu*, the aged sage would counsel his younger disciple, "Choose wisely, Grasshopper." The same counsel applies to use of life-narratives.

In my next chapter, I will explore more fully how people use stories to transform their lives. I will build on some of the insights of this chapter regarding the subtle and complicated relationship between story and life. To end this chapter, some thoughts on the wise use of story:

- any story can be an entry-point into the spiral of interpretation of life; the better the story, the fewer and less painful the revolutions of the spiral.
- story is a flexible, adjustable framework, used in dialogue with reality/experience.
- story offers resources for imaginative exploration of the world, not pre-packaged answers to our questions about the world.

As a counterpoint to all this caution, let me note the New Testament's use of story to interpret life. The New Testament is anything but cautious. Its authors boldly awaken our narrative imaginations, inviting us to risk taking its archetypal plots as road-maps for our path through life.

Here are a couple of quick examples. Jesus of Nazareth—a real, complex, historical person, living in a specific time and place, under distinctive historical circumstances. How would you even begin to tell his story? That question has obsessed New Testament scholars for more than a century—the so-called "Quest for the Historical Jesus."

How did the New Testament writers tell the story of Jesus? By clothing him in the archetypal plotlines and imagery from the Hebrew Bible! From the four Gospels to Paul to Hebrews, Jesus is imaged in terms of the storyline of the book of Exodus.[68] Apparently, that ur-narrative epic of liberation, journey, and community formation was just the lens needed to help us grasp the significance of Jesus.

Or consider New Testament books written to comfort readers who were despised and marginalized in ancient society. Books like Revelation. In the first century, from a Roman imperial standpoint, Christians were a minuscule, deviant minority, who "opposed the decrees of Caesar, by claiming there is another emperor—Jesus" (Acts 17:7). Accordingly, Christians received shame and hostility from the dominant culture.

---

67. Ibid., 79.
68. For the Exodus theme in the Gospels, see Swartley, *Story Shaping Story*.

How would the Roman Empire have interpreted the story of the first-century church? Probably as a dishonorable "tragedy"—the tragedy of futile and doomed resistance against the power and glory of the dominant culture.

How did the book of Revelation interpret the same story? By a complete reversal of the Roman imperial version! Faithful Christians are depicted, not as defeated, but as "victors" in an athletic (or military) contest. Such radical re-interpretations—of societal shame as a badge of honor—were not uncommon among religious minorities in antiquity.[69]

---

69. deSilva, *Hope of Glory*, 7–8.

# 12

# End-User Responsibility

IN OUR PREVIOUS CHAPTER, we searched for greater insight into the *intersection* between story and life. In this chapter, we will seek greater understanding of how stories *transform* lives.

We will start with an on-ramp into the territory of "consumer responses" to narratives. This will lead us into a catalog of positive transformational benefits experienced by end-users of narratives.

If you are seeking a story that you can live inside (a narrative home for your life), then this chapter may give you some thought-provoking pointers. The story you wish to inhabit—can that story offer you all the healthy effects of good narratives (effects listed later in this chapter)?

## VOYAGE-AND-RETURN

Reading a novel, or listening to a tale—these activities are stories. We open the book, enter the story-world, and close the book. Formally, this sequence mirrors the "voyage-and-return" plotline (discussed in chapter 8). But the analogy goes beyond the formal: "No book leaves us unchanged, for better or worse . . . The act of reading . . . posits an Elsewhere, another place beyond the present reality we inhabit. We read in order to travel, or be borne, to that other place and thus interrupt the curse of having only one life to lead."[1] When we re-emerge from the story-world, how are we different, and what changed us? Compare the paragraph just quoted with the following:

> I do not believe that any book can change your life; only you can. Two people read the same book, one is inspired while the other is bored. The issue is not the book but the person—what lies within each of us. The author's wisdom combined with the reader's inspiration and desire to change can lead to a new life for the reader.[2]

---

1. Collins, "*The Yearling* by Rawlings," 51.
2. Siegel, "*Human Comedy* by Saroyan," 154.

## Part 2: Stories Are ... and Stories Do ...

Variable reader-responses to the "same" book. A bit like the fundamentalist Christian view of the end-times: two people riding in the same car, one is raptured, the other remains.

When and how the story in the book intersects the story of our life—these objective realities factor big into the equation. But there's also the irreducible mystery of subjectivity, even idiosyncrasy, in our responses to literature.

Consider for a moment the response of the Gutres family in "The Gospel According to Mark," a short story by the Argentinian writer Jorge Luis Borges. The main character, Espinosa (whose name can mean "thorn" in Spanish) goes to live on a ranch in the outback of Argentina. The only folk for miles around are the Gutres, an illiterate family of Indian descent, who work the ranch. One day, Espinosa finds an old Bible in the ranch house. Each evening, around the meal table with the Gutres, he reads aloud from Mark's Gospel. The Gutres's growing fascination culminates with the question:

"The Roman soldiers who hammered in the nails—were they saved, too?"

"Yes," said Espinosa, whose theology was rather dim.[3]

That day, the Gutres built a cross using wooden beams taken from a shed. The final paragraph implies that Espinosa was crucified by the Gutres.

Saint Mark undoubtedly expected that many of his first-century Christian readers would be crucified. However, to read his Gospel as an invitation to perform a crucifixion—not what he would have expected.

Luis Borges's short story featured an extreme (and fictional) example of idiosyncratic response to narrative. However, real life routinely presents less extreme examples of idiosyncratic readings.

Consider the following response of a five-year-old boy to the fairy tale *Rapunzel*. In the tale, an (evil) enchantress imprisons the teenage girl Rapunzel in a tower. However, Rapunzel is rescued by a prince, who climbs the "rope" she provides by letting down her exceedingly long hair.

Bruno Bettelheim describes an interesting response to the tale.[4] A five-year-old boy, whose single mother worked all day, had a grandmother who took care of him. One day, Mom announces that Granny must go into hospital. The boy's reaction to the imminent loss of his caregiver? "Read me *Rapunzel*!" Apparently, two scenarios in the tale comforted him greatly. First, he interpreted the imprisonment as "being kept safe from all dangers." Second, he saw Rapunzel's long hair as the resourcefulness of one's own body when one needs a "lifeline."

How do you personally respond to the boy's ingenious response to *Rapunzel*?

Jesus often ended his parables with, "He who has ears to hear—let him hear." One senses that Jesus designed his parables for specific impacts. One could, perhaps, speak of their "intrinsic" meanings, accessible via the textual patterns created by their author. However, those meanings must be constructed by our "listening ears," and some will hear what others miss. And after we have heard, is there still more to hear?

At this juncture, I invite you to pause, and think of a story that powerfully impacted you. How did it change you? (How were you different after reading it, and what

---

3. Luis Borges, "Gospel According to Mark," 171.
4. Bettelheim, *Uses of Enchantment*, 16–17.

dimension of the story impacted you?) More generally, how do you personally *use* the stories that you read or hear?

## THE BOOK THAT CHANGED MY LIFE

Not mine, actually; seventy-one authors, mostly professional writers themselves, celebrating the books that transformed them.[5] That is a fairly decent sample size, even if skewed by profession (writers!) The books chosen were remarkably diverse, with only four duplicates. The usual suspects each showed up twice (*The Catcher in the Rye*; *To Kill a Mockingbird*), along with two essays on *The Great Gatsby*, plus two on *The Denial of Death* by Ernest Becker.

For anyone investigating how stories change lives, this collection of essays is pay dirt. Here, story meets life with indelible impact, and the end-users of narrative explain its transformative power.

So I combed through the collection for evidence. I asked each contributor, "How did the story impact you?" I distilled their answers to a phrase or sentence, which I wrote in pencil on the first page of each essay. Then I attempted to cluster these distilled answers into categories.

These categories generated a "top ten" list of ways that stories change lives (for the contributors). Were the results typical of readers in general? Suppose we pulled seventy-one random readers off the streets, and surveyed how books impact them. I suspect that most of the categories in the "top ten" would emerge from this different survey, but the rankings would vary. Looking at the list below, the number one category probably had something to do with the sample comprising professional writers! Anyway, here is the table of results, in which first place represents sixteen of the contributors, and tenth place represents three contributors (with the fifth spot a tie between two impacts):

How Stories Change Lives: The Experience of Seventy-One Writers

| Ranking of Impact | Type of Impact |
|---|---|
| 1 | inspire storytelling; inspire a search for one's own voice; awareness of word-power* |
| 2 | call to an alternative life-path; emulation of heroism |
| 3 | windows to the world: enlarged awareness and insight; expanded sense of possibilities |
| 4 | expose causality in life; make sense of history |
| 5 = | escape (from life's pains); enthrallment; vicarious living |
| 5 = | epiphany; crystallize experience; self-recognition |
| 6 | expose archetypal dimensions of existence; dig down to basic human experience |

5. Coady and Johannessen, *Book That Changed My Life*.

| Ranking of Impact | Type of Impact |
|---|---|
| 7 | inculcate or reinforce values and virtues |
| 8 | create empathy and human solidarity |
| 9 | give hope for positive change |
| 10 | dignify the mundane; bring transcendence to the mundane |

> \* These impacts (#1) all overlap two dimensions of story we discussed in chapter 7, namely, *medium* and *point of view*. According to one contributor, the essence of storytelling is a search for one's own *voice*: "Every great book is ultimately a metaphor for the act of writing" (Walbert, "*Charlotte's Web* by White," 174). In his inventory of story functions, William J. Bausch includes, "Stories . . . compel repetition," and "Stories restore the original power of the word" (Bausch, *Storytelling*, 30, 40).

When you glance at this listing of how stories change lives, which categories resonate most with your own experience? Would you supplement the list with additional ways that stories have changed you?

I myself will mention some additional functions of narrative in later chapters. Regardless of how we supplement the list, the categories seem fairly comprehensive of typical reader responses to narrative. (As confirmation, one might consult surveys of "Uses of Narrative" in standard guides to literature.[6])

This "top ten" impacts of narrative helped me to generate Part 3 of this book. As we continue, I will use the list of categories to drill down deeper toward the power-sources of narrative. This exploration will, of course, involve further explanation and illustration of the categories themselves.

You probably noticed that many of the categories overlap and interweave each other. Random example: an epiphany through reading (#5) may call us to a new life (#2) that expresses certain values and virtues (#7). This affirms the *holistic* quality of narrative; the multi-dimensional richness and wholeness of stories contributes to their power.

We also unearth the power of story by asking, Which *elements* of story help create all these life-changing responses in readers? To answer this question, I will re-group the "top ten" impacts of narrative, using the *five elements of story* that I introduced in chapter 7. In brief, I proposed that stories comprise the following elements:

| *setting* | time, place, circumstances; the "givens" (immutable dimensions) of the story-world |
|---|---|
| *character* | especially the protagonist, with whom most readers identify |
| *plot* | arc of tension, completed by crisis leading to resolution of initial problem |
| *point of view* | authorial evaluation of plot/character/setting (expressing the ideology [world and life view] of author) |
| *medium* | material form of the story (oral, written, film, theater, etc.); style/texture of presentation |

6. E.g., Ryken, *Windows to the World*; Rosenblatt, *Literature as Exploration*, 32–66; Lewis, *Experiment in Criticism*; cf. Bausch, *Storytelling*, 29–63.

"Elements" suggests a helpful analogy from chemistry. A combination of two gaseous elements, hydrogen + oxygen, generates a liquid ($H_2O$, or water). The whole is more than the sum of the parts. Likewise, in narrative, the impact comes from the interplay of the five elements. For example, many writers name Salinger's *Catcher in the Rye* as the book that inspired them to find their own voice. Here, *point of view* finds expression through the main *character*, Holden Caulfield, whose searing dismissal of "phonies" finds expression entirely through his distinctive idiom (i.e., linguistic *medium*).

This holistic awareness doesn't stop us from mapping relationships between the "five elements" of story and the "top ten" impacts of story. For each impact, we can single out the element(s) that have most "oomph." Combining the two preceding tables, I would (tentatively) suggest the following set of interactions between story element and story impact:

| *Story Elements* | *Contribution to Story Impact* |
| --- | --- |
| setting (story world) | window; escape; dignify the mundane |
| plot | reveal cause-and-effect; reveal archetype (essence) of life; give hope |
| plot + character (fusion) | epiphany; crystallize experience; call to life-path; emulate hero |
| character | empathy |
| point of view + medium/style (fusion) | inspire voice |
| point of view + plot + character (fusion) | inculcate values and virtues |

Let's pause here and consolidate our awareness of the range of powerful impacts from good stories. I invite you to turn back to the end of chapter 1 (to the section "Buffalo Soldier.") Back there, we listed numerous benefits of owning and articulating your personal life story. Suppose we compare these benefits with the list of story-impacts cataloged in this chapter. Do you sense the overlaps? And the implication—a well-told autobiography can do all the positive things we have been discussing in this chapter.

In the rest of this chapter, I will zero in on how stories can impact our *worldview*. Our basic assumptions about the world; whatever we "take for granted" about existence; our answers to life's fundamental questions. This stuff is high-stakes: change someone's worldview, you change their life. Screenwriter Robert McKee makes a big claim: "The world now consumes films, novels, theatre, and television in such quantities and with such ravenous hunger that the *story arts* have become humanity's prime source of inspiration, as it seeks to order chaos and gain insight into life."[7] Let us begin to explore the power of the "story arts" to shape worldview. As a guide, I will take four categories of "story impact" from the table above. (Given the holistic quality of story, I could use all ten categories of impact, but I'll leave some for later chapters, where I explore other ways that stories change us.) Here are the four perspectives on narrative impact that I will investigate as worldview transformers:

- story as window

7. McKee, *Story*, 12 (italics mine).

Part 2: Stories Are... and Stories Do...

- story as cause-and-effect
- story as values and virtues
- story as empathy

## WORLDVIEWS VIA STORY

### Story as Window

Plays in a theater feature a stage and a backdrop. Action in novels takes place in a *narrative world* conjured up, almost magically, by the writer's descriptions. "The narrative world is... a landscape, setting, or arena within which many (but not any) different things may happen—and a system of rules which determine what may or may not happen within a given story."[8]

Every story has background, constraining its characters and plotlines, bounding the action as firmly as the limits of the wooden stage in Shakespeare's Globe theater. When we open a book to read, we voyage into the narrative world created by the author. Eager to enter the adventure, we willingly suspend belief, accepting the givens of the narrated world on their own terms. Is magic possible or not? Is the world permeable to a supernatural beyond? What problems preceded the "Once upon a time"? What forms does evil take? What political and economic factors must characters reckon with?

Answers to these, and dozens of other questions, constitute the narrative world. When we return from our voyage of reading, how is our view of our own world different? Are we aware of evils we previously overlooked? Are we open to possible experiences we once dismissed? Are there dimensions of *realpolitik* we now take more seriously? To boil it down to one question, *How does the world of the story relate to our own world?*

This question sharply confronts the reader of so-called "realist" literature.[9] But, intriguingly, "fantasy" literature also poses the same question! Stories are windows, and any particular window offers an angle or a panorama not offered by other windows. For example, the world of traditional fairy-tales features some consistent givens, some immutable laws, some fixed assumptions about life. Could some of these actually be true?

As sane and deep a thinker as G. K. Chesterton replied "Yes!" In his chapter "The Ethics of Elfland," he asserts: "My first and last philosophy, that which I believe in with unbroken certainty, I learned in the nursery... The things I believed most then, the things I believe most now, are the things called fairy tales. They seem to me to be the entirely reasonable things... Fairyland is nothing but the sunny country of common sense."[10] Phew! Perhaps we'd better let Chesterton elaborate. In Fairyland, he came to understand "the pricelessness and the peril of life."[11] Pricelessness: a sense of wonder at the way things are, the "magic" of the natural world (apples fall to the ground!), and

---

8. Leitch, *What Stories Are*, 108–9.
9. See our brief discussion of literary realism in the previous chapter.
10. Chesterton, *Orthodoxy*, 54.
11. Ibid., 69.

sheer gratitude for the privilege of being alive.[12] Peril: the fragility of goodness and joy, the conditionality of privileged existence, lived constantly under the ubiquitous *If*.[13]

Chesterton goes on to explain how these "Ethics of Elfland" ran counter to the prevalent Western worldview of secular science. Agree with him or disagree, his experience singularly attests the power of stories to shape one's view of the world.

What about your own favorite novel or film? How does that story shape the way you view the world?

Our worldviews major on fixities, the screwed-down props of the world stage. But worldviews also provide us with understanding of how things change. Stories traffic in causality, our next topic for discussion.

## Story as Cause-and-Effect

"We are made in such a way that we continually look for the causes of things. The inevitable linearity of story makes narrative a powerful means of gratifying this need."[14] Accordingly, stories offer us insight into the dynamics of change.

Proverbs, generalizations about how the world really works, are ultra-compressed narratives of cause and effect. "Anxiety in a person's heart depresses it / But a good word gladdens it" (Prov 12:25). "Hope postponed sickens the heart / Advent of desire—a tree of life!" (Prov 13:12). "Abundant people—a king's adornment / Absence of people—a prince's ruin" (Prov 14:28). "A gift gains access for a person / And guides them into the presence of great people" (Prov 18:16).

These proverbial mini-narratives catalog cause-and-effect within a largely static world order. Other stories deal with change that overturns the static order of the world. Many storytellers would agree with Karl Marx's revolutionary insight: "The philosophers see their job as interpreting the world, but our job is to change the world." We can use Marx's dichotomy to pigeonhole stories into three types:[15]

| stories that *establish* worlds | myths |
| stories that *explore* worlds | most stories |
| stories that *overturn* worlds | counter-myths and parables |

The narrative arc turns on the crisis-moment, when a decisive action results in permanent change. Narrative rhetoric derives its power from this plot dynamic. The philosopher Plato, fearing this power, viewed storytellers as dangers to the social order.[16] Plato may have been on to something. Consider the rhetoric of vigilante movies, such as *Dirty Harry*, and *Death Wish*. These films trade on the counter-myth of redemptive

---

12. Ibid., 55–60.
13. Ibid., 60–64.
14. Abbott, *Introduction to Narrative*, 37.
15. Tilley, *Story Theology*, 39–54.
16. Cobley, *Narrative*, 60, 66.

violence. They assert the value of "justice," but deny that justice results from society's normal legal procedures of criminal prosecution.[17]

With this mention of the values embedded in stories, and the intersection of plot with point of view, we can turn to our next topic for discussion.

## Story as Values and Virtues

In narrative, values emerge where the plot intersects the author's point of view, and virtues where the author's point of view intersects characterization. In following the struggles of a sympathetic character, our beliefs about values and virtues may be formed.

Listen to Anne Perry's description of her favorite book (G. K. Chesterton's *The Man Who Was Thursday*): "[It] is above all a journey of the spirit where men love the good in the world enough to fight for it." For Perry, the book gave her "food, armor, ... a compass for the soul ... [and] light."[18]

In life, our real values emerge via the question, What is worth struggling to gain? Likewise, stories revolve around an escalating series of reversals in the protagonist's struggle to make reality conform to their values.[19] As things we fight for, values tend to be extremes, and so the positive value we seek pairs up with a negative value that we dread. Fears and longings, dreams and nightmares.[20] McKee culls the following list of binary values that drive the plot of many a film:[21]

| *Positive Value* | *Negative Value* |
|---|---|
| Life | Death |
| Love | Hate |
| Freedom | Slavery |
| Truth | Lie |
| Courage | Cowardice |
| Loyalty | Betrayal |
| Wisdom | Folly |
| Strength | Weakness |
| Excitement | Boredom |
| Right | Wrong |
| Good | Evil |
| Hope | Despair |
| Justice | Tyranny |
| Consciousness | Oblivion |

17. McKee, *Story*, 115–17, 129–30.
18. Perry, "Chesterton's *Man Who Was Thursday*," 138–39.
19. McKee, *Story*, 33–42.
20. Ryken, *Windows to the World*, 118.
21. McKee, *Story*, 34, 319–31.

| Positive Value | Negative Value |
|---|---|
| Communication | Alienation |
| Maturity | Immaturity |
| Success | Failure |
| Wealth | Poverty |

Interestingly, this (non-exhaustive) list may reveal the Western bias of the film industry. For example, the ancient Mediterranean cultures emphasized the following contrasts:

| Positive Value | Negative Value |
|---|---|
| Honor | Shame |
| Purity | Defilement |
| Order | Chaos |

Right here would be a good place to pause, and revisit your favorite film or novel. What are the central values enshrined in that story? And how do these values shape your own life?

Whatever the values that you and I struggle to realize, we know that reality doesn't always oblige. Our dreams may not materialize, or may be devoured by their nightmare opposites. Given this narrative context for values, we shouldn't be surprised if a particular archetypal plotline tends to revolve around a particular value. But the fit between plot type and value isn't a one-to-one mapping. For example, desire for justice confronted with an unsolved crime becomes a quest narrative. But justice confronted by a corrupt legal system may prompt a "dragon-slaying" storyline.

If value relates directly to plot, then virtue relates directly to character. Virtue answers the question, "What kind of person should I be?" Just as value comes in pairs of binary opposites, so does virtue. At least it did in the Greco-Roman world, when moralists produced lists of virtues and their corresponding vices. The New Testament tapped into such lists, in formulating qualifications for church leaders (1 Tim 3:2–3):

| Virtues | temperate; hospitable; gentle (etc.) |
|---|---|
| Vices | given to wine; covetous; quarrelsome (etc.) |

Stories teach us that a person's true character is only revealed under pressure, during an ordeal, and especially when facing a dilemma: the choice between irreconcilable goods, or the lesser of two evils.[22]

In other words, like value, virtue finds expression via plot. This linkage to plot explains the didactic power of narrative. Stories inculcate values and virtues indirectly; stories show rather than tell.[23] "A story is the living proof of an idea."[24]

---

22. Ibid., 249, 375.
23. Guroian, *Tending the Heart of Virtue*, 19–20, 37–38.
24. McKee, *Story*, 113.

At its simplest, narrative rhetoric fuses *value* and *cause*.[25] The resolution of tension presents a final state as a positive or a negative value, *and* the resolution answers the question of causality—how did this desirable/undesirable state emerge?

As such, stories are "experiments in living."[26] "The gift of story is the opportunity to live lives beyond our own, to desire and struggle in a myriad of worlds and times, at all the various depths of our being."[27]

Stories engage the moral imagination concretely, rather than dulling the soul with abstract principles. In his college and post-grad courses, Robert Coles uses literature to engage the students in ethical discussion. In one memorable discussion, a student identified exactly how she had been molded by reading William Carlos Williams's trilogy: "Williams's words have become my images and sounds, part of me. You don't do that with theories. You don't do that with a system of ideas. You do it with a story, because in a story—oh, like it says in the Bible, *the word becomes flesh*."[28] In identifying with a character and experiencing their choices vicariously, we can begin to internalize their virtues. Identification can also invoke our empathy, our sense of solidarity with the rest of humanity. We end this chapter with a brief look at the power of narrative to induce empathy.

## Story as Empathy

We seem to have a natural capacity to resonate with fellow-creatures, animate and inanimate. "Even the delicate poise of an architectural column or the symmetry of a Greek vase will be felt in the pull and balance of our own muscles."[29]

Screenwriters exploit this capacity, by encouraging us to identify with the protagonist early in the movie. Some screenwriters call this convention "saving the cat"; within the first twenty minutes of the film, the protagonist must perform an act we can admire.[30]

We should never underestimate the ethical benefit of experiencing empathy. C. S. Lewis considered this "enlargement of our being" a major blessing bestowed by literature.[31] In the absence of empathy, there seems no limit to the cruelty and horrors *homo sapiens* can perpetrate.[32]

In addition to the intrinsic benefits of empathy, identifying with the protagonist hooks us into a story, exposing us to the multiple impacts of narrative (such as formation of values and virtues, as discussed above).

---

25. Ibid., 115–17.
26. Ryken, *Windows to the World*, 139–41; cf. Guroian, *Tending the Heart of Virtue*, 26.
27. McKee, *Story*, 142.
28. Coles, *Call of Stories*, 128 (italics in original).
29. Rosenblatt, *Literature as Exploration*, 46.
30. Snyder, *Save The Cat*, xv–xvi.
31. Lewis, *Experiment in Criticism*, 137–41.
32. Kearney, *On Stories*, 139–40.

Empathy in the form of pity (Greek *eleos*) is a key component of the much-debated Aristotelian concept of catharsis. Tragic narrative, said Aristotle, rouses pity and fear (Greek *phobos*) and effects a catharsis (purification) of such emotions.[33] When we identify with the protagonist of tragedy, we vicariously share his vulnerability to the workings of fate: "Cathartic awe stops us in our tracks, throws us off kilter, deworlds us. The Greeks identified this with the detachment of the Olympian deities, enabling us to see through things, however troubling or terrible, to their inner or ultimate meaning."[34] Empathy for tragic figures can lead one to embrace a tragic *worldview*; there are contexts in which this might be preferable to some alternative worldviews.

For example, in human conflict, many of us are willing to virtually *demonize* our adversary. Even in a secular society, many resort to explanatory narratives with remarkable parallels to the demonization narratives of "superstition."[35] Such narratives invoke the hidden forces of demon possession to explain the sufferings of the victim. Similarly, many of us attribute all our problems to the negative self-image we internalized as a child, as if the negative voice of our parents "took possession" of our souls. Such explanations render our parents the equivalent of the demonic other. By contrast, the tragic worldview allows us to see the past through our parents' eyes, and to sympathize with their failings. "[The] tragic view of human failings as rigidified extensions of human strengths can be good medicine against the demonic outlook."[36]

## REVIEW AND PREVIEW

In this chapter, we have begun a systematic exploration of how stories change lives. Our exploration followed a simple two-dimensional map: on the *x*-axis, around ten typical *impacts* stories have on readers; on the *y*-axis, five *elements* of story. This map links story impact to story element(s), whilst recognizing the holistic experience of reading.

Using this map, we discussed story impact using four categories: story as window; story as cause-and-effect; story as values and virtues; story as empathy. Under all four categories, our chosen focus was the impact of stories on the formation of our *worldview*. Much more could have been said, but it's time to move on.

Part 3 of my book builds on the work of this chapter. Here is a preview of where we are going, as we explore territory mapped out by the other kinds of impact we experience through stories.

In chapter 13, we reflect on stories as a *call* to an alternative life-path (often involving emulation of heroism). This impact of story exposes *archetypal* dimensions of existence, digging down to basic human experience.

As an outgrowth of discussing narrative archetypes, chapter 14 examines personal identity in terms of the *self-images* that demarcate our roles in life.

---

33. Aristotle, *Poetics* 6.
34. Kearney, *On Stories*, 138.
35. Alon and Omer, "Demonic and Tragic Narratives," 33–37.
36. Ibid., 39.

Part 2: Stories Are . . . and Stories Do . . .

Discussion of narrative archetypes continues in chapters 15–17, which consider the impact of *cultural scripts* upon our identity and behavior.

Chapters 18–20 zoom in on *identity construction*, including reconstruction (personal healing), using the resources given by narrative. Various impacts of story come into play, including stories as *escape*, stories as *hope*, and stories as *empowering voices*.

Finally, chapter 21 explores story as *epiphany*, using this category as an entry-point for discussing meditative spiritual practices, and participation in the church calendar.

\* \* \* \* \*

# PART 3

How Stories Change Lives

# Spoiler Alert 3
(Overview of Part 3)

THIS PART BUILDS ON material in the previous part—especially from chapter 12, where we inventoried the rich and diverse ways that stories change lives. We will explore the life-transforming power of story in greater depth, and thereby enrich the resources of the reader who is seeking a healthy personal narrative. Part 3 will engage questions such as these:

- Can you live out the plots of classic literature?
- How is your *self-image* woven into a narrative?
- How do your personal *habits* fit into a story?
- How does the surrounding *culture* influence the stories you live?
- How are our psychological *problems* rooted in defective narratives?
- How can stories bring healing to our troubled psyches?
- What resources do humans have for constructing better personal narratives?
- What distinctive resources does Christianity provide for constructing a healthier personal identity?

Accordingly, the chapter flow of Part 3 goes like this. In chapter 13, I describe how ordinary people attempt to live out archetypal plotlines in their everyday lives. Chapter 14 continues this investigation, by focusing on archetypal self-images—the metaphors we use to crystallize our role in life's narrative.

Chapter 15 shifts focus from the panoramic to the microcosmic, by viewing personal daily habits as *scripts*. This introduction to "script theory" also provides a bridge into chapters 16 and 17, which zoom out from personal stories to cultural stories, examining some of the "cultural scripts" which shape everyday life in America.

Chapters 18–20 shift gears, exploring the dynamic processes whereby stories form our personal identities. Chapter 18 explores the negative impact of "bad" stories, while chapter 19 explores the positive impact of "good" stories. Chapter 20 discusses

Part 3: How Stories Change Lives

the challenges involved in building a narrative identity, and the resources available to help us. The chapter ends by discussing distinctively Christian resources for building a healthy narrative identity. Chapter 21 picks up where chapter 20 ended, by exploring in more depth some traditional Christian practices whereby the gospel story reshapes our personal stories.

\* \* \* \* \*

# 13

# Don Quixote Rides Again

TIME: 16TH CENTURY. PLACE: Spain. Protagonist: Don Quixote. Plot: Quest for heroic adventures, inspired by fervid consumption of stories of chivalry.

For many readers, Cervantes's classic novel *Don Quixote* (published 1605) symbolizes our delusional strivings to script our lives according to archetypal plotlines.

Indeed, Cervantes's satire skewers his hero on every page. The would-be knight dons a suit of rusty armor, and mounts a broken-down steed. Journeying out from his village, he espies scores of windmills in the distance. Giants! A summons to heroic combat! His travel companion, the worldly-wise Sancho Panza, insists they are windmills. Unpersuaded, Don Quixote spurs his horse toward the "giants." The sail of a mill catches his lance, whirling him airborne and throwing him to the ground. Still unpersuaded, Don Quixote reasons that an adversary must have used magic to transform the giants into windmills, in order to deprive the knight of the honor of victory.

Easy to join the narrator in laughter, and many readers have enjoyed the novel simply at that level. Others, though, reflect further. Witness the *Times Literary Supplement* (April 27, 1916):

> But, with more thought, comes a check to our frivolity. Is not all virtue and all goodness in the same case as Don Quixote? Does the author, after all, mean to say that the world is right, and those who try to better it are wrong? If that is what he means, how is it that at every step of our journey we come to like the Don better, until in the end we can hardly put a limit to our love and reverence for him? Is it possible that the criticism is double-edged, and that what we are celebrating with our laughter is the failure of the world?[1]

Emerging from Cervantes's novel, we may experience a familiar pull and tug. Like the Don, we may yearn for a classic script that gives value and direction to our lives. Like Sancho Panza, we may conclude that reality undermines all classic scripts.

I discussed that debate in chapter 11, so we need not revisit the dilemma here. Instead,ced, I will pick up a central thread from chapter 12, where I discussed seventy-one autobiographical snapshots from *The Book That Changed My Life* (edited by Coady and

---

1. Quoted in Slade, "Comments," 898.

Johannessen). For roughly 25 percent of the contributors, reading a particular story triggered life-changing events such as:

- a call to emulate the hero;
- a call to an alternative lifestyle;
- a call to walk closer to the archetypes of human experience.

Maybe your own experience resonates with this. Was there ever a book (or a film) whose main character so captivated you, that you wanted your life to "become" that role? Or has a film (or a novel) ever impacted you so deeply, that you made a drastic change in your daily choices? Or have you ever yearned for a deeper, more authentic self as a result of reading a story or watching a movie?

With good reason, Robert Coles titled one of his works, *The Call of Stories*. As Christopher Booker points out, the *call* functions as the gateway into many archetypal plotlines.[2] In other words: Don Quixote rides again.

## "THE STORY TAKES CARE OF THE REST"

When powerful plots invite us to change direction, we risk a journey whose outcome may surprise us. Experiencing a "call" is one type of "inciting incident" that propels us into new plotlines (recall the discussion of story structure in chapter 7). Musing on how stories change lives, Donald Miller recounts an *aha!* moment springing from conversation with friends: "Jordan said the story is what [ultimately] changes the character, not the inciting incident. 'The inciting incident is how you get them to do something,' Ben said. 'It's the doorway through which they can't return . . . *The story takes care of the rest*.'"[3] Think of the classic "quest" narrative. A character goes in search of a person, a place, a treasure—whatever might fill their void. At the end of their journey, what they find is different from (and better than) what they initially searched for. Indeed, one "how-to" guide for budding novelists asserts as dogma: "This plot [the quest] is about the character who makes the search, *not* about the object of the search itself. Your character is in the process of *changing* during the course of the story. What or who is she becoming?"[4] Think of other archetypal plotlines (discussed in chapter 8), and *how* their protagonists change through the course of the narrative. The following list is incomplete and simplistic. Hopefully, interested readers will generate their own fuller, more nuanced lists. (Think back to any *pivotal episode* in your own life, when some irreversible change took place within you. What events led up to that change? Who (or what) played the decisive part in changing you? Was the outcome different from what you had previously expected from life?)

---

2. Booker, *Seven Basic Plots*, 48, 65, 83.
3. Miller, *Million Miles*, 104 (italics mine).
4. Tobias, *20 Master Plots*, 70 (italics mine).

| Type of Transforming Episode | Plot Archetype |
|---|---|
| ordeal/test | quest<br>ascent<br>overcoming-the-monster |
| epiphany → seeing relationships with new eyes | comedy |
| exposure to an unfamiliar world | voyage-and-return |
| life-giving intervention by another character | rebirth |

If you want to change, heed the call of a story. If Abraham had known he would be asked to sacrifice his own son Isaac (Genesis 22), he would never have journeyed from Ur of the Chaldees (Gen 12:1–3). If he had stayed put in Ur, he would never have become the father of three world religions.

## PERSONAL MYTHS

"Every man invents a story for himself which he then often and with great cost to himself, takes to be his life."[5] Narrative psychologist Dan P. McAdams has spent decades collecting and analyzing these life stories or personal myths. McAdams has developed "interview protocols" which enable subjects to tell their life story in a manner that helps researchers.[6] Whilst recognizing the dangers of abstraction, we can establish a life story template of key elements (cf. my discussion of story elements in chapter 7):

**Life Story (Personal Myth) Template**

| ideological *setting* | assumptions about the *world stage* (e.g., its fairness or safety) |
|---|---|
| *character* | *self-images* encoding the subject's *role* |
| *plot* | *scenes* encapsulating *key moments*:<br>trigger incidents;<br>high points;<br>low points;<br>turning points<br>*(projected) ending*, visualizing the subject's *legacy* for future generations |
| thematic *point of view* | *values* determining the subject's *goals*<br>(in basic spheres of *work* and *relationships*) |

Throughout our lives, we are works in progress, and our personal myths adapt accordingly. At different stages of life, we may emphasize a particular theme: "Themes of identity (vs. role confusion) tend to predominate in memories from the teenage and emerging adult years, themes of intimacy (vs. isolation) are highest in the 20s, and themes of

---

5. Max Frisch, quoted in Wyatt, "Narrative in Psychoanalysis," 206.

6. Foley Center for the Study of Lives, "Life Story Interview." Cf. the summary of McAdams's model by Singer, "Heroin Addict," 255–56.

generativity (vs. stagnation) tend to show up in the midlife decades."[7] These shifting obsessions lure us into the plot that fits our stage of life.[8] Using the plot archetypes from chapter 8, we may risk a generalization:

| Stage of Life | Typical Plot of Personal Story |
|---|---|
| teens | *ascent* (striving for identity and independence) |
| twenties | *comedy* (facing the challenges of relationships) |
| mid-life | *quest* (for an enduring legacy) |

Other genres of life story may overlap with particular phases of life. For instance, "*dragon-slaying*" (good versus evil) often seems more compelling during the idealism of our youth. (Way back in my student days, there was a proverb: "If you aren't a Communist by the time you're twenty, there's something wrong with your heart; if you're still a Communist by the time you're forty, there's something wrong with your head.") The passage of time tends to erode youthful idealism. Black-and-white morality turns to grey. And the world (it turned out) wasn't as easy to fix as we had originally hoped and believed.

It may be worth pausing here, and reflecting upon the phases of your own life. Looking back, have particular phases been dominated by particular concerns? How have your ambitions altered over the years? What goals have you either abandoned or modified, and what provoked those changes? From your current vantage-point, do you regret the loss of any of your earlier storylines?

Not only do personal myths vary with age, they also vary with culture. Westerners tend to emphasize *individual* achievements, whilst members of Eastern cultures tend to underscore *collective* accomplishments.[9]

Our cultural location, our phase of life, our individual idiosyncrasies—all of these give texture and color to the personal myths woven over the course of our lives. Given all this diversity, the life story template (described above) offers an overarching unity. The template views your life story and mine as versions of the archetypal *quest*. What are we searching for? Meaning. Purpose. Significance. (Choose your own synonym.) In religious terms, immortality; in secular terms, a memorial, a legacy for future generations.

What will you pass on, how will you be remembered? Will your legacy be the product of individual achievement (e.g., a scientific discovery; an artistic product; wealth and property; etc.)? Or will your memorial emphasize the communal dimension (e.g., raising children; community service; membership of a religious tradition; etc.)?

If narrative psychology underscores the universality of the quest, so does genre criticism. "In essence we have told one another the same tale, one way or another, since the dawn of humanity, and that story could be usefully called *the Quest*."[10] This convergence of psychology and literature is no accident:

---

7. McAdams, "Personal Narratives," 250.

8. Cf. the correlations between life-stages and preferences for genres-of-literature proposed in Tilley, *Plot Snakes*, 2–14, and in Tilley, *Introduction to Plot*, 99.

9. McAdams, "Personal Narratives," 246–47.

10. McKee, *Story*, 196 (italics in original).

> Story is a metaphor for life, and to be alive is to be in seemingly perpetual conflict. As Jean-Paul Sartre expressed it, the essence of reality is scarcity, a universal and eternal lacking. There isn't enough of anything in this world to go around. Not enough food, not enough love, not enough justice, and never enough time. Time, as Heidegger observed, is the basic category of existence. We live in its ever-shrinking shadow, and if we are to achieve anything in our brief being that lets us die without feeling we've wasted our time, we will have to go into heady conflict with the forces of scarcity that deny our desires.[11]

When certain listeners hear the call of stories, their biographical script may take shape as a journey, a quest, a search for the elusive scarcity. For several contributors to *The Book That Changed My Life*, a story initiated their pilgrimage. For other contributors, the vertical image of ascent best captures their response to a narrative. They felt summoned upward, to fulfill their true potential.

Let us now hear from these (and other) "Don Quixotes," as they seek guidance from archetypal plots. Life and narrative are temporal media both; hence the power of elemental plotlines to reshape our *curricula vitae*. "Novels and stories are renderings of life; they can . . . point us in new directions, or give us the courage to stay a given course."[12]

## LIVING THE ARCHETYPES

Robert Coles believes we can "become our own appreciating and comprehending critics by learning to pull together the various incidents in our lives in such a way that they do, in fact, become an *old-fashioned story*."[13] The flesh-and-blood characters featured in this section would agree with Coles.

Before we reference their stories, a couple of caveats. Obviously, their inventory of personal myths is illustrative, not exhaustive.

More importantly, this section is descriptive, not prescriptive or normative. I am merely attempting to discern the human condition via the lens of narrative. Some of the stories I will recount come with the "Don't try this at home" label.

Regardless of whether or not you should want to imitate the various characters described below, I would invite you to reflect as you read the plot summaries of their lives. Do any of their storylines give you a narrative category for unifying your own experience of life? What about your family members, friends, and colleagues? Can you discern similarities to their own life stories in the narratives below?

For convenience, I will gather the personal myths under the "seven basic plots" (discussed in chapter 8), beginning with the "quest" archetype.

---

11. Ibid., 211.
12. Coles, *Call of Stories*, 159.
13. Ibid., 11 (italics mine).

PART 3: HOW STORIES CHANGE LIVES

## Quests

How do dry pages of print become a bucket of cold water in the face? Apocalyptic reading experiences unveil suppressed realities. One such reality: the basic plot of life is our struggle against inevitable death. For many readers, Ernest Becker's *The Denial of Death* (1973) was that epiphany.[14] Its thesis: uniquely human activities, from works of art to construction of civilizations, represent "our desperate and usually unconscious efforts to deny our impermanence, to run from our animal doom."[15]

The denial of death goads humans into quests for "immortality" (or the secular downsized versions, meaning and purpose). For award-winning chef Jacques Pépin, the summons came through reading Camus's existentialist classic, *The Myth of Sisyphus*. Pépin's take-home from Camus: "Even though the futility of our condition leads us all to the same end, we must and can dignify life through our deeds and behavior."[16]

Often, the quest takes a spiritual turn. Yale professor Carlos Eire, reading Thomas à Kempis's *The Imitation of Christ*, learned that the inevitability of death means "the only real treasures are intangible."[17] Brother Christopher seemed destined for a career in government, until a professor assigned *The Seven Storey Mountain* (the autobiography of the Trappist monk, Thomas Merton). This story "awakened a primal desire," leading Brother Christopher directly into the monastery.[18] For writer Anne Lamott, a book by Ram Dass empowered her quest: "I knew the day I read *The Only Dance There Is* that this was what I was going to do with my life: pursue spiritual truth."[19]

For others, the quest takes shape in creative activity, the struggle to beget beauty. One can speculate: is the art object "immortal?" Or, does creative activity itself connect the artist to the Creator? Alexandra Stoddard, a guru of the "Happiness Movement," drank in the wisdom of poet Rainer Maria Rilke (who had imbibed the artistic spirit from the sculptor Auguste Rodin). Stoddard noted that Rilke "was happiest when he was working, producing; not having written, but the actual writing, the creating, was all-important."[20]

Scientists, too, may be driven by a quest to realize an aesthetic ideal. A boiler-plate life script for many academics (whether in the sciences or the humanities) goes something like this:

> The protagonist encounters a grand question or problem in childhood or adolescence that guides his or her intellectual pursuits thereafter . . . The question gives birth to an idealized image of something or someone in the world that the protagonist longs to be, experience, make, or partake of in some manner. Over time, the protagonist commits the self to the realization of the image. As

---

14. Cheever, "*Denial of Death* by Becker," 37–38; Kurson, "*Denial of Death* by Becker," 93–94.
15. Ibid., 93.
16. Pépin, "*Myth of Sisyphus* by Camus," 135.
17. Eire, "*Imitation of Christ* by Kempis," 73.
18. Brother Christopher, "*Seven Storey Mountain* by Merton," 48.
19. Lamott, "*Only Dance* by Dass," 101.
20. Stoddard, "*Letters to a Young Poet* by Rilke," 166.

the image matures and develops in the mind and life of the protagonist, it . . . becomes elaborated into a personal aesthetic.[21]

A sixth-grade boy wanted to build a perfect robot, and he grew up to be a computer science professor. His work in robotics has a palpable aesthetic dimension: "[For him,] the beautiful robot is hip, small, and agile. His personal aesthetic privileges the qualities of agility over strength, speed over brute force, elegance over mass. These positive associations run toward youth, excitement, and freedom, but also toward self-control and functionality."[22]

Riddles are another kind of quest. As a genre, the riddle symbolizes our search for order in the world.[23] For some individuals, solving riddles becomes their life's quest. As a boy, I consumed the Sherlock Holmes detective stories, reading by flashlight under my quilt long after my parents had commanded "Lights out!" No mystery seemed beyond the reach of Holmes's powers of deduction.

During my research for this book, I came across a writer with an identical literary experience. Except that for Linda Fairstein, her enchantment with the fictional detective led her into thirty years of service in the homicide department of Manhattan's District Attorney's office.[24]

Existentialists. Spiritual seekers. Artists. Scientists. Detectives. All these (and others) embody the life script of the quest. But what happens when the quest falters? Not to worry. Help may be at hand—at least, it was during the self-help boom of the 1970s. That decade offered us a narrative solution to the "midlife crisis," via the writings of popular psychologist Gail Sheehy. Her books *Passages* (1977) and its sequel *Pathfinders* (1982) borrow resources from the archetypal quest (or "romance") script. Far from being a disaster, a midlife crisis can (we are told) become a turning point toward the truer realization of one's aspirations.[25]

In Sheehy's model, our life trajectory begins with youthful optimism about the personal "dream" we strive to realize. Mid-life is, typically, the time when reality pushes back via reminders of mortality (for instance, the death of one's parents). The ensuing feeling of futility brings us to a crisis, a crossroads.

Those who find a path beyond the crossroads must pass three tests, resembling those ordeals experienced by heroes in classic romances (and known by their Greek labels):

| first test | *agon* | the hero must confront the negative forces in battle |
| second test | *pathos* | the hero must suffer loss in the life-and-death struggle |
| third test | *anagnorisis* | the hero must recognize, by discovery or epiphany, the deeper meaning and truer realization of their quest |

21. McAdams and Logan, "Life Stories of Academics," 106.
22. Ibid., 94–95.
23. Tobias, *20 Master Plots*, 121.
24. Fairstein, "*Sherlock Holmes* by Doyle," 76
25. For summary and critical assessment of Sheehy's work, see: Murray, "Literary Pathfinding," 276–92; Murray, "Construction of Identity," 176–205.

One could, perhaps, "Christianize" this model by tweaking the second and third tests. In the *pathos* phase, one can ask oneself, was my personal dream a call from God, or (more likely) a self-gratifying or self-exalting fantasy? In the *anagnorisis* phase, one may become open to God-inspired scripts that replace one's youthful aspirations.[26]

Midlife crisis, reconfigured as the pivotal episode of a quest (or romance) script, may explain the upsurge of marathon running in the seventies and eighties. In 1983, fresh out of college, I enrolled in my first (and only) marathon. The whole 26.2 miles. Why? Aged twenty-three, I was not an obvious candidate for a midlife crisis. Then again, my post-college life was directionless. Living back home with my parents, I had failed to fulfill my "early promise" as a scholar.

My marathon experience meshed with the stories of many first-timers, especially the over-thirty crowd undergoing genuine mid-life crises. For such folk, the marathon was a romantic quest, culminating in an ordeal with transcendent rewards for the hero:

> Part of the shared mythology concerning the marathon were notions such as the "wall." Runners expected to encounter the "wall" near the end of the event, when their supplies of body energy would be exhausted and they could continue only by sheer will and commitment. If the will was sufficient, then entrants expected to be able to conquer this obstacle and experience the "runner's high," a euphoric feeling of invulnerability and transcendence of bodily limits.[27]

Viewing the marathon as a quest dovetails nicely with the "journey" metaphor often used for quests (and often a literal component of the genre's plotline). In spatial terms, the journey metaphor is unidirectional, orientated toward the endpoint (the "finishing line").

We can picture other narrative genres using spatial metaphors. In chapter 8, we discussed the plotline labeled "voyage-and-return" (a "round-trip" metaphor). This narrative archetype symbolizes the impact of disruptions of routine existence, by plunging the protagonist into a new world, from which the protagonist emerges enriched. Often the plunge is accidental or casual. But those who know the power of the plotline plunge very intentionally, hoping to return as a renewed self.

## Voyage-and-Return

Many people deliberately risk versions of this plot to generate an interesting life story. Writers seem especially vulnerable to this lure. Think of George Orwell (*Down and Out in Paris and London*), choosing to live on the streets with homeless vagrants, in order to chronicle the experience. Or Hemingway (surely the "patron saint" of this life-genre). Tracy Kidder testifies:

> I decided to become a writer because I wanted to be a romantic figure like Hemingway. He introduced me to the idea of the writer as himself a hero. It would be unfair . . . to blame him for the fact that I went to Vietnam as a soldier, but not entirely unfair to blame him for some of the romantic notions that were rattling around in my head when I went. At its best, his prose . . . made the

---

26. Cf. Tripp, *Lost in the Middle*.
27. Murray, "Construction of Identity," 184.

writing part of being a writer seem like the easy part. Once you'd performed heroic deeds ... you just told your story in declarative sentences strung together with lots of *ands*.[28]

The scripts lived by Orwell and Hemingway belong to an exceedingly broad and diverse cluster of narratives, which we may label *adventures*. According to psychologist Karl E. Scheibe, much of our behavior, individual and collective, only makes sense when viewed as adventures undertaken to generate life stories.[29]

Scheibe views *Don Quixote* from this perspective. The novel bubbled up from the cauldron stirred by Europe's sustained efforts to explore the globe.[30] Behind Don Quixote, the legends of King Arthur and his knights: "Lancelot and his mates leave the docile pleasures of the castle for the unpredictable adventures awaiting in the wild ... So strong is this story ... that our current attempts to construct self-narratives are still pulled and formed by its mythic force."[31]

These archetypes express our need to foreground novelty, variety, and risk whenever the background of routine and security stultifies us. Adventures offer thrills, a plotline of "fear, voluntary entry, and hope for survival."[32] If we live to tell the tale, the tale itself becomes our supreme gain. We have a life story. Other people will listen.

The genre of the lived adventure features innumerable specific tales: travel; roller-coaster rides; sport; gambling; etc. (the list is endless). The thrill, and the greater prize of a life story, may be experienced directly or vicariously. (In the interests of full disclosure: When my soccer team, Chelsea FC, at last [and against improbable odds] attained the "holy grail" by becoming champions of Europe, in a don't-dare-to-watch penalty kick shootout, my wife expected my reaction to be an unleashing of ecstatic euphoria. Instead, I sat with uncanny calmness, "reasoning" that, since I "shared" in Chelsea's triumph, none of the myriad problems in the rest of my life had any weight whatsoever.)

Scheibe highlights sport and gambling as the most popular modern American adventures. "Common games of sport and gambling are but stripped down, stylized and abbreviated dramas, inviting the direct or vicarious participation of masses of people seeking for some adventure, no matter how miniscule, to provide story matter for their lives."[33] Although my marathon-running script is now thirty years old, it still shapes my personal identity. Periodically, I retrieve my bronzed medallion, with its faded sash, and run my fingers over the icon that speaks of my ability to overcome.

According to Scheibe, sport and gambling have replaced warfare as the main sources of adventure. Like warfare, sport and gambling offer the prize of thrills and glory, plus a tale to tell.[34]

28. Kidder, "*Collected Stories* by Hemingway," 91 (italics in original).
29. Scheibe, "Self-Narratives and Adventure," 129–51.
30. Ibid., 132.
31. Ibid., 133.
32. Ibid., 136.
33. Ibid., 134.
34. Ibid., 129–31.

If adventures enable individuals to construct an identity, the same may be true of nations. Scheibe classifies Kennedy-era policies as a national striving for adventure.[35] Recall the intoxicating "brinkmanship" of the Cuban missile crisis. Or the "Space Race": What, apart from "winning," did America actually win by landing a man on the moon?

So far, we have discussed the quest and the voyage-and-return as common life scripts. Both involve spatial metaphors (journey; round trip). Let us now focus on another common life script, one involving a *vertical* spatial metaphor: the plotline of *ascent* (stereotypically, "rags-to-riches").

## Ascent

As we noted above, this plotline exerts a powerful tug upon adolescents. A time of awakening to literature coincides with a strong call to establish one's own identity and independence. Nothing like a good coming-of-age novel to draw out a fledgling voice. And no fictional character has given so much voice to so many readers as J. D. Salinger's creation Holden Caulfield (*The Catcher in the Rye*).[36]

Coles gives a poignant example of a teenage boy named Phil, afflicted with polio, bedridden in hospital, deprived of the use of both legs.[37] Denied action, Phil became an observer. And he observed through the lens provided by Holden Caulfield, in his merciless exposure of inauthentic people ("phonies"). How to be authentic, how to avoid becoming a "phony"—this became Phil's story of ascent.

Stories of ascent typically involve the struggle to transcend something *oppressive* in the social milieu of the protagonist. Charles Dickens, shaped by personal experience, became the master narrator of this genre. "Dickens had known the harsh life of poverty, even—when he was a child—debtor's prison, with his family."[38]

Oppressive social milieus can take many forms. As a teenager, NPR reporter Maureen Corrigan devoured Dickens's *David Copperfield*. The novel crystallized her dread of being "swallowed up in mediocrity," of being "buried alive in a lifetime of mindless work."[39]

As a teenager, I shared her dread of a lifetime of mindless work. Back in the seventies, my hope of ascent came not from fiction, but from biography. Specifically, the life of world chess champion Bobby Fischer. I was a good-enough chess player to be seduced by his script (but, sadly, nowhere near good enough to replicate his success on the sixty-four squares). The teenage Fischer always brought a pocket chess set to school, for use during "boring" classes. When teachers confiscated the chess set, he continued analyzing the moves in his head. Inspired by his example, I would bring a chess set to geography lessons, perching it ostentatiously upon my desk, inviting its confiscation in the hope of activating the Fischer script.

35. Ibid., 141–43.
36. E.g., Berg, "*Catcher in the Rye* by Salinger," 23–25; Hoffman, "*Catcher in the Rye* by Salinger," 84–85.
37. Coles, *The Call of Stories*, 37–39.
38. Ibid., 75.
39. Corrigan, "*David Copperfield* by Dickens," 59–61.

Looking back, I still have no regrets. The mental exertions of chess honed my analytical imagination (pretty useful for a professor). Even more, the monk-like dedication of the chess player kept me from many of the behavioral trainwrecks of my teenage peers.

Stories of ascent may have appeal beyond adolescence. In chapter 2, I give the backstory of this book. In essence, I view this book as the "protagonist" in a plot of ascent. The book (personified!) struggles to achieve mature expression (or at least adolescent vocalization) of the embryonic idea conceived shortly after my father's funeral in 2008. (I'll let the reader guess what is oppressive in the book's social milieu.)

In this chapter so far, we have explored life plots using the genres of ascent, voyage-and-return, and quest. The latter two (in particular) suggest that Don Quixote is alive, well, and mounted on horseback. By contrast, Saint George (the dragon-slayer) seems to have been thrown off his horse before arriving at battle. With the ascendancy of postmodernism, life plots based on the "dragon-slaying" archetype have dwindled, as the border between good and evil has grown fuzzy.

Not that this plotline is extinct. Hemingway's *For Whom the Bell Tolls* may still inspire solidarity with those who suffer and resistance against their oppressors.[40] Chesterton's *The Man Who Was Thursday* may still inspire resistance "against the anarchy in the world, against those who would destroy, whether by bombs or by indifference."[41]

## Dragon Slaying

In our time, one event universally labeled evil (at least on American soil) occurred on September 11, 2001. What were you doing that morning, just after nine o'clock Eastern Time? I was about to take a train into Manhattan to teach. Watching the twin towers collapse, I must have entered a trance-like mental state equivalent to shellshock. Eventually, I phoned one of my students, Chris. He was okay. But, no, he didn't think I should try to make it to Manhattan to teach my Hebrew class.

In the aftermath, I seriously contemplated converting my knowledge of ancient Hebrew into knowledge of Arabic. (The two languages are very similar.) I could work for the CIA, I reasoned, and help translate intercepted Arabic messages from terrorist networks.

A couple of years ago, I was at a dinner table with two randomly-chosen trustees of my seminary. Both, it transpired, had boys aged twenty-five who served in the armed forces. Not being overly-enthusiastic about the military myself, I asked what had motivated their sons' choice of career. Simultaneously, the trustees gave a one-word reply: 9/11.

There may still be dragons worth slaying. However, postmodernism can still warn us about the seductions of the good-versus-evil archetype. All too easily, the script can seduce us into legitimizing violence. By way of illustration, let us consider the phenomenon of Armenian terrorism. You probably need some backstory. Around the time of the Second World War, Turkish troops slaughtered over 1.5 million Armenians, an atrocity

---

40. McCain, "*For Whom the Bell Tolls* by Hemingway," 109–11.
41. Perry, "*Man Who Was Thursday* by Chesteron," 137.

"called the 'silent genocide' since it has always been denied by the Turkish government."[42] The 1970s witnessed a wave of Armenian terrorism "in response" to the silent genocide.

However, Armenian scholar Khachig Tölölyan refuses to reduce such terrorism to political protest. He argues that Armenian terrorism must be understood as an attempt to construct a narrative identity.[43] Robbed of their homeland by acts of genocide, the Armenian Diaspora preserved their identity by reciting the stories of national heroes. In Sunday School, Armenian-Americans would recite, "I am Armenian, I am Armenian, the grandchild of valiant Vartian."[44] Vartian who? The *fifth century* Armenian leader, who resisted unto death Persian attempts to impose the Zoroastrian religion upon his people. Armenian terrorists garb their actions in Vartian's clothing, leading Tölölyan to claim:

> [Armenian terrorism] is not the product of a particular individual's alienation, but the manifestation of a desire to give one's individual life an iconic centrality in the eyes of the community, which professes to value certain forms of behavior articulated in narratives.[45]

> The true audience of Armenian terrorism remains the Armenian Diaspora, whose fraying culture is constituted to a remarkable degree by old stories, and who see in contemporary terrorists Vartan's refusal to abandon cultural identity and national rights.[46]

If the downside of dragon-slaying narratives appears in the tendency to demonize the "other," the tendency of *comedic* plotlines works toward humanizing the other. Take Wilfred Owen's poem "Strange Meeting," written in response to the First World War. The poem imagines a deceased soldier descending into Hades. As he prods the slumbering corpses, one stands up. Who is he? This resident of Hades delivers a speech to the newly-arrived soldier, which terminates in the haunting identification, *"I am the enemy you killed, my friend."*[47]

## Comedy

In the classic comedic plotline, reconciliation happens via moments of recognition or epiphany, when a character learns to see the "other" in a new light. In life, comedic literature itself can provoke the insight that leads to reconciliation.

In 1963, Robert Coles's wife was teaching in Atlanta, Georgia, in one of the first racially desegregated schools in the South. "When Jane Austen wrote *Pride and Prejudice* she could not have known its possible value for Americans caught up in racial conflict."[48]

---

42. Kearney, *On Stories*, 141.
43. Tölölyan, "Motivation of the Terrorist," 99–118.
44. Ibid., 108.
45. Ibid., 111.
46. Ibid., 117.
47. Owen, "Strange Meeting," 96.
48. Coles, *Call of Stories*, 40.

Indeed, Austen's book was doubtless on the syllabus merely as a "classic," not with any agenda. Nevertheless, a white teenage student named Laura was able to connect the dots: "I guess a lot of us [white] folks are as proud as can be, and we've got our prejudices . . . There's prejudice going in both directions, and there's pride going in both directions."[49]

Racial conflict cries out, rather obviously, for true comedic resolution. Many (less obvious) situations also benefit from efforts to embody the wisdom enshrined in comedy. Consider the case of David, a thirty-five-year-old advertising executive.[50] Long and demanding hours at work have rendered him intolerant of his wife and children, and irritable toward them. David's solution? Run a marathon. Murray explains the narrative logic: "Briefly, 'comedy' involves the victory of youth and desire over age and death. Conflict in comedy usually deals with the repression of desire in society, which is released in the course of an adventure or festivity by means of which a healthier social unit is restored."[51] For David (and many like him), the marathon is the "adventure or festivity" that frees his identity from the corporate treadmill, rejuvenating him for a healthy relationship with his family.

Marathoners like David "shared the feeling of amused distance from the possible competitive role they might take in the event."[52] Festivity, leading to restored relationships, was the goal. How different from those competitors (discussed above) who viewed the marathon through the lenses of a romantic quest! For David, dropping out of the race when he encountered the "wall" would not undermine his identity. For those using the marathon to overcome a midlife crisis, dropping out would threaten to destroy their identity.

These case studies offer a valuable generalization: the meaning of an action to an agent depends entirely on the narrative they have chosen to inhabit.

In discussing comedic plotlines, we have noted that comedic literature (like *Pride and Prejudice*) can trigger the real-life epiphanies that promote social reconciliation. Similarly, real-life experiences of personal renewal may be triggered by reading stories of *rebirth*. In plots of this archetype, an externally-imposed affliction brings one into a death-like condition. Typically, a gift from outside oneself is needed to break the curse. Stories of rebirth can become the external gift that begets hope and provides deliverance from the deathly affliction.

## Rebirth

For many survivors of abuse, rebirth was experienced through reading Maya Angelou's *I Know Why the Caged Bird Sings*. One survivor testifies: "This book's pages dissolved the bars of my cage, and I felt myself fly free for the first time . . . [The book] instilled in me the pivotal message that I could transcend the nightmare . . . of abuse."[53]

---

49. Ibid., 43.
50. As discussed by Murray, "Construction of Identity," 185–86.
51. Ibid., 181.
52. Ibid., 186.
53. SARK, "*Caged Bird* by Angelou," 149–50.

A beautiful instance of the rebirth archetype lived out. Sadly (as with other plots), we often witness ugly distortions of the rebirth script. Christopher Booker describes the scenario:

> The archetype of Rebirth ... is certainly one which can exercise an enormously compelling hold over the ego, as we see whenever people imagine that they can escape in an outward fashion from some way of life that has become like a prison to them. They may imagine that by bailing out from an unsatisfactory marriage or job without properly understanding why their life has been unsatisfactory, they can "make a new start" which will solve all their difficulties.[54]

Quests. Adventures. Ascents. Dragon-Slayings. Comedies. Rebirths. Most of us, at some point, have heard (however faintly) the call to script our life according to one of these plotlines. But what of tragedy?

## Tragedy

A plot whose protagonist is destroyed by the greater forces of reality. Many of us end up there, unintentionally. With hindsight, we may trace how our choices have produced tragedy, and predictably so. Some of us even gain comfort from viewing our lives, retrospectively, in the image of the noble sufferer of certain types of tragedy.[55]

However, does anyone consciously start out seeking to embody a tragic storyline? To answer yes seems absurd ... until we consider the intellectual and artistic movement known as romanticism. Romanticism flourished in Europe from around 1760 to 1830.[56] Its legacy persists into the present.

Read the following description of romantic thinkers, and observe their enthusiastic embrace of the tragic plotline: "They believed in the necessity of fighting for your beliefs to the last breath in your body ... they believed in the value of martyrdom as such, no matter what the martyrdom was martyrdom for ... they believed that minorities were more holy than majorities, that failure was nobler than success."[57] In the nineteenth century, romanticism found a supreme artistic embodiment in Wagner's epic music drama *The Ring*:

> [Wagner's message] is the appalling nature of unsatisfiable desire, which must lead to the most fearful suffering and ultimately to the immolation in the most violent fashion of all those who are possessed by a desire which they can ... neither avoid nor satisfy. The result of this must be some kind of ultimate extinction: the waters of the Rhine rise and cover this violent, this chaotic, this unstoppable, this incurable disease by which all mortals are affected.[58]

---

54. Booker, *Seven Basic Plots*, 585–86.
55. Murray, "Construction of Identity," 198–200.
56. Berlin, *Roots of Romanticism*, 9.
57. Ibid., 10.
58. Ibid., 155.

In the twentieth century, romanticism expressed itself in the philosophy of existentialism.[59] Existentialism valorizes the heroic individual, who—in defiance of an intrinsically purposeless cosmos—attempts to create purpose by a pure act of will, a script akin to rolling a too-heavy rock to the top of a hill, only to watch gravity defeat the enterprise. "Tragedy 101" in a nutshell.

And then there is Jesus of Nazareth, who seems to have enthusiastically embraced a script with a strongly tragic dimension:

> Now they were on the way up to Jerusalem, and Jesus was leading them . . . And he took the twelve aside again, and began to tell them what was about to happen to him: "Look, we are going up to Jerusalem, and the Son of Man will be betrayed to the chief priests and scribes, who will condemn him to death and deliver him to the Gentiles, who will mock him, spit on him, whip him, and kill him." (Mark 10:32–34)[60]

To end our trek through the narrative archetypes, we should briefly mention the monomyth (discussed in chapter 7). Of all the storylines, this one claims to be the ur-narrative, the single plotline that can encompass all or most of the others.

## The Monomyth

No one has advanced the notion of subconscious archetypes more than Freud and Jung. No surprise, then, that both men structure their autobiographies according to the dictates of the monomyth. In constructing their life stories, some factual tweaking was necessary. The tweaking attests a deep desire for a personal identity validated by the monomyth:

> Jung repeatedly shows that in hero myths the protagonist is often cast-out from his own land to wander the world where he makes a great discovery with which he then returns to his people. The stories of both Freud's and Jung's self-analyses conform to this pattern. They left the normal terrain of consciousness on inward journeys of discovery where within the unconscious realm they grappled with the demons of human nature in order to return as enlightened souls to minister to humankind. Jung and Freud both knew the myth of the hero and the necessity of his being rejected. Each of them ennobled himself by accommodating his life story to its narrative pattern. Both men were extremely sensitive to criticism because each felt he had discovered the greatest of truths. They therefore took their reviewers' lack of universal acclaim or studied indifference as rejection. We need not follow them in this misreading which led them and their followers to produce the story of the rejected prophet for this tale is inconsistent with the actual reviews and the rapid acceptance of both men's ideas into the canon of Western thought.[61]

---

59. Ibid., 164–66.
60. For discussion of Mark's Gospel as tragedy, see Bilezikian, *Liberated Gospel*.
61. Steele, "Deconstructing Histories," 264.

Part 3: How Stories Change Lives

## BUT I STILL HAVEN'T FOUND WHAT I'M LOOKING FOR

Wait a second. If people are living stories, and if stories change lives, why are so many of us so screwed up? Are we choosing bad stories? Are our stories changing us for the worse? Good questions, generating more conflict than I can handle in one chapter. But I will offer three challenges to my fellow Don Quixotes out there. As in many a classic quest, these challenges are offered in ascending order of difficulty.

## Uniqueness

When constructing your personal life story, you can't buy it off the shelf, it must be tailored to fit your unique character plus setting. Listen to the wisdom of Michael Novak:

> We can impose a story upon events . . . we can understand a story as if it were something to copy, imitate, or follow like a predetermined script. To treat a story in this way, however, is to adopt it as if it were an abstract principle, to be followed by rote. Whereas a principle is honored in every observance, a story merely copied is a cliché. To avoid being hackneyed, a story must be fresh, unique, singular. Above all, it must spring from inner sources of creativity and perception. A story treated like a principle can be boring, rigid, and inflexible. But a story treated like a story is full of invention, surprise, and originality.[62]

Sadly, in the Christian community, there are many well-meaning folk eager to impose a one-size-fits-all narrative upon each and every one of us. (If you've spent any time in church, you know what I'm talking about.) In my early twenties, young in the faith, I wanted to resist the constrictive narratives on offer, but lacked the resources. Nevertheless, I continued to search for an authentic storyline. Encouragement came from a very strange place—the promise of Jesus in Revelation 2:17: "I will give him a white stone, and on the stone a new name written which no one knows except him who receives it."

If individuals must search for the "white stone" of authentic narrative identity, so must communities. "There are some masterplots, very loosely conceived, that would appear to be universal: the quest, the story of revenge, seasonal myths of death and regeneration. But the more culturally specific the masterplot, the greater its practical force in everyday life."[63]

The community-forming narratives of the four Gospels do indeed work with archetypes (see chapter 10 above). However, their diversity implies the need to find a version of the Jesus story that "fits." I love how the early church depicted the four canonical Gospels using the imagery of the four mythical beasts from Revelation 4:7. Each bears witness to Jesus, but in its own way. Mark roars like a lion. John soars like an eagle. Matthew, beginning with Jesus' genealogy, has a human face. Luke, beginning in the temple, has the face of a sacrificial beast, the ox.[64]

---

62. Novak, *Ascent of the Mountain*, 65.
63. Abbott, *Introduction to Narrative*, 43.
64. See the exploration of this symbolism in Burridge, *Four Gospels*.

My next challenge comes as a question. Do we need to be the protagonist? Or, does story-wisdom include acceptance of a "lesser" role? Along the lines, perhaps, of, Matthew 20:16 ("The last will be first, and the first last")?

## Minor Characters

Most of us can resonate with the opening sentence of Dickens's novel *David Copperfield*: "Whether I shall turn out to be the hero of my own life, or whether that station will be held by anybody else, these pages must show."[65]

In reality, we all belong to multiple dramas playing out simultaneously. In many of these dramas, we (temporarily!) adapt to playing lesser roles in scripts centered on other characters. Nevertheless, I tend to view these other scripts as less important than those in which I am the hero.

Let's grasp this nettle. If you imagine your life as a story, do you see yourself as the "main character"? If so, does this ever trouble you? Is assuming the role of "main character" the irreducible equivalent of egocentricity?

Whenever I discuss this book with (Reformed) Christians, and offer up the your-life-is-a-story proposal, I can pretty much guarantee they will fire back, "But *we are not* the main character!" (If only I had a nickel for every time . . . ) Obviously, they mean that *God* is (or should be) the "main character" in everyone's story. And, at some level, it's hard to disagree. (One only has to read, say, the letter of Paul to the Ephesians, to see how all of history unfolds "to the praise of God's glory.") I'm not questioning the doxological motivation of my Reformed friends.

However, I do wonder if our term "main character" gets used in different ways by different people. And—surprise—some of these usages may not be incompatible with the doxological concerns of Reformed folk.

When you hear the term "main character," what synonyms spring to mind? Does the term connote "hero"? Does it imply the "most important" agent? The game-changer? The (morally) best character? All these could be valid definitions—but they are not the only possible definitions.

Please read the next sentence very carefully. For a literary critic, "main character" need mean no more than a constant presence, *whose experiences give cohesion to the narrative arc* of the story. That is what (and all) I mean when I encourage readers to see themselves as protagonists in a plot.

On this definition, we may (from our own point of view) be the "main character" in our personal narrative. But that does not make us the best character, or the game-changer. For example, suppose we tell (like many Christians, Reformed or not) our personal narrative using a rebirth plot archetype ("born again!") Recall our discussion of the rebirth archetype (in chapter 8). In such narratives, the main character falls into a death-like state—perhaps through his/her own failings—and only returns to life through the loving intervention of another agent. The main character's downward slide

---

65. Quoted in Corrigan, "*David Copperfield* by Dickens," 60.

into powerlessness, and revival through the love of another, gives unity to the dramatic arc of the rebirth narrative.

Or consider a cinematic example. Who is the "main character" in the 1989 classic *Dead Poets Society*? Robin Williams, right? The charismatic school teacher, John Keating, whose inspiration made his boys' lives extraordinary. Well, Keating certainly was the catalyst, the game-changer, for his students. But (as the title of the film suggests), the plot can be seen as the students' coming-of-age, finding their voice. The archetype of ascent. The boys who (inspired by Keating) reconvened the Dead Poets Society—their collective experience provides the narrative arc of the film, giving coherence to the plot. In that sense, the boys are the main character. (As confirmation of this, recall how many key scenes Keating is absent from.)

To expand this discussion, consider the storyline of the Old Testament. From Exodus onwards, whose experiences give coherence to the dramatic arc? *Israel's*! So, from the point of view of narrative unity, Israel is the main character. And this observation is totally compatible with recognizing that—from other points of view—God is the main character. The game-changer. The morally superior agent.

As we (hopefully) learned in chapters 7–10 of this book: "point of view" is an essential element of story; any story can be told from multiple viewpoints, generating multiple plot descriptions; and the hologram of all these plot analyses helps bring out the riches of the meaning of the narrative.

Applied to Scripture (and to life): Even if history is (as some say) "*His*-story" (i.e., God's story), there are benefits (doxological and otherwise) to telling that story from multiple viewpoints. Including versions in which you and I, for a moment, get to be the "main character" (even if only in terms of plot coherence).

But back to the nagging question. If stories can (and should) be told from multiple viewpoints, are there merits in seeing myself as a "minor" character in the stories playing out around me? I believe so. (And, in case you are worried, nothing in this book need be thrown out if you take a vacation from being protagonist. You would simply start viewing life through the lenses of other agents, by asking how their experience can give narrative coherence to the events unfolding around you.)

How might we consciously function as a "minor" character in someone else's story? For guidance, we can turn to the literary critics, scholars who have cataloged the various functions of minor characters in literature.

For example, Claude Bremond lists the following ways we might interact with a "protagonist."[66] We might be an *influencer* of his/her thinking—toward wisdom or toward folly—in present time. Or we might function as an *enhancer* (or degrader) of his/her prospects in future time. Or we might be the *rewarder* (or retributor) of the protagonist's actions from his/her past time.

In my vocation as professor, I obtain guidance from V. Propp's study of Russian folktales.[67] He mentions two minor archetypal functions in quest narratives—the "dispatcher" and the "donor."

---

66. Bremond, *Logique du Récit*, 135, 160, 242–307.
67. Propp, *Morphology of the Folktale*, 32–42, 72–78, 110–11.

If I imagine my students as protagonists, here's how these minor roles help me become part of their story. The "dispatcher" informs the hero of the absence of something essential to life, and provokes the hero's journey to find what is missing. How (I ask myself) can I help students see their need for wisdom? (Especially those who already have all the answers before they arrive at seminary, and only enrolled for the diploma.) Once students begin their quest for wisdom, they eventually need a "donor"—someone who imparts a gift to be unwrapped in the future, in the hour of great need, to ensure the successful completion of their quest for wisdom. In class, I sometimes propose ideas that make little sense in students' present intellectual framework—ideas that may prove surprisingly helpful once that framework has collapsed.

Let me wrap up this discussion of roles with a question: Could one definition of "love" be the willingness to be a "minor character" in the stories of other people?

## Pointers

Finally, a troubling confession from a book expounding the moral value of great literature:

> Have you noticed what goes on when literature professors get together in a room? Are they saved by George Eliot or Chekhov, by Shakespeare or Dickens or Hardy, or even by Dostoevsky and Tolstoy, who tried like hell to save us all, poor bastards that we are? Tolstoy had one hell of a time trying to live up to his own ideals—and boy, did his wife and kids have to pay for the moral struggle he waged . . . So it isn't "the humanities," or something called "fiction" (or "poetry") that will save you . . . Books shouldn't be given *that* job, to save people.[68]

Sober words, which we tend to ignore. Our typical response to narrative: Copy this character! Live the plotline! Literature gets co-opted into our self-improvement projects.

But what if (as speculated in chapter 8) archetypal stories are merely pointers to a definitive narrative, the narrative of Jesus?

Unlike any other classic story, the story of Jesus offers us a *living relationship* with the protagonist. The implication is that his story becomes our story, if we are in union with him.[69] Christian baptism symbolizes our participation in Jesus' death and resurrection (Romans 6). In him, we actually get to live out the "monomyth." His death slaughters the dragon of all our egotistical vices. His resurrection rebirths us.

\* \* \* \* \*

---

68. William Carlos Williams, quoted in Coles, *Call of Stories*, 110–11 (italics in original).
69. Cf. Lucie-Smith, *Narrative Theology*, 197.

# 14

## A Self-Image Problem

### THE BREAKFAST CLUB

FIVE HIGH SCHOOL STUDENTS must spend their Saturday morning together in detention. Their punishment: write an essay. The topic: "Who you think you are."

This snapshot comprises the "inciting incident" from the 1985 movie *The Breakfast Club*. Initially, each of the five teenagers comes with a label: "the brain"; "the athlete"; "the basket case"; "the princess"; "the criminal." Partly imposed by others, these images govern the identity and behavior of the protagonists. By the end of the movie, the five have outgrown their labels. Their essay summarizes their new insight: "Each one of us is a brain . . . and an athlete . . . and a basket case . . . a princess . . . and a criminal."

When you were growing up, did others put any labels upon you? Or, perhaps you gave yourself a label? Whether imposed or self-defined, how did the label affect your identity and behavior?

In our previous chapter, we noted that each person's life story usually has a key metaphor or image for the *role* they play. In this chapter, we explore how stories change lives by giving us new self-images.

According to the philosopher Paul Ricoeur, we humans use two primary devices to navigate our way through the world: narrative and metaphor (story and symbol).[1] And the two are intimately connected, in symbiotic relationship.[2] Images derive from narrative, images evoke narrative. Think of the sacramental bread, wine, and water. The intersection of story and symbol, narrative and metaphor, word and image—this fusion releases energy that transforms us. To harness this energy, we will examine the intersection of story and self-image.

Names and labels. Some we inherit or receive, some we choose. What does your email handle reveal about you? Is it merely your given name(s) with some numerals thrown in, or does it reveal more of your sense of self?

In the West, our given names have become muted symbols—sounds that no longer evoke a particular image or activity or backstory. However, a little reflection often

---

1. See the summary of Ricoeur in Buttrick, "Story and Symbol," 104–5.
2. Eslinger, "Narrative and Imagery," 65–87.

highlights the narrative roots of a name. "Hill" and "Wood" were once the settings for the stories of ancient forebears. "Baker" and "Cooper" (maker of beer barrels) once determined ancestral roles in economic scripts. "Johnson" and "Williamson" tether their bearers to the backstories of William and of John.

In the world of the Bible, names were more than muted symbols. Names revealed a person's character traits, or their role in a story. Accordingly, changed names intersect changed stories.[3] If this is unfamiliar to you, I invite you to do a little research (say in the footnotes of a study bible) on the following transformations: Abram → Abraham (Gen 17:5); Jacob → Israel (Gen 32:28).

Nowadays, since our given names are often muted symbols, *labels* (selected or imposed) tend to be the stronger molders of our identity and behavior. In *The Breakfast Club*, imposed labels scripted the lives of the teenagers. The Brain was expected to get good grades. The Athlete was expected to perform on the field. The labels also identified tribal allegiances within the high school, and helped form tribal boundaries alienating student from student. The film's plot turned on the transcendence of these boundaries, in a comedic narrative of reconciliation. The story arc of bond-formation intersects the breakout from restrictive and divisive labels of self-image.

In the example just examined, character images (labels) drove the storyline. In other instances, storyline determines the image we inscribe on a character. Take storylines of the demise or failure of the main character. Do we view that character positively or negatively? Genre and narrator viewpoint come into play. Was demise the consequence of evil actions by the protagonist? Or was demise the result of social forces crushing the noble aspirations of the protagonist? These genres imagine the protagonist, respectively, as tragic *villain* or tragic *martyr*. Alternatively, was the protagonist's failure a consequence of their vain delusion? The satirical genre imagines the protagonist as a quasi-tragic *fool*.[4]

When you and I suffer decisive setbacks, do we imagine ourselves as martyr (frequently?), fool (sometimes?), or villain (rarely?).

The symbiosis of narrative and imagery extends beyond the plot/character interface. For instance, have you noticed how standard labels for plots often rely on imagery to capture the storyline? We describe several basic plots via spatial imagery (for example, stories of "ascent"; "voyage-and-return"; "journey"). Or, we encapsulate a plot via graphic imagery (for example, "slaying the dragon").

This phenomenon illustrates something bigger: the overlap between the temporal arts (like drama; film; novels; music; etc.) and the static arts (like painting; photography; sculpture; etc.) The static painting can freeze the temporal flow of narrative. And the freezing offers us space for contemplating the movement of time inherent to story.[5] Likewise, labeling a plot with a spatial metaphor like "journey" allows us to grasp the movement of the whole (from where, to where, via what route).

\* \* \* \* \*

3. For a summary of naming in the Bible, see Beeching, "Name," 1050–53.

4. For discussion of the intersections of tragedy and martyr, satire and fool, see Murray, "Construction of Identity," 198–99.

5. For discussion, see Crites, "Narrative Quality of Experience," 84–88.

We are characters in a story. Our characters have images. These images can propel the storyline. And the storyline can redefine the images. Self-image shapes our identity and behavior.

Let us explore these dynamics further, by reflecting on some additional archetypal images of the self. As an on-ramp, I invite you to consider the story of creation in Genesis 1.

In the beginning ... the earth was a formless, chaotic void (Gen 1:2). So, what did God do about it? Well, by a sequence of spoken actions, he produced increasing order out of chaos, as if he imagined structure, pattern and beauty—and then crafted these visions in his artist's studio. He brought definition into the darkness, by separating out spheres of existence, then filling them with entities appropriate for those environments.

At the apex of God's creation—humanity, male and female. Icons of God. Made "in the *image* of God" (Gen 1:26–27). Theologians have (of course!) pondered and probed the meaning of that primordial anthropology—"the image of God." Not to dismiss their investigations—but my proposal is fairly simple and story-based (of course!).

Being human—sharing God's image—means performing (in a finite fashion) the role that God performed in the story of Genesis 1. Bringing order out of chaos, or form out of formlessness. Perhaps as an artist, generating a creative product; or as a scientist, classifying and synthesizing phenomena.

Looking back over the phases of my own life story, the self-image of *ordering-the-chaos* contributes to my identity, my sense of personal continuity amidst the inevitable changes. Allow me to illustrate with some brief biographical snapshots.

My teenage years found me hunched over a chess board. Thirty-two pieces, sixty-four squares. Looks simple enough—but the multiple permutations of moves generate (literally) an astronomical number of possible games. People who've done the math tell us—the number of possible chess games exceeds the number of atoms in the universe!

Plenty of chaos, in other words—more combinations of moves than you can possibly encompass in your brain. Every move you make generates possibilities beyond the power of a super-computer to analyze. So—how do you figure out a successful string of moves, a sequence that leads to victory? Is there a magic formula, a "philosopher's stone"? In that quest lies the addictive power of the game of chess. On the occasions when the moves unfold like the notes of a Mozart symphony, the chess player feels like a master of the universe, a magician weaving enchanted spells.

Fast forward over a decade. I had quit my chess addiction "cold-turkey." I am enrolled in grad school, and seated in a cubicle in the cold basement of my school library. "Greek Linguistics" was my term paper. Laid out in front of me, on the desk of my cubicle—an apparently chaotic jumble of over fifty notecards (three-inches-by-five-inches). On each notecard, the Greek text of a dialogue from the Acts of the Apostles, with the speech-reporting verbs highlighted in yellow. A chaotic, random-looking jumble of variants—"said," "says," "answered," "answered and said" (to name but a few).

Staring at the note-cards, my body cold, my brain numb, I begin to entertain impious thoughts. Maybe "Saint" Luke (author of Acts) didn't really know what he was doing. Perhaps his word choices were the random product of authorial incompetence.

My professor believed otherwise, and had encouraged us to keep searching until we found a pattern of usage. Order amidst the chaos.

It was almost ten o'clock at night. The librarian was walking around the basement, switching off the lights. Suddenly, in the encroaching darkness—light ignited in my brain. I discerned a pattern behind the distribution of speech-verbs in Acts. That discovery felt like the magical insights from my chess-playing years. Inside the miniature kingdom of Greek verbs, I got to play a royal part, bringing the rule of grammatical law to the disorderly texts.

As a bonus, the "magical formula" I received that night became the touchstone that produced my PhD dissertation. And, as an off-shoot, my first published book.[6] Publishers typically reward authors with a few complimentary copies of the printed book. On Friday, July 11, 2014, a package (from Holland) arrived on my porch. Inside, virgin copies of my monograph, still in their shrink-wrapping. My attempt to bring order to the chaos of language phenomena. As I cautiously (with a Swiss army knife) cut through the shrink-wrap, I felt the humbling and awe-inspiring privilege of contact with the divine—contact experienced through living a finite version of the story of Genesis 1.

Well, that's enough of my story for now. As you look back on your own personal narrative, is there a self-image that provides a sense of continuity amidst all the changes?

As for the self-images evoked in my biographical snapshots—does all that stuff about royalty (not to mention wizardry) sound a bit too medieval (or maybe the result of reading too much Harry Potter)? Can such archaic images really help us navigate our course through life? I will explore this question in the section below. To get us there, I invite you to contemplate the following options:

- Consider these four modes of conscious experience: intellect; emotions; physical sensation; imagination/intuition/aesthetics. In which mode of experience do you feel most alive, most authentic, most *you*?

- Now consider these four basic activities: nurturing and organizing; fighting/protecting; building relationships/community; fixing/transforming? In which activity do you feel most alive, most authentic, most *you*?

Your thoughtful answers to these questions may help clarify your self-image, and the storyline you inhabit . . .

## ARCHETYPAL SELF-IMAGES

Magician. Warrior. Lover. King/Queen. Why do these four images recur in stories from vastly different times, places and cultures? In exploring this phenomenon, few scholars have mined deeper than Professor Robert L. Moore. He believes that the four images arise from "four modes of consciousness" proposed by Jung: intuition; sensation; emotion; reason. Moore provides a convenient summary at his own website.[7]

---

6. Smith, *Representation of Speech Events*.

7. Moore, "Theory and Discoveries." (Jung's "four modes of consciousness" are also the basis of the well-known Myers-Briggs Type Indicator personality test.)

Spoiler alert: I have no desire to elevate his hypothesis to any kind of normative status. I merely use his work to continue a conversation about the interplay of self-image and story in shaping our personal identities. The table below is my re-working of his material (most of the vocabulary is his).

| *Archetype* | Royalty | Warrior | Lover | Magician |
|---|---|---|---|---|
| *Mode of Consciousness* | reason | sensation | emotion | intuition |
| *Symbolic Sphere* | cosmos | field | garden | vessel |
| *Primal Activity* | nurturance: ordering; provision | aggression: protection; boundary-formation | affiliation: community; intimacy | wisdom: healing; transforming |

According to Moore, these four archetypal images represent four primal "energies" rooted in our DNA. Energy equals dynamism, drive. And it isn't too hard to see how these archetypal energies drive archetypal plots in real life. Suppose we brainstorm, and interface the table above with the "seven basic plots" discussed in chapter 8. How would images map onto plots? Here are my suggestions . . .

1. The *royal* image meshes with stories of ascent (construed as the protagonist's struggle to gain a sphere of influence, which they can order using their rational faculties).

2. The *warrior* image obviously belongs to "dragon-slaying" plots, dealing with stark external threats to life or well-being. The related activity of boundary formation meshes with the faculty of bodily sensation; from infancy upwards, our bodies educate us concerning the existence of boundaries.

    If we create a *survivor* sub-category of warrior, this meshes with plotlines of *adventure* (deliberate embodiments of "voyage-and-return.") Recall our discussion of war, sport, and amusement parks (in the previous chapter), where we viewed these exposures to danger as attempts to generate a heroic, high-adrenalin life story.

3. The image of self as *lover* is clearly a one-to-one fit for comedic plotlines.

4. The *magician* obviously inhabits quest narratives, since wisdom is frequently the explicit thing lacking and searched for. Furthermore, the magician's use of wisdom to heal or transform obviously meshes with plotlines of rebirth.

We have generated one plausible set of mappings from image to plot, distributing the four images over six of our seven plots. But what of *tragedy*? Well, Moore discusses immature and degenerate expressions of primal energies. For instance, he sees the tyrant as the distortion of the royal image, and the addict as the distortion of the lover image. These distorted images tend to generate tragic plotlines.

If you are anything like me, you probably have a dominant "energy" that you develop at the expense of the others. On his website, Moore offers us a warning:

> Some Jungians romanticize the archetypes. They encourage their clients to find and claim the *particular* archetype or myth that has organized their life. Life then becomes a process of affirming and living out this myth. However, our goal should not be to *identify* with an archetypal pattern, or to allow a mythic expression of it to make our lives what *it* will. For when we romantically *identify* with any archetype, we cease to be viable human beings moving towards wholeness [emphasis his].[8]

In the final clause from this quote ("moving towards wholeness"), Moore subsumes his four archetypal self-images into a narrative of psychic maturation and integration. This *meta*-narrative of *ascent* gives check-and-balance to the meaning of the four self-images. (In similar vein, Christopher Booker synthesizes several archetypal plots, as metaphors for the integration of "masculine" traits of rationality and strength with "feminine" traits of empathy and intuition.[9])

Once again, we see that overarching storylines interpret self-images. Implication: our labels and images of self multiply their power when plugged into a particular plotline.

What plotline does Moore advocate for our lives? An extended metaphor. Ascent/journey to a "center" of life-renewing power and integration; a movement from "chaos" to "cosmos"; an exodus from the "wasteland" to the "sacred space" symbolized by the mountain/city of ancient religions.

Moore gives this extended metaphor cutting-edge by targeting a particular form of *chaos*. He identifies a global malaise he labels "boy monsters." By this, he means male youth deprived of proper expression of "warrior energy," abandoned to destructive channeling of that energy (street gangs and fascist militias).

Modern society, he argues, leaves male youth without a tribe, without elders, and without proper initiation-rituals for directing their energies. If we cannot give our male youth a healthy tribe, with elders and rites-of-passage, the chaos of gangs and militias will only multiply. (Unsurprisingly, Moore is a major theorist behind the "men's movement.")

As a Christian storyteller, how do I react to the narrative Moore is advocating? Well, I can grant the "boy monster = problem" premise. I could also (perhaps) respond, Hey, maybe the *church* can become the tribe for such boys. After all, at its best, the church is a multi-generational institution, equipped with archetypal rites-of-passage (such as baptism).[10]

However, I am a bit reluctant to simply baptize Moore's narrative. After all, the meaning of self-images intersects the *particular* narrative they inhabit. Suppose, then, we bring the four archetypal images into conversation with the story of Scripture. Let's start with the Old Testament, and its major institutional figures.

Interestingly, there are four main players on Israel's stage: prophet, priest, king, and sage. (That plurality may testify to the danger of reliance on a single archetype as guide. For example, as Israel's narrative unfolds, God sent prophets—as a corrective for kings and priests, and as visionaries to overcome limited priestly and kingly perspectives.) How do the Israelite four match up with Moore's archetypes? There seems to be a fit, but

---

8. Moore, "Theory and Discoveries."
9. Booker, *Seven Basic Plots*, 267–69.
10. Cf. Lewis, *Crianza de un Caballero Moderno*.

not one-to-one. (No surprise here. Particular cultures always refract the light from our models via their own prisms.) The following table indicates potential overlaps:

| Old Testament Figure | Archetype |
|---|---|
| Priest | *lover* (empathy and reconciliation) |
| King | *king; warrior* |
| Sage | *magician; king* |
| Prophet | *warrior; magician* |

Solomon embodies the fusion of kingship and wisdom. David embodies the king/warrior fusion. (Moore recognizes that warrior and royal energies naturally ally, since the "focus and discipline" of the warrior gives "ability to follow the vision found in the royal line.")

The prophet is the real oddball. The warrior function finds expression in the "oracles against foreign nations," whereby Yahweh conducted a rhetorical jihad against idolatry.[11] The magician function finds expression in the visionary apocalyptic of the prophets, generating hope for national rebirth.

Thus far, Old Testament archetypal characters form part of the narrative grammar of the Christian story, since the New Testament writers use the images of prophet, priest, king, and sage as lenses for understanding the life of Jesus.

However, the life of Jesus means radical intensification and even redefinition of these four images. (Think of the priest-victim of Hebrews, or the king-crucified of the Gospels.)

Lastly, Moore's "monster boys" need more than a tribe of elders plus initiation rituals. That's a good story as far as it goes. But the Christian narrative offers an authentic union with the protagonist, Jesus. His distinctive energies (warrior, magician, lover, king) flow into us. Like branches nourished by the vine (John 15:1–10), we receive from him the integration and maturation of our misdirected energies. As his story (death, resurrection, ascension) becomes our story, we journey from chaos to cosmos, from wasteland to life-renewing sacred space.

In the final section of this chapter, we expand on the Christian use of narrative images as tools for personal transformation.

## THE WIZARD AND THE PORCUPINE

Most modern Western people regard metaphor as merely an ornamental luxury of verbal communication. You must, they believe, dispense with metaphor if you want to understand what is "really" being said.

Reversing this conventional wisdom, researchers George Lakoff and Mark Johnson have restored metaphor to the chief seat at the banquet table of life: "Metaphor is pervasive in everyday life, not just in language, but in thought and action. Our ordinary conceptual system, in terms of which we both think and act, is fundamentally metaphorical

---

11. Waltke, *Old Testament Theology*, 401–3.

in nature."¹² They illustrate this primacy by noting that our concept and practice of *argument* is governed by the metaphor of *war*: "Many of the things we *do* in arguing are partially structured by the concept of war . . . there is a verbal battle, and the structure of an argument—attack, defense, counter-attack, etc.—reflects this."¹³ The primacy of metaphor challenges our views of Christian ministry, of helping people to change. Especially in a postmodern context, argues Walter Brueggemann, few folk will be transformed by mere moral appeal or bare doctrinal argument: "In a conversation wherein doctrinal argument and moral suasion are operative, people in fact change by the offer of new models, images, and pictures of how the pieces of life fit together—models, images, and pictures that characteristically have the *particularity of narrative to carry them*."¹⁴ This last observation, on narrative as "carrying" powerful imagery into our lives, resonates with the following insight (by another scholar) on the use of religious metaphors:

> Using metaphors provides the *bridge* over which faith moves from the tradition of the community into the life of the individual.
>
> The process of *story-telling* provides the *bridge* for canonical images and metaphors from the community or tradition to the individual.¹⁵

Let's concretize all this in a real-life pastoral counseling case. My friend David Powlison is a sage (a magician, even). Powlison tells the story of Jim, who (reluctantly) approached him for marital counseling.¹⁶ Jim's wife found her husband cold, distant, self-protective. In this story of growing alienation, an upward turn followed Jim's epiphany: "I'm just an *old porcupine* and always have been."

This image of self-recognition captured Jim's prickly, isolationist behavior. A solitary, "outdoor animal," he loved to spend the evening working on garden projects, while his neglected wife languished indoors. In social contexts, Jim easily became defensive, shooting out his porcupine quills whenever he felt criticized.

Powlison offered Jim an alternative self-image: a sheep in God's flock. Unlike porcupines, sheep are collective animals, naturally congregating with other sheep. Unlike self-protective porcupines, sheep rely upon the shepherd for protection. The gospel narrative became the bridge for bringing the sheep metaphor into Jim's life. The story of the good shepherd, who seeks the wandering and isolated sheep, who lays down his life for that sheep, who brings the sheep into relationship with the flock.

By way of counterpoint, another case where someone discovered the destructive root metaphor of their life story, but could not relocate themselves inside a better story. Jefferson A. Singer tells the sad story of Rich, a habitually-relapsing heroin addict.¹⁷ Rich's childhood was disrupted by divorce, resulting from his Harvard-educated father's descent into alcoholism. Rich became a loner, a bookworm, who "imagined himself as

12. Lakoff and Johnson, *Metaphors We Live By*, 3.
13. Ibid., 4 (italics in original).
14. Brueggemann, *Texts Under Negotiation*, 24 (italics mine).
15. Tilley, *Story Theology*, 3 and 5 (italics mine).
16. Powlison, "Illustrative Counseling," 52–53.
17. Singer, "Heroin Addict," 253–77.

a scientist or physician, someone with mastery over the world . . . Rich called this image of himself the *Wizard*."[18]

Sadly, Rich's version of wizardry embodied an unrealistic belief in magical transformations, which eventually led him into drug addiction. "From an early age, he portrayed himself as looking for magical transformations that would bring him a sense of power."[19] Singer puts his finger on the Wizard's root problem: "A lack of insight into the daily application of one's labors toward a desired end. The immediate attraction of drugs for Rich fits nicely—they are . . . vehicles of magical transformation to a sense of mastery."[20]

Once addicted, the unrealistic "wizard" self-image constantly frustrated Rich's efforts at recovery.[21] In rehab, he consumed philosophical and spiritual literature, hoping for deliverance via sudden and instant enlightenment (a quick fix). It never came.

The Wizard's grip was strong. At one particularly low point, Rich seemed to sense the need to replace the unhelpful self-image with a humbler reality, namely, "A recovering drug addict . . . who needs to do an honest day's work and accept where I am in life."[22] However, Rich was unable to locate this embryonic self-image within a hopeful narrative.[23]

Why did the Porcupine change, whilst the Wizard remained trapped? Probe as deep as we may, mysteries will remain. But allow me some speculation. In archetypal "rebirth" plotlines, decisive change comes via a gift or agent external to the protagonist. (Think of folktales like *Snow White* or *Sleeping Beauty*.) However, secular western culture imagines the protagonist as a "solitary individual agent who must carry the entire weight of moral existence through the exercise of free choice."[24] This autonomous individual rebuffs the outside agent who offers the gift of a new narrative image of self. In other words, it's hard for the secular western self to receive God's grace.

To overcome this hardness, argues Rossi, the autonomous self must be immersed in the environment of *public* worship in the church, and exposed to *external* depictions of God's story.[25] In this sphere, word and sacrament (story and symbol) declare with authority, that "God effectively reshapes us, not willy-nilly, but in the image manifest in the life, death, and resurrection of his Son."[26]

Being reshaped in the image of Christ's death and resurrection. A simple phrase, but the story of the cross is no simple plotline. The New Testament writers ransack the imagery of their culture (Jewish/Greco-Roman), seeking analogies for Jesus' rewriting of the human narrative. Theologian Alister E. McGrath offers five images of the cross,

---

18. Ibid., 259 (italics mine).
19. Ibid.
20. Ibid.
21. Ibid., 261, 271.
22. Ibid., 270, 276.
23. Ibid., 270
24. Rossi, "Narrative, Worship, and Ethics," 242.
25. Ibid., 242–46.
26. Ibid., 244.

drawn from diverse spheres: battlefield; prison; law court; rehab clinic; hospital.[27] In the table below, I rework McGrath's images, highlighting their narrative embedding.

As you examine the right-hand column of the table ("Human Problem..."), which version (if any) of the human plight speaks loudest to you?

| Sphere of Imagery | Archetypal Plot | Human Problem → Resolution |
|---|---|---|
| battlefield | slaying dragon | death → immortality |
| prison | slaying dragon* | enslavement → liberation |
| law court | ascent | guilt/shame → vindication |
| rehab clinic | comedic | alienation → reconciliation |
| hospital | rebirth | sickness → healing |

\* Stories of rescue/escape may be viewed as subgenres of "dragon-slaying," since the monster frequently operates as captor ("holdfast"—Booker, *Seven Basic Plots*, 32).

Such hyper-abundance of meaning in the Cross, a treasury of resources for those charged with the care of souls. The multi-dimensional gospel encourages creative recombination of images and storylines, and fresh articulation of faith via narrative images. I end this chapter with one such attempt, a thoughtful effort by David Baily Harned.[28]

In brief, Harned interprets humans via three images defined by an integrating narrative. The images are: *player; sufferer; vandal*. The narrative: the biblical tale of "the two Adams."

First, the images of player and sufferer. Harned links these, respectively, to our fundamental senses of seeing and hearing. How so? Well, consider the different kinds of experience associated with each sense. For example, the dimensions of experience in the following table:[29]

| Experiences of Seeing | Experiences of Hearing |
|---|---|
| external focus | internal focus |
| creates a sense of distance | creates a sense of nearness |
| distinguishes self from others | experiences self in relation to others |
| focus on unchanging objects in space | focus on changing sounds in time |
| self as active ("swivels the lens") | self as passive (absorbs the sound) |
| self as free (looks where it wants) | self as bound (cannot shut out noise) |
| self as *agent* | self as *patient* |

With the last three pairs of contrasts (self as active free agent versus passive bound patient), we see the emergence of the player-versus-sufferer labels. As metaphors, each

---

27. McGrath, *What was God Doing on the Cross*, 45–85.
28. Harned, *Images for Self-Recognition*.
29. Based on ibid., 14–32.

self-image generates a multi-layered description of human life. What are some benefits of identifying oneself via these two metaphors?

## Self as Player

This metaphor takes life as a playing field (for games or sports) or a stage (recall our discussion of the "world stage" in chapter 11). Using this metaphor respects a primary means of socialization: early childhood play activities.[30] And childhood play, with its squabbles and selfishness, challenges our reliance upon sight. Even though our vision is angled and finite, we default to seeing things from our own point of view.[31] And so emerges the first benefit of adopting "player" as our self-image:

- The player image reminds us to play by the rules, to respect the rights of other players.

Other boons follow from taking the player self-image seriously, for instance:[32]

- Rules (laws) become the pre-condition for playing (flourishing), instead of chafing restrictions. In the words of Igor Stravinsky, "Whatever diminishes constraint diminishes strength."
- The self-image of player generates a relaxed, non-proprietary stance toward the world (God is the owner of the "stage," not us!).

Just as seeing and hearing work in tandem, so the image of sufferer complements that of player. Let us briefly discuss this second self-image.

## Self as Sufferer

This image, linked to the experience of hearing, also benefits those who take it seriously. Here are some of its boons:[33]

- a sense of accountability to external commands (encountered through the ear);
- openness to enrichment by other voices;
- solidarity and empathy with others;
- humility, from our sense of vulnerability and contingency.

Harned rightly insists that the player/sufferer images are complementary, just as our vision and hearing work together.[34] To unite the images, he makes use of a common idiom: "Authentic existence means *playing by ear*."[35]

---

30. Ibid., 6–7.
31. Ibid., 2–6.
32. Ibid., 6–7, 36–37.
33. Ibid., 43–62.
34. Ibid., 34–35.
35. Ibid., 62 (italics in original).

That said, he freely grants that even the complex fusion of player/sufferer cannot fully reveal who we are. "Neither the figure of the player nor the image of the sufferer can express the *bondage of the self to its own selfishness*."[36] To reveal this dimension of the human condition, we need another self-image: the *vandal*. Once a player decides to play by their own rules, they have all the potential to morph into a vandal.

## Self as Vandal

When sociologists and psychologists examine the literal vandalism disfiguring our urban environments, they search for a "cause." Harned dares to raise a specter few wish to face: ultimately, vandalism may have no cause beyond evil-for-evil's sake.[37]

A famous incident from Saint Augustine's biography encapsulates this perverse nihilism. "Close to the vineyard of his family there was a pear tree that belonged to a neighbor, a poor tree whose fruit had little appeal to either eye or palate. One night Augustine and a pack of friends stole whole armloads of the pears and threw them to a herd of swine."[38]

Player. Sufferer. Vandal. Does a fusion of these three images give us a true self-recognition? Not by themselves, nor even with any number of supplemental images. For one thing, images are plastic, moldable by their users. Many of us misuse the self-image of Sufferer by construing ourselves as mere blameless victims and refusing to take any responsibility whatsoever for our present condition.[39]

More fundamentally, "When images lose their *anchorage in stories*, they are divested of much of their significance and begin to drift aimlessly, growing enigmatic and increasingly indeterminate."[40] Accordingly, we need a narrative that defines and integrates the three images of self. Harned proposes the story of the "two Adams."

The Adam of the first three chapters of Genesis is player, sufferer, and vandal.[41] A player, Adam was a free agent, using his sense of sight to explore Eden, whilst bound by a command. A sufferer, Adam was constrained by the voice of God, heard announcing the prohibition and affirming the consequence of its violation. Lastly, Adam's choice to play by his own rules means that "the figure of the vandal lurks close by the precincts of the garden of Eden."[42]

The New Testament repeatedly images Jesus Christ as a second Adam, undoing the damage done by the first.[43] Engrafted into the story of Jesus' death and resurrection, we cease to be vandals, and become a distinctive kind of "suffering player":

- A *sufferer* . . . the life of the Christian (like medieval cathedrals) is cross-shaped.

36. Ibid., 77 (italics mine).
37. Ibid., 105–24.
38. Ibid., 123.
39. Cf. ibid., 63–64, on other misuses of the image of "sufferer."
40. Ibid., 133 (italics mine).
41. Ibid., 170.
42. Ibid., 177.
43. Rom 5:12–21; 1 Cor 15:20–22, 45–49; Phil 2:6–9.

Part 3: How Stories Change Lives

- *A player* . . . The practice of "make-believe" characterizes many play activities of children. As children, we naturally construct and inhabit worlds seen in our imaginations. The New Testament presents the cross, resurrection, and ascension of Jesus as the inauguration of a new world (recall our discussion in chapter 10). The Spirit invites us to live "as if" this new world is here, "already now," and to play according to the rules of the new creation.[44]

* * * * *

Our last two chapters have explored the *individual* life story. But when a group participates in a common narrative, change happens at the *collective* level (in addition to the individual level). In chapters 16 and 17, we will discuss "cultural scripts"—stories which shape societies and cultures, nations and tribes. As a bridge to that discussion, our next chapter examines our personal habits as behavioral "scripts," which govern our interaction with people and events on our "world stage."

---

44. Cf. Harned, *Images for Self-Recognition*, 201–6.

# 15

# According to Script

How do you react to stresses and setbacks? As your life unfolds, antagonistic forces threaten to derail you from your destiny. When you encounter failure (or the threat of failure), do your responses reveal any pattern?

In this chapter, we zoom in on the miniature scenes that make up the drama of a personal narrative. As a launchpad, we will examine habitual behaviors that recur in scene after scene after scene. Like the protagonist in the film *Groundhog Day*, we often find ourselves trapped in a repetitive pattern, perhaps a behavioral pattern that we don't even enjoy, or a pattern that harms us. What could explain such behaviors? The core of this chapter will explore the explanatory power of narrative to make sense of scenes that make little sense on their own. The meaning of scenes derives from the plot.

## FROM OCD TO BULIMIA

OK, let me get the usual disclaimers out of the way. I am not a professional psychologist. Nevertheless, looking through narrative lenses offers illuminating perspectives on psychological disorders. Let me begin with a story of behavior not uncommon in foster children.

The social worker from Child Protective Services brought a five-year-old girl to our house around midnight. Her father had recently gone to jail, and she was removed from her home when her mother tested positive for amphetamines (among other substances, legal and illegal). It was the beginning of October. The little girl had already been in two different elementary schools in two months. During that brief time, she had lived in three different apartments—two with her mother, one with a female relative. And now, at midnight, she was deposited in a home with complete strangers (even if we welcomed her with a warm bath and a sock monkey!)

During the first weeks in her new home, our foster child displayed a pronounced pattern of behavior. I'm not qualified to label it OCD (Obsessive-Compulsive Disorder)—but, if I ever needed a pop-psychology tag, that would have been my cliché of choice.

Observe the following scene, played out each day with minor variants. It's bedtime. The foster child is in her pajamas. Bathtime is over. Storytime is over. Still she cannot sleep.

So, as a foster parent in need of a little sleep myself, I confess I resorted to the "one-eyed baby-sitter." I plugged in a tiny DVD player and placed it on her bedroom bookshelf. I went to the living room, and returned with my go-to disc for kindergartners: Donald Duck. What's not to like? "*No-o-o . . . Not* Donald Duck!!" The ferocity of her reply surprised me. "OK, what else?" She demanded a "princess movie." Thankfully, we were well-stocked. I returned with a pile of DVD containers. *Barbie and the Musketeers* (a Barbie film with a feminist slant) met with her approval.

But then she insisted that I place the remaining DVD containers on her bookshelf. In the middle. I complied. Finally, I set down the grey remote control on top of the pile of DVDs. "*No-o-o . . . Not* on top of the DVDs! Put the remote by the side of the DVDs!"

At this point, I confess I got a little bit angry inside. (Who likes being bossed around by a five-year-old?) But I complied, and left the room so she could fall asleep watching *Barbie*.

Frustrating though it may be to foster parents, the foster child's excessive concern to micromanage her environment makes sense in terms of her past narrative. Changing apartments. Changing schools. Changing families. All change, all the time—and unwelcome changes, imposed by adults without reference to the preferences of the child. No wonder her default script becomes: bring order out of chaos. Impose my own order in my own miniature kingdom. Resist the patterns imposed by adults. The foster child strives to recover her (imagined) paradise of stability and tranquility, by resisting external forces of change, and manufacturing a physical and behavioral environment governed entirely by her own preferences.

* * * * *

Moving from children to adolescents, let us now reflect on a brave, candid article by Morwenna Jones, a student at Cambridge University.[1]

As an eighteen-year old, Morwenna was "little miss perfect." She had to be, to stand any chance of getting into Cambridge. Her grades were in the (English equivalent of) straight-A, 4.0 GPA territory.

However, a couple of years before heading to university, she had developed an eating disorder. She recalls "the seemingly endless piles of food I would consume and then bring up again afterwards."[2] This condition is known as bulimia.

Referred for counseling, Morwenna (very perceptively!) told the psychologist, "My condition was connected to an obsessive desire to be the best."[3]

Arriving at Cambridge, her problem intensified. From being the English equivalent of high school valedictorian, she was now surrounded by hundreds of peers of equal or greater brainpower. In Morwenna's words, "I was no longer special . . . Inside that

1. Jones, "How Cambridge University almost killed me."
2. Ibid., para. 2.
3. Ibid., para. 2.

[Cambridge] bubble, where perfection was the norm, falling short of my own expectations tormented me."[4]

As a result of her inner torment, her bulimia worsened, and she spiraled into depression. At her lowest point, she hid in her dormitory room for two whole weeks. Then she had to take a year of absence from her studies. Such "intermittence" is not uncommon among students at elite universities. Nor are eating disorders unusual; according to Morwenna, 28 percent of female students in her college experienced eating disorders.

Is bulimia simply a bizarrely inexplicable response to stresses and setbacks? Few people I know actually enjoy vomiting. And you don't need a doctorate in medicine to recognize the health dangers of the habit. So why do it?

In terms of archetypal plots, Morwenna was obviously and consciously living the storyline of *ascent* (to use the terminology of this book). The upward climb toward the pinnacle of perfection.

In the language of psychologist Silvan S. Tomkins (pioneer of "script theory"), Morwenna (and her fellow-bulimics) respond to failure by switching to a "doable" script.[5] In the academic hot-house, you may lose control of your grades. But you can still control your weight (provided you vomit up whatever you eat). When your perfectionist self-image takes a battering in every other realm, you can still embody the (cultural) norm of perfection in the realm of physical slenderness.

* * * * *

So far, we have analyzed a couple of examples of extreme behavior—in a five-year-old foster child, and an eighteen-year-old college student. For both, the habitual scenes they keep playing actually "make sense" in terms of the plotline of a bigger drama.

Indeed, the minor habitual scenes of your own life offer a window into the major storylines you are living. To unpack this relationship—between your life "scripts" and the "scenes" they generate and govern—we need a brief exploration of some narrative psychology.

## SCRIPT THEORY

You've probably figured out that I don't offer uncritical endorsements for anyone's theoretical models of human behavior. We are way too complex for the simple reductions of most models. That said, my love of Shakespeare draws me toward psychologies based on the world-as-stage metaphor. And so I have learned much from the model known as script theory. Here is my ultra-condensed version.[6]

As you go through life, new and unfamiliar circumstances confront you on a daily basis. What enables you to navigate these new scenes? The answer may be a mental

---

4. Ibid., para. 4.

5. "A *doable* script would prompt the individual to turn to something easy enough to accomplish" (Tomkins, "Script Theory," 187, [italics in original]).

6. My summary is based on ibid., 147–215. For a concise summary and affirmation of Tomkins's script theory, see McAdams, *Redemptive Self*, 222–24.

folder of scripts. Ways to play your role. Scripts inherited and acquired. Big scripts for major life goals, and small scripts for daily experiences on the way to your destiny. Your inventory of scripts governs your behavior in particular scenes.

So scripts are like road maps for navigating unfamiliar territory. But where do our scripts originate? Their roots are probably in childhood, reinforced by cultural patterns and norms, or in the *binarism* of positive and negative experiences. The growing child experiences "blessings" and "curses" in the biological, emotional, and social spheres. Pleasures and pains. Rewards and punishments. In terms of the archetypes of narrative imagery, we experience light and darkness, dreams and nightmares, feasts and famines, paradise and wilderness, "heaven" and "hell."

Over time, the child accumulates a strong personal sense of values, positive and negative. Especially if her culture reinforces these values. She knows what she would like to positively experience in the present and future, and what negatives she would like to avoid experiencing. Furthermore, she is developing a set of strategies to maximize the gain and minimize the pain. Her strategies likely overlap with culturally-approved means for reaching ends (unless she operates on the margins of social approval).

Her scripts enable her to play new and unfamiliar scenes, by giving her the formula "outcome = value + cause."[7] Her scripts tell her what is worth gaining or avoiding in any situation, and how to gain the desirable and avoid the dreadful. Scripts crystallize the plot-wisdom of ends and means. (It would be interesting to explore *proverbs* as embodiments of script theory.)

\* \* \* \* \*

Before we further develop this model, let's pause and consolidate. Here are some questions for reflection.

Think back to your most recent encounter with a new and unexpected situation. How did you react? What emotions did you experience? What pattern of behavior did you seem to default into? Did the situation pose a threat to any of your personal values/goals? Did the situation offer any opportunity for personal enrichment or progress? What were you seeking to gain/avoid in the outcome of the situation? How were your responses to the situation related to your values/goals?

Pulling all your answers together, do you now have clues to one of your personal scripts? If so, I invite you to further reflect on the origin of this script in your early experiences of life. Is the script reinforced by the cultural values and patterns you grew up with?

Script theory dovetails pretty well with the basic theses of my book. Most scripts, major or minor, can be seen as versions of the *archetypal plots* we discussed in chapter 8. This parallel, between scripts and archetypal plots, works both for big overall life-scripts and for smaller scene-governing scripts, because scenes are plots in miniature. Scenes tend toward the same basic five-phase structure of complete narratives (the five-act pattern discussed in chapter 7).[8]

---

7. A formula based on McKee, *Story*, 115–17.
8. Cf. ibid., 233, 257–59; Rainer, *Your Life as Story*, 264–66.

To illustrate the analogy between scripts and plot archetypes, consider the script which Tomkins labels "repetition with improvement"[9]; this is common among athletes (and performing artists), whose main satisfaction in life comes from constantly reaching higher peaks of achievement. Each peak rewards the competitor/performer with the familiar "high" of their youth, when they experienced recognition and a sense of excellence. Each day in training, the athlete pushes their limit. Their script governs their daily scenes in the gym. But the script may also govern their long-term trajectory, as they seek to ascend the Olympic podium. Whether daily in training, or over a lifetime of Olympic competition, their script is the archetypal plotline we have labeled *ascent*. This script empowers them to overcome barriers of physical pain in the gym. The script also allows them to autopilot through numerous daily decisions—what to eat; when to go to bed; etc. Will their diet and sleep habits help or hinder their ascent?

\* \* \* \* \*

We are now ready to contour the model of scripts, by sketching a scheme for the various kinds of script. This scheme will help us revisit the questions that began this chapter—how do you and I respond to stresses and setbacks?

Imagine a large rectangular stage in a theater where plays are performed. That stage, on which the actors move around, may illustrate a handy classification scheme for scripts. To grasp my spatial illustration, think of bigger and smaller chalk circles on the stage. Some big circles become occupied by almost every actor in the play; other small circles only feature one actor or action. So, the bigger the circle, the more universal the script. (This chalk-circle-on-a-stage metaphor would also show us how clusters of scripts may all be specific instances of a more general type.)

With this metaphor in mind, we may classify four different kinds of script: background scripts; ideological scripts; scripts for trajectories; scripts for responding to setbacks.

## Background Scripts

Imagine the empty rectangular stage, before any chalk circles appear. That rectangle would represent universally shared scripts, used by all actors (within a given society) and featuring the most basic and common daily actions. Scripts you and your anonymous neighbor have in common, regardless of your jobs, regardless of differences in your political or religious ideologies.

These scripts are ingrained habits that autopilot us through rudimentary spatial, temporal, and social tasks; awareness of which side of the road to drive on; how much time it takes to get to school; conventions for conducting a conversation; and so on.

We tend not to think about such tasks. Nevertheless, such scripts all embody the basic narrative properties of *means and ends in contexts*. For most of us, these scripts form the *background* to our more interesting personal scripts. (But for people with various disabilities, mastering elementary motor and social scripts may be the biggest challenge they face.)

9. Tomkins, "Script Theory," 164–65.

## Ideological Scripts

Now imagine a huge chalk circle, taking up most (but not all) of the stage. This represents the *ideological* script common to most members of a given society. Ideological scripts provide "an account of... central values, guidance for their realization, sanctions for their fulfillment, their violation, and their justification, and celebration."[10]

This is a big circle, because it validates and informs most of the smaller scripts we live out. But this circle doesn't take up all the stage, because to the left and right are smaller ideological circles, representing scripts followed by those on the cultural margins of society.

Whether mainstream or marginal, these "cultural scripts" provide the world-and-life-view that shapes our particular personal scripts. As we journey through life, these scripts are constant voices in our heads, saying things like "Fight for your rights" or "Defer to those in authority." (Cultural scripts will become the focus of our attention in chapters 16 and 17.)

Whatever our story, two narrative elements always feature: trajectory and setbacks. In other words, where we think we are going, and how we cope with obstacles encountered on the way. Our next two classes of scripts treat these elements in turn. (In terms of our chalk-circles-on-a-stage model, scripts that govern our trajectories, and scripts that govern our responses to setbacks, are smaller chalk circles inside the big circles of our ideological scripts. The big ideological scripts prescribe the values that govern the smaller scripts.)

## Scripts for Trajectories

These scripts govern small scenes of daily living, "episodes" of some length, and even lifelong personal narratives. Trajectory-scripts determine the benefits we seek, the price we are prepared to pay, and the risks we are willing to take. In terms of five-act dramas, such scripts focus on the outcome at the end of act five, the positive emotions of such outcomes, and the means of reaching those destinies.

To classify such scripts, we may start with our basic human tendency to view life-experiences through a grid of positive/negative values. (Blessing/cursing; life/death; dream/nightmare; feast/famine; paradise/wilderness; heaven/hell—however we subjectively define these contrasts.)

Then we may ask four questions: Are our scripts primarily about reproducing positive experiences? Or, are our scripts based on recognizing and repairing negative dimensions of life? Then again, are we haunted by past experiences which combined a perplexing fusion of the intensely positive and the intensely negative? Finally, are our scripts designed to deal with past experience(s) of overwhelmingly negative events?

Let us briefly examine four classes of script arising from our answers to these questions. As you read the following paragraphs, I invite you to reflect on your own tendencies. Are you more about seeking the blessings, or dealing with the curses of the human condition?

10. Ibid., 170.

## Accenting the Positive

Tomkins lists numerous scripts designed for (re-)experiencing positive states or psychological "affluence."[11] Individuals governed by such scripts tend to have enjoyed a large storehouse of positive experiences, and desire more of the same. As I glance over Tomkins's long list of "affluent" scripts, I notice three archetypal plots that typify these scripts: plots of *ascent; quests;* and the *adventure* or *"voyage-and-return."* To pick a random example, he describes "responsiveness scripts":

> [Scripts] in which the aim is not to seek rewarding experiences, but rather to be open *to* them, should they occur or reoccur. These sometimes occur poignantly among the elderly who feel they have cheated themselves of what they might have found exciting or enjoyable in their youth and attempt a first, never experienced childhood.[12]

This script is the real-life analog of the classic "voyage-and-return" plotline, in which the protagonist enters an unfamiliar world in the hope of experiencing something new and life-giving.

## Repairing the Negative

Even those of us blessed with a storehouse of positive memories will, sooner or later, encounter the "cursed" dimensions of life. Such encounters (experienced or observed) with suffering and evil can summon us into scripts of remediation.

Unlike the accent-the-positive scripts, remediation scripts major on addressing the stubborn reality of suffering and evil. Tomkins lists numerous "commitment" scripts, which empower us to battle the evil; to nurture the good despite the evil; to become stronger amidst the suffering; to become empathetic with sufferers.[13]

Classifying such scripts as plot archetypes, we may note an important contrast with the accent-the-positive scripts. Those were dominated by the quest, the ascent, and the voyage-and-return. By contrast, scripts of commitment-to-remediation accent the plot archetypes of *slaying-the-monster, rebirth,* and *comedy* (empathy and reconciliation).

All the major traditional religions address suffering and evil. At the risk of over-simplification, one could perhaps describe major religions as scripting a *death-and-rebirth* archetype as a pattern of remediation. Tomkins gives four examples: "sacrifice (Hebraic), confession (Christian), resignation (Hindu), and cessation of desire (Buddhism)."[14]

Scripts of remediation do include *quests* (e.g. for beauty amidst ugliness; for wisdom amidst folly). Plotlines of *ascent* often entail remediation—e.g., children of minorities who strive for success, to make up for the social humiliations experienced by their parents. The *voyage-and-return* plotline might also entail remediation, if respite/escape is the motive of the voyage into changed circumstances.

---

11. Ibid., 164–66.
12. Ibid., 165 (italics in original).
13. Ibid., 166–68, 179–84.
14. Ibid., 168.

## Ultra-Ambiguous Experiences

Some of us are haunted by past experiences which combined a perplexing fusion of the intensely positive and the intensely negative. Our scripts reflect this strange mixture of ultra-positive and ultra-negative emotions associated with the *same* event.

I witnessed these scripts first-hand when I lived in a dormitory for single guys, populated with an abundance of "nerdy" male seminary students. They (or should I say we?) nearly all shared a common experience, generating hyper-ambivalent responses. They invited a girl on a date, and she said yes! The days leading up to the date became a paradise of anticipation. Sadly, the evening did not produce the desired second date, leaving the male in the wilderness of rejection.

This experience, of intoxicating high inextricable from crashing low, produced numerous reactive scripts among the inhabitants of the dormitory. Looking back, the variety of scripts matches Tomkins's inventory remarkably well.[15]

Some men's script became a *utopian quest*—a self-defeating script aimed at recovering the (idealized) high and simultaneously eliminating the risk of rejection.

Others focused more on the negative side of the experience. Their scripts (bordering on misogyny) had dimensions of the archetype of "overcoming the monster," either by flight (from the "monster" of female rejection) into isolation, introversion, immersion in scholarship, or (more darkly) by vengeful fantasies of future dates in which the protagonist got to play the part of the rejecter. (This last version could also be construed as a plotline of *ascent*, if the protagonist's main goal is their own enhanced status.)

One guy became the perfect embodiment of Tomkins's "celebratory" script.[16] These scripts are a kind of *voyage-and-return* into the protagonist's memory-bank. The protagonist undertakes repeated mental revisits of both the ultra-positive and the ultra-negative dimensions of the trigger event (and uses their memories as a grid for interpreting new scenes). One student became a dorm legend for his manifestation of this script. He would eat dinner at a co-ed cafeteria, and return to the dorm to debrief. His reports went one of two ways. "There was this girl with a tattoo—and, man, I could tell that she *wanted* me!" Alternatively: "There was this preppy-looking girl—and I knew right away that I *disgusted* her."

## Toxic Experiences

Some among us are victims of events where there is no mix of positive and negative experiences—only the overwhelmingly negative—experiences of extremes of intimidation and humiliation. Tomkins offers a brief discussion of the scripts that tend to be lived out by such victims. Reading his account, I was struck by the *loss of narrative options* for these victims.[17] No utopian quests. No hope of remediation. Mostly scripts of damage-limitation.

* * * * *

15. Ibid., 168–69, 204–5.
16. Ibid., 204.
17. Ibid., 169.

To round out our summary of script theory, we turn to a folder of scripts that revisit the questions we asked at the start of this chapter. General questions of how you and I respond to stresses and setbacks encountered as we live out our "trajectory" scripts.

## Scripts for Responding to Setbacks

These are scripts that we use to handle the negative emotions arising from roadblocks to our goals. In terms of chalk circles on the "stage" of life, these scripts appear *inside* the circle of ideological scripts. They also *overlap* with trajectory scripts. Here's how. Trajectories focus on positive outcomes, and positive outcomes feed positive emotions. For some folk, the positive emotion becomes an *end in itself*, the desired outcome of their major scripts. Furthermore, some scripts offer reduction of negative feelings as a byproduct of some other outcome. (For example, the "American Dream" offers a "white picket fence" home. Positively, this scripts attainment of social status. But the byproduct may be reduction of fear through dwelling in a gated community.)

So, then—how do you personally handle stresses and setbacks, and the negative emotions these events tend to generate? Do you resort to the script that Tomkins calls *sedative*? For example: "A cigarette is but one of many types of sedative act. One may attempt self-sedation via alcohol, drugs, eating, aggression, sex, travel, driving, walking, running, watching TV, conversation, reading, introversion, music, or a favored place."[18] In terms of our plot archetypes, sedative scripts are microcosms of the *quest* for "paradise restored"—with paradise defined as the emotional equilibrium that preceded a disconcerting event.

Probably all of us resort to some form of sedative script at some points in our week. (And that may not be inherently bad; perhaps the fourth commandment, instituting "Sabbath rest," counts as a legitimate form of sedative script.)

Nevertheless, script theory informs us that we have a degree of choice in our responses to setbacks. There are alternatives to sedative scripts. Narrative wisdom affirms this. Have you noticed the typical structure of act one of narratives? A setting is established, and then comes a trigger event. This inciting incident upsets the equilibrium of the protagonist's world.[19] Then comes a phase in which they contemplate a response. At the end of that phase comes the *call* or summons into a specific plotline. The trigger is not usually the call. The protagonist can (to some extent) choose how to script their response to the disruptive event.

With this in mind, let us list Tomkins's inventory of *non-sedative* alternatives for managing our negative emotions.[20] Please note: I am not primarily listing these as recommendations! Rather, I intend the list as a tool for self-examination. As you read the inventory of scripts, I invite you to ponder your own habitual responses to stresses and setbacks. What might your scripts tell you about your bigger life story? (I will refrain

---

18. Ibid., 186.
19. Mckee, *Story*, 189–94.
20. Tomkins, "Script Theory," 187–88.

from classifying the scripts via their plotline archetypes, but you are welcome to do so, since that exercise may help you get a handle on your own life story.)

When you've encountered setbacks, have you ever minimized or suppressed your negative reaction? Have you ever practiced some form of denial? ("It's no big deal!") Some cultures emphasize keeping our emotions under control. If we grew up in such a culture, our scripted response to setbacks may be a *stoic* effort to dam up the torrent of emotions before they burst forth.

Then again, some personal narratives recognize that the road to glory is paved with suffering. ("No pain, no gain!") Do you have an umbrella narrative sturdy enough to withstand the storms, to motivate you to keep going despite antagonism? The various *commitment* scripts (discussed above) offer such resources—including the scripts of traditional religions.

By contrast, some of us develop the habit of quitting in the face of adversity. Perhaps these scripts of *resignation* are a form of damage-limitation—e.g., protecting our battered self-esteem.

Midway between dogged perseverance and resignation would come the switch to a *doable* script. (Recall the above discussion of the perfectionist university student, who compensated for struggling to maintain straight A-grades by adopting the "bulimic script" for achieving another kind of perfection—control over her weight.)

Perhaps, when you fail, your tendency is to assume personal responsibility. Then you may be attracted to *power* scripts, in which you work to increase your competence, to ensure success at the next attempt.

The opposite response would be to attribute your failure to "bad luck." This may result in an *opportunist* script, in which you wait for "better luck" to arrive.

Another batch of scripts majors on actions designed to prevent future recurrence of negative scenes. *Insurance* scripts make small behavioral modifications as a hedge against future setbacks. *Prudential* scripts reduce the amount of risk we are willing to take. *Boldness* scripts take big risks, in the hope of getting to a place where the negatives of life are outweighed by a mass of positives. *Gambling* scripts take small risks, hoping for the psychological equivalent of a winning lottery ticket.

Sometimes our setbacks trigger responses of a more *philosophical* nature. We may seek greater wisdom, by learning to factor in the cost of negative emotions in whatever we do. Or we may undertake a more radical re-evaluation of ourselves, of others, and our place in the world.

Then again, in some individuals, setbacks provoke responses rather more *pathological* in nature. Some of us develop a morbid obsession, constantly replaying the mental movie of the negative event (hoping for a better outcome?). Others sign up for a "jihad," mobilizing all their resources to eliminate the source of the negative event. Still others embark on a utopian quest to create a paradise of perpetual shelter from the negative event and its analogs.

\* \* \* \* \*

Scripts, habits, rituals. Our brief tour of script theory has sketched some major contours of repetitive human behavior. To end this chapter, a brief look at ritualized responses to suffering, through the lens of biblical poetry.

## RITUALS OF LAMENTATION

Our tour of script theory ended by listing typical human responses to setbacks. The authors of the Old Testament were no strangers to suffering. Interestingly, their preferred response was to write poetry! In doing so, they gave us a rich inheritance of wisdom in dealing with setbacks. The poetic form ritualizes the grieving process, and thereby generates a script for dealing with suffering.

Lamentations is a little-read poetic book of Scripture. The book reflects on the traumatic event of the destruction of Jerusalem at the hands of the Babylonians. Even fewer people read it in Hebrew. But, if you do, you notice something remarkable: the "acrostic" structure of chapters 1–2 and 4. The first verse starts with the (Hebrew) letter A, and each new verse begins with the next letter of the Hebrew alphabet. (In the central chapter 3, this pattern is tripled: three verses begin with A, the next three with B, and so on. The Hebrew equivalent of an "A through Z" of grief.) The grieving poet thereby gives full vent to his sorrows, and at the same time imposes some self-discipline. He doesn't rant at random (how can you, when your sentences must follow the sequence of the alphabet!) The formal pattern guided ancient Israelites into the structure of grieving.

The *Psalms* provide us with many more examples of the poetry of suffering. A big chunk of Psalms 1–150 are known as *laments*. Their disciplined poetic form, their careful literary structure, make them perfect scripts for dealing with setbacks.

Let me illustrate. I invite you to read Psalm 13. Pay special attention to the narrative flow of the poem.

The poet begins by talking to God—an honest, full-disclosure, three-hundred-and-sixty-degree declaration of his sufferings. Bordering on insistence, impertinence—four times he repeats the question, "How long?" The repetition symbolizes the psyche of the sufferer—we suspect that God is not really listening . . . but maybe if we repeat ourselves enough, he will.

The poet inventories the multiple dimensions of his plight. God has forgotten him; the divine countenance is hidden. In the heart of the poet—deliberations and sorrows. In the outside world—the exaltation of his adversaries.

In narrative terms, this is the frustration phase of the story. Next comes crisis. The poet faces the worst: death. Twice he cries out for illumination, epiphany, lest death overcome him.

Perhaps in answer to his cry comes a glimmer of light. The poet dares to express trust in God's covenant-faithfulness, joy in God's acts-of-deliverance.

Finally, he reinforces this hope by a commitment to sing in celebration of God's provision.

Now, I am not offering this psalm as a one-size-fits-all script for handling setbacks (after all, we have many different psalms of lament, contoured to the complexities of suffering); nevertheless, it may help to outline the structure of Psalm 13 as an example of a biblical script for handling adversity:

- Honest, full disclosure of suffering; including impatience with God.
- Facing the worst; desperate cry for light and hope.
- Remembering the *metanarrative*. ("Covenant faithfulness" evokes God's promises to Abraham and to David, among other references; "salvation" connotes God's interventions in history, like the Exodus.)
- Celebrating the rekindled hope.

*****

The Psalms offer us wonderful scripts for coping with adversity, perhaps because they are microcosms of the entire biblical story. The whole of Scripture could be viewed as a script for coping with adversity. (Perhaps that is why theologians speak of the Bible as "*redemptive* revelation from God.")

With this in mind, let us revisit the story of the perfectionist university student from the opening section of this chapter. Recall the direct link between her perfection and her bulimia.

What were some scriptural alternatives to her bulimic script? Let's not minimize the agonies of perfectionism. Rather, let's brainstorm, by using perfectionism as an entry-point into the story and the scripts of the Bible. Here are three almost random thoughts:

1. Academic attainment is symbolized by the gown, the robe of success. (In some American high-school graduations, I have witnessed the symbolism of perfection: students with 4.0 GPA get a special-color hood, distinguishing them from their "imperfect" peers!)

   The gospel also uses clothing as a symbol of perfection. Galatians 3:27 tells us that, in the ritual (script) of baptism, we clothe ourselves with Christ's identity, his perfection.

2. In addition to the perfectionism of weight-control, bulimia may have a purgative or cleansing "function."

   The gospel is rich in the imagery of purification. Think of the foot-washing ritual (script) in John 13—a ritual continued to this day in the liturgies of many churches. (I discuss John 13 at greater length in chapter 22 of this book.)

3. For students at elite universities, perfection is bound up with place. (In my day in England, students who got into good universities, but failed to get into Oxford/Cambridge, were known as "Oxbridge Rejects.")

   The gospel also uses place to symbolize perfection, especially in the New Testament book known as Hebrews. This book loves the vocabulary of perfection and connects this perfection with the notion of sacred space. According to Hebrews, Jesus functions as a high priest, mystically inducting Christians into the holiest of abodes, the perfect abode of God. (I explore Hebrews further in chapter 23 of this book.)

\* \* \* \* \*

This chapter mentioned the central importance of *ideological scripts*. These narratives, common to an entire culture (or to "tribes" within that culture), are the big chalk circles on the stage of life. Our personal scripts tend to operate as variants of the big umbrella cultural scripts.

Cultural scripts are so important, because they set boundaries for the smaller personal scripts we live by. Accordingly, the next two chapters take a closer look at ideological scripts.

# 16

# A Better Life

## FROM KINDERGARTEN TO CULTURAL SCRIPTS

IN THIS CHAPTER, we begin to zoom the lens out, from individuals to society, from autobiography to cultural scripts. Let us start with a couple of snapshots from early childhood development, and then fast-forward into adulthood.

How fundamental is *narrative* for the human psyche? Absolutely essential, according to some recent branches of cognitive psychology. Take *language acquisition* in young children. Narrative appears to play a crucial developmental role. Hearing stories and (re-)telling stories helps children grasp concepts such as agency and sequence. In this process, toddlers acquire grammatical knowledge, such as use of pronouns and verb tenses.[1] A study of toddler development revealed this tendency: "Much of Emily's early [language] acquisition seemed to be driven by a need to fix and to express *narrative structure*—the order of human events and what difference they made to the narrator/protagonist."[2] According to script theory, narrative also guides the child in her growing self-understanding and interactions with the world. Observing infant efforts to *re-experience pleasurable scenes*, Sylvan S. Tomkins comments: "She is doing what she will continue to try to do all her life—to command the scenes she wishes to play. Like Charlie Chaplain, she will try to write, direct, produce, criticize, and promote the scenes in which she casts herself as hero."[3] As we grow into adulthood, our society offers us cultural scripts within which we can live, move, and have our being. These scripts shape our identity, our values, and our decisions.

Narrative psychologist Dan P. McAdams catalogs numerous "upbeat" scripts available to modern Americans as part of their cultural legacy.[4] There is the "atonement" script (rooted in Puritan spiritual autobiographies); the "emancipation" script (rooted in African American slave narratives); the "upward mobility" script (rooted in numerous rags-to-riches stories); the "recovery" script (popularized in twelve-step programs).

---

1. Bruner, *Acts of Meaning*, 75–80, 87–94.
2. Ibid., 90 (italics mine).
3. Tomkins, "Script Theory," 150.
4. McAdams, *Redemptive Self*, 42.

## THE AMERICAN DREAM

By way of concrete illustration of the workings of a cultural script, I offer my own narrative analysis of a predominant option, namely, "the American Dream."

As you read my thumbnail sketch, I invite you—assuming for now that you live in the USA—to pause and reflect: To what extent is your life story shaped by some version of this upward-mobility script?

Then again, perhaps your biography has unfolded in reaction against the perceived shallowness of the dominant cultural script of upward mobility. Thinking back to chapter 5 of this book, perhaps you resonated with the characters from the novel *Generation X*. If so, how successful have you been in your search for a more authentic personal narrative? Has the dominant culture continued to exert a hold over you in some ways?

Alternatively, maybe you live outside the USA, in a culture with very different values. If so, I invite you to reflect on the American Dream from your own perspective. Is the "rags to riches" storyline attractive to you in any way? What defects in the script are clearly visible from your own cultural vantage point?

Staple components of biographical narratives might include these elements: family origins; personal destiny; setting; causal connections; plotline archetype; symbols/imagery. If we analyze the American Dream via these categories, the following (somewhat caricatured) story emerges:

| *family origins* | not so important; neither an obstacle to success, nor a determinant of success |
| --- | --- |
| *personal destiny* | financial security; property ownership; career success |
| *setting* | America; land of opportunity; a level playing field, canceling any disadvantages due to unfortunate origins |
| *causal connections* | meritocratic; individual effort earns/deserves success; hard work pays off |
| *plotline archetype* | ascent; rags to riches |
| *symbol/imagery* | the "white picket fence" |

This caricature illustrates the prevalence and the mythic power of cultural scripts.[5] Whether we borrow an existing narrative, or fashion our own, living inside a story comes naturally to us as humans. Reduced to its bare bones, script theory posits that "Human beings are fundamentally like playwrights who create scripts in which they play the leading roles. From the earliest weeks of life onward . . . people unconsciously fashion *scripts* to organize and make sense of their lives and to set the stage for future action."[6]

\* \* \* \* \*

---

5. Ironically, when I first drafted this chapter in 2009, thousands of white-picket-fenced homes were being lost to foreclosure, as the hard-working owners were unable to maintain their steep mortgage payments.

6. McAdams, *Redemptive Self*, 222 (italics in original).

Credit for coining the phrase "the American Dream" goes to James Truslow Adams, in his 1931 work *The Epic of America*. Written over eighty years ago, some of his words have a prophetic ring:

> [The American Dream is] that dream of a land in which life should be better and richer and fuller for everyone, with opportunity for each according to ability or achievement. It is a difficult dream for the European upper classes to interpret adequately, and too *many of us ourselves have grown weary and mistrustful of it. It is not a dream of motor cars and high wages merely,* but a dream of social order in which each man and woman shall be able to attain to the fullest stature of which they are innately capable, and be recognized by others for what they are, regardless of the fortuitous circumstances of birth or position.[7]

Among the affluent, many of can testify to the anomie of a cultural script reduced to "motor cars and high wages merely." However, for many living south of the American border, Adams's vision still calls out its siren song. Many are willing to hazard an illegal border crossing in search of a better life.

## A BETTER LIFE

Drugs. Gangs. Violence. Kidnapping. Poverty. There are many reasons for Mexicans to run into the arms of America in search of a better life. An example is found in Carlos, the protagonist from the Oscar-nominated 2011 film *A Better Life*.

Single parent Carlos lives in California, and works seven days a week to support his teenage son Luis. "*Undocumentado*," an illegal immigrant, Carlos's career option equals low-paid yard-work.

But he dreams the American Dream. If only he could afford a truck. Then he could hire day laborers. He would be the *jefe*, the boss, a businessman. Then hire a lawyer to file for citizenship.

In the film, dream collides with reality. Carlos's wife left him for a wealthier man. His son Luis flirts with gang membership. Carlos slinks around in fear of the police ("Show me your ID!").

The film asks hard questions. Is Carlos's life in America better than it was in Mexico? What makes a better life?

Dallas (where I used to reside) is home to thousands like Carlos. Perhaps for some, the frustration of their dream provokes questions. When and where is the better life?

Abraham became the father of three world religions. Like Carlos, he left his country, his tribe, his parents, in search of somewhere better. Abraham wandered restless in the land of promise. Frustrations multiplied. His nephew gets kidnapped. Famine wastes the land. Local residents steal Abraham's well.

The New Testament book of Hebrews likes the word "better." According to Hebrews, Abraham searched for the land of promise, but found something better. He came to desire "a better [country]—that is, a heavenly one" (Heb 11:16). He looked forward to "the city having foundations, whose architect and maker is God" (Heb 11:10).

---

7. Adams, *Epic of America*, 214–15 (italics mine).

We all know people like Carlos, whose dream has become frustration. Is the frustration an invitation to embrace the faith of Abraham, to seek the better, heavenly country?

Suppose someone told Carlos the story of Abraham. And suppose Carlos embraced the vision of Abraham. Then, perhaps, Carlos could teach us. For if failing to reach the American Dream is frustrating, attaining it may be worse. What's the profit if someone gains the world, but loses their soul?

Sensing the emptiness of the American Dream, some members of the counterculture embrace Eastern religious alternatives . . . involving dropping out of the "rat-race" and cessation of materialistic and egocentric desires.

This is not the place to engage Eastern religious perspectives. But I do wonder if the American Dream is more a distortion of proper God-given desires, than a simple falsehood to be rejected through cessation of ambition.

In terms of plotline archetypes, the American Dream is a *quest for paradise*, and/or a narrative of *ascent*. Could those ambitions be redirected into truer and more satisfying storylines? Such "morphing" of the "desire line" of our personal narratives often typifies the truly meaningful biography.[8] Let's briefly explore this trajectory.

*Paradise*: could desire be redirected toward the restoration of paradise promised in the Bible? Along the lines of Hebrews, inviting the reader to imitate Abraham in a quest for a better (that is, "heavenly") country. (I explore Hebrews further in chapter 23 of this book.)

*Ascent*: instead of increased social status, could our ambition for ascent be channeled into growth in virtue, culminating in what 2 Peter 1:4 boldly asserts: "participation in the divine nature," no less. (For further exploration of 2 Peter 1, I invite you to turn back to the end of chapter 2 of this book.)

\* \* \* \* \*

In this chapter, we have introduced the notion of cultural scripts. In our next chapter, we deepen our analysis of these powerful masterplots.

---

8. Rainer, *Your Life as Story*, 45–46, 68, 80.

# 17

# American Graffiti

## NO PAIN, NO GAIN?

CULTURES ARE STORIES. IN this chapter, I explore the power of narrative as a tool for analyzing cultures. In the previous chapter, I outlined the American Dream as a prevalent cultural script. For over a century, the dream has been nourished by countless "rags to riches" tales. For some, the dream comes true. In 2008, Americans elected Barack Obama, a person of color, as president. For many, this proves that America really is a land of unbounded opportunity, where anyone, regardless of race or religion, can ascend to the oval office.

Cultural scripts are powerful. They tap into something very basic, very archetypal—just as the seven genres of story (discussed in chapter 8) tap into fundamental dimensions of human existence. The rhetorical power of a cultural script derives from its convincing use of archetypal plotlines:

> We seem to connect our thinking about life, and particularly about our own lives, to a number of *masterplots* that we may or may not be fully aware of. To the extent that our values and identity are linked to a masterplot, that masterplot can have strong rhetorical impact.
>
> The more culturally specific the masterplot, the greater its practical force in everyday life. All national cultures have their masterplots, some of which are local variations on universal masterplots.
>
> It is tempting to see these masterplots as a kind of cultural glue that holds societies together.[1]

Cultural glue. Practical force in everyday life. Strong rhetorical impact. Anything this powerful is worth harnessing, and harnessing requires understanding. Let's enter the forcefield of cultural scripts and reflect on the dimensions of their power.[2]

Past. Present. Future. We live, inescapably, on a timeline. Looking backwards, looking forwards, or in the existential moment—cultural masterplots serve as our

---

1. Abbott, *Introduction to Narrative*, 42–44 (italics mine).
2. My reflections are indebted to Novak, *Ascent of the Mountain*, 104–8.

indispensable guide. They are our collective storehouses of *values and virtues* (whose formation via stories we discussed in chapter 12).

Looking back on our life, how can we measure our performance up to the present? Cultural scripts tell us, here are the roles approved by society, and here's how you embody these roles.

Looking forward, how do we choose our next goal? Cultural scripts filter the options. Widespread aimlessness in society warns us that our national myths are losing their plausibility.

In the existential moment, an unexpected circumstance, how should we behave? Cultural scripts offer a "style guide" for the minutiae of human interactions. We will illustrate this shortly, by studying how four different ethnic groups react to the experience of hospitalization.

Cultural stories not only shape individual lives; they also function as our collective conscience. Versions of our national history can crystallize collective experience with epiphanic effect. Pulitzer prizewinner David Halberstam exposed the tragic *hubris* of the Vietnam war.[3] For many Americans, such narratives led to a painful soul-searching and a questioning of the unquestioned goodness and rightness of US foreign policy.

Competing versions of our national masterplot either undergird or undermine collective morale. One can present the European settlement of America as a heroic journey out of the decay of the old world. Equally, one can tell of the genocide of the Native American. "We wiped out 90% of the native population—even using Gatling guns against Sioux and Cheyenne villages in the last years of the conflict."[4]

Stories that support a culture, stories that challenge a culture—we will shortly examine both kinds, using the book of Revelation as example. First, however, let's illustrate the impact of cultural scripts in the minutiae of individual lives.

How do you respond to the experience of physical pain requiring hospitalization? Apparently, your ethnic background and its cultural script may play a decisive role.[5] Wait a second! Are we about to commit the sin of stereotyping? Well, I would not be citing this material, except for the fact that some patients in the study stereotyped themselves by self-castigation for failure to "live up" to their ethnic script![6] So, with this disclaimer, here is my narrative digest of the study of hospital patients from four ethnic backgrounds:

| Ethnic Background | Typical Responses to Pain | Cultural Master-Plots |
| --- | --- | --- |
| "Old American" | don't cry, it's impractical<br>suffer alone<br>activist co-operation with treatment<br>resist germs as "invaders" | utilitarianism<br>rugged individualism<br>optimism<br>"slaying dragon [disease]" |

---

3. Halberstam, *Best and Brightest*.
4. Junger, "*Bury My Heart* by Brown," 87.
5. The following summary is based on a study cited in Novak, *Unmeltable Ethnics*, 38–46.
6. "People try to be what they are not. They try to live up to a cultural type not their own. They ride roughshod over their own instinctive gropings. Self-hatred is profound." (Ibid., 39.)

## Part 3: How Stories Change Lives

| Ethnic Background | Typical Responses to Pain | Cultural Master-Plots |
|---|---|---|
| Jewish | fears the worst<br>complains; gathers community<br>dramatizes pain | pessimism<br>comedic (suffering unites)<br>tragic |
| Irish | inward struggle of the soul<br>endure test of manhood | ascent via ordeal<br>stoicism |
| Italian | resents interruption of pleasures<br>craves sympathy from nurses | epicurean ("*carpe diem*")<br>Italian mother as Madonna |

More poignantly, another researcher recounts a medical exam undergone by a Jewish survivor of Auschwitz.[7] To navigate the indignity of the exam, the patient constantly told his doctor stories from the concentration camp. "The stories are tokens of the man, talismans of the salient and defining history which has shaped him. They... are invoked as touchstones of his presence."[8]

Let's pause and solidify the link between our cultural scripts and our responses to physical suffering. I invite you to think back to your last major illness or hospitalization. What inner beliefs did this suffering bring to the surface? What behavior did the trial trigger in you? Next, reflect on your cultural or ethnic heritage. How are your beliefs about physical suffering, and your behavioral responses, shaped by your heritage?

\* \* \* \* \*

Having looked at individuals using cultural scripts as behavioral guides, now let us turn to the collective impact of cultural masterplots. We may pigeonhole stories into three types, by determining their ideological stance (positive, "neutral," negative) toward the dominant culture:[9]

| positive | stories that establish worlds | myths |
|---|---|---|
| "neutral" | stories that explore worlds | most stories |
| negative | stories that overturn worlds | counter-myths and parables |

We may illustrate myth and counter-myth by accessing the backstory behind the book of Revelation, which we will do in our next section, exploring Revelation as a clash of narratives.

## MY NAME IS GLADIATOR

After its superscription, Revelation 1:4 begins sounding exactly like any of the letters of the New Testament (especially those of Paul): "John, to the seven churches in Asia, grace to you and peace..."

---

7. Young, "Narrative Embodiments," 152–65.
8. Ibid., 162.
9. Tilley, *Story Theology*, 39–54.

This matters. The letter parallel invites us to ask the same questions of Revelation that we would ask of a Pauline letter. What is the backstory? What were the circumstances of the first audience? What overarching problem confronted the seven churches of Asia Minor?

The answer is pretty obvious. The seven churches of Asia Minor were a tiny, despised religious sect, experiencing the oppression of the Roman Empire.

Western Turkey, the location of these seven churches, was a strong center of the Roman imperial cult, whose temples proclaimed the divinity of the emperors and the divine right of Roman dominion.

Any self-respecting Empire needs a compelling *foundational story* to legitimize its power. For Rome, that story was supplied by the epic poet Virgil, whose *Aeneid* was penned a couple of decades before the birth of Jesus.

Virgil's epic is a powerful story of the *rebirth* of a civilization. Of a *quest* for a homeland for the ancestors of the Roman people. The epic foreshadows the *ascent* of the Roman empire, rising from the dust to dominate the known world.

Virgil's story is structured around the epic *journey* of the hero Aeneas. When ancient Troy was destroyed by the Greeks, Aeneas led a small band of exiles across the Mediterranean in search of a new homeland. Through tribulation, testing, and battle, Aeneas and his warriors eventually establish themselves in Italy, as the nucleus of the future Roman empire. The *journey* and *battle* plotline allows Virgil to depict the hand of divine providence behind Aeneas's success, thereby legitimizing Roman imperial dominion.

Virgil includes "eschatological" anticipations of the reign of Caesar Augustus (emperor at the time Jesus was born). In book 6, Aeneas receives a vision of the destiny of his descendants:

> Now turn your gaze here and let it rest upon
> Your family of Romans. Here is Caesar,
> And here are all the descendants of Julius
> Destined to come under heavens great dome.
> And here is the man promised to you,
> *Augustus Caesar*, born of the gods,
> Who will establish again a Golden Age
> In the fields of Latium . . .
> And will expand his dominion . . .
> Beyond our familiar stars,
> Beyond the yearly path of the sun . . .[10]

In book 8, Virgil anticipates the enthronement of Augustus:

> Caesar entered Rome in triple triumph . . .
> The streets rang with joyful festivities . . .
> Caesar himself . . . reviewed the gifts from the *world's nations* . . .
> The conquered people marched on past

---

10. Virgil, *Aeneid* 6.935–46 (italics added).

PART 3: HOW STORIES CHANGE LIVES

> In long procession, each as different in their clothes and gear
> As in *the tongues they spoke* . . .
> The loose-robed African people,
> The quivered Scythians . . .[11]

Compare and contrast this vision with Revelation 7:9–10:

> After this I looked, and behold!
> A great crowd that no one could number,
> from every nation, tribe, people, and language,
> stood before the throne and before the Lamb . . .
> They cry out in a loud voice, saying:
> "Salvation belongs to our God who sits on the throne, and to the Lamb!"

Can you feel the *cultural rhetoric* of Revelation in this scene? In place of Caesar's triumphal procession, the triumphal procession of the Lamb (who was slain by the Roman practice of crucifixion).

Using a multiplicity of such rhetorical devices, Revelation systematically *deconstructs* the Roman imperial myth, replacing it with the ultimate truth of the story of the gospel.

This is what *apocalyptic* literature does. Apocalypses *unveil* the truth behind appearances. They expose false stories, and replace them with true stories.

The Roman empire presented itself to the conquered world as a benefactor, an agent of universal peace (the *Pax Romana*). Think of the opening scenes of the Russell Crowe movie *Gladiator*. Crowe plays the Roman general Maximus Meridius, who is leading an assault on the Germanic tribes. The legions line up on one side of a river, the Germans on the other. At Maximus's command, all hell breaks loose. Roman catapults hurl burning missiles onto the helpless Germans, who are then dismembered by Roman swords. This R-rated scene of violence then switches to Italy, where Maximus is received in honor by the emperor, and thanked for "extending the *peace of Rome* to the German tribes"![12]

In much the same way as *Gladiator*, the Book of Revelation exposes the dark underbelly of Roman imperial rule. One of Revelation's most effective rhetorical moves may be described as "A Tale of Two Cities." Using Babylon to depict Rome, and Jerusalem to depict the church, Revelation compiles a sustained set of contrasts, turning the glory of Rome into shame, and turning the shame of the church into honor. Let's itemize some of these contrasts, in the form of Babylon versus Jerusalem:[13]

| Babylon (Rome) | Jerusalem (church) |
|---|---|
| whore | bride |
| beast | lamb |

---

11. Virgil, *Aeneid* 8.18–35 (italics added).
12. Scott, *Gladiator*.
13. Howard-Brook and Gwyther, *Unveiling Empire*, 160.

| Babylon (Rome) | Jerusalem (church) |
|---|---|
| clothed in scarlet | clothed in linen |
| name of Babylon on forehead | name of God on forehead |
| abode of demons | abode of God |
| nations intoxicated | nations healed |
| nations deceived | nations walk in the light |
| weeping and wailing | no tears or sorrow |
| burnt ruin | everlasting garden |

Let's now refocus all these observations in narrative terms.

Based on Virgil's *Aeneid*, and other empire-glorifying cultural artifacts, Rome depicted its story as virtually a *paradise restored*, the development of a golden age of universal peace.

The book of Revelation essentially rewrites Rome's cultural script. Instead of paradise restored, we read *decline and fall*. Revelation unveils the true story of Rome as tragedy. The *hubris*, pride, vainglory inevitably meets its nemesis: "Fallen, fallen is Babylon the Great . . . Her sins piled up to heaven, And God remembered her injustice" (Rev 18:2, 5). By contrast, the story of the church is celebrated as a triumph of light over darkness, a non-violent slaying of the dragon, in which the Saints "were victorious because of the blood of the lamb" (Rev 12:11). The story of *Christus Victor*, so to speak.

Having reflected on the role of story in the rhetoric of Revelation, let us now fast-forward two thousand years and reflect on the underlying narratives of two competing American cultural scripts.

## A CAPPUCCINO, WITH A SHOT OF POSTMODERNISM

For the purpose of identifying prevalent contemporary cultural scripts, I am indebted to a book by Steve Wilkens and Mark L. Sanford, entitled *Hidden Worldviews: Eight Cultural Stories that Shape our Lives*. The authors have two main theses, which resonate strongly with me:

1. World- and life-view is, for most people, absorbed unconsciously via daily social/cultural interactions (imbibed via "coffee at Starbucks");
2. Worldviews all have *story* at their core. The story shapes identity and behavior.

Let's take a couple of the contemporary worldviews identified by Wilkens and Sanford, and supplement their study by highlighting the *narrative underpinning* of the worldviews.

One prevalent worldview in America today, especially among religious conservatives, is *nationalism*. (This ideology goes beyond patriotism, or natural affection for one's homeland.) As an Englishman and a green card, I need to tread carefully here. So I will begin with a narrative analysis of one form of *English* nationalism (and hopefully convince my American friends that I am not immune to the emotive tug of nationalist sentiments!).

Part 3: How Stories Change Lives

Perhaps you recall the closing scene of the film *Chariots of Fire*. The film ends with the funeral of Harold Abrams, Olympic 100m champion. His funeral service ends with a singing of the hymn "Jerusalem," taken from words penned by the poet William Blake, circa 1800:

> And did those feet in ancient time
> Walk upon England's mountains green?
> And was the holy Lamb of God
> On England's pleasant pastures seen?
> And did the countenance divine
> Shine forth upon our clouded hills?
> And was Jerusalem builded here
> Among these dark Satanic mills?
>
> Bring me my bow of burning gold
> Bring me my arrows of desire
> Bring me my spear: O clouds unfold!
> Bring me my chariot of fire
>
> I will not cease from mental fight
> Nor shall my sword sleep in my hand
> Til we have built Jerusalem
> In England's green and pleasant land

Here is the storyline of the poem (which functions as an alternative national anthem of England):

- *backstory* (legendary): Jesus visited England (the mystical site of Glastonbury, perhaps), establishing a New Jerusalem paradise there
- *conflict*: the Industrial Revolution produces "dark satanic mills," destroying paradise
- *resolution*: reader is summoned to spiritual warfare to reestablish paradise

The consequences of living in this story are fairly harmless (unless, I suppose, you happen to be a property developer!): conservationism; listed buildings of architectural value; zoning restrictions to preserve the "greenbelt."

Given England's lack of political clout in the world, this seems a fairly tame form of nationalism (but perhaps I am biased).

With this illustration out of the way, let me now offer a narrative analysis of American nationalism. Wilkens and Sanford offer us four diagnostic questions for detecting American nationalism: *"You may be a nationalist if . . . "*

1. You believe that God's plan for the world would suffer greatly if America ceased to exist in fifty years;
2. You cannot fathom how an American Christian could refuse to pledge allegiance to the flag, or to sing the national anthem;

3. You believe the Declaration of Independence states eternal truths, or that the Constitution cannot be improved upon;

4. You believe America needs to return to "how things were" during some "golden age."

I know that, for many Christian readers (including several of my friends), these four convictions are inextricably woven into the fabric of faith. If that is true for you, I invite you to pause and reflect on how these beliefs provide you with a cultural script. Presumably, these values affect the way you vote. But how about where you choose to live, where you go to church, or how you educate your children? Cultural scripts have enormous power and reach. Perhaps you recall certain American sports-commentators of the 1990s, who denounced soccer as a game tainted by "European" and "socialist" influences.

In terms of a narrative analysis of American nationalism, all four convictions listed above rest on the power of underlying masterplots, and associated archetypal images:

1. This invokes a conglomerate of narrative images: "city on a hill"; "manifest destiny"; millennialism. The colonial era *quest* for an American paradise filters down to a current world role for the US: as agent of political *rebirth*, bringing democracy to the planet; "*slaying the dragon*" (via the War on Terror)

2. The Stars and Stripes, the Star-Spangled Banner—a powerful symbol invoking a cultural story (of liberation from the "ogre" in the form of the English monarchy)

3. America has often compared its story to Israel's. Is reverence for the Constitution parallel to ancient Judaism's veneration of Torah?

4. This conviction views recent American history via the plot archetype "voyage [into darkness] and return [into light]." Such a narrative assumes the return is feasible: the 1960s were merely a dark episode (a "bad trip," so to speak)

From the "thesis" of American nationalism, let us turn to its "antithesis," namely, "postmodern tribalism." This worldview also draws much of its power from a narrative interpretation of reality.

Those who embrace a "postmodern tribal" view experience the American story in terms of *disillusionment*. They embrace a cynical *realpolitik* script, which depicts *tragic* flaws in the American experiment. In this version of American history, American social experience is an anti-comedy, a dis-integration, a movement from the exalted idealism of *E Pluribus Unum* to the harsh realism of "Every Tribe for Itself."

In terms of narrative metaphors, the dis-integrative trajectory goes from melting pot, to multicultural mosaic, to tribalized war zone. These three phases of the story are worth fleshing out:[14]

1. America starts as a *melting pot*, a nation of immigrants from diverse lands, whose identities-of-origin get melted down and remolded on American soil. The

---

14. My analysis is indebted to the chapter on "Postmodern Tribalism" in Wilkens and Sanford, *Hidden Worldviews*, 139–59.

immigrant arrives, for example, as an Italian; her children grow up hyphenated, Italian-American; her grandchildren drop the hyphen—they are simply American.

This is the *dream*like phase of the story. "Give me your tired, your poor, your huddled masses yearning to breathe free." Equal opportunity to live the American Dream.

2. The second phase, the *multicultural mosaic*, reflects a dual *frustration* with the ideal inscribed on the Statue of Liberty. On the one hand, many immigrants feel a loss of identity and roots when they Americanize. On the other hand, the American Dream seemed to work better if you were Caucasian, and not so well if you were Black or Hispanic.

3. In the postmodern viewpoint, this second phase of multicultural awareness is an unstable middle term, which soon breaks down as different social groups grow more and more aware of their irreconcilable differences.

Once we are *dis-illusioned*, we can embrace the *tribal phase* of American society. Welcome to a politicized war zone. My identity comes from my tribe: Gay; Lesbian; Black; Hispanic. My tribe has its agenda; your tribe has a contrary agenda.

The rules of society are not written to give equal opportunity, but to bolster the agenda of whoever has the most power.

In the backstory of American nationalism, America came into being by "slaying the monster" of (English) oppression. In the backstory of postmodern tribalism, America *is* the monster of oppression!

In this postmodern script, America is governed by raw power, cosmetically concealed by an ideology of justice and equality.

In this script, all the tribes are in a competition for the "limited good" of power. Life within this story reduces to a constant politicized struggle to protect my tribe from oppression by others. The weapon of choice in this struggle? Victimhood! In a perverse secularized parody of Paul's "when I am weak, I am strong," power now goes to the tribe who can demonstrate maximum oppression at the hands of others.

As an ironic aside, many conservative Christians—who most naturally tend toward nationalism—are increasingly seeing themselves as an oppressed tribe, victimized by the likes of the ACLU trying to keep nativity scenes out of public spaces.

For what it's worth, I also see the same subculture of victimhood among some evangelicals in England, who are preoccupied with the allegedly preferential treatment given to Muslims.

Does any of this disillusionment resonate with you? If so, I invite you to reflect on the ways this cynical, tribalized narrative generates a cultural script. Are your voting habits determined by the story of your "tribe" (or maybe you think voting is a waste of time)? How much time do you spend on the web and on social media, seeking out folk with similar scripts to yourself? Do your choices of food and clothing serve to reinforce your "tribal" identity?

* * * * *

Tribalism. Nationalism. Which story is the truth? Such questions are hard to answer. But I have to confess, at the present time, reality *feels* closer to the experience described in the postmodern tribal narrative. I perceive this in the loss of civil discourse, the harshly polarized rhetoric from the right and the left of the political spectrums.

However, if the postmodern tribal narrative is the truth, I find that profoundly depressing. That is not a story I wish to inhabit.

## BABEL UNDONE

So I have been searching for a better story. Just as the book of Revelation subverted the Roman narrative with the story of Jesus, I believe that we today can discern and live a better story than the discredited nationalism or the demoralizing tribalism.

I have seen glimpses of this new story. Both in the pages of Scripture, fully written, and a (very) rough draft of a chapter in the life of a church my family used to attend.

Around a decade ago, a wealthy, totally Anglo, Presbyterian church in a major Texan metropolis decided to plant a Reformed church for the huge Hispanic population. That population is, of course, served by the Pentecostal and Roman Catholic denominations, but no Hispanic Reformed church existed in that city.

A core group of immigrants from Mexico developed around the bilingual pastor, and began regular worship services.

But events didn't unfold according to the script from the Presbyterian "church planting" manual. Along with abundant Latino growth came a mixed multitude of representatives of virtually every continent on the planet. White Americans. An Englishman. Albanians. A Croatian. Ethiopians. Koreans.

When the sponsors of the church plant wanted us to keep emphasizing a Latino focus, it was our Hispanic brothers and sisters themselves who protested, "No! We like belonging to a multi-ethnic community!"

Was the original vision of the church plant *too tribal*? I give my wife Dawn the credit. She was the first to discern the alternative story that God appeared to be scripting before our eyes. (Sadly, this alternative plotline never came to fruition–but that, as they say, is another story.) She calls the post-tribal narrative "Babel Undone," and here are the CliffsNotes.

Genesis chapters 4–11 chronicle the ripple effects of the exile from Eden. Fratricidal violence. The law of the jungle. And then Babel. In God's sight, the scattering of humanity into dis-integrated tribes was a lesser evil when compared with a monolithic self-exalting humanity.

But the effects of Babel were not without evil. A re-unification of the tribes is hinted at in the very next chapter of Genesis, when God promises to Abraham, "In you, all the families of the earth will be blessed" (Gen 12:3).

Despite that seed promise, the next long phase of the Abrahamic plotline has a strong ethno-centric strand. Mosaic law puts up high walls for *goyim* (non-Jews) to climb over. Circumcision. Dietary restrictions.

Despite the self-protective ethnocentricity of the bearers of the promise, faint foreshadowings occur. The story of Ruth the Moabitess. Jonah's reluctant mission to the Assyrians. And then there is the very strange form of Zionism advocated in Psalm 87:2–6:

> The Lord loves the gates of Zion . . .
> Glorious things are spoken about you, O City of God.
> I memorialize Rahab and Babylon as those who know me;
> Behold, Philistia and Tyre, with Cush—"This one was born there" . . .
> The Lord records while registering peoples [plural],
> "This one was born there."

At the time of Jesus, the Roman empire kept tribal hostilities under the surface, but racial tension was ever-present. Mutual contempt between Jew and Gentile is well-documented. The Greeks despised other cultures as "barbarians." The Abrahamic promise, of a seed that unifies the tribes, seems more remote than ever before.

And then the cross. In Colossians and Ephesians, Paul sees the cross as a cosmic act of reconciliation, a breaking down of the Berlin Wall that separates tribes, the creation of a unified humanity.

At Pentecost, the linguistic confusion of Babel is transcended by the Spirit-empowered proclamation of the narrative of God, and Pentecost foreshadows the culmination of "Babel Undone" that we read from Revelation 7:9–10:

> Behold! A great crowd that no one could number,
> from every nation, *tribe*, people, and language,
> stood before the throne and before the Lamb . . .
> They cry out in a loud voice, saying:
> "Salvation belongs to our God who sits on the throne, and to the Lamb!"

If our churches can live out this post-tribal narrative, it could be our very best apologetic in a cynical postmodern world.

\* \* \* \* \*

This chapter hinges on a simple but profound concept. Our daily lives operate under the umbrella of cultural scripts. Some scripts are ethnic, some reflect the dominant culture, others the counterculture. All these scripts rely on *narratives* about our "tribe," our nation, our world.

As the twenty-first century unfolds, cultural pluralism increases, the plethora of competing scripts multiplies, and many of us become paralyzed by disorientation and confusion.

In this context, the American church also seems to be struggling to find a script. A way of embodying the ancient Christian narrative in the postmodern world.

I am a fellow-participant in this search, not the guy with the quick fix. (Sorry if that disappoints some of you.) The best I can do at present: provide you with an overall framework of narrative wisdom, and drop a few specific hints (e.g., the storyline of "Babel Undone").

So, to end this chapter, I offer less in the way of prescription, and more in the way of a sociological narrative written to further the quest for better scripts.

## CULTURE WARS AND SECTARIAN SCRIPTS

The "culture wars" of the 1960s (the hippies/students versus the establishment) and the 1980s (the rise of the "moral majority") made big waves in the ocean of American history. The ripple effects continue down to the present. (The ideological conflict between tribalism and nationalism, discussed in this chapter, looks like one of those ripples.)

The protagonists and antagonists of the culture wars (depending on which side you are on) usually get labeled "Left" and "Right." And the church has (mostly) failed to transcend this simplified polarization.

Looking at the struggle between the Christian Left and the Christian Right, we immediately see the *competing narratives* at the heart of the struggle. James Davison Hunter captures this clash of narratives as concisely as anyone:

> Like politically conservative Christians, politically progressive Christians also are defined by and operate within a reading of myth and history. If conservatives are animated by a mythic ideal of the *right ordering* of society, and thus see modern history as a decline from order to disorder, progressives have always been animated by the myth of *equality and community* and therefore see history as an ongoing struggle to realize these ideals.[15]

Let's fill in some of the details of this thumbnail sketch of two competing narrative visions for America. The chart below indicates how narrative elements form the core of the progressive and the conservative worldviews.[16]

|  | *Progressive Christians* | *Conservative Christians* |
|---|---|---|
| *masterplot for current action* | holy war (liberation from oppression); comedic (social and racial reconciliation) | holy war (re-ordering chaos) |
| *historical inspiration* | American Revolution as part of a wider emancipation story (French Revolution ideals of liberty, equality, fraternity) | American Revolution as founding of a Christian nation (or a nation heavily influenced by Christianity) |
| *temporal orientation* | future (eschatological kingdom of God as ideal to work toward) | past ("golden age" of America governed by Constitution/Judeo-Christian morality) |
| *heroes* | multi-national: Frederick Douglass, Martin Luther King, Mother Teresa, Nelson Mandela | American: George Washington/Founding Fathers |
| *biblical role models* | Prophets (broadsides against the wealthy) | Moses (founder of a nation, lawgiver) |

15. Hunter, *Change the World*, 132 (italics mine).
16. Based on ibid., 112–15, 117–18, 132–36, 141–43.

## Part 3: How Stories Change Lives

|  | *Progressive Christians* | *Conservative Christians* |
|---|---|---|
| *anecdotes of atrocity*\* | vindictive behavior of the religious Right | vindictive behavior of the secular government |
| \* "Stories are always the most poignant way to communicate to people . . . " (Hunter, *Change the World*, 118). |||

By focusing on the narrative elements of these worldviews, I trust we have highlighted the selectivity practiced by the storytellers of both camps. (There is always more than one way to tell any story, including the American story.)

We could extend this set of narrative contrasts, but I would rather shift attention to what the Christian Right and the Christian Left have in common. Both have some sort of sense of ownership of America. The Right (obviously) because of the "Christian nation" conviction. The Left may eschew such rhetoric, but their donning of the mantle of the Hebrew "prophet" implies a megaphone voicing Yahweh's warnings to his kingdom.

But what if both versions of Christianity are becoming disenfranchised? This has long been the situation in many European countries (Germany; England; etc.), where only the tiniest sliver of the population attends church. Projecting into the not-too-distant future, one suspects that the USA is not far behind the European trend.

If we are, in reality, witnessing the shrinking of the size and influence of the American church, what might this new ("post-Constantinian") setting imply for our Christian scripts?

The social marginalization of the church means that our setting mirrors (in some respects) the setting of the ancient church of the first century. Perhaps, then, we might take some cues from how our ancient forebears scripted their interaction with the dominant culture.

In order to map out the range of options, we may borrow from sociological research on how "sects" relate to the dominant culture. (I get that some of you might be uncomfortable with the term "sect"; I use it in the neutral sense, denoting small communities of religious minorities.) The following list of seven scripts is adapted (with minor modifications) from the work of Derek Tidball:[17]

**Sociological Model: How "Sects" Relate to the Dominant Culture**

| conversionist | rescues people from "evils" of main culture |
|---|---|
| revolutionist | waits for destruction of "evil" culture |
| introversionist | insulates individuals from "evil" culture |
| reinterpreting | re-interprets marginalization as a badge of honor |
| wonder-working | reliance on miracles to cope with socioeconomic disadvantage |
| reformist | accepts status quo; works to modify its "evils" |
| utopian | works to ultimately eliminate "evil" status quo |

---

17. Tidball, *Social Context*, chapter 8.

The early church developed a wide range of responses to the challenge of living as a religious minority in the Roman Empire. Arguably, all of the seven scripts (from the list above) appeared in the primitive church (except the utopian).

In terms of a viable current option, I personally am most intrigued by the analogy offered by the Pastoral Letters (1–2 Timothy and Titus). Under the above scheme, these letters would appear to be:

- *Conversionist*: emphasizing that salvation delivers from vice to virtue.

- *Reformist*: safeguards the stability of the Greco-Roman social order; works within the framework of Greco-Roman society to promote a Christianized version of the nobler values of Greco-Roman society.

If you go to church, I invite you to ponder this list of seven cultural scripts for religious minorities. Which (if any) do you see operating in the ideology of your church?

\* \* \* \* \*

This chapter has taken a panoramic view of cultural scripts—the big umbrellas under which our personal narratives develop. The next three chapters zoom the lens closer, using the topical heading "Selves Under Construction." We explore further ways in which narratives contour our personal identity. We begin this close-up focus in chapter 18, which examines how flawed narratives contribute to psychological problems.

# 18

# Selves under Construction (1)
## Losing the Plot

STORIES HAVE POWER—MORE THAN we imagine. Have you ever paused to consider the negative power of a wrong story?

> Our thoughts are a shorthand version of a longer life story, says author Byron Katie... Sometimes we tell ourselves the wrong story, one that keeps us from realizing our full potential, while making us miserable at the same time. Examples might include, "I will always be overweight," "My partner doesn't love me," or "I'm stuck here."[1]

Think of your own common self-talk (or ask someone who has to listen to you on a regular basis!) What are some of your most frequent shorthand expressions to describe your life? How are these phrases windows into your version of a life story? Does your "plotline summary" have any negative impact on how you think and behave?

In this chapter, we explore some of the negative consequences of defective life stories. What happens to people who lack a life-shaping narrative, or who inhabit a flawed narrative? Psychological malaise (various kinds, in varying degrees). To illustrate, let's look at the story of the Sculptor.[2] An individual with a painful past, translated into a fatally flawed script, guaranteed to produce frustration in the present and into the foreseeable future.

As an infant, the Sculptor was unable to digest milk. The heaven of feeding at his mother's breast soon turned into the hell of uncontrolled projectile vomiting. A repeated scene, leaving an impression that reinforced and magnified itself with every cycle. "Distress, pain, pleasure, and terror were tightly fused."[3]

When he turned three, these formative scenes of infancy were compounded by the birth of baby sister, consuming maternal attention. When baby sister occupied the paradise of his mother, he withdrew to his room and refused to speak. Isolation was better than the torture of witnessing his mother betray him by breastfeeding little sister.

1. Fertig, "Healing Power of Story," 19.
2. My version culls from and simplifies the account by Tomkins, "Script Theory," 201–15.
3. Ibid., 202.

Aged four, the Sculptor became fascinated with the creation story of Genesis 1. This fascination intersected hearing his mother often describe his little sister as "perfectly *sculpted*."[4]

The story of creation. A mother who gave life to a "perfectly sculpted" sibling. These narratives inspired his adult work as a creative sculptor. Rather strangely, however, he took to hoarding numerous finished pieces, refusing to exhibit his beautiful artifacts!

How can we make sense of the Sculptor's biography?

Tomkins views human life in terms of formative *scenes* and overarching *scripts*.[5] (See our discussion of script theory, in chapter 15.) To radically simplify: Beginning in early infancy, experiences of pleasure and pain (especially when repeated and magnified) are scenes that generate scripts (preferred habitual responses to present and future scenes of pain or pleasure).

This basic dualism, grounded in the positive and negative values of pleasure and pain, resonates with "Literary Criticism 101." Stories oscillate around the protagonist's fears and longings, nightmares and dreams.[6]

In terms of scenes generating scripts, painful scenes may have more influence than pleasurable ones. "Negative events produce more cognitive activity in general and more efforts to engage in causal reasoning, compared to positive events. At the level of the life story, negative events seem to demand an explanation."[7]

OK, so back to the Sculptor. His biography may be the outworking of a fairly common script (one discussed in Tomkins, "Script Theory," 196–201). In terms of narrative archetypes, the Sculptor is trapped by a tragic quest for paradise restored.[8] In his story, "paradise" equals a euphoric state analogous to feeding at his mother's breast—before the "expulsion from Eden" associated first with projectile vomiting, and then with the unwelcome arrival of baby sister.

The tragedy arises from the fusion of incompatible goals (positive and negative). He seeks entry to an idealized heaven *and* avoidance of anything that feels remotely like hell. This script generates endless no-win scenarios, where his achievement of his negative goal automatically voids his positive goal.

For instance, his childhood strategy of *retreat* protects him from the unbearable pain of witnessing his sibling "usurp" maternal attention, but excludes him from the paradise of mother's presence.

In adulthood, the creative activity of *sculpture* appears to be an attempt to usurp the life-giving power of the mother, thereby re-entering paradise. But the *hoarding* of his sculptures precludes anyone validating his creativity, and so undermines his sense of paradise—even if hoarding protects him from the pain of rejection in the form of critical reviews, and from having to share the maternal life-giving power with others (as he had

---

4. Ibid., 206 (italics mine).
5. Ibid., 148, 150, 153–55.
6. Rkyen, *Windows to the World*, 118–19.
7. McAdams, "Personal Narratives," 253.
8. Tomkins explicitly invokes the archetypes of *tragedy* and *paradise restored* in his explanation of the Sculptor (Tomkins "Script Theory," 197, 206).

been forced to share his mother with his baby sister). Intriguingly, a number of great artists had a hoarding habit (e.g., Hemmingway; Picasso).[9]

* * * * *

The Sculptor's bizarre, self-frustrating behavior (hoarding his creative product) may exemplify (in extreme form) a more universal tendency. Cáit O'Dwyer discusses the *"someday"/"if only"* life stories (utopian projection or nostalgic reminiscence).[10] The two often combine. The utopian hope goads the protagonist into deluded quests ("Someday, X will happen and everything will be OK"). The fixation on an equally idealized past paralyzes the protagonist ("If only X hadn't happened back then, everything would now be OK").

Before reading on, you may wish to pause and reflect on your own self-talk. Do you have a version of the "someday"/"if only" storylines? If so, how does this belief impact your feelings, your self-image, your decisions, or your behavior?

My own story has included an unrealistic quest for idealized place, manifesting both sides of the "someday"/"if only" script. Once this script entangles you, escaping its delusions becomes next-to-impossible. For me, researching, writing, and reflecting on this book revealed the multiple threads that tangle this script into every strand of my story.

Where to begin? In unraveling tangled yarn, you grab a random thread and pull. So let's start in a Barnes & Noble bookstore, in a suburb of Philadelphia, in the mid-nineties. I'm combing the shelves at random, and notice Thomas Hardy's novel *Jude the Obscure*. Ten years earlier, a friend had recommended it. So I pick it up, find the comfy chair, and start reading. Three hours later, I'm still reading. (I did purchase that copy, eventually.) What gripped me? Back in chapter 1 of this book, narrator #5 observed, "It can take a long time to figure out why a particular story so grabs your heart." But Hardy's plot offers me a big clue. It's about Jude's failed quest to gain access to the University of "Christminster" (a transparent renaming of Oxford). How I suffered along with the man who found the way back into paradise blocked by angels wielding fiery swords!

Another strand: Is it coincidental that my first published scholarly essay dealt with the theme of sacred space?[11] Place is so powerful, it can almost become a metaphor for one's identity and life story (as many case studies document).[12]

In earlier scenes from my childhood, inability to find my place (outside my home) surfaced early and often. In kindergarten, we sat on low chairs with four children to a table. Opposite me, a sweet little girl. Each day, at 11:00 a.m., milk was served at our tables. One day, I accidentally spilled my milk. It deluged across the table, soaking my sweet little neighbor. She started crying. Our teacher let out a yell of accusation. "Adrian! Why did you do that! Get a cloth and clean it up!"

---

9. Ibid., 214.
10. O'Dwyer, *Imagining One's Future*, 205–12.
11. Smith, "Fifth Gospel."
12. E.g., Crossley, "Sense of Place," 279–94.

But it was an accident. Traumatized at the unjust rebuke, I sobbed out the incident to my mother after school. Up to that incident, I had enjoyed my kindergarten. But now, I never ever wanted to return. My mother agreed with me (!) . . . and so I experienced my first exile from paradise.

A year later, we moved to a small village in rural England, and I enrolled in an elementary school. Up to age eleven, this village and school was my new paradise. Wonderful teachers. No homework. Gangs (non-criminal) of friends. Captain of the soccer team. Chess champion. What was not to like?

At age eleven, a big "mistake" exiled me once more from paradise. Back then, English children took a standardized test, which determined your destination for middle school (and probably the rest of your life). Pass the test, you got to go to the state-run equivalent of a college prep school. Fail the test, you got to go to a school where the most intellectually challenging subjects were woodwork and metalwork.

I passed the test. Why did I label this a "mistake"? Well, all (100 percent) of my friends from our village were forced to enroll in the school that taught woodwork and metalwork. I alone bussed many miles to the college prep school. And was I lonely. Even though I made the soccer team, and ranked first in my class academically (they used to rank students back then), I was miserable to the point of depression. I hated spending the evening doing homework, when my old friends were outside kicking a soccer ball. I hated the pressure to perform, to live up to my number one ranking.

I lasted less than a year. One morning, in early spring, I told my mother, "I don't want to go to school today!" Once more, she agreed with me (!) . . . and I was back to the wilderness in my search for a place outside my home.

These early childhood scenes probably explain my particular version of the "someday"/"if only" script (the search for a "commonwealth" where I can be a "citizen"). However, informed by my Christian faith, I do wonder if those early scenes merely surface a deeper, "collective subconscious" memory of a primordial loss of paradise.

In seeking extrication from the tangles of "someday"/"if only," the narrative of Hebrews is helping me. Plotline summary: Here, we have no enduring city, but seek an eternal city, whose builder and maker is God (Heb 11:10; 13:14). Jumping ahead, I have a meditation on "place" in Hebrews in chapter 23 of this book.

Back to my childhood "wilderness wanderings." My next school cost my parents money. It was founded centuries ago, and one illustrious pupil was William Penn (founder of Pennsylvania). It was a boarding school, so I had to live away from home. (We got to go home at the weekends.) Issues of identity and place soon surfaced. In many respects, I actually enjoyed being at school during the week. They taught me Greek and Latin, and let me play a ton of soccer. However, I felt an unresolved contradiction. I also loved returning home at the weekends, and I came to dread the Sunday evening drives back to school. Looking back, I think I understand the struggle between two place-related identities. Was I the Monday-Friday kid, living away from my family, or was I the Weekend kid, back with family?

My strategy for coping with this tension will lead us into discussion of other malaises connected with flawed scripts and lack of scripts.

PART 3: HOW STORIES CHANGE LIVES

One philosopher of narrative has said, "Deprive children of stories and you leave them *unscripted, anxious* stutterers in their actions as in their words."[13]

Was I anxious about my place? Definitely. Was the real me the weekend inhabitant of my family home, or the weekday inhabitant of my boarding school? Unscripted? It felt that way. As a disturbing illustration of what the scriptless may do, here's what happened next.

Back in my (garden of Eden) elementary school, one of my teachers had made a curious entry on my report card. "Adrian's occasional mild *misbehavior,* far from being a cause for concern, is actually a sign that he *feels at home* in the school." Just the script for my hour of need!

In my post-Edenic boarding school, I cautiously improvised that script. Perhaps some mild misbehavior (acceptable to the authorities—"Boys will be boys") might re-establish my sense of place. And it worked. Some mild pranks won the awe of the other boys, and even some of the younger teachers nostalgic for their youth. I began to feel at home. The problem with that script, however, soon emerged. After mild pranks, what do you do for an encore? The misbehavior escalated, culminating in the official reason for my expulsion: "Adrian has instigated an orgy of *vandalism*."[14]

\* \* \* \* \*

If the absence of a narrative script can produce anxiety, the availability of too many competing and mutually cancelling scripts can produce apathy:

> In a pluralistic culture, in which many stories are simultaneously and powerfully presented to the young, a certain confusion, malaise, and loss of confidence often result. No one story commands allegiance. Action, therefore, lacking a story to give it significance, seems pointless. Why bother to do anything at all? . . . The young often begin to sleep a lot. Not to have any story to live out is to experience nothingness: the primal formlessness of human life below the threshold of narrative structuring.[15]

Then again, an entire grab bag of psychological malaise intersects not the absence of story, nor the cancelling effect of competing stories, but the prison-house of a particularly paralyzing kind of story. Nihilism; depression; fatalism; paranoia. Whilst these malaises may have several complex causes, they are bound together by a simple script. For believers in this simple narrative, their life story simply cannot have any kind of positive outcome. Tragedy, without any redeeming epilogue.

MacIntyre pinpoints the narrative roots of *nihilism*: "When someone complains—as do some of those who attempt or commit suicide—that his or her life is meaningless, he or she is often and perhaps characteristically complaining that the narrative of their

---

13. MacIntyre, "Virtues," 101–2 (italics mine).
14. Cf. the discussion of the self as vandal in chapter 14.
15. Novak, *Ascent of the Mountain*, 52.

life has become unintelligible to them, that it lacks any point, any movement toward a climax or *telos*."[16]

As one who has struggled with *depression* (see chapter 2, above), I resonate with MacIntyre. For me, the mire of depression resembled that phase of folk tales (like Snow White or Sleeping Beauty) when the protagonist is asleep, paralyzed under a spell. Ultimately, my depression was failure of belief, or failure of imagination. In my many struggles inside the dark cloud, one sign always foreshadowed eventual release: I got a tiny glimpse of a positive future for myself, a story with a role worth playing.

In glimpsing a potentially positive next chapter to my story, you could say I got lucky (or maybe received grace). After all, I inhabited a culture which retains a storehouse of upbeat narratives. Not all cultures have this treasury (and maybe ours is losing it). Brian Sutton-Smith illustrates how the ability to form stories with positive endings intersects cultural heritage. Building on his research into how children create fictional narratives, he offers this generalization: "We have detected four stages in the way children come to deal with their characters and their conflicts. The conflicts are usually over villainy (attack, threat . . . ) or deprivation (loss of love, food . . . )."[17] The four stages represent progressively greater triumphs of the fictional protagonist, from zero to maximal.[18] Many stories feature zero response by the protagonist to the threat or loss. In others, the protagonist responds but fails. In a third kind of story, the threat/loss is nullified. The fourth kind resolves in a complete transformation ("happily ever after"), in which the threat/loss can never reappear.

Sutton-Smith notes that some *fatalistic* cultures fail to generate stories of nullification or transformation: "From . . . cross-cultural evidence . . . it is also clear that there are many societies in which no such belief in one's ability to overcome the *fates* exists, and in these cultures the stories do not rise above the first or second levels."[19]

Even Western culture, so richly stocked with redemptive narratives,[20] has occasionally developed fatalistic scripts bordering on *paranoia*.[21] In the fifteenth century, mass outbreaks of pestilence generated a subculture obsessed with the specter of death, the grim reaper scything down men and women in their prime. In the twentieth century, as the USA and USSR stockpiled weapons of mass destruction, the specter of thermonuclear cataclysm haunted large subsets of the population.

Despite these collective examples, paranoia in its purest form exists in the isolated individual. An old joke captures the frustration of dealing with a paranoiac, who bats away any challenge with the response, "You too would be paranoid if the whole world was against you!"

We all need life narratives to navigate the world: to synthesize the fixity of the past with the relative openness of the future; to explain the presence of good and evil; to relate

---

16. MacIntyre, "Virtues," 103 (italics in original).
17. Sutton-Smith, "Children's Fiction Making," 83.
18. Ibid., 83–87.
19. Ibid., 87 (italics mine).
20. For discussion of some of these upbeat scripts, see McAdams, *Redemptive Self*.
21. Keen, "Paranoia and Cataclysmic Narratives," 180–81, 189–90.

ourselves to other people.[22] The paranoiac imposes upon life a skewed form of narrative coherence, where the inevitable triumph of evil (in cataclysmic form) "makes sense" of everything (like conspiracy theories, for their adherents).[23] However, the weight of being the sole guardian of the "true" narrative crushes the narrator: "The narrative of cataclysm ... articulates the futurelessness and the loneliness of paranoia. This narratizing effort attempts to mediate past and future, good and evil, self and other, and it fails on all three accounts. The future cannot redeem us, good will not survive evil, and my loneliness will not be healed."[24]

As we begin to wrap up this chapter, let us review and summarize. We've proposed that various kinds of psychological malaise (e.g., anxiety; apathy) intersect the absence of a plausible life narrative. Other malaises (e.g., nihilism, depression, fatalism, paranoia) afflict protagonists who adhere to narratives that lack a positive resolution. In addition, many of us are deluded and/or paralyzed by some version of the "someday"/"if only" script.

To supplement these proposals, let us take note of a generic type of unhappiness that accompanies life stories which ignores basic distinctions between past and future.[25] Put bluntly, the past is fixed and the future (relatively) open. Accordingly, the narrative of our past can and should have greater depth and fixity than the narrative we improvise in the present and tentatively project into the future. Our mental health requires it. "Psychic strength includes both a strong sense of self-identity, rooted in the past, and an equally strong power of self-transcendence, directed toward the future."[26]

When we forget or suppress our past, or ignore our past in our scramble to reach the future, our identity "contracts to the thinness of its personal pronoun."[27]

Conversely, when we cryogenically freeze our past identity, our past storyline, and rigidly extrapolate this self into the future, we resist the very possibility of beneficial growth or change.[28]

As a final illustration, we may mention problems that result from certain kinds of *backstory*—namely, inherited scripts from previous generations, which overshadow and inhibit the emergence of our own story.

We all arrive on the world stage with a backstory—the lingering impact of storylines lived by previous generations. And this may not be a bad thing. It can even be positive, a form of inheritance, a gift of stability and direction. Our inherited scripts can enable us to improvise a healthy version of our own personal narrative.

If our lives are a drama, then act one establishes the setting, the givens, such as time, place, and cast of characters, and any backstory bequeathed by previous generations. So it's always worth asking, "What narrative did my parents, my ethnic group, my nation pass on to me? Does this inherited narrative empower or paralyze my own story?"

22. Ibid., 176.
23. Ibid., 178–79.
24. Ibid., 188.
25. Crites, "Storytime," 152–73.
26. Ibid., 171.
27. Ibid., 172.
28. Ibid.

During the summer of 2014, we had the opportunity to witness (in most excruciating form) the negative impact of an overpowering backstory.

Brazil. A nation for whom soccer is virtually a religion. In 2014, the host nation for (arguably) the greatest sporting circus on earth, the World Cup. An event televised to billions worldwide.

Brazil had hosted the tournament once before, in 1950. There, in their country's soccer stadium, the cathedral of their national obsession, they drank the bitter cup of a humiliating defeat to their South American rivals, Uruguay, who defeated Brazil 2–1 and became world champions on Brazilian soil.

The national psyche was deeply scarred. Never again, they vowed—not in our house. The "ghost story" of 1950 initially had a positive impact. It drove generations of Brazilian soccer geniuses to unprecedented accomplishments. Over the subsequent decades, in tournaments held on other nations' soil, Brazil racked up an unmatched total of five world crowns. Their superstars became so famous, they needed no more than one name for the purposes of identification (a bit like Jesus or Moses): Pele, Zico, Socrates, Ronaldo, Ronaldinho.

In 2014, Brazil had the opportunity to exorcise the ghosts of 1950. The World Cup returned, at last, to Brazilian soil. New stadiums were constructed, at great expense. A soccer squad was assembled. Not the best Brazilian side ever—but with home field advantage in every game, surely a real contender.

As Brazil progressed nervously through the tournament, the ghosts of 1950 became more and more palpable. The national psyche was tortured by hope. Eventually, the Brazil team was one step away from the final. The coveted trophy was so close, they could almost reach out and touch it. Only semifinal opponents Germany stood in their way.

I watched the semifinal on a big-screen TV, in a local pub, surrounded by a rowdy multinational crowd. I expected a tight game. Instead, a surreal result. One of the greatest humiliations in the history of the sport. Germany 7, Brazil 1. No typo, you read it correctly. (To contextualize: think of a Super Bowl final, with a 49–7 blow-out.)

How can one explain such a disaster? Were the Germans really that good? (The narrowness of their victory in the final, versus Argentina, suggested otherwise.) Were the Brazilians really that bad (with talented players like Oscar in their team)?

Narrative psychology would propose an alternative explanation. Brazil was crushed by the burden of their backstory. The ghosts of 1950 returned—on steroids—to haunt them.

Against Germany, Brazil played a kamikaze game, as if pure passion could trump sound tactics. Brazil had to win, they must win, to exorcise the spirits of the past. The overbearing backstory was more than they could bear, and they collapsed into soccer dysfunctionality.

\* \* \* \* \*

This chapter has floated a simple thesis: psychological malaise accompanies defective life stories. We've only drilled a few inches down this potentially very rich mine of wisdom.

But hopefully we've illustrated the value of narrative as a critical tool for diagnosing the ills of the soul. Here are our examples of this, in condensed tabular form:

| Defective Life Story | Psychological Malaise |
| --- | --- |
| "someday..." <br> "if only..." | delusion <br> paralysis |
| absence of script <br> over-abundance of scripts | anxiety <br> apathy |
| lack of positive ending | nihilism; depression; fatalism; paranoia |
| indeterminate past <br> fossilized future | shrunken identity <br> obstruction of positive growth or change |
| overbearing backstories | unbearable burdens → dysfunction |

At this juncture, I invite you to take an honest look at your own life. Most of us don't visit psychotherapists—but all of us (in varying degrees) experience psychological problems and exhibit harmful behavior-patterns.

Are you able to clearly identify some of your own problematic traits, mental and behavioral? If so, are you able to see connections between your problems and the *story* you repeat to yourself about your life?

\* \* \* \* \*

If defective personal narratives contribute to a range of psychological problems, then the upbeat counterpoint involves the healing power of better stories. In our next chapter, we investigate some of the rich healing potential of good stories.

# 19

## Selves under Construction (2)
### Healing Plots

IF DEFECTIVE LIFE STORIES contribute to psychological malaise, the antidote seems obvious: "A growing number of clinical and counseling psychologists are beginning to see psychotherapy as fundamentally a process of *story reformulation and repair*."[1]

For example, in the penal system, rehabilitation of criminals requires life stories that "acknowledge wrongdoing, manage shame, and point the way to a reformed life."[2]

Likewise, some group therapy programs for heroin addicts rely upon a narrative: "A first phase in which the newcomer understands his problems and finds the will to solve them . . . a second phase in which he finds alternative behaviors . . . a third phase in which he, by continuous practice . . . makes the new behaviors his own."[3] In terms of archetypal plots, the addict is summoned into a quest narrative: "Wisdom is the most rewarding prize waiting at the end of the path."[4] The phases of this narrative, reinforced by weekly therapy sessions, intentionally replace the "magic fatalism" of the addict's narrative, namely the passive wait for a one-shot fix that solves their problems.[5]

In this chapter, I reflect on narrative's "inherent" power to heal. Whence the therapeutic power of story? Obviously, we mean "good" stories, given my previous chapter on defective life scripts! Narrative psychologist McAdams affirms the axiom, "Some stories are better than others."[6] In chapter 8 of this book, I express my Christian hunch that all good stories are allegories of the one great story. Still, we gain wisdom from exploring the narrative texture of any healing story.

Let's begin with an inventory: What are some basic gifts conferred by a good life story? *Stability and wholeness* tag many of the benefits. Who am I? Identity ceases if I dissolve into flux and indeterminacy. Story gives basic coordinates for stable identity.

---

1. McAdams, "Personal Narratives," 248 (italics mine).
2. Ibid.
3. Fasulo, "Theories of Self," 328.
4. Ibid.
5. Ibid., 335.
6. McAdams, "Personal Narratives," 247.

*First*, since we live in time, story preserves our identity over time. Story integrates our past, present, and future.[7] Plot interprets personal change via metaphors ("evolution"; "transformation"; "reinvention") that conserve the thread of selfhood.

*Second*, story gives us a role, a script, often compressed into a dominant self-image. Real-time situations present miniature crises, with numerous forks in the road. Our role, our self-image, symbolizes a plotline compass that keeps us on a particular track.

*Third*, story integrates the contradictory aspects of self.[8] Unfolded in plot, our inconsistencies often make sense as compensations for the built-in limitations of our dominant script.

If you own an articulate personal narrative, I invite you to pause and reflect on the numerous psychological benefits your story gives you. Or, if you are someone who lacks a strong and clear sense of your own identity, I invite you to think about the stories you consume, and the stories you narrate about yourself. Perhaps there is something about these narratives which limits their power to help form a healthy identity?

In conferring all the stabilizing and integrating psychological benefits we've been listing, our life stories act like protagonists in archetypal plots. A good life story images the opening chapter of Genesis, bringing order from the chaos we experience as voice- and event-bombardment. A good life story constructs a narrative world for us to indwell, and thereby functions as a quest for "place."

Ancient cultures grasped the power of story better than scientific cultures. The Ute tribe of Native Americans used to roam the elk trails on the heights of the Rocky Mountains of Colorado. The Ute told stories about their environment—stories that viewed the elk trails as life-giving beings, and stories that viewed the mountain heights as near to the abode of the gods. Easy to smile condescendingly at the superstition—but not so easy to find replacement stories that affirm *our* place in the cosmos.

\* \* \* \* \*

So far, we've inventoried some general benefits of owning a life story. Let us now shift to some experiential dimensions of reading/watching/hearing (and telling) stories, and tease out some healing benefits of this experience.

In chapter 12, we looked at multiple ways that readers experience stories as blessings. Here's a subset of these blessings, a list that opens vistas onto the healing power of narrative:

- escape
- dignifying the mundane
- hope
- establishing a personal point of view

Let's explore these healing dynamics. When we watch a film, or read a novel, we are like a character in an archetypal plot of "voyage-and-return." Like the little yellow guy in

7. Crites, "Storytime," 155–70.
8. McAdams, "Personal Narratives," 244.

Google Maps, we explore the unfamiliar terrain of the world of the story. Then we exit the virtual world of the story, and return to our own life. Let's investigate this experience, using the checklist (above) of some of the typical outcomes of immersion in novels and films. As we investigate, I will prompt you to contemplate your own consumption of stories, and ponder the benefits they confer (or don't confer).

## ESCAPISM

*Escapism*! That's bad, right? Well, it depends. C. S. Lewis aptly notes that every act of reading involves escape, in the sense of mental projection into the world conjured up by the text.[9] According to Lewis, there are two kinds of escapist readers. One egocentric (and baser), one self-transcending (and nobler). The former reads narrative for "egoistic castle-building"—the vicarious thrill of imagining the protagonist's exploits (erotic; military; entrepreneurial; etc.) as one's own.[10] The latter seeks the "enlargement of our being" that comes from exposure to other worlds and viewpoints.[11] Of this kind of escape, Lewis writes: "Here, as in worship, as in love, in moral action, and in knowing, I transcend myself; and am never more myself than when I do."[12] Defenders of the nobler kind of literary escapism use "re-" words to describe the benefits of a temporary sojourn from the pain and boredom of our own existence.[13] Recreate. Reinvigorate. Regroup. Re-form. All imply an eventual return, from the story-world, better equipped to deal with our own world. (What about your own escapist reading and viewing? How does it impact your functioning in the real world?)

And then there's *rest*. Have you noticed how novels often follow scenes of intense action with "downtime" for the characters (and the readers)? Tolkien's hobbits, exhausted from battling goblins, rest up in elven sanctuaries. For many readers, entry into the story-world of a text offers the mental and emotional equivalent of an elven sanctuary. Here, the *aesthetics* of narrative provide balm for the soul; the "emotional equilibrium" that follows a "complete aesthetic experience."[14] Lewis almost drools over the *poetics* of narrative—"the balance and contrast and the unified multiplicity of its successive parts."[15] Reading becomes mental choreography, as we work through the plot's "rests and movements, the quickenings and slowings, the easier and the more arduous passages," with psychic benefits akin to those of regular bodily exercise.[16]

This *shalom*, associated with narrative aesthetics, may have even deeper dimensions. Bausch discusses the holistic, integrative properties of story—the power of narrative to link right brain and left brain; to bridge the unconscious world of dreams and

---

9. Lewis, *Experiment in Criticism*, 68.
10. Ibid., 52–55.
11. Ibid., 137.
12. Ibid., 141.
13. Cf. Bausch, *Storytelling*, 43–46.
14. Rosenblatt, *Literature as Exploration*, 52.
15. Lewis, *Experiment in Criticism*, 132.
16. Ibid., 134.

the conscious world of reason.[17] Narrative language evokes logic and analysis, and also arouses feelings and imagination. Our reason tracks narrative's temporal sequence and cause and effect; our fantasy entertains its imagery and symbols.

Narrative's access to our subconscious was utilized by psychologist Bruno Bettelheim, in his work with severely disturbed children.[18] He found that classic fairy tales were balm to the souls of his young patients. Interestingly, he concluded that the healing power of archetypal stories is best experienced *subconsciously* by the child, without the intrusive didacticism of parental analysis.[19]

When we return from the enchanted world of narrative, and re-enter our own mundane existence, what are some of the resources we bring back with us? When we put the novel down, or exit the cinema, perhaps we've experienced the power of story to dignify the mundane.

## DIGNIFY THE MUNDANE

Some of the enchantment of the story rubs off on our own world. If something in the story we read intersects something in our own life, our own life may start to glow with whatever glory the story possesses. (Think of your own favorite film. Where does the beauty of the "silver screen" shine onto your own humdrum realities?)

Finding a fit between a valorized narrative genre and our own circumstances confers considerable dignity upon us: "Just to be in the cast of a narrated drama which comes to be taken as exemplary or paradigmatic is some assurance of social *immortality*."[20] From another angle, stories (including the most fantastical) borrow elements from our everyday world, and use them to construct a transcendent world, whose glories reflect back onto the everyday elements. Stories are a *sacramental* medium: "Stories hint that our taken-for-granted realities may, in fact, be fraught with surprise. There are 'rumors of angels' and grace abounding in our world. If a frog might be a prince, a lost sailor an angel, a pilgrim the Christ, then all of creation may be a sacramental presence pointing to 'Something More.'"[21] Furthermore, since most stories told by humankind have positive resolutions, we often emerge from the world of narrative with renewed hope.[22]

## HOPE

The dynamics of tracking the plot intensify the consolation of hope. Tolkien (in *Tree and Leaf*) describes the archetypal upbeat ending: "A sudden joyous 'turn.' . . . However fantastic or terrible the adventure, it can give to child or man that hears it, when the

---

17. Bausch, *Storytelling*, 22–26, 38–39, 47–54.
18. Bettelheim, *Uses of Enchantment*.
19. Ibid., 18, 153–55.
20. Turner, "Social Dramas," 155 (italics mine).
21. Bausch, *Storytelling*, 196–97.
22. Ibid., 46, 60–62.

'turn' comes, a catch of breath, a beat and lifting of the heart, near to tears."[23] The film producers of Hollywood recognize the enormous emotional impact of this archetypal plot structure. Whether for base commercial or noble philosophical reasons, their films rely on the same upbeat plotlines as classic fairy tales and the Judeo-Christian narratives. (Ironic, given the tendency of conservative Christianity to demonize Hollywood.) Screenwriting guru Robert McKee gives his take:

> Hollywood filmmakers tend to be overly (some would say foolishly) optimistic about the capacity of life to change—especially for the better. Consequently, to express this vision they rely on the Archplot and an inordinately high percentage of positive endings. Non-Hollywood filmmakers tend to be overly (some would say chicly) pessimistic about change, professing that the more life changes, the more it stays the same, or, worse, that change brings suffering. Consequently, to express the futility, meaninglessness, or destructiveness of change, they tend to make static, Nonplot portraiture or extreme . . . Antiplots with negative endings.[24]

If the films that supply your metaphors for life are (credibly) optimistic, you gain a strong psychological resource. From the perspective of his work with severely disturbed children, Bettelheim affirms: "Only *hope* for the future can sustain us in the adversities we unavoidably encounter."[25] From working with heroin addicts, Jefferson A. Singer concluded that recovery hinged on the patient's ability to construct a *hopeful* life story.[26] Modern narrative psychology merely affirms what ancient wisdom has known all along. Bettelheim describes the function of optimistic fairy tales in Hindu therapy, where the tales are allegories of the inner life:

> In traditional Hindu medicine a fairy tale giving form to this particular problem was offered to a psychically disoriented person, for his meditation. It was expected that through contemplating the story the disturbed person would be led to visualize both the nature of the impasse in living from which he suffered, and the possibility of its resolution. From what a particular tale implied about man's despair, hopes, and methods of overcoming tribulations, the patient could discover not only a way out of his distress but also a way to find himself, as the hero of the story did.[27]

Perhaps your own favorite novel or film has an upbeat ending. If so, how did the narrative's image of hope translate into your own life story? Or did you experience the poignancy of disconnect between the beauty of well-told tales and the non-resolution of life's problems?

As we wind down this chapter, a brief reminder of where we have been. We've traced the "voyage-and-return" of the reader of stories. Escaping into the narrative world of a text, we find rest from the pain and frustration of our mundane existence. Returning

23. Quoted in Bettelheim, *Uses of Enchantment*, 143.
24. McKee, *Story*, 60.
25. Bettelheim, *Uses of Enchantment*, 4 (italics mine).
26. Singer, "Heroin Addict," 256, 270, 273–74.
27. Bettelheim, *Uses of Enchantment*, 25.

from the narrative world, we may find ourselves renewed. The story we have read may lend dignity to our mundane situation. The story may renew hope for our future.

Lastly, the story may have given us resources for establishing a personal point of view.

## ESTABLISHING A PERSONAL POINT OF VIEW

Narratives give us tools for constructing a life-affirming personal story. Through narrative, we find perspective for healing the pain of our past. "Story... helps the person to go back, not to change an unchangeable situation, but to *reinterpret it creatively*."[28]

By reading other stories, we learn to tell our own unique story. We become "a subjective storytelling 'I' whose stories about personal experience become part and parcel of a storied 'me.'"[29]

Many of us have been captivated by classic "coming-of-age" stories, because their plot emboldens our search for our own voice, our own identity, our own story. (Think of the power of J. D. Salinger's *Catcher in the Rye*, or the poignancy of the movie *Dead Poets Society*.) Perhaps there's a particular book or film that established and empowered your own view of the world. If so, you may benefit from contemplating that story's impact on you. Was the story simply a one-time trigger for change, or do you return to it for further guidance? If you've followed its script, have you encountered limits to its wisdom?

Through the temporary sojourn of reading, we gain a self-transcending viewpoint on our own situation. We get the lens of distance, of an external perspective. Likewise, the construction of a personal narrative can give us space for viewing ourselves more clearly. To that end, some "narrative therapists" even recommend the strange-sounding device of telling our own story in the *third-person*! ("Adrian has been struggling to meet a publisher's deadline.") Apparently, when used to recount negative episodes, the third-person viewpoint helps reduce anger and blood pressure.[30]

*Point-of-view* is integral to narrative (see chapters 7 and 12). We have all suffered injustices. Many of us have been victims of crime. Left untold, these events hover over an abyss of non-being. Storytelling memorializes the events. They matter, and they cannot be swept under the rug of an historical void. As narrators, we can bring the events under *our* evaluation, our point of view. Notice the positive shift. In the act of injustice, it subjected me. I was passive. But in the act of telling, we become active, we become the subject. And we get to evaluate the event, not as a brute fact, something that "simply happened," but as an injustice, a crime, an outrage.

To illustrate how story can bestow the healing gift of personal point of view, let us mention the Freedom Writers.[31] In the 1990s, Long Beach, California was dubbed the "Gangsta-Rap capital" of the USA. Walking to school, teenagers risked the cross fire of gun battles between rival gangs. Every teenager knew someone who had perished in

---

28. Bausch, *Storytelling*, 25 (italics mine).
29. McAdams, "Personal Narratives," 244.
30. Kamps, "Story That Can Change Your Life," 122.
31. Freedom Writers, *Freedom Writers Diary*.

gang violence. As a new teacher, Erin Gruwell found her class overwhelmed by apathy. She wrote, "To some of these kids, death seems more real than a diploma."[32]

Nevertheless, Gruwell found a way to motivate her students. She assigned two classic diaries, written by teens under the dark shadow of war. *Anne Frank: The Diary of a Young Girl*; and *Zlata's Diary: A Child's Life in Sarajevo*. Seeing so many stark parallels between these lives and the lives of her students, Gruwell wrote, "I think they'll be surprised how life mirrors art."[33]

The result: her students began to devour literature voraciously. They began to write their own diaries. They found their own voices. They abandoned the fatalistic belief that violence and racism are inevitable. They began to believe that stories could change the world. Read the book (*Freedom Writers Diary*) for yourself; or, at the very least, rent the movie adaptation (starring Hilary Swank).

\* \* \* \* \*

In this chapter, we explored some of the healing dimensions "inherent" to good stories. In our next chapter, we will investigate the quest for a healthy narrative identity. What are some of the challenges, resources, and processes involved in seeking our storied self?

---

32. Ibid., 49.
33. Ibid., 50.

## 20

## Selves under Construction (3)
A Work in Progress

IN THE LAST TWO chapters, we have felt out the power of story to shape our identity—both for good and for ill. Chapter 18 underscored the harmful effects of owning a defective personal narrative. Chapter 19, as a counterpoint, highlighted the healing power of healthy narratives.

Accordingly, finding our true selves entails "putting off" a defective narrative identity and "putting on" a healthy narrative identity (cf. Ephesians 4:20–24).

In this process, what are some of the *challenges* we face, and what are some of the *resources* that come to our aid? You may recall, back in chapters 3 and 4, our outline of the work of constructing a personal life story. The present chapter explores additional dimensions of that process.

\* \* \* \* \*

"What are you writing?" My friends at church often ask me that question; I usually reply, "A book about how our lives are like stories." Receiving my usual response, Dr. Atkinson observed, "Hmm . . . our lives may be like stories . . . But we only get to read one page at a time!"

While I'm watching a film (time for a nerdy confession), I cannot resist the temptation to figure out if the film belongs to a genre or subgenre of "the seven basic plots" (see chapter 8 above). At least half the time (especially with thoughtful films), the ending undercuts my initial hunch. What begins (say) as a battle against evil ends up being more about reconciliation between father and son.

These two anecdotes throw down a gauntlet to folks busy constructing a life narrative for themselves. How do we handle the indeterminacy (from our perspective) of the future?

Furthermore, this unpredictability co-exists with teleology (our sense that outcomes are designed, that events are funneled toward a goal). We anticipate "a future in which certain possibilities beckon us forward and others repel us, some seem already foreclosed and others perhaps inevitable."[1]

This tension (unpredictability plus teleology) gets intensified, not reduced, for those of us who embrace the Christian metanarrative. We indwell a paradoxical story: the kingdom of heaven is already here, and yet it isn't. (See chapter 10 above.) The implications for personal identity: "I am unfinished."[2]

As you peer into the uncertainties of your future, what silhouettes emerge in the fog? Imagine yourself five years from now—what images popped into your brain? How was your five-years-further-along self different from the present you? And how was this projection a clue to the storyline you inhabit?

Narrative psychology recognizes that our *quest for personal identity* may begin in adolescence and early adulthood—but the holy grail may prove elusive. "Into and through the midlife years, adults continue to refashion their narrative understandings of themselves."[3]

Let's see if the quest metaphor can guide us. The stories we project into the future must respect the future's uncertainty. Our projected scripts feel like "unchoreographed dance" or "improvisatory jazz."[4] Yet the dance, the jazz, needs a "point of departure, the launching pad for the great leap into the unknown."[5] What moves us forward? The beckoning into an archetypal plot: "Each [of us] is scheming and scurrying with all his might, in pursuit of what utopian dreams? what pile of gold for his golden years? what applause from his peers? what dark fantasy? what erotic adventure? what bright wings?"[6] The quest metaphor says to us, Yes, embark upon your pursuit, by all means—but recognize that the prize will transcend your initial objective. The initial lures are merely "realistic surrogates of the great hope we can scarcely name."[7]

\* \* \* \* \*

In this chapter, we explore some of the *challenges* we face in the quest for a personal narrative that can ground our identity. A narrative that makes sense of our past, and offers hope and direction as we move into the uncertain future.

In facing these challenges, what are some basic *resources* available to us? Consider the following checklist:

> How does one acquire a story? The culture in which one is born already has an image of time, of the self, of heroism, of ambition, of fulfillment. It burns its heroes and archetypes deeply into one's psyche. The tendencies and fears of one's parents, the figures one hears described in church, the living force of teachers and uncles and grandparents and neighbors, the example of companions along

1. MacIntyre, "Virtues," 101.
2. Cf. McLaren, *Generous Orthodoxy*, 289–97.
3. McAdams, "Personal Narratives," 252.
4. Crites, "Storytime," 164.
5. Ibid.
6. Ibid., 164–65.
7. Ibid., 170.

the way, the tales read in books or visualized in legend, cinema, the arts: all such influences impress one's imagination with possible courses of action, possible styles of life.[8]

Such lists do not exhaust the sources of our life scripts. We can sprinkle some other influences into the mix, and get the following (non-exhaustive) inventory of influences:

- cultural scripts (see chapters 15–17)
- the arts: stories in the form of novels, films, plays, etc.
- role models (from real life)
- daily conversations (oral storytelling)
- virtual conversations (online storytelling)
- rituals (see below)
- games (e.g., most video games are "dragon slaying" or "quest" narratives)
- role-play[9]
- replayed memories (e.g., "the Sculptor" [discussed in chapter 18])[10]
- dreams and daydreams[11]

All of the above impact us on a daily basis, more than we realize. Picking one at random: who are your real-life role models? Suppose you were to compile a select list of real people you have tried to emulate. Perhaps their character inspired you, or their conduct lit up the path to wisdom. What "plot genre" best describes the trajectory of their life, and how does that trajectory compare with your own story?

If you began to contemplate the other multiple influences in the list above, would this non-exhaustive list start to seem exhausting to you? Does its multi-vocal bombardment of scripts seem like over-choice, a bit like trying to find a breakfast cereal in a supermarket aisle?[12]

Actually, most of the listed sources of scripts have been around for millennia, and people survived with their identities intact. However, the twentieth century immersed us in an accelerated culture, in which script bombardment increased exponentially. Let's tabulate three cultural epochs to illustrate the problem:[13]

---

8. Novak, *Ascent of the Mountain*, 49. Compare the checklist given by Sarbin: "Human beings construct identities not only out of their *reading*, like Don Quixote, but also out of imaginings stirred by *orally told tales* or by the direct or vicarious witnessing of the actions of *role models* [italics mine]" (Sarbin, "Narrative as Root Metaphor," 17).

9. See Gordon, "Repetition and Identity," 133–57.

10. Sylvan S. Tomkins highlights "positive and negative *celebratory* scripts," which use memory to "describe, explain, and celebrate the nuclear scene that was once so wonderful and then turned so bad *and* the continuing family of scenes which have been repeated again and again and which cast a long shadow over the future" (Tomkins, "Script Theory," 204 [emphasis his]).

11. Cf. Crites, "Storytime," 169–70.

12. Cf. page 56 of this book on the problem of choosing from an excess of available stories.

13. Adapted from McLeod, "Storytelling in Postpsychological Counseling," 18.

| *Traditional* Society | *Modern* Society | *Postmodern* Society |
|---|---|---|
| *oral* culture | *print* culture | *digital* culture (TV, internet, computer games) |
| relatively limited stock of mythic-religious stories | wide range of stories (novels; newspapers) | limitless choice of stories (global narrative industry) |

Facebook. Twitter. Email. Voicemail. Feel overwhelmed? Join the club. Kenneth Gergen (a psychologist) coined two terms that describe the disorientation felt in the electronic village. "Multiphrenia" (i.e., schizophrenia on steroids); "the Saturated Self."[14] Our identity gets molded by two-way traffic: stories we tell and stories we hear in daily social interactions. When the quantity of that traffic increases exponentially, and the kind of traffic diversifies pluralistically, the self-image equivalent of a multi-car pileup looms ahead.

Hardcore postmoderns go one step beyond Gergen, and affirm (or celebrate?) the death of the stable self. "Rather than cementing an identity as an ontology of the person . . . [we] start from the assumption that narratives form something like a playground—a ground that allows us to test out identity categories."[15] McAdams summarizes the views of advocates of the "dialogical self": "Narrative identity is akin to a polyphonic novel that is authored by many different voices within the person, all of whom engage in dialogue with each other and with flesh-and-blood characters in the external world."[16]

\* \* \* \* \*

Even if we disagree with these postmodern denials of coherent personal identity, we must still take seriously the *shaping power of conversational stories*. Informal social interactions (real or virtual) give us the platform for telling the story called "this is who I am." For every weekly sermon that Christian teens fidget through, they have thirty, sixty or a hundred digital social media interactions. To an extent far greater than most of us realize, "selves are 'talked into being'" via mundane everyday discourse.[17]

Let's give a concrete example. As a writer, my eyes and ears are always open for material. (Don't tell me your personal stories, if you wish them to remain private!) Here's some material I heard riding the subway. The speaker: Yolanda, a young African-American lady (single mom?) The addressee: a girl, around ten years old (her daughter?) The discourse went something like this:

> Them bitches in my hair salon, they done me wrong.
> Rich lady comes in, they sez to me, "Yolanda! You sweep up the hair!"
> I'm new, so I don't get no say.
> So I'm sweeping the floor.
> Rich lady sits down.

---

14. For a synopsis of Gergen, see Holstein and Gubrium, *Self We Live By*, 58–60.
15. Bamberg et al., "Introduction," 6.
16. McAdams, "Personal Narratives," 243.
17. Holstein and Gubrium, *Self We Live By*, 124.

> One of them bitches gets to cut her hair, and gets her big fat tip.
> Bitches only ever let me work the poor customers.
> But them bitches are going down!
> Once I work there another month, I'm getting in their faces, and they're going down!

Listening to this narrative, I sympathized with Yolanda. I've had jobs where I was low down the pecking order. That said, I did wonder about the impact of Yolanda's narrative upon her ten-year-old auditor. Heard on a daily basis, what view of the world might this story convey?

In microcosm, Yolanda's narrative projects a classic plotline of "ascent" (see chapter 8 above). Rags-to-riches (or at least higher tips). Setting, inciting incident, pivot, and destination—the anecdote has them all. Auditors interpret stories subjectively, but here's the worldview I felt Yolanda conveyed:

| Setting | "social Darwinism" (law of the jungle) |
| Value | necessity of money |
| Change | the brave self is all you can rely upon |

This was a very one-sided conversation. Usually, however, there's two-way traffic. Our *audience* impacts the telling of the tale in which our identity takes shape. The self-image we project, and the plotline we own—both are impacted by our audience.

When a group of teenagers share stories, the need to "hold the floor" is paramount. This social constraint tends to skew the way narrators depict themselves. Suppose the narrator participated in a traumatic event. How do they describe their role? McAdams notes a bias toward extreme images of self: "as brave and courageous (John Wayne), [or] caring and concerned (Florence Nightingale)."[18]

Audience also shapes the plotline we own (or are allowed to own). Take the stories typically told in support groups for caregivers married to patients with Alzheimer's disease.[19] Caregiver narratives oscillate between two extreme plotlines. One, with caregiver as "martyr," is a subgenre of tragedy. (The caregiver fights a losing battle, persevering in a relationship that becomes increasingly one-sided and one-dimensional.) At the opposite pole, caregivers who position themselves as "realists." Their I-have-my-own-life-to-live plotline is a subgenre of rebirth narratives, in which they project a future freed from the increasingly futile caregiving that consumed their identity.

My job isn't to pass judgment on either narrative. Rather, I would simply note that caregivers tend to feel guilty about voicing the second plotline. Accordingly, the second plotline probably doesn't get voiced without a sympathetic audience who affirms its validity from inside their own narrative.

Perhaps you too experience a tension—between the story told by your internal narrator, and the versions of your story you are "allowed" to tell in public. When you narrate your story (in conversation with friends, family, colleagues), do you feel constrained to

---

18. McAdams, "Personal Narratives," 245.
19. Holstein and Gubrium, *Self We Live By*, 113–16.

imagine yourself, your struggles, and your goals by using conventional idioms? How big is the gap between the "real you" and the socially-acceptable version of yourself?

In sum, constructing our narrative identity is a *collaborative* effort. It happens in conversations, in which our audience shapes our story (and we shape theirs).[20]

Let me offer a powerful example of this multi-vocal experience—a true clash of narratives.[21] Our protagonist: Tom, "a 66-year-old married, middle-class White man . . . diagnosed with a *chronic depressive* personality."[22] ECT didn't work. Medication didn't work. More in desperation than hope, Tom's psychiatric unit handed him over to narrative therapist Stephen Madigan.

The latter encouraged Tom to tell his own story in his own words. Since retirement, Tom had felt "bored and unaccomplished."[23] The hospital treatments had only increased his sense of futility. Tom reached the point of questioning if his life was worth living. Interestingly, though, an unquenched passion for gardening flickered amidst the despair.

Madigan took the unusual step of inviting Tom's friends to write Tom letters of encouragement, containing these upbeat narratives:

> In the letter could you relay an experience you have had with Tom that you see as neither boring nor unaccomplished, and indicate what kind of future you would like to enjoy alongside Tom.[24]

In response: forty-one letters, with hopeful counter-narratives about Tom. Emboldened by these alternative scripts, Tom held a celebration party, and checked himself out of the psychiatric unit.

Taking a birds-eye view, we can approximate Tom's journey as the "rebirth" archetype (discussed in chapter 8 above). Here are the phases of his story:

1. *inciting incident*: retirement
2. *dream phase*: delayed impact (of cessation of satisfying work, plus excess time for morbid thoughts)
3. *frustration phase*: growing paralysis, induced by rehearsing a narrative-of-failure
4. *nightmare phase*: "living death": near-hopelessness, reinforced by the *narrative* of "chronic depression"
5. *rebirth*: triggered by hopeful *counter-stories*; residual passion for gardening; positive memories and hopes expressed by forty-one friends.

Notice how *narratives* shaped Tom's identity in the phases labeled frustration, nightmare, and rebirth. Furthermore, the last two phases involve a "mortal combat" between two opposite stories, one told by the psychiatric establishment, the other told by Tom's friends (building on the glimmer of hope still in Tom).

---

20. For examples, see ibid., 142–52.
21. Adapted from McLeod, "Storytelling in Postpsychological Therapy," 19–22.
22. Ibid., 19 (italics mine).
23. Ibid., 20.
24. Quoted in ibid., 21.

PART 3: HOW STORIES CHANGE LIVES

\* \* \* \* \*

The *dialogic* quality of personal narratives; the *unpredictability* of the future. Two reasons why our life stories remain works in progress. Our narrative selves "are on the way to becoming authentic, as long as they continue to transcend themselves and recast themselves in the light of every new step of self-discovery."[25]

A personal narrative gives you a stable identity. But personal narratives themselves can be unstable, subject to *flux*. Here are some further reasons for this flux:[26]

- instability of autobiographical *memory*
- accumulation of new *experiences*
- shifting viewpoints due to *aging*

The passage of time can expose the limited point of view inherent in our stories. McLaren gives poignant testimony to this experience, in his chapter, "The Seven Jesuses I Have Known."[27] In his pilgrimage through various Christian traditions, McLaren kept encountering gaps in how particular traditions imagine Jesus. (The proverbial blind men feeling an elephant.)

Our stories frequently organize around a dominant image, but time exposes that image as a lens that limits us. Our life-text, centered on a particular image, generates a subtext based on the opposite image. Biographies of academics neatly illustrate this dialectical process.[28]

In sixth grade, Dennett dreamed of building the perfect robot.[29] Through grad school, he was lured by an image of elegance: perfectly-regulated robotic movement. This aesthetic quest has dominated his professional life. Intriguingly, though, his private life differs. A series of (largely unsuccessful) relationships with women; all his partners being spontaneous, passionate (and highly unstable) types. The opposite of robots. Dennett's quest, driven by an image of control, was successful in the professional sphere. But the successful quest left a void: the absence of spontaneity, which he compensated for in his private life, via his repeated choice of out-of-control partners.

Dennett's life story unfolded through the pull-and-tug of competing desires and values. The emotional austerity of his professional life, versus the emotional excess of his private life. His turbulent romantic relationships represent a kind of "Mardi Gras" for the engineer. (The cultural script of Mardi Gras institutionalizes a time of carnival and feasting prior to the season of austerity of Lent.)

How does this resonate with your own story? Are there some areas of life where you compensate for the limitations of your major script? If so, what does this tension reveal about your values? How has the pull-and-tug shaped the big decisions over the course of your life?

25. Wyatt, "Narrative in Psychoanalysis," 207.
26. McAdams, "Personal Narratives," 246.
27. McLaren, *Generous Orthodoxy*, 43–67.
28. McAdams and Logan, "Life Stories of Academics," 89–107.
29. Dennett's story is taken from ibid., 90–96.

The story of Dennett the robot-designer also hints at a broader reason why we often need to revise our personal narrative. This reason surfaced in chapter 11 of this book: the approximate fit between tidy narrative genres and the messiness of the real world.

In order to plan our life trajectory, we need a plot. But standard plots are merely ways of entering into conversation with our past, a conversation where our past threatens to have the last word: "While local and broader narrative formats offer familiar or conventional guidelines for how stories might unfold, they do not determine individual storylines. Who and what we are is not frozen in available discourses of subjectivity."[30] This dialectic, between genre and reality, is neatly illustrated by the "narrative elasticity" of the standard recovery template offered in Alcoholics Anonymous meetings.[31] In the standard AA narrative template, "hitting bottom" is the crucial turning point. Before you can receive help—runs the original script—you must reach a point of total despair, where you realize alcohol is costing you everything, up to and including your very life.

However, in later versions of its script, AA modifies its template, as a result of its work among milder alcoholics. AA now recognizes gradations: some alcoholics only hit a "high bottom," while others hit (the original) "low bottom." One patient employs an elevator metaphor to capture this relativity. Descent into alcoholism is like a downward trip in an elevator; you never know how many floors (bottoms) lie beneath you.

In sum, narrative thinking is "an heuristic activity because it is open-ended, constructive, and involves varying kinds of uncertainty."[32] Accordingly, the quest for our story has inbuilt frustrations. But can we make progress, despite these frustrations?

* * * * *

The journey into a true story is rarely smooth. But the journey metaphor sheds light on the process. A journey into a true story implies an exodus out of a false (or inadequate) story. So let's focus briefly on deceptive stories, and the possibility of escaping from self-deception.

Traditional psychology, with its "mechanistic worldview," attempts to explain self-deception by positing "mechanisms" such as "repression" and "dissociation."[33] These mechanisms supposedly confer some benefit on the self-deceived individual. But what benefit, exactly? Sarbin concludes that these traditional concepts "have no explanatory power."[34]

Narrative psychology appears to offer a sharper account of self-deception. Sarbin argues that self-deceivers, like all of us, rely on narratives to explain their role in the world. They are the protagonists in the stories they tell. Their stories rely on the standard narrative elements of contexts and causes. Only, in the case of self-deceivers, key contexts get skewed (or omitted), and erroneous causes get attached to events. The benefit

---

30. Holstein and Gubrium, *Self We Live By*, 107.
31. Ibid., 120–23.
32. Robinson and Hawpe, "Narrative Thinking," 117.
33. My discussion is based on Sarbin, "Narrative as Root Metaphor," 16–17.
34. Ibid., 16.

accrued from these narrative distortions? Protecting or enhancing the identity or image of the protagonist.

Thankfully, "narrative repair" can and does happen.[35] True contexts and causes, distorted by self-deceiving storytellers, can be re-affirmed. Establishing truth about context and cause will have ripple effects. Stories have elements, but stories are wholes. Modify any element, and you are on the way into an alternative story.

What are some other goads that prod us out of inadequate stories and into better stories? Here's a partial list (paraphrased from Novak's discussion):[36]

- the nagging insistence of our unconscious mind;
- lack of good fruit from living the story—e.g., absence of impact on world, absence of peace with others, absence of peace with oneself;
- inability of our story to absorb new experiences;
- internal conflict between elements of our story;
- our stories fail to predict consequences;
- our stories fail to explain the behavior of other people;
- the stronger positive appeal of an alternative story.

As you were reading over this "nagging" list, did any of the items prod you toward a critique of your current life story? If so, you may wish to pause and consolidate the insight.

Alternatively, you may wish to think back to pivotal moments in the past, when you "jumped ship" from one story into another. What triggered the radical change?

Once we start moving away from an inferior story, we may (hopefully!) be on the road to a better story. In the quest for this holy grail, what are some criteria for "my best story"? Before reading on, I invite you to pause and answer that question for yourself. In your own estimate, what benefits would a truly good life story confer upon you? What traits must a worthwhile personal narrative possess?

Narrative psychologists have wrestled with this question, and some have written a "template" for a healthy version of the personal life story. Admittedly, their template has a distinctly secular feel. How much true wisdom do they offer? You decide. Here's the proposal.[37] A healthy personal narrative has these dimensions:

- coherence: the story elements hang together;
- complexity: the story incorporates setbacks, and personal inconsistencies;
- power to infuse life with a sense of unity and purpose;
- power to promote maturity and mental health;

---

35. Robinson and Hawpe, "Narrative Thinking," 121–23.

36. Novak, *Ascent of the Mountain*, 72.

37. I'm borrowing the template from Singer, "Heroin Addict," 255–56, 273 (using a mix of his own wording plus my paraphrasing). Singer borrows from McAdams—cf. McAdams, "Personal Narratives," 247–48 ("Some Stories are Better Than Others").

- power to promote professional and relational satisfaction, and a balance between work life and family life;
- "generativity": the prospect of leaving a legacy for future generations;
- a personal image that is positive, and largely tolerant of oneself;
- memories of positive turning points;
- an ideological setting that affirms the basic security and fairness of one's world.

Or, consider the following version, which Novak calls a "Christian-humanist story."[38] He proposes that "my story" should be:

- Unique to me. "We can impose a story upon events, and . . . we can understand a story as if it were something to copy, imitate, or follow like a predetermined script . . . [But] a story merely copied is a cliché. To avoid being hackneyed, a story must be fresh, unique, singular."[39]
- Appropriate to my own possibilities and potential.
- Appropriate to the stories of my family/community.
- Appropriate to the times (i.e., relevant to the general cultural story around me).

OK, some of you will say, "How do these guys validate their criteria for a 'better story'? What's the criterion for their criteria?" Good question. And the answer, according to Novak, is "a second-level story."[40] (You didn't think you would escape the inescapability of story that easily, did you?)

Consider the following criteria (offered by Stanley Hauerwas and David Burrell):

> Any story which we adopt, or allow to adopt us, will have to display:
> (1) power to release us from destructive alternatives;
> (2) ways of seeing through current distortions;
> (3) room to keep us from having to resort to violence;
> (4) as sense for the tragic: how meaning transcends power.[41]

What's the criterion for these criteria? They are generated by Hauerwas's reading of the four Gospels (the story of Jesus' non-violent victory over evil).

Here is a criterion I can fully resonate with. The story of Jesus is the ultimate touchstone of a good story. To end this chapter, let us reflect on some of the processes through which the story of Jesus can reshape our personal and communal narratives.

\* \* \* \* \*

---

38. Novak, *Ascent of the Mountain*, 61–62.
39. Ibid., 65.
40. Ibid., 61–62.
41. Hauerwas and Burrell, "From System to Story," 185.

## Part 3: How Stories Change Lives

"The Holy Scriptures are story-shaped. Reality is story-shaped. The world is story-shaped. Our lives are story-shaped."[42] Indeed, we humans may literally (biochemically) be hardwired for and by stories.

As evidence, consider the research of Paul J. Zak, a neuroeconomist (yes, this is apparently an academic discipline nowadays). Zak showed participants a short, poignant film about a father coming to terms with his toddler's losing battle with cancer.[43] The film was classically crafted to follow the five-phase dramatic arc of tension (discussed in chapter 7 of this book). The result: viewers' brains showed increased levels of cortisol (the chemical associated with distress) and oxytocin (the chemical associated with empathy). However, if viewers were presented instead with merely the bare, undramatized facts of the account, this produced little if any emotional or chemical response.

Accordingly, when God re-shapes us, He uses the gospel narrative—in many *media*. Here are some of the rich media through which we internalize the gospel narrative. Formal expositions of Scripture. Private meditation upon Scripture. The church year. Prayer. Ritual. Conversation with fellow-disciples.

We won't discuss all of these here, since many of them feature elsewhere in the book. Here are the cross-references for some of these topics:

- *Expositions of Scripture*: In Part 4, I provide extended commentary on several biblical texts, as a lens for exploring various dimensions of a life lived inside the biblical narrative.

- *Meditation upon Scripture*: In the next chapter, I discuss the practice of using our imagination to enter the world of the Gospel narratives.

- *The church year*: The next chapter also discusses inhabiting the church calendar as a mode of internalizing the Christian narrative.

- *Conversation with fellow-disciples*: In the present chapter, I highlighted the power of everyday conversation to shape our identity. We all need trusted dialogue partners who can share our struggle to connect our broken life stories to the healing narrative of Jesus.[44]

Which leaves *prayer* and *ritual*—two powerful means for internalizing the story of Jesus.

We don't always think of prayer as participation in God's narrative, perhaps because our prayers are so atomized ("Lord, please speed up my recovery from my bout of flu!"). However, if we undertake a study of prayer in Luke-Acts, paying attention to the strategic plotline location of its major prayers, a striking conclusion emerges: "Luke associates prayer with the movement of God's redemptive drama, with gaining or disclosing insight into the reality of that drama and its central character, and with preparation

---

42. Peterson, *Eat This Book*, 62.

43. Zak, "Empathy." (My thanks to my former student, Yuce Kabakci, for bringing this to my attention.)

44. For further discussion of the art of Christian conversation, see Powlison, *Speaking the Truth*.

for participation in the same drama."[45] Prayer, then, is a means for fusing our story with God's story.[46] So is *ritual* (which, of course, overlaps prayer).

I like rituals. This book would not have been written without one. I wanted to start writing at the beginning of the summer of 2012. But first I needed a tidy office desk. So I enacted my biannual, end-of-semester "phase marking" ritual. I sort through all the accumulation of materials cluttering my desk. Some I file away, others I discard. Then, to symbolize the start of a fresh phase of my work, I spray-clean the desk (with eco-friendly, lemon verbena fragrance cleanser). Then, and only then, am I psychologically ready to begin my summer writing projects.

Daniel Taylor discusses the overlap between narrative and ritual:

> [The] power of stories derives in part from their partaking in the character of ritual. Rituals are those things we do over and over again . . . Sacred rituals are those that tie us somehow to the transcendent, to everlasting things that are larger than ourselves. Human beings always have been and always will be creatures of ritual. There is something comforting in chosen repetition . . . it may begin as early as the unborn child's familiarity with the mother's heartbeat. It is reinforced by the rhythms of day and night, and of the seasons. At its most fundamental, *ritual is a vote against chaos and randomness and arbitrary death*.[47]

Many rituals embody narratives, so performing the ritual powerfully shapes our narrative identity. The "recovery script" (for strugglers with addiction) usually gets reinforced by the rituals of group therapy. For example, the AA meeting, with its ritualized confessions and autobiographical accounts of "hitting bottom."[48] Likewise, for recovering heroin addicts, the weekly ritual of group therapy session "is devised specifically to replace with an orderly time the 'fatal' time in which addicts live, the wait for events that would, in their hopes, solve the problem in one shot and forever."[49]

We should never underestimate the power of religious rituals that embody and perform narratives. I learned this at an academic conference in San Francisco in 2011. Skimming through the program booklet, I confess I was bored with a capital "B." I'd been attending this annual conference for years, and its lectures had become the same old thing. But, on Saturday morning, one session lured me in. The topic: esoteric knowledge in the Western tradition. Esoteric means you can't know it until you try it. The opposite of the neutral objective stance of the Enlightenment.

Well, some of the learned speakers turned out to be practitioners of neo-pagan religions. Very esoteric. But I'll never forget the sociology PhD who spoke about rituals performed at "fire festivals." At night, around a fire, a circle of dancers traverses the elliptical patterns of the planetary orbits. The dancing continues until sunrise, when the new dawn confirms that the fire dance has worked a spiritual alchemy: "the leaden dross of the dancer's life has been transmuted into gold."

---

45. Bartholomew and Holt, "Prayer in Luke," 357.
46. For how this works out in contemporary practice, see Miller, *Praying Life*.
47. Taylor, *Healing Power of Stories*, 121 (italics mine).
48. Cf. Holstein and Gubrium, *Self We Live By*, 120–23.
49. Fasulo, "Theories of Self, 335.

Not that I'm recommending it, of course.[50] But it did make me ponder: are we Christians making enough use of our own rituals that embody the redemptive narrative of the gospel?

Let's end the chapter with mention of a couple of our obvious Christian rituals: song and Eucharist. Let's start with the Psalter. The psalms, of course, were originally poems set to music. The parallel rhythmic structure of Hebrew poetry, plus the enhancement of music, intensifies the affective power of the material. And much of the material of the Psalter is narrative. Many psalms are compressed autobiographical narratives, in which the psalmist struggles before God, trying to make sense of his troubled life story. Many other psalms are dramatic recitals of the mighty acts of God in history.

The rhythms of Hebrew poetry shaped the hymnody of the primitive church; the well-known nativity hymns in Luke 1–2, for example. In addition, many scholars detect hymn fragments in some of the letters. One of my favorites: Col 1:1–15. This hymn celebrates the comedic plotline of cosmic reconciliation, in which Christ ushers in a reign of universal peace under God. Perhaps this hymn was in mind in Col 3:16, where Paul encourages the ritual of sacred song as a means of internalizing the gospel narrative.

Lastly, the Eucharist. Liturgical scholars have noticed the narrative performance dimensions of our celebration of the Lord's Supper. For example, S. W. Sykes highlights the "story grammar" of the Eucharist:[51]

| Setting | thanksgiving to the Father (creation) |
| --- | --- |
| Theme | memorial of the Son (redemption) |
| Plot | communion of the faithful (church) |
| Resolution | meal of the kingdom (eschatology) |

I like to think of the Eucharist as "a tale of two feasts," encompassing the grand sweep of salvation history. The Passover/Exodus echoes root the church deeply in the ancient covenant narrative of Abraham, Isaac, and Jacob. The prospective dimension of the feast looks forward to the end-time banquet, celebrating the final victory over death, announced poetically in Isaiah 25:6–8. When I participate in the Eucharist, I participate in the sweeping metanarrative that runs from Exodus to New Creation.

According to Robert W. Jenson, recovering the regular celebration of the Lord's Supper and its surrounding liturgy may be the single most important task for any church that wants to communicate with the postmodern world.[52] Jenson points out that postmodern people no longer inhabit a "narratable world." (Recall our discussion, in chapter 5, of postmodernism as the loss of the "grand narrative.") For postmodern thinkers, there is no big-umbrella story under which all humanity can shelter. There is no overarching coherence to world history. Accordingly, the claim of the Christian gospel frequently

---

50. Those interested in a Christian analog might wish to consider the church's use of the *labyrinth*. The labyrinth is a circular path, marked by stones, leading to a center. Walking the labyrinth in prayer/meditation can ritualize the Christian pilgrimage toward God. (With all such rituals, the *metanarrative* they embody would seem crucial for determining if they are helpful or not.)

51. Sykes, "Story and Eucharist," 370.

52. Jenson, "How The World Lost Its Story."

falls on deaf ears. In this context, Jenson offers a thoughtful response: "If the church does not *find* her hearers antecedently inhabiting a narratable world, then the church must herself *be* that world."[53] How, exactly, can the church be the embodiment of a narrative world? Through the liturgy of the Lord's Supper, which symbolizes and enacts the great drama of Scripture, the true story of the whole world: "In the postmodern world, if a congregation or churchly agency wants to be "relevant," here is the first step: it must recover the classic liturgy of the church, in all its dramatic density, sensual actuality, and brutal realism."[54]

* * * * *

Before we leave this chapter, I cannot resist briefly mentioning another (re-)emerging medium for indwelling God's story. I'm referring to the contemporary recovery of an ancient practice—the memorization of scripture for oral recitation in community.

This practice recognizes that the Bible was the product of an oral (mass illiterate) culture. Back then, most written texts were scripts for public performance. So think of the four Gospels as dramas to be reanimated, with voice and gesture, in a communal setting. Or the letters of Paul as speeches in the classical tradition, to be "channeled" by a sympathetic interpreter, whose vocalization and gesture embodied the virtual presence of Paul in the church gathering.

In response to these insights, I helped form a "troupe" of performers of Scripture. Our basic method: 1) select a sequence of texts, from Genesis to Revelation, which work together to highlight the narrative arcs of Scripture; 2) internalize and embody these texts, via interpretative vocalization and gesture; 3) perform the sequence for a live audience.

You have probably never experienced anything like this, neither as a performer nor as an audience member. But the feedback we get, from both performers and audience, typically goes like this: "You enabled me to dwell in God's story in a new and fresh way."[55]

The Christian tradition offers us an abundant, multimedia heritage—a treasury of practices for indwelling God's story. This chapter ended with a brief investigation of some of these practices. Our investigation continues in the next chapter, under the rubric of *epiphany experiences*—life-changing *aha!* moments, which can anchor and direct our unfolding personal narratives.

---

53. Ibid., 22 (italics in original).
54. Ibid.
55. For more on the power of performing the story of Scripture, see Novelli, *Shaped by the Story*.

# 21

# Twelfth Night

**BOLTS OF LIGHTENING**

"Every short story is an *epiphany*—for the main character, or the reader, or both," proclaimed a short story journal perched on the coffee table of my ultra-literate friend Robyn. The bare quote was evidently an epiphany for me, since I rushed home and scribbled it down.

Leland Ryken describes the overlap of epiphanies and plot structure: "Storytellers . . . tend to structure stories around one or more moments of *epiphany* ("revelation," "insight"). Usually there is an epiphany near the end of the story."[1]

Self-recognitions. Crystallizations of experience. Flinging open the doors of perception onto the world. Stories catalyze these *aha!* moments, thereby changing lives.[2] Think back to the last time a novel or a film did this for you. What changed as a result?

These experiences can affirm or disturb us. They confirm our identity or overturn us.[3] Contrasting versions of the story of Jesus illustrate these effects. The modern Jesus (a product of nineteenth-century moral and sentimental religion) confirmed our own basic niceness. That Jesus merely had the teacher's knack of pithy distillations of what right-thinking folk already thought. By contrast, the Gospels depict an apocalyptic Jesus who overturns our assumptions, much as he did the tables of the money-changers in the temple (Mark 11:15).

"Midwives of epiphanies." As a one-line job description of artists, one could do worse. Walker Percy describes this function of art: "In art, whether it's poetry, fiction or painting, you are telling the reader or the listener something he already knows but which he doesn't quite know that he knows, so that in the action of communication he experiences a recognition, a feeling that he has been there before, a shock of recognition."[4] Via

---

1. Ryken, *Windows to the World*, 93 (italics in original).

2. For many personal descriptions of this experience of reading, see Coady and Johannessen, *Book That Changed My Life*, which I engage in chapter 12.

3. Terence W. Tilley uses these opposite effects to classify narrative genres: "*Myths* are stories that set up worlds. Their polar opposites are *parables*, stories that upset worlds" (Tilley, *Story Theology*, 39, italics in original).

4. Quoted in Cremeens, "Walker Percy," 279.

what formal aesthetic devices does art birth such recognitions? If we writers could bottle the formula, what royalties would await! We can offer a couple of thoughts (even if these fall short of a magic formula). First, stories involve readers in the movement of narrative time toward a crisis, and this temporal funneling helps beget new insights. Second, stories work holistically, by an integrated appeal to all the faculties of our soul. Robert McKee witnesses to this power: "Story is first, last, and always the experience of aesthetic emotion—the simultaneous encounter of thought and feeling. When an idea wraps itself around an emotional charge, it becomes all the more powerful, all the more profound, all the more memorable."[5] Third, a paradox aptly stated by Ezra Pound: "Art does not avoid universals, it strikes at them all the harder in that it strikes through particulars."[6] Rather than explain this, I will illustrate through particulars—two of the most famous epiphanies in literature.

Let's begin with an episode from the life of the Old Testament figure, King David. While his troops are away on the battlefield, David commences an extra-marital affair with Bathsheba (wife of Uriah, one of David's soldiers). Their affair results in a pregnancy. As a cover up, David engineers the death of Uriah (2 Sam 11).

Then the prophet Nathan comes to David, and delivers one of the briefest and most effective sermons ever preached:

> In a certain city, there dwelt two men, one rich, one poor.
> The rich man abounded in sheep and cattle.
> The poor man only had one little lamb, which was "like a daughter" to him.
> One day, a traveler visited the rich man. Rather than use his own flocks or herds, the rich man took the little lamb from the poor man, and made it into a meal for the traveler. (2 Sam 12:1–4, my paraphrase)

David's anger was kindled. "That man deserves death! He must pay compensation worth four lambs!" Nathan's response: "You are that man!" (2 Sam 12:5–7.) Trapped by his own reaction to the parable, David confesses, "I have sinned against Yahweh!" (2 Sam 12:13.)

Equally dramatic are the scenes from Shakespeare's *Hamlet*. A traveling theater arrives at the royal court of Denmark. The arrival of the players sets Hamlet scheming, in an attempt to confirm that the King of Denmark did in fact poison Hamlet's father:

> I have heard that guilty creatures, sitting at a play,
> Have by the very cunning of the scene
> Been struck so to the soul that presently
> They have proclaimed their malefactions . . .
> The play's the thing
> Wherein I'll catch the conscience of the king.[7]

---

5. McKee, *Story*, 111.

6. Quoted in Ford, "System, Story, Performance," 215. Cf. Ryken, *Windows to the World*, 25, 119.

7. *Hamlet* 2.2.

## Part 3: How Stories Change Lives

Hamlet duly persuades the players to include a murder-by-poison scene in their performance before the royal court. As anticipated, the guilty king ups and leaves upon witnessing the reenactment of his crime.[8]

Some have witnessed real-life parallels to this scene from Shakespeare. Commenting on performances of Sophocles's *Oedipus Tyrannos*, Christopher Booker writes:

> It has been observed how simply watching this play, showing a man having to face up to his own guilt, can in some spectators evoke a long-repressed sense of guilt about their own lives. I recall how, during a particularly powerful production of the play at Stratford-on-Avon in the 1950s, a good many people in the audience, as the tragedy moved towards its climax, could evidently take no more and stole out of the theater. Although these people had not literally killed their fathers and married their mothers, the more general sense of unease the play aroused became too much to bear.[9]

*Epiphanies occur at the intersection of stories.* An external narrative collides with our internal version of events, calling us to radically reevaluate our life story. For Robert Coles's students, John Cheever's short stories catalyze these *oh-no* moments:

> I read Cheever . . . as if I'm on one of those suburban trains of his, headed home to Westchester or Connecticut, or any pretty, woodsy American township, and I'm just sitting there, in the plushest car, having a drink and looking forward to a swimming party, and feeling glad inside, because out of the corner of my eye I can see the [*Wall Street*] *Journal*, and by God, the market has been up for a month—but all of a sudden the train stops, and there's Cheever, standing outside the train, in front of it, in the middle of the tracks, maybe telling us that we're in trouble, because the train isn't going where we thought, and it might plunge off the track any minute, and we'll end up in hell. Is that a momentary "bad thought?" Should I shrug it off and have another drink? Or have I been given a chance of a lifetime: to change trains, change my destination?[10]

This *oh-no* experience *reframes the plot archetype* of the reader's life story. He had been cruising along comfortably, inside the plotline of ascent (to the "good life"), the American Dream. Cheever's stories enable something like an out-of-body-experience, allowing the reader an external viewpoint on his own life trajectory. Instead of a plotline of ascent, he sees himself in the nightmare phase of a "voyage-and-return" archetype (discussed in chapter 8 above). In this crisis, can he "change trains," and return to the self that was lost during his story of ascent?

If "secular" epiphanies are collisions of narratives, how much more so the "religious" kind. Stephen Crites uses a convergence-of-tracks metaphor to describe such experiences:

> The narrative quality of experience has three dimensions, the sacred story, the mundane story, and the temporal form of experience itself: three narrative tracks, each constantly reflecting and affecting the course of the others. And sometimes the tracks cross, causing a burst of light like a comet entering our

8. *Hamlet* 3.2
9. Booker, *Seven Basic Plots*, 520, n. 2.
10. Quoted in Coles, *Call of Stories*, 159.

atmosphere. Such a luminous moment, in which sacred, mundane, and personal are inseparably conjoined, we call *symbolic* in a special sense.[11]

This sense, of one's life story taken up into a sacred story, tends to be a pivotal event. Emergence from a crisis, or summons into a new script, or both/and. Without one such moment, I would not be writing this book (see chapter 2, "A Graveyard Shift"). Meditating on the Feast of Epiphany (January 6th), Luci Shaw writes poignantly of her own emergence from darkness into light.[12] Her experience deserves to be retold.

Vancouver, Canada, where she taught poetry at a college, was the geographical setting for Luci's story. Abandonment—the theme of her story. Feeling abandoned—first by an absentee father, then by the untimely death of her husband, and ultimately by God. Into this darkness, some "absurd" counsel from a trusted friend. "Whoever tries to save their life will lose it, and whoever loses their life will save it. Luci, the path leading out from the pit of abandonment is the way of self-abandonment." What could this mean?

A few days later, a young mother was about to carpool with Luci. Preoccupied with stowing stroller and diaper bag, Luci perched her spiral-bound journal on the roof of the vehicle. When they reached their destination—no journal. Lost—her journal, the treasure-chest of her most precious thoughts, an extension of her identity.

"God, if you really want me to abandon my self in this way, then I will accept this loss as from your hand."

Found—Luci's journal. Rain-soaked and tire-marked, but found—by a close friend walking across the college campus. Recognizing the divine handprint, Luci wrote: "If I am willing to abandon my will to God, broken like the spine of this journal, imprinted with God's own tire-track signature, he will give it back, and my identity with it."[13] During this time frame, her geographical setting provoked a metaphor of this experience. The Cascade Mountains lie concealed by rain clouds, invisible for much of the year. Driving to college one morning, a sea breeze swept back the cloudy curtain to reveal Mount Baker in all its undeniable glory: "It's God, showing me a metaphor of himself. I mean—he's there, whether I see him or not. It's almost as if he's lying in wait to surprise me. And the wind is like the Spirit, sweeping away my foggy doubt, opening my eyes, revealing the reality of God."[14]

Does Luci's experience resonate with yours? Or, are you thinking "Bully for her; but stuff like that never happens to *me*"? Many of us hunger after clear, heaven-sent guideposts for our pilgrimage. Discouragingly, conventional wisdom says that these bolts of lightening are unmanufacturable and unrepeatable.[15]

Allow me to tweak (rather than overturn) the conventional wisdom. Even if we cannot manufacture epiphanies, can we at least increase our openness, and structure our lives expectantly? Let me offer some "secular" analogies:

---

11. Crites, "Narrative Quality of Experience," 81 (italics in original).

12. Shaw, "Epiphany," 40–48.

13. Ibid., 47–48.

14. Ibid., 41.

15. No one has expressed this conventional wisdom better than C. S. Lewis, in his poem "The Day with a White Mark" (quoted in ibid., 43).

"An artist is a lightning rod, someone who walks around in open fields during thunder storms, waiting to be struck by a bolt from the heavens." This is my paraphrase of someone who deserves credit (but whose name escapes me). The quote implies both the artist's dependence upon inspiration, and their deliberate self-exposure to sources of inspiration.

Or, take the common experience of arriving at knowledge. Philosophers like Esther Lightcap Meek have wrestled with the question, How do people come to knowledge?[16] She concludes that we do not arrive at knowledge in a logical, linear, deductive manner. Rather, coming to know is a story-like experience.

Something in our context piques our curiosity, sending us on a quest to make sense of things. We search our context for clues, and struggle to fit them into a pattern. Our struggle resolves via the epiphany of intuitive insight; we have an "*aha!* Now I see it!" moment.

Such "secular" epiphanies are a daily occurrence. Could they be a common grace allegory of the religious kind? Does attainment of mundane knowledge via "epiphany" teach us that heavenly enlightenment awaits those willing to begin the quest?

According to my reading of the Christian story, epiphanies may be available by the bucketload for those who seek. I'm not saying they can be manufactured. But earnest seekers may find.

In chapter 10, I offered my thumbnail sketch of the Christian story. That thumbnail plotline pivots on two epiphanies of Jesus. According to the New Testament, his first advent (incarnation; cross; resurrection; ascension) is an apocalypse, a breach of heavenly glory into history. His second advent, with glory infinite and complete, hovers over history, and from time to time breaks into our experience. The book of Acts attests this permeability of heaven and earth. On the mundane stage of the Greco-Roman world, epiphanies of all kinds break in with alarming regularity:

> The continued earthly activity of the exalted Jesus provides the basis for the episodic plot of Acts. Although taking many forms—spirit invasions, deeds accomplished in the name of Jesus, dreams, visions, angelophanies, Christophanies, miracles, sermons—the *miniapocalypses* all disclose key information to key characters at key junctures in the narrative, divinely emboldening the human agents to do the exploits of the exalted Jesus.[17]

Within such a worldview, perhaps C. S. Lewis's "peacock-colored days" may not be so unusual after all. In the next two sections of this chapter, I will explore practices which can expose us to heavenly lightening bolts (even if they do not guarantee an epiphany). We will reflect upon the spiritual benefits of indwelling the church calendar, and of indwelling the Scriptures through the art of meditation.

---

16. Meek, *Loving to Know*.
17. Newman, "Acts," 440 (italics mine).

## A PARTRIDGE IN A PEAR TREE

"Tell me the old, old story," says the old, old hymn. But we can tell it once too often. Some stories, through no fault of their own, become dead metaphors (the Prodigal Son; the Good Samaritan).

Maybe the Wedding at Cana (John 2:1–11) can slide into that category. Not that it should. "Even the most 'simple' of stories is embedded in a network of relations that are sometimes astounding in their complexity."[18] This is especially true for the Gospel of John.

Last year, the over-familiar Wedding-at-Cana episode sprung to life for me. Why not, I wondered, read the story from the viewpoint of "the mother of Jesus"? After all, she gets first billing in the *dramatis personae* (verses 1–2). And, following the inciting incident ("the wine ran out"), she takes the initiative to solve the problem (verse 3). From her point of view, the story is a miniature quest. A search for an external, life-renewing boon, in the context of its acutely-felt absence. (In first-century Palestine, insufficient wine at a wedding was acute social embarrassment.)

Her quest follows the standard arc of tension. Initial optimism (verse 3): Just ask Jesus! (Note that, in John's narrative world, Jesus has *not* performed any miracle yet (verse 11). So her request was along more mundane lines. Maybe Jesus, a local Rabbi (John 1:38), had some connections, could pull some strings.)

Initial optimism encounters frustration, confronted with Jesus' enigmatic reply (verse 4): "What do you and I have in common, Woman? My hour has not yet arrived."

Undeterred, she enlists the servants in her quest (verse 5). At this critical moment, the camera slows, zooming in on the six stone jars used for Jewish purification rituals (verse 6). At Jesus' command, these are filled with water to the brim (verse 7).

You know the plotline resolution (verse 10): from the water in the stone jars, a hyper-abundance of vintage wine (not the cheaper plonk generally reserved for drunken guests). For Jesus' disciples, epiphany: "the beginning of signs" whereby he "revealed his glory" (verse 11). An intrusion into history of Isaiah's end-time banquet feast, serving choicest wine (Isa 25:6–8).

A mundane quest for festal wine leads to experience of the transcendent (endtime wine). In John's sacramental worldview, the mundane can always open a door to the transcendent.

What of our own mundane searches for whatever is lacking? Can God use our initial trajectories as points of entry into a story that culminates in manifestation of glory? Perhaps you can recall an experience somewhat like Mary's—when an ordinary activity took on profound meaning, connecting you to a bigger and truly meaningful story.

\* \* \* \* \*

On the first day of Christmas
My true-love gave to me

---

18. Cobley, *Narrative*, 2.

## Part 3: How Stories Change Lives

A partridge in a pear tree.

A bizarre gift? Not if one grasps the symbolism. Back in the Old Testament story, David spent years as a refugee, fleeing Saul's obsessive and murderous pursuit. David described the experience as being hunted down like a partridge (1 Sam 26:20). In David's eventual kingship, the messianic ideal took concrete shape. Connecting the dots, the partridge became an ancient symbol of Christ.

The song goes on to celebrate the twelve days of Christmas, ushered in by the Feast of the Incarnation (December 25th) and culminating in the Feast of the Epiphany (January 6th). Nowadays, few churches even bother with Twelfth Night. However, "In Shakespeare's England, Twelfth Night was such a big day that special entertainments were composed just for that occasion."[19] (Think of the Shakespeare comedy of the same name.) Traditionally, Epiphany celebrated the cluster of events that revealed Christ's glory, including his baptism, the visit of the Magi, and the miraculous wine at the Wedding of Cana.[20]

Before we dive into the calendar of the Christian year, let's reflect on our modern secular experience of *time*. Have you noticed how time often feels like a string of undifferentiated, unhighlighted moments—"one damn thing after another"?[21] Or have you experienced both a sense of having too little time, *and* a sense of time needing to be filled? Bruce Chilton describes this modern malaise, a product of industrial, clock-driven society:

> There is a deeper temporal paradox in a society constrained by time: people often feel they have time they do not know what to do with. When we are not too busy to be happy, or even to be aware of the degree of our unhappiness, time appears as something to be filled. Unfilled, time is a threat, and under that threat people commonly speak of being depressed.[22]

Calendars, like stories, structure time. Our calendars are icons of our life story. What are the peak events on your annual calendar? Do the holidays and festivals you celebrate connect you to a bigger story—or are they just "one damn thing after another?"[23]

As our Western society has lost its grand narrative, so our calendars of public events have lost their power to bestow a worthwhile rhythm on our lives. Some of us find comfort in "tribal" calendars. Like the narrative pattern of "seasons" created by professional sports. The English soccer season starts in late August, building tension through a fixture-clogged December, and peaking in May ("the business-end of the season," in soccer parlance). At Stamford Bridge, the home field of my team, Chelsea FC, the fans fly blue banners (the club color), emblazoned with statements of identity. "Chelsea Our Religion," reads one. Another used to defy political correctness, with the assertion that following Chelsea is "One True Religion."

---

19. Bevis, "January 6 Epiphany," 167.
20. Ibid., 165.
21. Bennett, *History Boys*, 85, 106 (expletive modified).
22. Chilton, *Redeeming Time*, 5.
23. Bennett, *History Boys*, 85, 106 (expletive modified).

In the 1980s (before the advent of online printable DIY calendars), I used to dream of making a truly meaningful calendar. One in which every day matters, every day commemorates a truly significant event. Armed with such a calendar, I would arise every morning, and step onto a world stage bursting with potential. "Just think, *today* "xyz" happened! If something that *big* happened once, something big could happen again, today!" Little did I know:

> Christians inherited a Roman calendar that was perfectly adequate for ... calculating the equinox, for setting a wedding day. But the Roman stories attached to the Roman calendar were not at all adequate. So from early days Christians told stories of Jesus and their experience with him. As the stories were told and retold, they clustered around the calendar and pushed the Roman stories off; they were better stories ... The "Roman" year slowly gave way to a "Christian" year.[24]

Genius! What better way to remind us that we inhabit God's story? The church calendar reinforces the link between the sacred and the mundane. The seasons of Christmas and Easter (for inhabitants of the northern hemisphere) fuse the natural as with the supernatural. In the dark of winter, the light of the world is born. As the earth regenerates in spring, we celebrate the resurrection.

When we recover the marking of time by the events of the gospel, we recover the sense that our lives are expressions of Christ's story:

> The Christian year is divided into two parts, roughly equal—our Lord's half-year and the Christian's half-year. Our Lord's half-year, from Advent to Ascension, tells the stories of our Lord's arrival, life, death, and resurrection. The Christian's half-year (from Pentecost to Christ the King) tells the stories of our reception of his Spirit, our participation in the Trinity, our long discipleship as a communion of saints, our death and resurrection under the overarching sovereignty of Christ.[25]

A beloved low-church colleague of mine (whose denomination has a Puritan aversion to anything "Catholic") took skeptical aim at the church's calendar. "Twenty-five long weeks between Pentecost and Advent, with nothing from the Jesus story. Nothing but the five-and-twenty Sundays after Trinity. Seems like a very long time!"

Without missing a beat, I shot back. "But that's the whole point! We calendarize the inherent tension of the New Testament story. From Trinity Sunday to Advent, the Church inhabits between-time, wilderness time, awaiting God-With-Us."

The New Testament describes both advents of Christ, past and future, as *epiphanies*. His first epiphany "abolishes death, and shines forth life and immortality" (2 Tim 1:10). His second epiphany will "judge the living and the dead" (2 Tim 4:1). The second completes what the first inaugurates. The first foreshadows the second.

The structure of the church year habituates us to yearn for epiphanies, for inbreakings of the unbroken realm, for a taste of the milk-and-honey of paradise during our long pilgrimage through the wilderness:

---

24. Peterson, Introduction to *Christian Year*, viii.
25. Ibid.

> The early Christians believed that the rhythm of the year gave us a perfect opportunity to re-enact the story of our salvation. In the holy days and seasons of the church year, the life of Christ and the entirety of human history are recapitulated. The eternal is aligned with the here and now . . . Finally, the long season of "ordinary time" after Pentecost reminds us of the story we are living now: the church in time. At the end of ordinary time we look to the end of time . . . and then with Advent we begin the cycle again.[26]

## IN THE HOUSE OF THE GALILEAN

I have described the act of reading stories as a kind of plotline, a "voyage-and-return" to a strange country, the narrative world of the text. Stories summon our imagination, transporting us to another time, place, and point of view. The experience can literally enthrall. Hear the testimony of a first-time teenage reader of Tolkien's *The Lord of the Rings*:

> I can't remember starting the book, but I can remember finishing it. I cried. How dare it come to an end? Only 1,086 pages? I wanted it to go on and on, not because I had escaped into another world . . . but because I had been utterly captivated by the romance, the fantasy, the sheer epic enormity of the thing. More a prisoner than an escapee![27]

For some of us, reading the Bible was once like that. Once. But then something changes, usually imperceptibly. Over-familiarity? A utilitarian search for nuggets of morality or doctrine embedded in the stories? Seminary training, with its idealized stance of objective observer, applying scientific rules of interpretation? Whatever the cause(s), we have lost our first love (Rev 2:4).

Is there a remedy? The default Christian response to the problem advocates greater self-discipline. A stoic system of read-through-Scripture in one year. Don Hudson exposes the flaw in this behaviorist regimen:

> If the Bible really is the story of God, why must I treat myself like some prisoner in a labor camp who must discipline himself to do the dreaded duty of reading his Bible again? If you were an outsider hearing most Christians talk about *reading* their Bibles, you would think they were speaking of root canals or tax audits.[28]

Is there a way back to the garden, a gateway to a "second naiveté"? Suppose we discard our critical filters, abandon our quest for utilitarian moral/doctrinal nuggets, and give ourselves to Scripture like an expectant reader of Tolkien? Use our imaginations to enter and inhabit the narrative world of the text. Adopt a "childish" reading strategy as our entry into the kingdom of God (Mark 10:15).

If we follow our imaginations into the text, we may find our pathway converges with the venerable reading practices of the pre-modern church. The practice known in the Latin as *lectio divina* ("spiritual reading"), with its four connected phases: read;

---

26. Bevis, "Church Year," 11.
27. Base, "*Lord of the Rings* by Tolkien," 19.
28. Hudson, "Bring Your Story," 74 (italics in original).

meditate; pray; contemplate. In the twelfth century, the ancient four-dimensional practice was crystallized by a European monk, Guigo the Second:

> Reading, as it were, puts solid food in our mouths, meditation chews it and breaks it down, prayer obtains the flavour of it and contemplation is the very sweetness which makes us glad and refreshes us.[29]

It's the second phase, meditation (which "chews it and breaks it down") that especially interests me. Rumination, using the imagination to fix the sacred story in the memory, so that it becomes a part of us.[30]

Commenting on Tolkien's narrative world, C. S. Lewis remarked, "Here are beauties which pierce like swords or burn like cold iron."[31] When we enter Tolkien's Middle-Earth, we experience its beauties via the full range of our sensory imagination.

When we enter the strange world of Scripture, we let the text become the tour-guide for our imagination. Visualizing whatever the text pictures. Hearing its echoes and cadences. Feeling the textures of its physical settings. Richard L. Pratt describes the use of sensory imagery in Old Testament narratives:[32] "Through the use of vivid imagery, they [the Old Testament narrators] invited their readers to have imaginative, sensory experiences of the past."[33]

In the history of the church, no one has unlocked the potential of this imaginative reading strategy more than Ignatius of Loyola (c. 1491–1556). Taken with discernment, we may learn much from him. Let us begin with a bit of his backstory.

Born into the Spanish nobility, Ignatius's early education took place in an atmosphere of late-medieval courts and knights (think *Don Quixote*, maybe). The chivalrous ideals he imbibed, he later transmuted into a model for Christian service (a knight in the court of King Jesus).[34]

In his youth, Ignatius was a nominal Catholic. "He did not live in keeping with his belief or guard himself from sins; he was particularly careless about gambling, affairs with women, and the use of arms."[35]

Around the age of thirty, Ignatius experienced a profound conversion and call. The precipitating incident: an injury received on military duty, when a cannonball shattered his leg. During his convalescence (in Loyala, Spain), he devoured spiritual literature: Jacobus, *The Golden Legends* (a popular collection of biographies of the saints); Ludolph, *Life of Christ*. The latter inspired the framework for Ignatius's famous *Spiritual Exercises*, with its encouragement of imaginative contemplation of scenes from the Gospels.

After convalescence, Ignatius set out on a lengthy pilgrimage to Jerusalem. On the way, he spent almost a year living as a hermit in a cave at Manresa, Spain. During this year, he developed the practice of prayerful contemplation that would emerge in his

---

29. Quoted in Peterson, *Eat This Book*, 91, n. 1.
30. Peterson offers a helpful brief description of the practice (ibid., 98–102).
31. Quoted on back cover of Tolkien, *Two Towers*.
32. Pratt, *He Gave Us Stories*, 169–76.
33. Ibid., 169.
34. Lonsdale, "Ignatian Spirituality," 355.
35. Quoted in Gnass, *Ignatius of Loyala*, 15.

*Exercises*. At Manresa, mystical experiences profoundly shaped his calling, and these epiphanies also inspired the *Exercises*. In his third-person autobiography, Ignatius describes these epiphanies:

> While he was seated there [by the river], the eyes of his understanding began to be opened; though he did not see any vision, he understood and knew many things, both spiritual things and matters of faith and learning, and this was with so great an enlightenment that everything seemed new to him . . . He experienced a great clarity in his understanding. This was such that in the whole course of his life, through sixty-two years, even if he gathered up all the many helps he had had from God . . . and added them together, he does not think they would amount to as much as he had received at that one time.[36]

In his *Exercises*, Ignatius invites us to use all five elements of our sensory imagination to enter and inhabit the story of Jesus as told in the canonical Gospels. Embarking in faith on this pilgrimage, we may experience epiphanies which change the direction of our life.

Indeed, the last fifty years witnessed resurgence of the devout use of the *Exercises*, across the ecclesiastical spectrum.[37] (Protestant practioners will tend to bracket out the distinctively Roman Catholic bits of Ignatius.) The staunchly Reformed writer, Hughes Oliphant Old, recognizes the pedagogical wisdom of Ignatius's approach: "Modern experts in the theory of communication marvel at the holistic approach of these exercises. By playing on the full range of senses, the oral, the visual, the tactile, these exercises were most effective in motivating the religious energies of Catholics."[38] Evelyn Underhill attests the power of the *Exercises*:

> In his humble meditations on the mysteries of Faith, his deliberate picturings of the scenes of the Incarnation and Passion, the devout Christian truly experiences the "tender mercy" of the Absolute, inviting the soul to life-giving acts of faith, hope, and love. The continued success of the *Spiritual Exercises* of St. Ignatius . . . depends almost entirely on the way in which the soul is thus brought in its solitude into direct imaginative contact with the mysteries of the Life of Christ; and through and in this searching experience is compelled to a total capitulation to the Divine.[39]

Despite these testimonies, one Protestant tradition would remain suspicious of Ignatian practices. The Puritans tended to view the imagination as "the primary inlet for error and temptation," and regarded mental images of Christ as violations of the second commandment.[40] However, there was a "minority report": Puritans who took a more positive view of mental images of Christ; and this positive view was cautiously advocated by their great descendant, Jonathan Edwards.[41] Furthermore, the famous nineteenth-century

---

36. Quoted in Olin, *Autobiography of St. Ignatius*, 39–40.
37. Lonsdale, "Ignatian Spirituality," 356.
38. Old, *Age of the Reformation*, 185.
39. Underhill, *Worship*, 175.
40. La Shell, "Imagination and Idol," 309, 314–15.
41. Ibid., 316–18.

Baptist preacher, C. H. Spurgeon, saturated his sermons with appeals to all five senses—including appeals to visualize Jesus.[42]

To my Puritan friends, I simply say: Is the human imagination any more corrupt than the human intellect? Is the left brain purer and more reliable than the right brain? Would the Word, the Divine Wisdom, who took on the fullness of human flesh to restore us to wholeness, deny the full use of our faculties in our quest for healing?

\* \* \* \* \*

I close this chapter with material based on my journal entries from Winter, 2010. In that season, I meditated on the Gospels using a critically-modified (Protestant) form of Ignatian practice. There follows an edited record of my pilgrimage (with added commentary):

Yeshua became my Rabbi. Or maybe I enrolled in his yeshiva. Stepping through that door was somewhat like Abram's journey from Ur. Neither knew our destiny; both felt a summons we could not ignore.

"Encounter Jesus as Rabbi," said the idea in my head. I decided to respond as if to the living voice of God. (If you need to stick a dismissive label on my experience—"*subjective*," intoned with skepticism—allow me to help you. I am a professional theologian. I read books by scholars who think of Jesus as a *sage*. Maybe one of those books planted the idea in my head.)

> God of God
> Light of light
> Very God of very God
> Begotten not made
> Being of one substance with the Father

I love the Nicene Creed. Its cadence and imagery transfix me. I confess what it says about Yeshua. Its lofty truth makes me crane my neck heavenwards—like visiting a gothic cathedral, leaning backwards to absorb the panoramic ceiling.

The Creed embodies what theologians like to call "Christology from above." Start with the divinity of Jesus, and work downward to his humanity. The modern alternative is "Christology from below." Start with Yeshua of Nazareth: human; Jewish; inhabiting the Roman empire.

"Encounter Jesus as Rabbi," said the idea in my head. Why did this lure feel like a gentle magnet? Maybe a rabbi seemed more knowable than "being of one substance with the Father." Perhaps I would find it somewhat easier to converse with a rabbi. After all, isn't my job—seminary professor—the ancient rabbi in modern garb? Then again, maybe the truth is—despite my earned doctorate—I am in many ways a fool. Via an encounter with Yeshua the Sage, would God meet this fool at his point of need?

In the Gospels, Yeshua's original disciples called him "Rabbi"; that was how they could relate to him, in a category familiar to them. I trusted that Yeshua would welcome me if I, too, approached him as my Rabbi. So I enrolled in his yeshiva.

---

42. Adams, *Sense Appeal in Sermons*, 13.

## Part 3: How Stories Change Lives

This next part of my story will sound weird to many in my Presbyterian/ Reformed tradition. (Perhaps the part about listening to voices in my head has already established some unease.) My journey to the House of the Galilean will not seem alien to readers from other traditions—in particular, those familiar with the spiritual exercises of Ignatius of Loyala.

Over the course of several weeks, I journeyed back to ancient Galilee to encounter Yeshua the Sage. Each day began with an imaginative walk. I pictured myself walking down a dusty street through a small Galilean village. (It helps to have toured the Holy Land; otherwise, illustrated Bible dictionaries may prove useful.) I felt the hot Middle-Eastern sun on my neck; smelled the animals jostling with the human traffic; paused to enjoy the shade of a palm tree. At the end of the street, my destiny. The yeshiva. Flat-roofed; secluded by a courtyard. Entering the narrow doorway, I am refreshed by the cool of the dim interior. The Rabbi sits at a table. He doesn't notice me at first. His rich, resonant voice intones Torah; he sways gently, in a rhythm of body expressing the soul of the sacred words. He senses my presence. I greet him; he beckons me to sit down, as if he had been expecting my arrival.

At this point in my story, I would like to pause briefly, and muse on why I think this imaginative ritual proved helpful to me. Minimally—like any prelude to meditation—it cleared my mind of other thoughts. The imagery of "walk" or "journey" perhaps reminded me of the pilgrim-quality of the Christian life. More specifically, as I traversed the Galilean village, I realized that "The word became flesh, and dwelt among us" (John 1:14). He is not distant from mundane experiences, but meets us in and through the mundane. Lastly, by imaginatively daring to cross the threshold of his yeshiva, I reminded my unbelief that he does not reject me in my folly, but waits to instruct me in wisdom.

What did I learn in the yeshiva? Each day, as I sat in the presence of Yeshua, I read a story from one of the four Gospels. As I read, I asked Yeshua for the wisdom to discern where this particular episode from his life intersects my life. I crept through the story, visualizing its scenery, hearing its dialogue, exploring the texture of its language.

Each episode in the Gospels is like a raindrop on the grass in the early morning sun. View the raindrop from an appropriate angle, and it captures the full spectrum of rainbow light. Likewise, each Gospel story, when it comes into focus, is a microcosm of God's epic drama.

As I sat patiently in the yeshiva, I took the Gospel episode in my fingers, like a rare diamond, and turned it slowly in the sunlight, until its multi-hued glory blazed forth. I shared the joy of discovery with my Rabbi, and awaited the benediction of his smile.

I wish I had written down more of what I learned. But writing was wearisome to me in that season. Handling a pen, or typing a keyboard, seemed too much a part of the long, long story of the academic treadmill. The term papers, the dissertation, the lectures—year after year after year. Writing seemed alien to the cooling restfulness of my time in the yeshiva.

But I have preserved some of the insights I received. One of them developed as a meditation on John 13, reworked into a chapter in Part 4 of this book.

\* \* \* \* \*

Epiphany, or life-changing insight, is a typical strand of many literary narratives. In real life, many individual and communal narratives turn on a moment of epiphany. Epiphanies (theophanies) are woven into the tapestry of the Bible.

This present chapter is a bridge to the next part of my book, in which I share some of my formal meditations on texts of Holy Scripture. These meditations all engage the Bible as an overarching story. Entering and emerging from that story, I have often been changed as if by theophany. Maybe not Moses-and-Burning-Bush theophany, but the palpable presence of God nevertheless. In attempting to give verbal form to my meditations, I recognize that, apart from the energy of the Holy Spirit in the reader, they remain ink on a page. But I trust that the Spirit may honor my attempts to witness to the story of Yeshua.

# PART 4

The World is a Dark Place—
Stories Bring Light

# Spoiler Alert 4
(Overview of Part 4)

"Stories are light. Light is precious in a world so dark."[1] Every sixth of January, the Christian feast of Epiphany (discussed in our previous chapter) celebrates the public manifestation of Jesus Christ, the Light of the World. This manifestation was objective, a historical event. But the manifestation of Light is also a subjective event, an epiphany within the soul.

Part 4 of my book is a quartet of expositions of Scripture texts, designed to facilitate epiphany, or "collision of narratives." These expositions attempt to give room for the Spirit to grant epiphanies, insights that allow the reader to gain a new identity "in Christ," insights that reshape our personal narratives with the luminous glory of the gospel narrative.

I cannot know your unique personal story. If I did, perhaps I could unearth a scriptural story or scene that would seem to have been written "just for you." Instead, I have to rely on archetypal storylines—common narrative arcs that find a point of contact in the experience of many/most humans.

For instance, my book has discussed narratives of rebirth, quests for paradise, scripts of ascent, and scripts of adventure (the "voyage-and-return" archetype).

These four plots all resurface in Part 4. Many scriptural texts feature these archetypes. Furthermore, many of my readers are seeking to live such narratives, or would locate themselves midpoint in such dramas.

For instance, do any of the following desires intersect your current struggles?

- "I wish I could just start over, *wipe the slate clean*, be free from the burden of my past."
- "I wish I could find my *place* in life; somewhere I could thrive, realize my potential."
- "I wish I could be *in charge*, be the one making decisions."
- "I wish I could experience something *out of the ordinary*, have an encounter with the spirit realm."

1. DiCamillo, *Tale of Despereaux*, 81.

These desires are points-of-contact for the expositions of Scripture in this part of my book. We will explore how biblical texts intersect, answer, or challenge and reshape such desires.

Our expositions start with these common personal desires, and move from there into different dimensions of life lived inside the gospel narrative. Each exposition contemplates, from different angles, the new narrative identity found "in Christ." The trait that unifies the quartet turns out to be the *Cross of Jesus*.

Here are the titles and texts featured in Part 4, along with "sneak peeks" into their contents:

- Chapter 22, "A Clean Slate" (John 13):

    This chapter has a point of contact with any reader whose personal story is dominated by *shame/guilt*. By imaginatively entering the "rebirthing" scene from John 13, we are freed from a life story that keeps us chained to the past.

- Chapter 23, "Redefining Your Personal Space" (Hebrews):

    This chapter explores the *spatial imagery* that we often use to tell our personal stories. With this point of contact, I unpack the way that Hebrews uses spatial metaphors to transform the identity and role of the reader. Hebrews intersects the archetypal quest-for-paradise plotline—and offers sustenance to those whose journey takes them through the wilderness.

- Chapter 24, "The Men Who Would Be King" (Mark's Gospel):

    This chapter engages our "royal" scripts, rooted in the archetypal image of self as king (cf. our discussion in chapter 14). These plotlines of personal *ascent* spring from our desire to be in control, to reorder the world, as well as our thirst for status and glory.

- Chapter 25, "Out of Body Experiences" (Ezekiel 1):

    This chapter finds a point of contact in those religious seekers whose story is a quest for epiphany (mystical/transcendent experience). The prophet Ezekiel recounts his version of a mystical adventure, a life-transforming "voyage-and-return" into the realm of the supernatural.

At the end of each chapter, I include questions for reflection and discussion, designed to help the reader interface the gospel story with their own story.

## EXCURSUS: CLASH OF NARRATIVES

Now seems a good time for consolidating this concept—introduced in chapter 2, and mentioned above—namely, how the gospel narrative "collides" with our own personal narratives. "Collision" or "clash" imagines some kind of challenge which emerges from the gospel story and confronts us with new possibilities for existence.

This excursus presents a partial and preliminary inventory of the "angles of impact" of this existential collision. (If you have responded in the past to the Christian message,

I invite you to pause and ask yourself, "What did the gospel do to my personal story?") Here are some of the possibilities:

1. A version of the gospel story provides a *satisfying resolution* to the story you already indwell. The gospel offers a solution to the insoluble problem you recognize so well, one you have tried to solve in many ways—all unsuccessful. (Obvious examples: lifelong struggles with shame or guilt.)

2. A version of the gospel story provokes you to *morph your "desire line"*—i.e., offers you a different and better version of what you are seeking,[2] analogous to the experience of the main character in the film *Mr. Holland's Opus*. Plotline summary: A musician desires to write "the great twentieth-century American symphony," at which he labors for decades, all the while working in his "day job" as a high school music teacher. At the end of his career, he realizes his true "opus" was generations of students in whom he had inspired the love of music.

3. A version of the gospel story *subverts* or deconstructs (via irony) your personal myth (Mark's Gospel seems to function this way).

4. A version of the gospel story "*seduces*" you to abandon your story for the sake of a plot genre of greater beauty. In response to Jesus, you "jump ship" from one genre of life story into another. I wonder if that's what happened to the tax-collector-turned-benefactor named Zacchaeus (Luke 19:1–10). This well-known Sunday school character, upon encountering Jesus, jumps out of a life story of personal ascent (via wealth and power) and into a liberating story of seeking justice and mercy for the poor. Zacchaeus was perhaps seduced by the beauty of the storyline of Jubilee, announced by Jesus in Luke 4:16–21.

5. *Etc.* . . . (You fill in the blank).

---

2. I borrow the concept of "morphing your desire line" from memoir coach Rainer (*Your Life as Story*).

# 22

# A Clean Slate
(John 13)

"I wish I could just start over, wipe the slate clean, be free from the burden of my past."

Does this desire express the longing of your heart?

Guilt. Shame. Trauma. Failure. Looking back regretfully and annotating the past with "If only . . .". Hard to stop such negative memories from popping up in our brains. But if we are moving forward with our lives, we tend to treat such intrusions like the moles in the arcade game Whack-the-Mole. They pop up, we instinctively push them back down.

However, for some of us, our negative memories won't stay down. They define who we are, they determine our life story (or so we think). Perhaps we replay the negative memory over and over (hoping for a better outcome?). Our life story seems written in stone, finished before it got started. No new chapter seems possible, only variations on a demoralizing theme.

If this is our personal narrative, and we ever dare to hope, our hope probably centers on a future gift of *rebirth*. This narrative archetype crystallizes the promise of John's Gospel. The thirteenth chapter of John's account invites us to witness—and participate in—a "rebirthing" scene. I invite you into that scene via my meditation that follows the text below:

> It was just before the feast of the Passover. Jesus knew that his hour had come to cross over from this world to the Father. He had always loved his own who were in the world; now he showed them the perfection of his love.
>
> It was mealtime. The devil had already motivated Judas to betray Jesus. Now Jesus knew that the Father had placed everything into his hands; that he had come from God, and to God he was returning.
>
> So he got up from the meal, laid down his garments, and took a towel and tied it round himself. Then he poured water into a wash-basin, and began to wash his disciples' feet, and wipe them with the towel he was wrapped in.

So he came to Simon Peter, who said to him, "Master—you—my feet—you're really going to wash them?"

Jesus responded, "What I am doing, you do not comprehend now; but you will understand it later."

Peter said, "There is no way you will ever wash my feet!"

Jesus replied, "Unless I wash you, you cannot share in my inheritance."

Simon Peter said, "OK, then not only my feet, but also my hands and my head!"

Jesus said, "The person who has been bathed has no need to be washed, but is clean all over. And you disciples are clean—but not everyone." (For he knew who was about to betray him; that is why he said, "You are not all clean.")

When he had washed their feet, and taken up his garments, and returned to the table, he said to them, "Do you know what I have done for you? You call me "Teacher" and "Master"—and you do well, for I am. If I, Master and Teacher, have washed your feet, you also must wash one another's feet. For I have given you a pattern, so that, just as I have done for you, you should do also.

"Truly, truly, I say to you, a servant is not greater than his master, nor is the person sent greater than the one who sent him. Since you know these things, you will be blessed if you do them.

"I am not speaking about all of you. I know whom I have chosen; but the scripture must be fulfilled, that says, "The one eating my bread lifted up his heel against me." In truth, I am telling you before it happens, so that, when it happens, you may believe that I am.

"Truly, truly I say to you: the person who receives someone I send, receives me; and the person who receives me, receives the one who sent me." (John 13:1–20, my paraphrase)

Let us take off our shoes, for we are on holy ground. The text you just read is the Holy of Holies. Here, as nowhere else, resides the awesome mystery of the gospel.

As we step inside this sacred text, I offer two questions to guide our path. First, why does John's Gospel *not* include the institution of the Lord's Supper? Second, does Jesus really expect his followers to wash their neighbor's feet?

Ritual foot-washing is a venerable part of the Church's liturgy. Every Maundy Thursday, priests in some traditions ceremoniously wash the feet of twelve men.

English monarchs used to perform the ceremony for twelve paupers—"after the yeomen of the laundry had first washed the feet of the paupers with warm water and sweet herbs."[1]

Is this what Jesus commanded his followers to do? I think this question relates to our other question. The scene in John 13 strongly resembles familiar passages from Matthew, Mark, and Luke. The Passover. The supper. Jesus' final meal alone with the Twelve. One who would betray him.

Given all these similarities, why does John fail to narrate the institution of the Lord's Supper?

\* \* \* \* \*

---

1. Hoskyns and Davey, *Fourth Gospel*, 444.

## Part 4: The World is a Dark Place—Stories Bring Light

The fourth Gospel. The strange Gospel. Ancient tradition says, "Last of all John, perceiving that the bodily facts had been made plain in the other Gospels . . . composed a spiritual gospel."

In the fourth Gospel, nothing is surface. Everything has depth:

> "'Destroy this temple, and in three days I will raise it.'
> 'Forty-six years it took to build this temple!'
> But he was speaking about his body as the temple." (John 2:19-21)

The fourth Gospel *ends* by asserting that its source was an eyewitness. Yet it *begins* from a transcendent viewpoint, beyond the reach of any eyewitness: "In the beginning was the Word. The Word was with God, and the Word was God" (John 1:1).

What the Apostles saw, heard, and touched—the speech and actions of the incarnate Word—this is narrated, in the fourth Gospel, from the transcendent viewpoint of eternity.

And so, as John narrates Jesus' final meal with the Twelve, we enter the depths of the eternal significance of that last supper.

*****

I invite *you* to imagine yourself in the scene from John 13. Imagine *yourself* seated at the meal-table:

> Loaves of bread. Jars of wine. Shadows on the wall, cast by the flickering oil-lamps. Eating. Drinking. Conversation with friends.
>
> Suddenly the room goes quiet. Jesus gets up from the table. He lays down his garments, and puts on the clothing of a slave.
>
> Hear the water splashing in the bowl! Through him, all things were made; without him, nothing was made that has been made.
>
> He draws near to you. Jesus touches your feet. He washes your feet with his hands. Is this where you want to cry out with Peter, "No! You cannot be washing my feet!" Isn't this why it can be such a struggle to really and personally trust the good news?
>
> The Son of God humbles himself to wash *your* feet! Does anything in the entire Bible so capture the wonder of the gospel? What a tangible assurance of forgiveness and acceptance!

*****

Many of us spend our whole lives feeling polluted. Something clings to us, like dirt we cannot shake off. But this shame can be our gateway into the symbolic power of John 13.

In antiquity, a person's sandaled feet presented the greatest challenge for cleanliness. In the daily walk, the feet inevitably got dirty! Accordingly, shoes and feet naturally entered the lexicon and rituals associated with purity:

> "Take off your *shoes*, for you are on holy ground." (Exod 3:5)
> "Shake the dust off your *feet*." (Matt 10:14)

The feet became a metaphor of behavior and lifestyle:

> "*Feet* swift to shed blood" (Rom 3:15)
>
> "*Walking* in the truth" (2 John 4; 3 John 3–4)

Purity deals with boundaries, often spatially imaged. Some cultures today express this when they expect visitors to remove their shoes at the threshold of the home. The guest is only welcome once they have removed the shoe, the symbol of defilement.

Sadly, church can so easily become a place where we are not welcome until we have removed our impurity!

We speak of the "purity" of our doctrine, and those of us defiled by theology that is less than 100 percent pure feel permanently unclean, permanently unwelcome, and permanently under suspicion as outsiders.

By contrast, Jesus washes our feet, thereby assuring us that we are clean in his sight. Only the apostasy of a Judas could make us unclean.

The foot-washing in John 13 is an *enacted parable of the cross*. Unless Jesus washes us, we cannot share his inheritance. If he washes us, we can and do share his inheritance.

When John describes the foot-washing, he speaks of Jesus "laying down" and "taking up" garments. Elsewhere, John uses the same language for Jesus' death and resurrection.

This is why there is *no* institution of the Lord's Supper in the fourth Gospel. The Lord's Supper is a symbol of the cross; the foot-washing in John 13 is the meaning of the cross.

\* \* \* \* \*

Did Jesus expect his followers to wash one another's feet?

In John 13, Jesus gives his disciples the *strongest assurance* of their welcome, their wholeness. He conveys this gift of assurance through the symbolic action of the foot-washing. Christians are sent by Jesus to continue his ministry: "Whoever receives the person Jesus sends, receives Jesus" (John 13:20).

Jesus is a priest. All believers share his priestly vocation. One important priestly function is *declaring clean* whatever and whomever God has cleansed.

Bringing assurance of cleanness to fellow-lepers is a priestly service. Helping one another enjoy this gift of assurance is one of the greatest privileges of the body of Christ.

In the worship services of some churches, we institutionalize this ministry via the ritual of "the peace": "The peace of Christ be with you / And also with you."

Here is a concrete expression of mutual priestly service, wherein Christians wash away the dirt from one another's feet, declaring to spiritual sisters and brothers that, whom Christ has cleansed, let no one call unholy.

\* \* \* \* \*

Rebirth stories use numerous images to focus the life-changing experience. *Purification* is one of the most powerful of these narrative images. Purification of our life story implies freedom from the pollution of the past, and freedom to live a new story.

When we meditate upon the foot-washing scene from John 13, we potentially undertake the "Hero's Journey" (described in chapter 7 of this book). As previously stated, Joseph Campbell said, "In the cave you fear to enter, lies the treasure that you seek."[2] If we dare to hope, dare to trust the cleansing power of Jesus, we can "return" from John 13 with a new identity. We can be transformed from a "leper" into a foot-washer, a priest.

As a foot-washer, our old toxic memories, our old wounds, are taken up into a new story. The memories are both killed and rebirthed. When killed, they lose their power to define and demoralize us. Rebirthed, we don't so much *forget* them, but we can "repurpose" them. Once we have been cleansed by Jesus, our memories of pollution become reminders of the power and love of Jesus. Our polluted memories also connect us to those still in need of cleansing, and motivate our priestly ministry of "washing their feet" by inviting them into the story of Jesus. (The next chapter explores further dimensions of the Christian's priestly identity, via a meditation on Hebrews.)

\* \* \* \* \*

## QUESTIONS FOR REFLECTION AND DISCUSSION

1. Imagine Jesus washing your feet. Does it make you feel uncomfortable? If so, why?
2. Is there anything shameful in your past you would just rather forget? Anything you find difficult to bring before God?
3. Have you ever felt unworthy, unaccepted, or excluded in church? Do you believe that Jesus welcomes you, even if his people may not?
4. If your church shares "the peace," is it a meaningless ritual, or an authentic affirmation that everyone is welcome in God's house?
5. Do you believe that you need to "clean up" your life *before* you can enjoy a relationship with God?
6. "You are all clean through the word I have spoken to you" (John 15:3). If you have responded to the gospel, do you still struggle to believe this statement by Jesus? If so, why do you find it difficult to embrace what Jesus said?

---

2. Quoted in Winkler, "What Makes a Hero?"

# 23

# Redefining Your Personal Space
(Hebrews)

"I WISH I COULD find my *place* in life: somewhere I could thrive, realize my potential."

Does this ambition intersect your own life story? Perhaps your quest for place was literal. Does your story hinge on your *going* somewhere, in search of something that could only be found there? Or do you dream of going there in the future, one day? Maybe your search for a proper environment is more metaphorical, involving not a journey, but a reshaping of your current setting.

Whether literal or metaphorical, the search for place defines many biographies. In chapters 9 and 18 of this book, I mentioned that the specter of an imagined paradise has haunted my own narrative for decades.

The nineteenth-century English essayist Charles Lamb eloquently expressed the yearning for an academic paradise in his essay "Oxford in the Vacation."[1] Lamb was a frustrated scholar, denied the academic opportunities commensurate with his abilities. He spent more than thirty dull years working as a clerk in the accounting office of the East India Company. Granted one week's vacation a year, he tended to spend this precious time at the ancient universities of Cambridge and Oxford. Of his visits to the latter, he writes:

> [I am] here in the heart of learning, under the shadow of the mighty Bodley [Library]. I can here play the gentleman, enact the student. To such a one as myself, who has been defrauded in his young years of the sweet food of academic institution, nowhere is so pleasant, to while away a few idle weeks, as one or other of the Universities . . . Here I can take my walks unmolested, and fancy myself of what degree or standing I please . . . I can rise at the chapel-bell, and dream that it rings for *me*.[2]

Lamb's poignant confession mirrors a scene from my own life, in details almost embarrassing. The year 2004 was an extremely low point in my academic career (for details, consult the next chapter of this book). In my early forties, my doctoral dissertation barely

---

1. Lamb, *Essays of Elia*, 10–16.
2. Ibid., 12 (italics in original).

Part 4: The World is a Dark Place—Stories Bring Light

begun, I was neither literally nor metaphorically in the place envisioned over a decade earlier, when my grad school marathon had begun.

I was living in America, voluntarily exiled from my English homeland. My father's hospitalization required my return. I spent a couple of weeks visiting. As the visit ended, I took a day off, and boarded the train for "one . . . of the Universities" (using Lamb's nineteenth-century idiom, that predated the proliferation of degree-granting institutions).

My odds of ever teaching there were exceedingly small (and diminishing by the year). Had I squandered an opportunity of a proper academic career, many irretrievable years ago? What fateful, regretful decisions!

In that entire noble city, there was—perhaps—one academic institution where, with the requisite dose of enormous good fortune, I could conceivably teach (provided I finished my dissertation). Street map in hand, I made the long pilgrimage to the outskirts of the old city, to locate this hall of learning. Rather like Charles Lamb almost two hundred years before me, I touched the orange brick façade of the school, in the vain hope that this "magical" contact would somehow fuse my story to its more substantial history.

\* \* \* \* \*

My story is one of voluntary exile to the USA, in search of a paradise I have not yet found. At times I feel virtually homeless. At such times, I often turn to the New Testament document known as Hebrews. There, in a first-century sermon, God seems to say to me, "Homeless? We can work with that!"

Hebrews is a profound illustration of the power of place (literal, metaphorical) to reshape our personal identity, and to give us a new role in life. Hebrews offers true consolation for anyone whose paradise-quest has taken a wrong turn into the wilderness.

The rest of this chapter contemplates the importance of place in everyone's personal narrative, and explores the new "spatial identity" offered to us by the author of Hebrews.

\* \* \* \* \*

Geographical space. Location. Environment. For each one of us, location is a very big part of our life story.

Suppose you were a Mexican immigrant living in America. Think of what the place called America might mean to you. Perhaps "America" would represent economic opportunity. But perhaps, if you were an *undocumentado*, an illegal immigrant, "America" would mean uncertainty; constant anxiety every time you drive in the vicinity of a police vehicle.

Whether opportunity or uncertainty, the environment known as America would play a major part in shaping your life story.

Location plays a big part in shaping everyone's life story. Indeed, we often use various locations as figures of speech to characterize our situation or circumstances.

For example, if we are unhappy at school, or bored in our job, or unfulfilled in our marriage, we might say, "My school is a prison" or "This job is a prison" or "My marriage is a prison."

When we speak this way, we are using a location (prison) as an image to describe or summarize our life story.

Consequently, the way we label or imagine our environment has great power to shape our *identity* and our role in life.

If we view school as a "prison," for exmaple, our identity may become, "I am a powerless victim of my circumstances."

Alternatively, if we view our marriage as a "prison," our role in the story may become "I need to break out of this jail by getting a divorce!"

Here I would invite you to pause and contemplate your own self-talk (or ask for input from people who regularly listen to you). In talking about your life, do you commonly use any *spatial* images to describe your place in life? If so, what do these images reveal about your life story? How do they impact your identity?

Environment (geographical or metaphorical) can, of course, shape our sense of self in positive ways.

For example, whenever I return to England, I love to visit the ancient university towns of Oxford and Cambridge. I love to walk along the cobbled medieval streets, and touch the ancient stone walls of the colleges. I enter the bookshops, and listen to the students conversing about history, art, and literature.

The cities of Oxford and Cambridge are *symbols* of noble culture and civilization. When I visit them, the beauty and ambience of the cities inspires me, grips me, shapes me. I hunger to feed on great literature, to listen to great music, to converse with great philosophers.

Our environment shapes our identity; our images of our environment shape our identity. With these simple but profound notions, we have built an on-ramp to the biblical book called Hebrews.

\* \* \* \* \*

When we turn to the New Testament letter known as Hebrews, we are given a *new map* of the world. The gospel gives us a new set of spatial images for picturing and experiencing life. To truly appreciate these positives, we must first paint a negative backdrop.

Hebrews was written for a small congregation of Christians who were at a difficult place in life. The Roman empire was not an easy place for Christians. The empire had executed Jesus as a criminal, so Christian allegiance was seen as disloyalty to the empire.

Such disloyalty had negative consequences. The consequences for the first listeners to Hebrews appear in chapter 10, where the author summarizes their experience:

> Remember the former days in which, having been illuminated, you endured a struggle with sufferings: sometimes shamed in public with insults and afflictions; sometimes as companions of those so treated. For you sympathized with prisoners, and accepted the plundering of your property. (Heb 10:32–24)

These listeners were marginalized and despised in society. Their life story included public humiliation, imprisonment, and confiscation of their property. Initially, they had endured this with faith—but now their faith was being eroded by the passage of time that brought no betterment of their condition.

The author of Hebrews was a pastor, writing to help these demoralized and discouraged listeners. The pastor searched the Old Testament for a spatial image of this demoralized place in life . . . and the analogy he found was Israel's wanderings in the *wilderness*:

> We must be afraid—in case, with an enduring promise to enter God's rest, any of you seem to miss out.
> For we, too, have received good news—just like the Israelites in the wilderness.
> But the word they heard did not benefit them, because they did not combine hearing with faithfulness.
> Now we—the faithful—do enter into God's rest, just as he said in the psalm:
> "As I swore in my anger: No way those Israelites will enter into my rest!"—speaking about his rest, even though his work was finished at the foundation of the universe.
> For he spoke elsewhere about the seventh day, saying:
> "And God rested on the seventh day from all his works."
> Yet in the psalm he said, "No way those Israelites will enter into my rest!"
> Since, then, it remains for someone to enter into God's rest
> (and the first generation failed to enter because of unfaithfulness),
> God, many years later, appointed another opportunity—"Today!"—
> saying in a psalm, through David:
> "Today—if you hear his voice, do not harden your hearts!"
> Now, obviously, if Joshua (in the Conquest of Canaan) had obtained true rest for Israel, God would not have spoken of another opportunity (many years later).
> So, then: there remains a sabbath rest for the people of God; for the person who has entered into rest has rested from their labors (just like God).
> So, then: let us strive to enter into that rest, so that no one stumbles by following the pattern of Israel's unfaithfulness. (Heb 4:1–11, my paraphrase)

The wilderness, the desert—this bleak location perfectly described the spiritual condition of the listeners. Unrelenting monotony of scenery. Privation of food and drink. Such is life in a desert. Spiritually and metaphorically speaking, such was life for the first listeners to Hebrews.

Yet the Old Testament story of the wilderness matched their ancient Christian situation even more exactly. When God brought Israel out of Egypt at the Exodus, he led them through the wilderness before they could reach the Promised Land.

Consequently, the wilderness represented imperfection, frustration, not yet reaching one's goal. Wilderness became a place where faith was severely tested: Is God with us in our hardship? In all these ways, wilderness was the realistic image of life for those ancient Christians who first heard Hebrews.

All this might seem very negative. Was the pastor trying to make the listeners feel even worse? No! By using wilderness to describe their situation, he was actually offering them consolation! Why? Because, in the Old Testament story of the wilderness, God was present in a very special way.

In the wilderness, the people dwelt in tents—the symbol of a nomadic existence. So God dwelt in a sacred tent in the midst of his people. Like his people, God too became a nomad.

Hebrews chapter 9 describes the sacred tent for us:

> The first covenant had regulations for worship and the material sanctuary.
> 
> For a tent was prepared: the first part (in which were the lampstand, the table, and the sacred bread), which is called "the holy place."
> 
> And behind the second veil, the part of the tent which is called "the most holy place," which had the golden censer, and the ark of the covenant covered entirely with gold, in which were the golden vessel that had the manna, Aaron's rod that blossomed, and the tablets of the covenant. And above it, the glorious Cherubim, overshadowing the mercy seat. (Heb 9:1–5)

This description creates a sense of reverence. To sense the impact, think of any place where you have sensed the presence of God in a most intense manner. Think of the most beautiful cathedral, or of the grandest mountain range (whatever best represents the sacred for you).

This feeling of reverence—that is what the sacred tent evoked. The lavish gold furnishings adorned a dwelling-place of highest value. The tent also evoked sacred memories of God's involvement with his people. The stone tablets of the covenant said, "I rescued you from slavery in Egypt." The jar of manna said, "I have nourished you on your weary journey."

The architecture of the tent heightened the sense of the holy. A curtain separated the outer sanctuary from the inmost sanctuary. This curtain was a warning sign: "Access strictly limited!" The people knew that God was in their midst, yet he remained distant.

Only one person, the high priest, had the privilege of entering the inmost sanctuary. But the message of the New Testament is that now, through Jesus, *all* of us may have free access to that most holy place, the place where God's grace and glory exceed the beauty of gold or any other symbol of eternity.

When your path through life takes you through the deserted places (loneliness, failure, loss, boredom, or futility) do you ever indulge in *escapism*? And, if so, do you feel guilty about your escapist thoughts and behavior?

Most of the Christian preachers and moralists that I know tend to denounce escapism. But is the evil of escapism in the forms it tends to take (addictions, vices, irresponsibility) rather than the practice itself?

My reading of Hebrews leads me to conclude that God actually encouraged the first-century listeners to indulge in a form of divinely-approved escapism. An imaginative entry into a sacred space that transcended the bleak circumstances of their real world. (And, as we shall see later in this chapter, their escapism would enable them to function better in their temporal environment.)

Think of Hebrews's activation of the imagination as a form of meditation. To center myself amidst stressful circumstances, I often practice the following ritual. I imagine Jesus, clad in the robes of the high priest, inducting me into the most holy place of the sacred tent. Using the description provided by Hebrews (and the Old Testament), I imaginatively explore the holy of holies, and allow the imagery to wash over my frazzled neurons. Gradually, noise and distractions diminish, and I experience a zone of tranquility. The storylines evoked by the symbols (manna, covenant-inscriptions, curtains decorated with emblems of paradise) gradually seep into my sense of self, inspiring new possibilities for when I exit the realm of meditation.

\* \* \* \* \*

The message of Hebrews is as follows: Is your life story taking you through a bleak and barren wilderness? Don't despair. Through Jesus, through the exercise of faith in him, you can legitimately escape to the most glorious place in the universe, the epicenter of the entire cosmos.

Indeed, Hebrews gives an even better picture of the Christian's true environment. The sacred tent was temporary, impermanent. The heavenly *city* is the Christian's permanent, ultimate, and perfect environment.

Chapter 12 of Hebrews uses sublime poetry to open our eyes to this greater environment that actually surrounds us right now. In most audacious terms, it addressed its ancient Christian listener:

> You have already, now, drawn near to Mount Zion, city of the living God, heavenly Jerusalem;
>
>> and to myriads of angels in victory celebration, and to the assembly whose names are registered in heaven, who inherit God's promises;
>>
>> and to a judge—the universal God, who will accept you and not condemn you,
>>
>> and to the spirits of righteous, perfected people;
>>
>> and to Jesus—mediator of a new covenant;
>>
>> and to his sprinkled *blood that speaks*—not of vengeance, like Abel killed by Cain, but of forgiveness, reconciliation, peace with God. (Heb 12:22–24, my paraphrase, italics mine)

Hebrews dares to situate the Christian reader in the suburbs of heavenly Jerusalem. Thankfully, with a claim like that, the writer more than hints at how this locality may be reached. This transcendent environment manifests itself wherever the blood of Christ is speaking.

Blood speaking? How? Well, blood symbolizes vitality, and it symbolizes death. The blood of Christ speaks of his noble life and sacrificial death.

When his purity makes contact with our impurity, he consecrates us so that we may enter boldly and confidently into the presence of God. Through Jesus, the gate of the holy city is flung wide open for us to enter in.

Wherever the blood of Jesus is speaking, wherever the holy and imperishable gospel is encountered, the eternal city—the heavenly Jerusalem—graciously invades our personal space. In church. Where the Lord's Supper witnesses to the blood of Christ. Where the Scriptures are encountered in reading, exposition, prayer, confession, and song.

But not only in church. Even when we occupy the "secular" realm, the heavenly city surrounds us. Through the channel of our faith-filled imaginations, its sacred energy and joyful celebrations can transform our mundane space into holy ground.

\* \* \* \* \*

Our environment shapes who we are and what we do. When I visit the cities of Oxford and Cambridge, I become more like a person of culture. As a Christian, I travel spiritually to the most holy place; I go on a spiritual pilgrimage to the heavenly city. Jesus, my mediator, brings me to the place where God lives.

This spiritual environment re-shapes who we are and what we do. By faith, we enter the most holy place. This is the place for *priests*, special people consecrated for special tasks.

When our spiritual abode is the most holy place, the place for priests, we *become* priests. The holy environment shapes us for the glorious and honorable role of priesthood.

In the ancient world (especially the world of Judaism), a priest was an honorable role with glorious privileges. The priest enjoyed special access to God. The priest mediated God's grace to needy people. The priest led the people in the worship of God. The priest was a bridge between the ordinary and the transcendent.

Hebrews chapter 13 tells the average Christian, "You are a priest!" It says, "Through Jesus, let us continuously offer up to God *a sacrifice of praise*—namely, the fruit of lips that confess his name. And do not neglect to do good and to share, for God takes pleasure in *such sacrifices*" (Heb 13:15–16, italics mine).

Hebrews uses the terminology of sacrifice, the terminology reserved for priestly activity, to describe mundane actions of kindness and simple doxological language!

Do you sense the audacity of Hebrews's act of reimaging its listeners? The dregs of Roman society, the bottom of the social pyramid—reimagined as priests! The outcasts of Roman civilization—recast as citizens of the heavenly Jerusalem!

What difference might it make in your life if every mundane action received the glow of transcendent significance?

In my (previous) church in Dallas there are two young ladies, Paulina and Saradeli, who lead the communal singing of hymns. When they lead the congregation in singing praise to God's name, Paulina and Saradeli are priests! They have the most glorious role in the universe.

A former member of this church in Dallas was Pepe, a gifted chef. When Pepe prepared seafood salad for the communal meal, Pepe was a priest! He had the most glorious role in the universe.

Last month, I spoke at a church in central Pennsylvania. In the front row, sat a young man called David, a man with Down Syndrome. (I nearly wrote that he "suffered" from Down Syndrome—but rapidly deleted it for the reason that follows.) I had never spoken in that church before, and was not sure how well my message would be received. After I was done speaking, David came up to me and introduced himself in barely-intelligible (but profoundly eloquent) speech. "My name is David. My brother is

Peter, and my dog is Mattie. *I want you to be my friend.*" One of the priestly jobs involves bringing outsiders into the community of God's people. David is a priest. He has the most glorious role in the universe.

* * * * *

According to Orthodox theologian Alexander Schmemann, nothing captures the primordial purpose of being human better than the role of priest to God's creation:

> The first, the basic definition of man is that he is *the priest*. He stands in the center of the world and unifies it in his act of blessing God, of both receiving the world from God and offering it to God—and by filling the world with this eucharist, he transforms his life, the one that he receives from the world, into life in God, into communion with Him. The world was created as "matter," the material of one all-embracing eucharist, and man was created as the priest of this cosmic sacrament.[3]

Hebrews offers us a place where we can thrive, where we can fulfill our potential, where we can become who we were created to be.

* * * * *

## QUESTIONS FOR REFLECTION AND DISCUSSION

1. Is there a special place strongly connected to your identity? If so, where and why?
2. Are there any spatial metaphors you consistently use to describe your life?
3. Is God distant in your experience? What do you make of Hebrews's claim that Christians can, right now, enjoy unrestricted access to God's presence?
4. Where is home for you? Have you ever adopted the mindset of Hebrews—a pilgrim, passing through this world, on the way to your true home? If you adopted the pilgrim mindset, how might that affect your lifestyle?
5. What privileges and activities spring to mind when you hear the word "priest"? If priest is a positive image in your estimation, do you ever think of your Christian service as a priestly activity?
6. As the priest of God's creation, humankind's role is to offer up the world to God, and to receive it back as a blessing. Have you consecrated your talents and resources to God?

---

3. Schmemann, *Sacraments and Orthodoxy*, 15 (italics in original).

# 24

# The Men Who Would Be King
(Mark's Gospel)

AMERICA IS NO LONGER a British colony, but a democratic republic. The British monarchy may be reduced to a figurehead, a tourist attraction. The idea of kingship may seem outmoded. However, scratch beneath the surface of our personal narratives, and the *regal archetype* appears to be alive and kicking.

Metaphors crystallize plotlines, and the images of "king" and "kingdom" can bring many of our life stories into sharper focus. The role of kings, in the traditional narratives, overlaps many of the tasks we feel called to. Struggling for good versus evil. Ordering chaos by shaping culture or establishing rules. The quest for a "kingdom" can echo the primordial yearning for lost paradise. The comedic storyline of social integration can also dovetail with the rise of a "king," a charismatic figure around whom the people rally. And, intersecting all these stories, the "rags to riches" drama of *personal ascent*, in which you and I get the lead role, the occupant of the throne.

Our personal stories of ascent are often justified by our desire to use power/authority for good. Therein lies the seduction of narratives of personal ascent. It's good for me to be king, since my rule will re-order the world to make it a better place. In this script, our climb to status starts out as a means to an end, but can easily become an end in itself.

As a seminary professor with a PhD, I have faced that struggle. As did all my peers in grad school. We coveted the rare professorships, not for the honor (of course), but for the good we could do from a position of influence.

I was probably corrupted sooner than most. My pursuit of a PhD was always haunted by a backstory of "unfulfilled potential," of having been identified by middle-school teachers as "gifted and talented," and having done little, if anything, to demonstrate the truth of their assessment, resulting in a life-long burden "to prove myself to myself."

Here is a snippet from my story. Doubtless you are less egotistical than me, but perhaps my narrative may resonate with your own experience in some manner. (Warning: the next paragraphs include some boasting. Please read them as hyperbolic, and as ironic—cf. Paul's boasting in 2 Cor 11:1—12:13.)

## Part 4: The World is a Dark Place—Stories Bring Light

Back in the nineties, I enthusiastically enrolled in a graduate school, one that prided itself on virtually being an "Ivy League" seminary. (After all, its roots were deep in Princeton Seminary, so why not exult?)

As a PhD student, I was soon appointed Lecturer in Greek and Hebrew. (Grad schools do that sort of thing; it's cheaper to pay adjuncts by the course, than hire a full-time professor.) I received glowing reviews from my Greek and Hebrew classes. "The seminary should hire you as a *professor*!" When I aced my doctoral exams, I was told by my prof, "Your performance ranks in the top three of all of our doctoral students from the last decade."

There was another student in the program, who rather flew under the radar screen of academic distinction. He was competent, if not eye-catching. In the words used to describe King David's second-string warriors, "He did not rank with the three" (2 Sam 23:19). In his defense, he worked thirty hours a week (in addition to full-time studies) to feed his wife and three children.

Anyway, he had graduated before I started my dissertation, and landed a job at a seminary I had never heard of. One January, a sudden vacancy in their New Testament department led him to kindly phone me and invite me to apply for the position at his school. I interviewed, got the job, and showed up in June to teach summer Greek.

Whereas my old school had been (sort of) Ivy League, my new school seemed (pretty much) Community College in comparison. But I made the colossal mistake of microwaving my "Ivy League" lectures, and serving them up to students unable to digest them. That summer, I earned the worst course evaluations I have ever received. How the mighty have fallen!

I was summoned into the Dean's office, and was told that "Your teaching performance must drastically improve, or your contract will not be renewed!" Worse news followed in the fall, a change in policy by the school's credentialing agency. No longer were schools like mine allowed to have "ABDs" on faculty ("All-But-Dissertation"—an acronym for PhD students with an unfinished thesis). Once again, I was summoned into the Dean's office: "Finish your dissertation promptly, or your contract will not be renewed!"

That gloomiest of semesters ended with a Christmas chapel service. The faculty donned our academic regalia (they all had their doctoral hoods, apart from me). We lined up for our ceremonial procession into the sanctuary. An usher handed me a program, and I glanced at the list of Awards for Excellence. This list recognized outstanding accomplishments amongst students and faculty. There in bold font, the "Teacher of the Year Award," given to my less-than-totally-distinguished colleague from grad school. (Sidebar: he thoroughly deserved it. He was and is an excellent, innovative lecturer. He has also published many scholarly works, far exceeding my own meager production.)

As I fruitlessly attempted to pray down the pangs of envy that were searing my soul, the Dean called me over. "We have a custom for our Christmas chapel. As the faculty process into the sanctuary, the school sings the hymn, "Lift High the Cross." The crucifer [cross-bearer] walks at the head of the procession. Our custom requires the *most junior* faculty member to carry the cross. That would be you, Mr. Smith."

So my peer from grad school got Teacher of the Year, and I got to carry the cross.

This story is obviously (at least from my own point of view!) a long way from a happy ending. To get us there, I need to splice in another story, one that I was teaching in my Gospels class that semester. As I carried the cross into the chapel, I reflected on the collision of the narrative I was living with the narrative I was teaching my students.

Let's press the pause button on my own story of (failed) ascent, and add a shorthand version of the biblical story of kingship. When we are done, I will tie in the loose threads of my own story.

\* \* \* \* \*

"Adam" and "humanity." They are the same word in Hebrew; his story is our story. Adam; a royal figure. From dust to dominion—an ancient metaphor of enthronement.[1] Ruling the animals—a kingly privilege (cf. 1 Kgs 10:22). Bearing God's image and likeness—words inscribed on ancient statues of kings.

"Eat the fruit of knowledge. Be more like God. Why settle for vassal, when you could be the Great King?" (cf. Gen 3:5).

From dominion to dust. The exiled keeper of the royal garden (cf. Eccl 2:5–6) now cuts his hands on thorns and thistles.

Adam. Humanity. The regal reality is lost, and yet the royal ideal remains. The quest for a true king propels the plotline of the biblical narrative.

Fast forward to the time of Samuel. The royal ideal resurfaces. "Establish for us a king to rule us, like all the nations!" (1 Sam 8:5, 19–20). Samuel tried to warn them (1 Sam 8:11–18). Conscription. Taxation. Enslavement. The king would rewrite the royal script; he would import too much of himself into the role.

Royal reality may disappoint, but the royal ideal burned bright. Israel's poets give voice to the royal ideal:

> O God, grant your justice to the king,
> and your righteousness to the royal son.
>
> He will judge your people in righteousness,
> and your afflicted ones with justice.
>
> The mountains will bring wholeness to the people,
> and the hills, righteousness.
>
> He will vindicate the afflicted among the people,
> save the children of the poor,
> and crush the oppressor. (Ps 72:1–4)

Fast forward to the vision of Daniel (Dan 7:1–8). Pagan imperialism. Perversion of kingship. Bestial Babylon. Bestial Rome. An apocalyptic slideshow of grotesque images. "Rulers of the gentiles lord it over them, and their great ones exercise authority over them" (Mark 10:42). Subjects trampled underfoot, devoured by iron teeth (Dan 7:7).

---

1. Thanks to my colleague Douglas Green for sharing this insight.

Bestial conduct, bestial images. Multiple heads, multiple horns. Grotesque, unnatural, winged predators. Where is the Adamic ideal, a king in God's true image and likeness? "One like a *son of man*, coming with the clouds of heaven . . . His dominion is an eternal dominion that will not pass away, and his kingdom is one that will never be destroyed" (Dan 7:13–14). The greater the perversion of kingship, the stronger the royal ideal.

Fast forward to the Greco-Roman world. Enter the horror story envisioned by Daniel. Time: 167 BC. Place: Jerusalem. As the story unfolds, we shall witness the near-extinction of Judaism, and the rescripting of the royal ideal.

At this point in the story, Israel is virtually a colony within a sector of the Greek empire. Cultural Hellenization threatens to absorb the Jewish way of life (1 Macc 1:10–15; 2 Macc 4:7–15).[2]

Daniel's apocalyptic nightmare unfolds. Cultural imperialism intensifies, reinforced by the swords and spears of the Greek ruler Antiochus Epiphanes (Dan 11:29–32).

Judaism is under siege, its sacred symbols outlawed and defiled. Torah scrolls—confiscated and burnt. Circumcision and Sabbath-keeping—capital crimes. Jewish mouths force-fed unclean meat. The Temple itself, the epicenter of Jewish purity, turned into a shrine for unclean sacrifices to Zeus (1 Macc 1:41–63; 2 Macc 6:1–11; 6:18; 7:1).

How Israel needs a hero! Cue Mattathias, a priest with five sons—including one Judas Maccabeus. This family leaves defiled Jerusalem for the nearby city of Modein. Soldiers from Antiochus Epiphanes march into Modein. Their mission: compel the leaders of Modein to offer pagan sacrifices as tokens of loyalty to their Greek overlords. "A man—a Jew—came forward . . . to offer sacrifice . . . according to the king's orders. And Mattathias saw, was filled with *zeal* . . . and ran and slaughtered the man upon the altar. Simultaneously, he killed the king's official (who was compelling them to sacrifice) and overturned the altar. Mattathias was full of *zeal* for the law of God, just like Phinehas" (1 Macc 2:23–26, italics mine).

*The Zealot script emerges*, rewriting the royal script.

Maccabean Zealots. God was on their side. Through relentless guerilla warfare, Judas Maccabeus and his brothers progressively expelled the Greek imperialists.

Early in the campaign, in 164 BC, the Temple was purified and rededicated (1 Macc 4:36–59). At this inaugural Hanukkah, the Jews, "holding beautiful branches and also *palm* leaves, lifted up *hymns* to him who had prospered the purification of his own place" (2 Macc 10:7, italics mine).

Palms and Psalms. This Maccabean motif accompanied the eventual independence of Israel. In 141 BC, "the yoke of the Gentiles was removed from Israel" (1 Macc 13:41). Within a year, the last Gentile troops were expelled from their citadel inside Jerusalem. "The Jews entered it . . . with *praise and palm branches* . . . with *hymns* and songs, because a great enemy had been smashed out of Israel" (1 Macc 13:51, italics mine).

---

2. The apocryphal books 1 and 2 Maccabees are found in the Greek Old Testament. They do not belong to the Protestant canon of Scripture. Nevertheless, they provide invaluable background for the New Testament.

## The Men Who Would Be King

History abounds in ironies. The Maccabean story has two ironic twists. First, the Maccabean dynasty emerged in opposition to the Hellenization of Judaism. But over time, the Maccabean kings took on an eerie resemblance to their Hellenistic counterparts.[3]

Second, in their quest to remove the Greek yoke, the Maccabean leaders sought alliance with the Romans (1 Macc 8). In 63 BC, the Roman empire extinguished Israel's hard-won freedom, and Israel once again shouldered the imperial yoke.

But Israel's royal ideal endured, fortified by memories of the Maccabean zealot script.

Fast forward to the Gospel according to Mark. Immediately, Jesus heralds the arrival of a new era: "The time is fulfilled, and the kingdom of God has come near" (Mark 1:15). Jewish ears reverberate with Daniel's prophecies (Dan 7:22; 12:4, 7). Israel's time has come. Rome's time is over.

Mark's script unfolds with breathless pace. An apocalyptic slideshow flashes across the screen.[4] The power of heaven invades the earth. Exorcisms expel the demonic powers reckoned to support Rome.[5] Demon hordes named "*Legion*" drowned like the armies of Egypt (Mark 5:9–13; Exod 14:26–28).[6]

What's that about a mustard seed? Contemptibly small? Surely that's only temporary! (See Mark 4:30–32.)

Mark's script unfolds with breathless pace. The kingdom of God has come near, so near that the disciples can confidently expect its establishment within their lifetime (Mark 9:1). How natural, then, the request of James and John. In Messiah's kingdom, they want the seats on the right and the left of the throne (Mark 10:37; cf. Luke 22:29–30). As the royal script unfolds, they seek the role of best supporting actor!

As Jesus enters Jerusalem, the jostling crowds wave leafy branches, and shout, "Blessed is the coming kingdom of our father David!" (Mark 11:8–10). Palms and psalms. The Maccabean Zealot script reactivated.

James and John know the time must be near. Rome replaced by Israel. The "last" will be "first"!

*The Cross.* Brutal symbol of Roman imperial domination. Deconstruction of the Maccabean script. Crucifixion of the Zealot script. Above the Cross, the victim's crime: "The King of the Jews" (Mark 15:26). A billboard for Roman power; public derision of James's and John's dreams.

If sheer volume of text is an index of author intent, then Mark's message about the Cross becomes clear. His account majors, in excruciating detail, on the *humiliation and shaming* of the one who embodied the royal ideal. Mark's unrelenting narrative depicts Jesus' humiliation so forcefully that commentary might dilute the message:

> Pontius Pilate . . . after flogging Jesus . . . handed him over to be crucified.
>
> The soldiers took Jesus inside the courtyard . . .

---

3. Scott, *Jewish Backgrounds*, 86–87.

4. Hays, *Moral Vision of the New Testament*, 89.

5. Second Temple Judaism saw evil spirits behind pagan empires (Reid, "Principalities and Powers," 750–51).

6. The defeat of *Legion* (a fairly transparent reference to Roman armies) "could hardly have been read in Mark's time without political overtones" (Boring, *Mark*, 151).

> They clothed him in purple, then twisted thorns into a crown and put it on him.
>
> Then they addressed him: "Greetings, King of the Jews!"
>
> They kept hitting him on the head with a staff and spitting on him.
>
> Falling on their knees, they "revered" him.
>
> And when they had ridiculed him, they removed the purple robe . . .
>
> Then they took him outside to crucify him . . .
>
> And they crucified him.
>
> Dividing up his garments, they cast lots to determine who got what.
>
> It was the third hour when they crucified him.
>
> The written notice of the accusation against him read: "The King of the Jews."
>
> They crucified two thieves with him, one on his right and one on his left.
>
> Passersby reviled him . . .
>
> The chief priests and the teachers of the law also ridiculed him . . .
>
> "This Christ, this King of Israel—let him come down now from the cross, that we may see and believe!"
>
> Those crucified with him also insulted him. (Mark 15:15–32)

In his narrative of crucifixion, Mark takes the life-script of James and John, and tears that script to shreds. Participation in the royal ideal? The role of best supporting actor? The men who would be king? Torn up. Ripped apart. Shredded.

In this deconstructive narrative, Mark also subverts the James and John in you and in me. James and John represent the triumphal life-script of the Christian reader.[7]

Irony plays a big part in Mark's subversion of our royal life-scripts. James and John coveted the places to the left and right of Jesus at his coronation (Mark 10:37). When Jesus is crowned (with thorns), under a placard reading "The King of the Jews," who gets the places to his left and right? Two thieves! (Mark 10:27.)

Irony continues. The disciples have fled the scene. Peter has betrayed his Messiah. Who confesses the crucified Jesus as "Son of God," a title denoting the Emperor of Rome? A Roman centurion! (Mark 15:39.)

In Mark's paradoxical universe, these radically subversive ironies actually point to redemption. Mark's deconstruction is ultimately reconstruction.

Whoever clings onto their own story will lose it; whoever abandons their own story for the sake of Jesus will, paradoxically, redeem their story (cf. Mark 8:35).

Jesus rewrote the royal script. The gospel overwrites our own royal scripts with the subversive anti-Messiah story of Jesus.

In the Gospel of Mark, three interrelated symbols convey this fusion of narratives: cross, cup, and baptism. Want to follow Jesus? Take up your cross! (Mark 8:34.) Do you, like James and John, want a part in the kingdom of glory? Then you must share Christ's cup and baptism (Mark 10:37–39).[8]

---

7. For discussion of the disciples as foils for the Christian reader, see Tannehill, "Disciples in Mark," 392–95.

8. "These metaphors (cup and baptism) could hardly be used in the Markan community without evoking Christian baptism and the Eucharist, in which every Christian participates" (Boring, *Mark*, 301).

When we, by faith, identify with Messiah crucified, we enter a plotline of reversal leading to restoration. No more, the role of best actor. No more Maccabean or Zealot power-politics. No more Adam, grasping at equality with God.[9] The Cross of Jesus crucifies our self-centered royal scripts, and so restores us to our proper place in God's universe.

The Cross generates a mustard-seed kingdom, despicable by Greco-Roman imperial standards. In the kingdom of the Cross, first equals last, and greatness equals slave-service (Mark 9:35; 10:42–45).

The Cross inaugurates a contemptible, paradoxical, non-kingdom kingdom. Messiah's story of humiliation rescripts our egocentric, self-glorifying lives.

The Cross subverts Roman imperial tyranny, and all other tyranny, because the cross humbles the ego that builds empires in its own image.

\* \* \* \* \*

Time to return to my unfinished biographical snippet from the start of this chapter. We left our "hero" in the throes of "crucifixion"—well, carrying the cross, if only in ceremonial procession. This ritual symbolized (for me) a semester of humiliation, something I had not yet experienced in my academic career.

I could have reacted in one of two ways. Tempting, very tempting, was the path of pouting: "This 'community college' is beneath me, anyway. Who cares about their dumb awards?", followed by grinding out my dissertation, padding my resumé, and exiting for academic pastures more in keeping with my Ivy League pretensions.

Thankfully (and doubtless prompted by the Holy Spirit), I chose to bear my "cross." Instead of pouting and bolstering my shattered self-image, I embraced the "death" experience. (After all, isn't that the wisdom we learn from the "monomyth," the "hero's journey" template, the blueprint of all good stories? See chapter 7.) Out of the death experience comes new life, and wisdom to share following our "return" from the ordeal.

So I asked myself, "Is there a way I could change my teaching style to connect with the local students?" (Perhaps I could learn something from The Teacher of the Year!)

So I did. Out went the big academic technical terms from my lectures. Instead of "metanarrative," I spoke of "God's big story." Instead of info-packed, two hour lectures, delivered without a pause for breath, I went with less-is-more. Less lecturing, more time for classroom discussion. Genuine conversation with the class, not mere Q&A.

In sum, the crucifixion of our pride is never enjoyable. But, in my case, it was followed by my resurrection as a teacher.

## QUESTIONS FOR REFLECTION AND DISCUSSION

1. The dream of James and John centered on the glory of political and military triumph. Do any of your personal dreams resonate positively with their triumphalism?

---

9. Cf. Phil 2:6, as exposited by Wright, *Climax of the Covenant*, 82–92.

2. The dream of James and John had a legitimate religious component. (After all, God had promised a kingdom to Israel!) Do any of your triumphalist dreams weave a good religious motive into your personal desire for glory?

3. If you are a conservative evangelical, do you employ "kingdom" language to legitimate your own personal agenda?

4. Re-read Mark's account of the crucifixion. How does this account make you feel?

5. How do you feel about Mark's version of the Christian life as "bearing your cross"?

6. In the current episode of your life, is God frustrating your desire for glory?

7. For a Christian, are there any acceptable forms of personal ambition? If so, can you give examples? What makes them acceptable?

# 25

## Out-of-Body Experiences
(Ezekiel 1)

"What's on your bucket list?" asked the preacher at summer youth camp. I was in the audience, chaperoning high-school students from my church. Sitting next to me was Dulce. Never an avid note-taker during sermons, Dulce started scribbling frantically in her notebook. Intrigued by this unusual development, I glanced over. She was compiling her "bucket list," and was already down to number seventeen. Number one on her list of do-this-before-I-die? "Find out if aliens are real."

Dulce is not alone in her fascination with extraterrestrials. We even see this obsession on the History Channel, which recently seems to have been taken over by shows with titles like *Ancient Aliens*. Going back over a few decades, some of the most popular movies tap into this fascination. *Close Encounters of the Third Kind* (1977); *E.T. the Extra-Terrestrial* (1982); *Contact* (1997). Likewise, UFO "sightings" (and stories of alien abductions) never cease.

What might explain this striking cultural phenomenon? At the risk of over-simplifying, I would suggest that obsession with aliens arises at the apex of modern secular culture, and compensates for the loss of the transcendent. Technological, scientific civilization tends to eliminate the mysterious and the numinous from our lives. Everything receives a natural explanation, in terms of ordinary causes and effects. The transcendent world recedes into nowhere, displaced by the visible, material, tangible realm. In place of the old-fashioned notion of the soul, with its access to the beyond, we have neuroscience, imprisoning the self inside our craniums.

But our hunger for transcendence does not recede. Instead, this desire mutates, expressing itself in forms adapted to scientific culture. The ancient Greeks created gods in their own image—superheroes on steroids. Similarly, when modern scientific culture imagines transcendent beings, these entities are super-sophisticated versions of ourselves. The classic alien (think Roswell) has a super-sized cranium, and arrives on earth via other-worldly technologies.

UFOs are not the only phenomenon generated by late modern culture to compensate for the loss of the transcendent. Alongside this high-tech version of transcendence,

## Part 4: The World is a Dark Place—Stories Bring Light

we also observe the revival of more traditional interests in the mystical and the supernatural. Neo-pagan religions ("witchcraft," in more traditional parlance) are making a comeback in the West. Turning to the Christian context, the last hundred years has witnessed the burgeoning of Pentecostal and Charismatic churches, with their unapologetic emphasis on supernatural experiences and encounters.

This chapter taps into contemporary thirst for the transcendent. I will investigate one of the most influential mystical encounters recorded in the pages of Scripture. To get us started, I invite you to go find a Bible, and read the "throne vision" narrated in the first chapter of Ezekiel.

\* \* \* \* \*

As you were reading the strange account of the prophet's experience, what was your honest gut response? Was it dismissal? Or maybe curiosity?

I once studied such narratives in an academic setting: Lutheran Seminary in Germantown, PA. After we heard some "throne vision" narratives read out loud, the professor welcomed honest personal responses from the class.

The first response came from a tattooed and pierced male (presumably a youth pastor). "Dude!" he exclaimed. "What had the prophet been *smoking*?"

Others were a bit more respectful. They wondered, "Are such experiences for real?" "Could something like that ever happen to me?" "Do people today have mystical encounters akin to Ezekiel's?"

In this chapter, I will explore the meaning of Ezekiel's throne vision, with annotations for those of you seeking mystical encounters of your own.

\* \* \* \* \*

What do scriptural theophanies reveal about God, and about experiencing God?

Ezekiel's vision is kaleidoscopic. Successive images superimpose upon each other. First a thunderstorm; then four-winged, four-faced creatures; then chariot wheels; and finally, a celestial throne. The sequence has a holistic, aesthetic impact.

Hebrew *apocalyptic* imagery loves kaleidoscopic representation. Rather than reproduce a single, graphic image in the mind's eye, Hebrew apocalyptic generates an overwhelming thread of hyper-text linkages. The layers upon layers of images activate the deepest *cultural memories* of Israel's religion. *In the act of self-disclosure, God meets us "where we are at"; he enters into our story.*

Two-and-a-half millennia before the internet and worldwide web, ancient Hebrew scribes loved to thread together multiple related scriptures. This "inspired threading" intensifies and expands our experience as readers of the text.

Ezekiel's report of his vision hyper-texts into an overwhelming multiplicity of scriptural images:

- the storm-theophany on Mount Sinai
- the throne-vision of Isaiah, with its winged creatures

- the fiery torch of the Abrahamic covenant
- the divine chariot of the Psalter
- the heavenly firmament of Genesis 1
- the crystal pavement of Exodus 24
- the rainbow of the Flood

All these echoes remind us of the cosmic drama of God's unfolding covenant. In other words, Ezekiel experienced God via the foundational images of Israel's faith. God communicated with the prophet using familiar symbols. *Our mystical encounters with God find meaning within the matrix of God's story, the overarching narrative of scripture.*

One might also say that Ezekiel's experience had a *culture-specific dimension*. Archaeological finds have disclosed numerous fascinating parallels to the imagery of Ezekiel. Learned commentaries conveniently reproduce some of these archaeological discoveries that shed light on our text:

- statues of celestial beings, some with two faces and others with four faces
- statues of hybrid creatures, supporting the heavenly dome
- hybrids with four wings, and bodies combining the form of a man and the form of a bull

This culture-specific dimension means that *our* experience of God will differ from Ezekiel's. We may not get to see the wheels with eyes on their rims. (Sorry if that disappoints you!)

Indeed, Ezekiel's report takes great care to *safeguard the transcendence of God*, whose infinite glory is beyond the scope of any creaturely imagery. Notice the careful language: Ezekiel saw, not the glory itself, but the "appearance of the likeness of the glory of Yahweh" (Ezek 1:28).

That said, let us briefly explore some of the *symbolism* of the images.

The wings, the wheels, the number four—all seem to depict the radical *freedom* of God. This freedom is expressed by the effortless motion afforded by the wings and the wheels. The number four suggests the universal scope of God's freedom—a freedom that operates to the four corners of the earth, that matches the freedom of the four winds (north, south, east, and west).

In addition, the "hypertext links" that we noted speak of the *faithfulness* of God. The God encountered by Ezekiel is the creator, the one who made eternal promises to Abraham, the one who formed Israel at Mount Sinai.

In the rest of the book of Ezekiel, God's freedom operates as an expression of his faithfulness, and his faithfulness is an expression of his freedom. He acts not because of any merit in his people, but for his own name's sake.

The faithfulness of God, the freedom of God. Ezekiel's mystical experience reflected these basic divine character-traits. These same traits have implications for our own encounters with the divine.

God's freedom means that we cannot use magic formulae to manipulate the presence of God. God shows up when, where, and how he pleases.

On the other hand, God's faithfulness holds out real hope for all who sincerely seek his presence. God's covenant faithfulness crystallizes in his promise, "I will be with you." This promise was incarnate in Jesus, called Immanuel, "God with us." Seek, and you will find.

\* \* \* \* \*

So far, we have scratched the surface of the profound symbolism of Ezekiel's opening chapter. Ezekiel's throne vision entered into and shaped the stories of two ancient religions, Judaism and Christianity. To explore the influence of the prophet's encounter, I will *trace the trajectory* of the throne vision, from the initial experience of the prophet, through its literary representation in the canonical book, on to the ripple effects of Ezekiel 1 in ancient Judaism, and into the New Testament. This storyline will yield new insights for anyone searching for the transcendent.

Ezekiel's *initial experience* led into the call of the prophet in chapters 2–3. For the prophet Ezekiel, his experience of the throne vision functioned to equip him for his prophetic ministry. Mystical experience cannot be an end in itself. Such encounters are a means to an end, an empowerment for a role in God's unfolding drama. Thrill-seeking, experience-for-its-own-sake, is never encouraged in Scripture.

Ezekiel's Hebrew name means "God strengthens," and the vision of God's radical freedom gave the prophet strength to declare a dreadful consequence of God's freedom. Ezekiel was strengthened for the unpleasant task of announcing that Yahweh, in his freedom, would abandon Jerusalem to the violence of the expanding Babylonian Empire.

This was no capricious act on Yahweh's part. It reflected the terms of the covenant. Israel had polluted the land with unworthy and ignoble religious and moral practices. Now Yahweh would remove his glory and protection from that polluted place.

Turning from the impact on the prophet, let us consider the impact of chapter 1 upon his *first readers*.

The book of Ezekiel incorporates numerous visions received by the prophet, and some of these are dated *after* the destruction of Jerusalem in 586 BC. The book of Ezekiel has two halves, the first half majoring on a message of doom, and the second half majoring on a message of hope. The initial readers of Ezekiel had lived through the doom (the destruction of Jerusalem), and were awaiting the hope of restoration.

For those first readers of Ezekiel, chapter 1 functioned to convince them that God is free to realize the promises and the hope which form the encouragement of the second half of the book. (The prophetic hope of a "paradise restored" storyline.)

Readers (ancient and modern) encounter the throne of Yahweh via its literary representation—a *different medium* from the direct visual-auditory experience of the prophet. But—here's a big question—is the *existential impact* different? After all, "The word of God is living and energetic, sharper than any two-edged sword" (Heb 4:12).

Can our experience as readers approach the intensity of the prophet's encounter?

Ezekiel promises that God will do many mighty deeds in the future. God will take away his people's stony hearts, and give them a heart of flesh. God will put his Spirit inside his people, and wash us clean with pure water.

These actions of God have a singular purpose: that we "may know that He is Yahweh," that He is faithful to His promises. This knowledge is highly existential in character.

Ezekiel envisions a more intense, more permanent presence of God's glory among His people. The book ends with a vision of a holy city, named "Yahweh is there."

One might venture to say that the promises of the book of Ezekiel actually encourage those readers who desired an experience of God akin to Ezekiel's . . .

. . . And such readers were not uncommon in ancient Judaism. After Ezekiel's day, Judaism developed a strain of mysticism which modern scholars label *Chariot Mysticism* (in reference to the chariot wheels of Ezekiel 1).

In Jewish Chariot Mysticism, meditation on the text of Ezekiel 1 became a springboard for a mystical experience, in which the mystic *allegedly* ascended to the throne of Yahweh, and saw visions of glory like Ezekiel's! And those who saw the divine glory were *transformed* by it.

This form of mysticism *feeds into the New Testament* in many places:

- Revelation 4–5 is an obvious point of contact. John's vision of the throne of God and the Lamb is clearly patterned after Ezekiel's experience.

- And then there is chapter 3 of John's Gospel, where Jesus says: "No one has ever ascended into heaven, except the one who descended from heaven—the Son of Man. Just as Moses lifted up the serpent in the desert, so the Son of Man must be lifted up, so that everyone who believes in him may have eternal life" (John 3:13–14). Is Jesus contesting the claims of the Jewish Chariot Mystics? Is Jesus claiming that he, uniquely, has that kind of access to God? Is Jesus saying that, through the Cross, we too may enjoy that kind of access to God?

- And then there's the conversion and commission of the Apostle Paul, on the road to Damascus. Acts 9 describes his experience in terms that echo Ezekiel 1: the glorious light; the heavenly voice; Paul's response of falling to the ground.

Intriguingly, there is evidence in 2 Corinthians (chapter 12) that Paul—like many others trained by the Rabbis—may, at one time, have practiced something akin to the techniques of Chariot Mysticism.[1] Paul speaks of (what may have been) an out-of-body experience, of being caught up into the third heaven, of being caught up into paradise, and of hearing the ineffable language of paradise (2 Cor 12:2–4).

Unlike modern rationalists, Paul is not interested in denying the reality of such experiences. Instead of denying such experiences, he takes a completely unexpected tack. Remarkably, Paul, in 2 Corinthians, does *not* dwell on the details of his experience of mystical exaltation.

---

1. See: Bowker, "Visions of Paul," 172; Morray-Jones, "Paul's Heavenly Ascent," 283, 291–92; Scott, "Merkabah Mysticism in Paul," 260–81.

Rather, in a move that deconstructs Chariot Mysticism, Paul says that an *experience of humiliation*—a "thorn in the flesh"—became the means for gaining a deeper knowledge of God (2 Cor 12:7–10).

Through weakness, Paul deepened his union with Christ—the one who definitively ascended into the highest heaven: "God was in Christ, reconciling the world to himself" (2 Cor 5:19). In the Cross of Christ, through the weakness of Christ, God stooped down to the lowest level of humanity, the most abased and shameful level, in order that he might raise our weakness to glory.

For the Chariot Mystics, those granted a vision of the glory were *transformed* into its likeness. Paul writes, "We all . . . contemplating the glory of the Lord Jesus, are being *transformed* into the same image, from glory to glory" (2 Cor 3:18).

Ezekiel had a vision symbolic of God's freedom and faithfulness. In the Cross and Resurrection of Jesus, God's freedom and faithfulness find their ultimate expression.

When we become painfully aware of our weakness, our frailty, our sin, our shame—then we can identify more closely with the crucified one: "Him—who knew no sin—God caused to be sin on our behalf" (2 Cor 5:21). And if we participate in his Cross, we will also participate in his exaltation to the third heaven, to the very throne-room of God.

*For the Christian, meditation on the Cross of Jesus becomes the ultimate "mystical chariot"—a practice which opens up for us an unsurpassable vision of the greatness and glory of God.*

In our meditation upon the Cross of Christ, the Lord's Supper gives wings (so to speak) to our "mystical chariot." God created the grain and the grape as a cosmic parable of the Cross and Resurrection of Christ. The grain—crushed and ground—becomes life-sustaining food. The grape—squeezed and oppressed—becomes the wine of joy. As one partakes of the Lord's Supper, the heavens may open, and one may behold the glory of God.

\* \* \* \* \*

This chapter taps into the growing hunger for transcendence that arises when the forces of materialism and secularization threaten to drive the numinous from the cosmos. By exploring the storyline triggered by Ezekiel's throne vision, I have tried to gather some scraps of "journey advice" for would-be mystical travelers. To end the chapter, let me gather these scraps of wisdom together as summaries of what we might learn:

- In the act of self-disclosure, God meets us "where we are at"; he enters into our story.
- Our mystical encounters with God find meaning within the matrix of God's story, the overarching narrative of scripture.
- God's freedom means we cannot use magic formulae to manipulate the presence of God. God shows up when, where, and how he pleases.
- God's faithfulness holds out real hope for all who sincerely seek his presence. God's covenant faithfulness crystallizes in his promise, "I will be with you." This promise was incarnate in Jesus, called Immanuel, "God with us." Seek, and you will find.

- Mystical experience cannot be an end in itself. Such encounters are a means to an end, an empowerment for a role in God's unfolding drama. Thrill-seeking, experience for its own sake, is never encouraged in Scripture.
- According to Paul, we are more likely to encounter the heavenly power of God in our weakness and shame than in our strength and exaltation.
- For the Christian, meditation on the cross of Jesus becomes the ultimate "mystical chariot"—a practice which opens up for us an unsurpassable vision of the greatness and glory of God.
- As one partakes of the Lord's Supper, the heavens may open, and one may behold the glory of God.

\* \* \* \* \*

## QUESTIONS FOR REFLECTION AND DISCUSSION

1. Have you ever had a powerful, mystical experience of God?
2. Do you seek intense, undeniable encounters with God?
3. If God granted you a supernatural sense of his presence, would this strengthen your faith? Would it change how you live?
4. Paul seemed to believe that the Cross of Jesus, and the Christian's experience of weakness, actually channel more heavenly power than Ezekiel's throne vision! Does this make any sense to you, or does the paradox of power-in-weakness seem absurd to you?
5. In the current episode of your life, what vulnerabilities and weaknesses are being revealed in you?[2] Do you see these as an opportunity to identify with Christ's shame and death, in order to later share in his life and glory?
6. Have you ever experienced powerlessness and shame, and in that experience identified more closely with Jesus? Did you experience God's power in an unexpected way?

---

2. As I was finishing my third draft of this chapter (on Wednesday, December 18, 2014), I got a phone call from England, informing me that my aged mother had passed away unexpectedly. As I was processing my loss, I took great comfort from knowing that she has ascended to the glorious scene envisioned by Ezekiel.

# PART 5

Sequels and Backstory

# Spoiler Alert 5
(Overview of Part 5)

THIS BOOK IS A story embedded in bigger stories. Your story, my story, and a broader cultural narrative.

For you, the reader, putting the book down is like the exit from a "voyage-and-return" plotline. You have traveled into the foreign mental terrain of the author. I hope the experience has changed you for the better. I hope you emerged with more power to embody a meaningful life story.

Perhaps you would like to explore the themes of my book in greater depth. If so, additional resources are described in chapter 26 (a select annotated bibliography). These books helped me to write my own, by helping me ponder the "life = story" equation.

Many of the books mentioned offer a gateway into a broader cultural narrative—namely, the multi-disciplinary *recovery of the centrality of story* during the final quarter of the twentieth century. Almost independently, in fields like religion and psychology, leading thinkers had an epiphany: life = story.

Ripple effects from this recovery eventually drifted into my own backyard pond. In 1992, I enrolled in Westminster Theological Seminary in Philadelphia. During my long education there, a seed was planted that eventually sprouted into this book.

Chapter 27 includes that backstory, and allows me to end my book with reflections on the benefits of consciously indwelling a *multi-generation plotline*. Reflecting on the deep roots of my work, I began to feel like the literary equivalent of an Olympic torch-bearer. I received the flame from my forerunners, and pass the torch to successors.

As you read my final chapter, I hope it will catalyze reflections on the trans-generational strands embroidered into your own personal narrative:

- Whose labors are you continuing?
- To whom will you pass the torch?
- What legacy, what inheritance, what story-to-be-finished will you bestow upon the generation(s) that follow you?

# 26

# Artists Don't Borrow—They Steal
## (a select annotated bibliography)

My book interfaces three main disciplines:

- biblical and theological studies (especially research that takes the Bible as story);
- literary criticism ("English Literature 101");
- narrative psychology.

Under such headings (plus other miscellaneous categories), this chapter lists a selection of the books and essays that were especially stimulating during my research. I also offer light annotations of most items (for a comprehensive bibliography of the materials referenced in my footnotes, please consult the bibliography at the end of this book).

Needless to say, with such a broad range of authors, I am not in agreement with everything that each of them says! However, rather than nit-pick each one, I simply offer the list with this general disclaimer. Read wisely!

## LITERARY CRITICISM, FILM CRITICISM, THEATER CRITICISM

Abbot, H. Porter. *The Cambridge Introduction to Narrative.* Cambridge: Cambridge University Press, 2002.

> We all need one readable guide that answers the question, What *is* narrative? This lucid work should suffice. Connects story to life through discussions of cultural masterplots and narrative rhetoric.

Balthasar, Hans Urs von. *Prolegomena.* Vol. 1 of *Theodrama: Theological Dramatic Theory.* Translated by Graham Harrison. San Francisco: Ignatius, 1988.

> Distills two millennia of reflection on theater as a metaphor for life.

Booker, Christopher. *The Seven Basic Plots: Why We Tell Stories.* London: Continuum, 2004.

> Argues that most stories belong to one of these genres: overcoming the monster; rags to riches; quest; voyage-and-return; comedy; tragedy; rebirth. Attempts an explanation (Jungian) of why the human mind resorts to these patterns for storytelling (discussed in chapter 8 of my book).

McKee, Robert. *Story: Substance, Structure, and the Principles of Screenwriting*. New York: HarperCollins, 1997.

> Views the "arch-plot" as a universal template for storytelling, and unpacks the phases of its classical design.

Ryken, Leland. *Windows to the World: Literature in Christian Perspective*. Eugene, OR: Wipf & Stock, 2000.

> Solid discussion of the multiple ways that narrative impacts and enriches the reader.

Tilley, Allen. *An Introduction to Plot in the Modes of Experience*. Jacksonville, FL: Stone Snake, 2009.

> Views plot as an experience of readers (rather than characters). Images plot structure as a "snake," tracking the oscillations from initial disordering to final order in the narrative world. Argues that plot phases reflect five psycho-biological life stages: birth; puberty; adulthood; midlife; death. Classifies plot genres in terms of the operative mode of causality of the storyline (discussed in chapter 8 of my book).

## BIBLE AS LITERATURE

Bilezikian, Gilbert B. *The Liberated Gospel: A Comparison of the Gospel of Mark and Greek Tragedy*. Eugene, OR: Wipf & Stock, 2010.

> Views Mark's Gospel as a flexible adaptation of the genre and dramatic devices of classical Greek tragedy.

Frye, Northrop. *The Great Code: The Bible and Literature*. New York: Harcourt Brace Jovanovich, 1981.

> If you can get beyond the word "myth," this work offers a soaring panorama of the archetypal imagery of the biblical epic.

Rhoads, David, et al. *Mark as Story: An Introduction to the Narrative of a Gospel*. 3rd ed. Minneapolis: Fortress, 2012.

> A classic application of "Eng Lit 101," exploring the artistic patterns that shape the narrative rhetoric of Mark's Gospel.

Ryken, Leland, and Tremper Longman III, eds. *A Complete Literary Guide to the Bible*. Grand Rapids: Zondervan, 1993.

> General essays on the literary appreciation of the Bible, plus concise treatments of the literary artistry of most of the books of the biblical canon.

## BIBLICAL META-NARRATIVES

Bartholomew, Craig G., and Michael W. Goheen. *The True Story of the Whole World: Finding Your Place in the Biblical Drama*. Grand Rapids: Faith Alive Christian Resources, 2009.

> Concise, readable unfolding of the biblical drama from Genesis to Revelation. Uses the establishment of God's kingdom as the plotline to integrate the whole.

Gombis, Timothy G. *The Drama of Ephesians: Participating in the Triumph of God.* Downers Grove, IL: InterVarsity, 2010.

> Interprets Ephesians against the backdrop of the Old Testament plotline of "overcoming the monster." According to Gombis, Ephesians construes the "monster" as "systemic evil." As the subtitle suggests, Gombis has much practical advice on how this version of God's story can reshape the story of one's church.

Longman, Tremper III, and Daniel G. Reid. *God is a Warrior.* Studies in Old Testament Biblical Theology. Grand Rapids: Zondervan, 1995.

> Traces the archetypal plotline of "overcoming the monster," following the trajectory from the Old Testament into the New Testament.

Smith, Adrian T. "The Fifth Gospel." In *Eyes to See, Ears to Hear: Essays in Memory of J. Alan Groves,* edited by Peter Enns et al., 77–91. Phillipsburg, NJ: Presbyterian & Reformed, 2010.

> In this essay, I explore the paradise-lost-and-restored plotline of the Bible. I hint at some practical implications of owning this storyline.

Strom, Mark. *The Symphony of Scripture: Making Sense of the Bible's Many Themes.* Phillipsburg, NJ: Presbyterian & Reformed, 1990.

> From Genesis to Revelation, multiple plotlines unfold. Strom finds harmony in this multiplicity: "Jesus Christ is the key to understanding this unity in diversity." (Ibid., 15.)

## NARRATIVE THEOLOGY

Brueggemann, Walter. *Texts Under Negotiation: The Bible and Postmodern Imagination.* Minneapolis: Fortress, 1993.

> Takes the Bible as a resource for imagining oneself into God's "counter-drama" (in opposition to the dominant cultural script of consumerism).

Hauerwas, Stanley, and L. Gregory Jones, eds. *Why Narrative? Readings in Narrative Theology.* Grand Rapids: Eerdmans, 1989.

> Seminal essays representing the "narrative theology" movement that emerged during the final quarter of the twentieth century.

Hays, Richard B. *The Moral Vision of the New Testament: A Contemporary Introduction to New Testament Ethics.* New York: HarperCollins, 1996.

> The New Testament writers explored the ethical implications of the Christian metanarrative. Hays explains this trajectory from story to behavioral scripts, and describes the texture of the "narrative world" projected by the New Testament.

Lucie-Smith, Alexander. *Narrative Theology and Moral Theology: The Infinite Horizon.* Burlington, VT: Ashgate, 2007.

> Argues that ethics are not grounded in timeless abstract principles; rather, ethics derive from an overarching story.

Tilley, Terence W. *Story Theology*. Collegeville, MN: Liturgical, 1990.

> Argues that metaphors, explicated by narratives, are the most basic component of religious belief.

## ORAL STORYTELLING

Ellis, Elizabeth. *From Plot to Narrative: A Step-by-Step Process of Story Creation and Enhancement*. Little Rock, AR: Parkhurst Brothers, 2012.

> A gifted storyteller, Ellis walks us through the basics of crafting compelling oral narratives.

Novelli, Michael. *Shaped by the Story: Helping Students Encounter God in a New Way*. Grand Rapids: Zondervan, 2008.

> Based on the author's experience in youth ministry. Novelli recounts his years of fruitless attempts to interest teens in the Bible. Then a missionary to oral cultures introduced him to "storying." Novelli's youth ministry was transformed when he began to retell, sequentially, key episodes from the biblical epic.

## "AUTOBIOGRAPHIES": PERSONAL QUESTS FOR A LIFE STORY

Coupland, Douglas. *Generation X*. New York: St. Martin's, 1991.

> Poignant witness to the loss of narrative amongst post-boomers. Discussed in chapter 5 of my book.

Miller, Donald. *A Million Miles in a Thousand Years: What I Learned While Editing My Life*. Nashville: Thomas Nelson, 2009.

> Utilizes Robert McKee's book *Story* (see above) as a basis for constructing and living a meaningful personal narrative.

## WRITING YOUR PERSONAL MEMOIR

Allender, Dan B. *To Be Told: Know Your Story, Shape Your Life*. Colorado Springs, CO: Waterbrook, 2005.

> Written from the standpoint of Christian faith. Uses a "paradise partially restored" construal of the biblical plotline to help readers frame their life story. Especially helpful for those, like Allender, whose early chapters were shattered by the intrusion of evil (discussed in chapter 3 of my book).

Rainer, Tristine. *Your Life as Story: Discovering the "New Autobiography" and Writing Memoir as Literature*. New York: Jeremy P. Tarcher, 1997.

> Based on "nine essential elements of story structure." Engagingly written by an autobiography coach. Very lucid and helpful (even if the author's postmodern individualism surfaces on some pages). Discussed in chapter 3 of my book.

Part 5: Sequels and Backstory

## CULTURAL SCRIPTS

Hunter, James Davison. *To Change the World: The Irony, Tragedy, and Possibility of Christianity in the Late Modern World.* Oxford: Oxford University Press, 2010.

> Essay II discusses the church's engagement with American politics. Hunter shows how the Christian Right, Christian Left, and neo-Anabaptists all rely upon their own particular "myth" to fuel their critique of American society.

McAdams, Dan P. *The Redemptive Self: Stories Americans Live By.* Oxford: Oxford University Press, 2006.

> Discusses the numerous "upbeat" cultural scripts that enable many Americans to overcome adversity.

Wilkens, Steve and Mark L. Sanford. *Hidden Worldviews: Eight Cultural Stories that Shape our Lives.* Downers Grove, IL: InterVarsity, 2009.

> I discuss two of the cultural stories (nationalism; postmodern tribalism) in chapter 17 of my book.

## NARRATIVE PSYCHOLOGY

As I was starting to explore this important field, the following materials provided me with a solid introduction:

McAdams, Dan P. "Personal Narratives and the Life Story." In *Handbook of Personality: Theory and Research*, 3rd ed., edited by Oliver P. John et al., 242–58. New York: Guilford, 2008.

> Concise introduction to the narrative psychology movement that emerged in the last quarter of the twentieth century. States six principles held in common by most narrative psychologists.

Sarbin, Theodore R., ed. *Narrative Psychology: The Storied Nature of Human Conduct.* New York: Praeger, 1986.

> A collection of seminal essays from the emerging discipline of narrative psychology. Includes examples of personal searches for a life narrative, and discusses the problem of distortion of reality in autobiographical narratives.

Tomkins, Silvan S. "Script Theory." In *The Emergence of Personality*, edited by Joel Aronoff et al., 147–216. New York: Springer, 1987.

> A detailed inventory of micro and macro "scripts" that humans use to navigate the "scenes" of life. (see my discussion of "the Sculptor," in chapter 18 of this book).

In addition, the American Psychological Association has produced numerous multi-author volumes that explore the growing discipline of narrative psychology. Here is a random sampling of chapters I found especially interesting:

Alon, Nahi, and Haim Omer. "Demonic and Tragic Narratives in Psychotherapy." In *Healing Plots: The Narrative Basis of Psychotherapy*, edited by Amia Lieblich et al., 29–47. Washington, DC: American Psychological Association, 2004.

>According to the authors, many popular forms of psychotherapy employ secular versions of "demonic narratives" (akin to those found in traditional religions). The authors argue that, in many cases, patients would benefit from viewing life through the lens of classical tragedy.

Crossley, Michele L. "Sense of Place and its Import for Life Transitions: The Case of HIV-Positive Individuals." In *Turns in the Road: Narrative Studies of Lives in Transition*, edited by Dan P. McAdams et al., 279–94. Washington, DC: American Psychological Association, 2001.

>In the author's own words, "We all live with culturally saturated images of places of Paradise and places of Hell" (ibid., 294). Her case studies of HIV-positive individuals show how place (geographical location) can function as a metaphor of one's life story.

McAdams, Dan P., and Regina L. Logan. "Creative Work, Love, and the Dialectic in Selected Life Stories of Academics." In *Identity and Story: Creating Self in Narrative*, edited by Dan P. McAdams et al., 89–107. Washington, DC: American Psychological Association, 2006.

>The authors describe typical academic research as a life-long quest for an intellectual product that symbolizes an ideal world. However, the concrete, aesthetic image of the ideal is finite. The finite ideal suggests an opposite image, generating a dialectic between two contrasting images of the ideal. One image may govern the professional life, while its opposite governs (by way of compensation) the personal relationships of the academic.

McLeod, John. "The Significance of Narrative and Storytelling in Postpsychological Counseling and Therapy." In *Healing Plots: The Narrative Basis of Psychotherapy*, edited by Amia Lieblich et al., 11–27. Washington, DC: American Psychological Association, 2004.

>In the author's own words, "A central theme in narrative therapy is that of enabling the person to reauthor his or her life story as a means of resisting the control or subjugation of dominant cultural narratives" (ibid., 13). McLeod sees mainstream psychology as a dominant narrative to be resisted. He gives the example of Tom's "depression" (discussed in chapter 20 of my book).

Singer, Jefferson A. "Living in the Amber Cloud: A Life Story Analysis of a Heroin Addict." In *Turns in the Road: Narrative Studies of Lives in Transition*, edited by Dan P. McAdams et al., 253–77. Washington, DC: American Psychological Association, 2001.

>The author attempts to delineate the essential components of a healthy life story. A case study of a typical heroin addict shows how the addict constructs a personal narrative that becomes an enemy of their own recovery.

This growing scholarship on narrative psychology has begun to trickle down into popular magazines. Here are some interesting random examples of such popularization (unannotated):

Huston, Matt, et al. "Insights: Past Meets Present." *Psychology Today* 49/3 (May-June 2016) 9–21.
Kamps, Louisa. "The Story That Can Change Your Life." *Good Housekeeping* (July 2008) 119–25.
Thomas, Susan Gregory, et al. "Rewrite Your Life." *Psychology Today* 49/3 (May-June 2016) 50–59.

## NARRATIVE THERAPY

Bettelheim, Bruno. *The Uses of Enchantment: The Meaning and Importance of Fairy Tales*. New York: Alfred A. Knopf, 1976.

> Despite some Freudian interpretations, this book attests the power of classic fairy tales to interface with the deep needs of children.

Coles, Robert. *The Call of Stories: Teaching and the Moral Imagination*. Boston: Houghton Mifflin, 1989.

> Compelling anecdotal illustrations of the power of classic literature to minister to the human condition at every stage of life.

Freedom Writers with Erin Gruwell. *The Freedom Writers Diary: How a Teacher and 150 Teens used Writing to Change Themselves and the World Around Them*. New York: Broadway, 1999.

> Inspiring evidence of the power of narrative (in the form of diaries). Anne Frank's diary inspires contemporary American teens to tell their own stories as a way of resisting the fatalism, bigotry, and violence that surrounds them.

Taylor, Daniel. *The Healing Power of Stories: Creating Yourself Through the Stories of Your Life*. New York: Doubleday, 1996.

> Well-written and wise discussion of how stories give us a purpose and a place in the world, and how stories shape our character and behavior.

## BIBLICAL COUNSELING (USING NARRATIVE PARADIGMS)

Emlet, Michael R. *CrossTalk: Where Life & Scripture Meet*. Greensboro, NC: New Growth, 2009.

> Many Christian counselors view the Bible as a collection of laws or human exemplars. Others view the Bible as a "system of doctrine," or as a collection of abstract timeless principles. Emlet disagrees. He sees Scripture as a Christ-centered (and cross-centered) narrative for reshaping the broken narrative of the counselee.

Powlison, David. *Speaking the Truth in Love: Counseling in Community*. Greensboro, NC: New Growth, 2005.

> The stories we tell in daily conversations powerfully mold our identity and behavior. Powlison shows us how to inject biblical wisdom into our daily interactions.

Tripp, Paul David. *Lost in the Middle: Midlife and the Grace of God*. Wapwallopen, PA: Shepherd, 2004.

> Views midlife crisis as an opportunity to cease being captain of our own ship, and submit to God's redemptive narrative.

## THE CHURCH CALENDAR

Pennoyer, Greg, and Gregory Wolfe, eds. *God With Us: Rediscovering the Meaning of Christmas*. Brewster, MA: Paraclete, 2007.

> From Advent to Epiphany, the history of the feast days of the Christmas season is recounted, and illustrated with beautiful paintings by Christian artists. Meditations explore the meaning of the Jesus story celebrated in the feasts.

Peterson, Eugene H., ed. *Stories for the Christian Year*. New York: Collier, 1994.

> Numerous authors contemplate the meaning of the special days of the church calendar (Advent, Epiphany, Lent, Pentecost, etc.). The authors show how this calendar can connect the story of Jesus to the stories of our lives.

## THE ART OF MEDITATION INTO GOD'S STORY

Peterson, Eugene H. *Eat This Book: A Conversation in the Art of Spiritual Reading*. Grand Rapids: Eerdmans, 2006.

> A contemporary treatment of the ancient practice of *lectio divina*. Meditation involves the use of our imagination to fix the sacred story in the memory, so that the story can begin to reshape us.

## PRAYING YOUR WAY INTO GOD'S STORY

Miller, Paul E. *A Praying Life: Connecting with God in a Distracting World*. Colorado Springs, CO: NavPress, 2009.

> Part 4 focuses on prayer as connecting one's life to God's redeeming narrative.

# 27

# From Seed to Tree

### A BENCH BY THE RIVERBANK

"A POEM IS NEVER finished; it is only abandoned," to paraphrase the French poet Valéry—who uttered wisdom for prose writers too. The author's journey embodies the Aristotelian dramatic unity of beginning, middle, and end. Books are birthed by a trigger-incident (and usually ended by a publisher's deadline!).

This book was triggered by the death of my father (see chapter 2). In a strange coincidence ("inclusion" is the literary term), my mother passed away the day before I started to redraft this final chapter. That same week, our foster-child was moved to the home of someone in her biological family.

So, naturally, I am still thinking about family generations as I write. What cultural inheritance, what "scripts," did my parents pass down to me? With my father, that's easy to answer. Every day, I turn to his dog-eared, leather-bound Book of Common Prayer (recall my discussion of the church calendar in chapter 21). Through the devotional discipline of the Prayer Book, I keep his Anglican faith alive (notwithstanding my ordination in a Presbyterian denomination).

We all have biological families, but many of us have spiritual families too. Like our parents, our spiritual or intellectual forebears bequeath us a rich inheritance. As an on-ramp to this chapter, I invite you to ponder the many benefits of consciously indwelling a *multi-generation plotline*.

Reflecting on the deep philosophical roots of this book, I began to feel like the literary equivalent of an Olympic torch-bearer. I received the flame from my forerunners, and pass the torch to successors.

As you read my final chapter, I hope it will catalyze reflections on the trans-generational strands embroidered into your own personal narrative:

- Whose labors are you continuing?
- To whom will you pass the torch?
- What legacy, what inheritance, what story-to-be-finished will you bestow upon the generation(s) that follow you?

\* \* \* \* \*

Last summer, amidst the majesty and tranquility of the Rocky Mountains, I was struck by a powerful composite image of *multi-generational storylines.* Through the small town of Estes Park (Colorado), there flows the pure water of a mountain river. Local boutiques and cafés take advantage of this beautiful scenery by opening their back porches onto the river-walk. Outside a Starbucks, you can sit on a sturdy wood-and-iron bench, sip your coffee, and watch hummingbirds hover just above the fast-flowing waters.

The bench is inscribed in memory of Bob Quick (1921–2013), World War II veteran and great-grandparent. I wondered what wartime narratives—heroic or tragic—had passed down his family line.

Together, river and bench symbolized for me the power of multi-generational plotlines.

The narrow river, pounding over rocks, was sonorous and rhythmic. Its cadences overcame the competing noise of traffic, and created a restful acoustic space for me. In that rest, my mind began to free-associate, moving from the power of the river to the power of narrative.

The moving river represented the movement of time. I pondered, Whence the river's force? From its pure and noble source in the Rocky Mountains, from which it powered down through the valley. Likewise, a storyline that spans the generations derives strength and power from its venerable source.

The river continued to flow, with urgency, out of the town of Estes Park, bringing its tranquil rhythm to those beyond the bench where I sat. Similarly, a story sustained over generations gathers momentum, carrying its rhythms, its "script," far into the future.

If the river represented time, the sturdy bench stood for a freeze-frame image of narrative. The inscription offered tantalizing CliffsNotes, a plotline summary of the life of a war veteran, passing down his hard-won wisdom through his children, grandchildren, and great-grandchildren.

\* \* \* \* \*

The benefits of belonging to a multi-generational plotline are numerous. But perhaps these benefits are felt most poignantly at *times of transition*: disruptions, new beginnings, the onset of demise.

At such times, we instinctively seek the compass of a bigger story. A narrative that began before our own, and that will continue after we are gone. That was the instinct of those who wrote the Scriptures. At major transitions in the life of the religious community, authors arose who gave the community a compass, by tethering the communal identity and lifestyle to a multi-generational narrative.

Let's briefly consider three different types of transition, and interface these critical moments with examples of Scripture narratives that arose in response.

## Disruptions

Externally-enforced, unwanted change. Think back to the last time you experienced a major disruption. What roots from the past did you cling to for continuity and comfort?

The deeper the trauma, the deeper the fissure of individual or communal identity—the deeper the narrative roots needed to tether us to sanity. That appears to be the testimony of 1-2 Chronicles, written in response to the enforced exile of Israel to Babylon.

Chronicles's last recorded event is the decree of the Persian king Cyrus, permitting Jewish exiles to return and rebuild their temple in Jerusalem. Back in their land, but scarred by the exile—what was their narrative response? Chronicles tells a very different story from the parallel material in Samuel and Kings. Dealing with the radical discontinuity of the exile, Chronicles emphasizes the profound continuities between the present and the remote past. Emphasizing the constancy of God, and the primordial identity of Israel—an identity that exile cannot erase.

Here are some of the storytelling devices that Chronicles uses to emphasize the continuity of Jewish identity:

- The present is linked to antiquity, via nine (yes, nine!) chapters of *genealogies* . . . going all the way back to Adam.

- The past is mined for patterns of history, to generate a script for the present. The script is summarized in 2 Chr 7:14 (a verse that—for some reason—often appears in bumper-sticker form on American automobiles): "If my people . . . humble themselves, pray, seek my face, and turn from their evil ways—then I will hear from heaven, forgive their sin, and heal their land." In retelling Israel's story, Chronicles delights in showing how this pattern (repentance → restoration) repeats itself.

- The present is anchored to the past by glorifying those institutions that persist. The Jews of Chronicles's day no longer have a king—but they do have the rebuilt temple and its rituals. Chronicles's narrative glorifies the temple and its rites.

## New Beginnings

Voluntary, self-generated change. Think back to your last major new beginning. What scripts from the past guided you into the uncharted waters? As you embarked upon personal change, what did you cling to from your past to conserve your identity?

In the first century, Christianity faced a "PR" problem—it looked like a new religion. Why was that bad? Doesn't latest = best? Isn't the iPhone 7 automatically better than the iPhone 6? Well, the cultural values of antiquity totally inverted the modern dogma of progress. In antiquity, religions required pedigree. The older the better. First-century Christians faced an identity crisis, as they embarked on living out a religion markedly different in many ways from its Jewish parent.

Luke's response (in two volumes, Luke and *Acts*): Root Christianity as deeply as possible in the venerable religion of Judaism. Here are just a few of the storytelling devices whereby Luke-Acts constructs a robust, deep-rooted narrative identity for the early church:

- Take Jesus' genealogy all the way back to Adam (cf. Chronicles, discussed above).

- Articulate the story of Jesus as the fulfillment of the entire Hebrew Bible (Luke 24:27, 44). Christianity may be a new story, but it climaxes an old story.

- Pattern characters on Old Testament figures. In Luke 1, Zechariah and Elizabeth walk onstage in the literary garments of Abraham and Sarah. Jesus reprises the miracles of the prophets Elijah and Elisha. And so on.

- Pattern the history of the church on the history of Jesus. Luke's second volume (Acts) abounds in literary parallels with his first volume (the third Gospel). Jesus goes on a journey to Jerusalem; Paul goes on a journey to Rome. Jesus emerges alive from the tomb; Paul, facing a watery tomb, emerges alive from the ocean storm and shipwreck in Acts 27. And so on.

The overall effect, on the first-century Christian, of Luke's patterning Jesus on the Old Testament narratives, and the church on the Jesus narratives? An unshakeable sense of continuing the true story of the whole world.

## The Onset of Demise

When did you last face the death of a storyline you were living? How did you attempt to conserve the gist of that story's enduring value?

As a seminary professor in my mid-fifties (how did the hair turn grey so fast?), I developed a special affinity for the Paul that wrote the Pastoral Letters (1–2 Timothy and Titus). I see this Paul as obsessed with issues of continuity, legacy, and succession. Paul is like a trustee, gifting a precious inheritance to his inheritors. What could he pass on to the church, as it emerged from the cocoon of Judaism and faced the cultural might of the Greco-Roman world, without the guiding hand of the Apostles?

I believe the Pastoral Letters are his response to the crisis of his own demise. His passing of the torch to the next generation. These letters seek to preserve Paul's legacy, to tie his life and labors into the future, by developing a three-fold cord: successors (Timothy, Titus, and others like them), crystallized truth, and institutional structure.

Here are some hints of the legacy-conserving devices of the Pastoral Letters:

- a strong sense of the trans-generational continuity of "the faith."[1]

- successors as Paul's "children in the faith."[2]

- crystallized, portable truth: a "good deposit" of "faithful sayings."[3]

---

1. 2 Tim 1:3, 5; 2 Tim 2:2.
2. 1 Tim 1:2; Titus 1:4.
3. 2 Tim 1:13–14; Titus 3:8 (back-referencing verses 3 to 7).

- institutional structure: the church, God's household, as "pillar and foundation of the truth."[4] A mechanism for preserving and propagating the crystallized truth of the "faithful sayings."

With the trans-generational narrative of the Pastoral Letters in hand, the churchmen who succeeded Paul were able to navigate the choppy waters of the second century, and preserve the faith intact down to our own time. A remarkable legacy.

\* \* \* \* \*

"The powerful play goes on, and you may contribute a verse."[5] Some projects are simply too massive to complete within one person's lifetime. (Think of medieval cathedrals, which often took over a century to finish.) Multi-generation plots enable us to "contribute a verse" to the ongoing "powerful play."

When we hear the call to walk onstage into a multi-generational drama, something intriguing can happen to our sense of identity. We become a bigger person. Our individual identity merges into a *corporate character*. That character embodies our predecessors and followers, and the role that they/we play in a trans-generational plot. In the Old Testament, individual Israelites felt that they shared the destiny of the macro-character "Israel." This collective entity was summoned onto the world stage by "the God of Abraham, Isaac, and Jacob" (Exod 3:6) in order to be a "light to the nations" (Isa 42:6; 49:6).

As a reaction against Western individualism, *community* has become something of a buzz-word of late. (Think of all the "Community Churches" that have sprung up in suburban America.) Shared narrative constitutes community. "A community exists where a narrative account exists of a *we* which persists through its experiences and actions."[6]

Do you identify with any particular group narrative? If so, how many generations does the group narrative span? Viewing the group as the protagonist, what kind of plot is the narrative? What phase of the plot is your group currently living through?

Throughout this book, we have explored narrative from the viewpoint of archetypal plots. In principle, a *group* can function as a protagonist in any of the basic plots (just like an individual). Even if the plot spans several generations, the collective protagonist can undergo all the phases we normally associate with the individual hero. Calling. Journey. Crisis. Resolution.

As individual participants in group narratives, we enter (and exit) the stage at a particular phase of the unfolding plotline. (Saint Paul describes the growth of a church—a plotline of ascent—using an agricultural metaphor to capture the nuances of individual roles. "I planted, Apollos watered—but God caused the growth" [1 Cor 3:6].)

To end this chapter (and this book), I would like to share with you something of the backstory of my book. The group narrative that nourished my writing. The bigger, multi-generational plotline which gives meaning to my work.

---

4. 1 Tim 3:15.
5. Whitman, "O Me! O Life!"
6. Carr, "Narrative and the Real World," 130 (italics in original).

Regardless of how many (or how few) copies this book sells, it flows as a rivulet of a very powerful stream, cascading down from an elevated source. Here, in condensed form, is the story behind my book.

## BACKSTORY

September, 1992. I had barely set foot on the Philadelphia campus of Westminster Theological Seminary. A throwaway line from a brilliant professor. "Eschatology governs protology." Translated: Revelation explains Genesis. Ends clarify beginnings.

For readers of the epic *Harry Potter* series, book seven is a rollercoaster of *aha!* moments. Disconnected episodes from books one to six suddenly cohere. Expectations unravel and rethread.

For movie watchers, *The Usual Suspects* culminates in a recognition-scene that literally causes a character (and maybe the viewer!) to drop their coffee cup in amazement.

In fiction and in film, the ending gives clarity and coherence to all the earlier episodes. In this respect, life imitates art. From the vantage-point of the harvest, we understand the seed.

September, 2009. I sit in my office at Redeemer Seminary in Dallas, typing the first draft of this chapter. Westminster Seminary, my *alma mater*, is celebrating its eightieth anniversary. Fourscore years. A complex interplay of subplots. A *dramatis personae* spanning three generations.

One particular subplot has now matured from seed to tree. That tree has budded, and is producing its first-fruits. I write as a participant in this quest for wisdom, as one who has tasted its slow-ripening fruit. From the vantage-point of the harvest, so many earlier phases now make sense. The planting and watering, the patient fertilizing, the grafting and pruning—all these phases connect, all were necessary, all make sense in the light of their end-product.

As you read my version of one strand of Westminster's story, I hope that you grow in appreciation of the intellectual foundations of my book, and that you too can find a worthwhile multi-generational storyline to inhabit.

## Planting the Seed: Biblical Theology 1.0

Geerhardus Vos was never on faculty at Westminster. He remained at Princeton when Westminster began in 1929. Nevertheless, Vos has been a major player in the Westminster story. He planted a seed idea that was cultivated over the generations at Westminster.

The seed Vos planted was the discipline known (in academic circles) as "biblical theology." For Vos, biblical theology "deals with the *process* of the self-revelation of God deposited in the Bible."[7] The Bible did not drop out of the sky in one sixty-six-book dollop. Rather, it grew over time, in a story of emerging God-given insights.

This dynamic emphasis on process opens the door to fresh ways of reading the Bible. Ways that transcend the "concordance" practice of reading the Bible as a topical

---

7. Vos, *Biblical Theology*, 5 (italics mine).

encyclopedia (supposedly containing nuggets of wisdom on everything from Anorexia to Zenophobia). Instead of seeing Scripture as a repository of proof-texts, Vos emphasized the way the Scriptures developed over time. "In Biblical Theology the principle is one of historical ... construction. Biblical Theology draws a *line* of development."[8]

Along with this geometric metaphor, Vos also used an organic metaphor for biblical theology:

> The organic nature of the process of revelation ... is from seed-form to the attainment of full growth ... [F]rom the organic character of revelation we can explain its increasing multiformity, the latter being everywhere a symptom of the development of organic life.[9]

This organic metaphor leads Vos to underscore the *practical* concerns of biblical theology:

> God's self-revelation to us was not made for a primarily intellectual purpose ... He has caused His revelation to take place in the milieu of the historical life of a people. The circle of revelation is not a school, but a "covenant" ... All that God disclosed of Himself has come in response to the practical religious needs of His people as these emerged in the course of history.[10]

In sum, Vos bequeathed us two powerful, interrelated concepts: a dynamic, developmental way of understanding the Bible; a "situational" perspective that highlights Scripture's sensitivity to practical, existential human needs.

Taking up this legacy of Vos, later generations of scholars at Westminster furthered the fusion of these two ideas: the Bible as an unfolding revelatory process; a revelatory process that engages the full spectrum of human needs.

## Green Shoots: Biblical Theology 2.0

The seed ideas of Vos's biblical theology fell on fertile soil at Westminster. Over the decades, the seed grew, being cultivated by men such as Edmund P. Clowney.

Clowney taught "practical theology" at Westminster from 1952–1984 (and served as president from 1966–1982). He is a pivotal figure in our story, one who significantly enriched biblical theology in many dimensions.

Firstly, Clowney underscored the *Christocentric* character of the unfolding of biblical revelation.[11] So imaginative, so compelling were his visions of Jesus in the Law, Prophets, and Writings, tempting speculation that Clowney himself had journeyed to Emmaus and heard Jesus expound the Old Testament (Luke 24:27)!

Secondly, Clowney emphasized the *practical utility* of biblical theology. Harvie Conn describes this dimension of Clowney's contribution:

> He brought to every course biblical insights shaped by his studies in the history of special revelation. Whether homiletics or Christian education, missions or

---

8. Ibid., 16 (italics in original).
9. Ibid., 7.
10. Ibid., 7–8.
11. Clowney, *Unfolding Mystery*.

ecclesiology, each class moved from Genesis through Revelation, drawing together the whole of Scripture with new insights that pointed in a fresh way to Christ and His redemptive purposes.[12]

Thirdly, Clowney begins to articulate biblical theology via more explicit use of "story" vocabulary: "The Bible is the greatest storybook, not just because it is full of wonderful stories but because it tells one *great* story, the story of Jesus."[13] This appreciation of narrative dovetailed with Clowney's strong aesthetic sensibilities. As a gifted amateur painter, he was well-equipped to appreciate the artistic dimensions of the biblical story:

> The rich literary art in the Scriptures displays the wealth of allusiveness in which God's revelation is given. Symbolism appears not only in metaphorical language but also in the elaborate patterns of the Old Testament ceremonial cultus. It is also evident in the accounts of redemptive history and in the shaping of redemptive history itself. Design in the pattern of the tabernacle points to the larger design of God's wisdom in his plan for the redemption of sinners.[14]

Sensitivity to narrative, sensitivity to literary artistry—the door opens to the next phase of biblical theology at Westminster.

## First-Fruits: The Bible as Literature (Biblical Theology 3.0)

Tremper Longman III taught Old Testament at Westminster for almost two decades in the eighties and nineties. He was adept at tracing a biblical theme, Clowney-style, from Genesis to Revelation.[15] Longman also shared Clowney's instincts on the practicality of biblical theology.[16]

However, from the vantage point of our story, Longman advances the plot in two related areas: appreciation of the Bible as literature; awareness of the transformative power of narrative.

Longman's book *Literary Approaches to Biblical Interpretation* might have been subtitled "English Literature 101 Meets the Bible." Genre. Point of View. Narrator. Setting. Plot. Characterization. Irony. Dialogue. Type-Scene. Style. Reader-Response. Longman employs these staples of literary criticism, giving us a holographic appreciation of the artistry of biblical narrative.

Push the pause button. Rewind. Here is something new. An injection of steroids into a burgeoning biblical theology. Vos's progressive revelation and Clowney's unfolding mystery—now seen as *narrative theology* in embryo. Longman gave us new tools for retelling the biblical story.

---

12. Conn, Foreword to *Practical Theology*, xi.
13. Clowney, *Unfolding Mystery*, 9 (italics in original).
14. Clowney, "Living Art," 251.
15. E.g., the theme of "holy warfare" (see Longman and Reid, *God is a Warrior*).
16. E.g., Longman addresses the challenge of how to handle difficult people in a redemptive manner, by applying lessons from his study of Jesus as the culmination and transformation of the "divine warrior" theme. (See Allender and Longman, *Bold Love*.)

The scales fall from our eyes. Our Sunday School teachers were right: the Bible is best appreciated as *story*! Longman zeros in on the vital significance of the literary form or genre of Scripture:

> Exactly how does the Bible address the whole person? How does it penetrate our souls? It speaks powerfully and intimately through stories and poetry. Consider the form in which God has chosen to give us His Word. Have you noticed that the Bible isn't a philosophical treatise or a systematic theology . . . Also notice that the Bible is not a confession of faith . . . God could have chosen to tell us about Himself through catechism and confession, but He wisely decided not to do so . . . The Bible speaks to the whole person. Its stories seize our imaginations . . . The events and images do more than simply inform us; they suck us into the "story" of our God, bringing us into His life.[17]

The seed has germinated. The green shoots have become a sapling, whose flowers are budding. Longman anticipates the harvest: a robust narrative theology, in dialogue with our personal and communal narratives: "Our lives are stories. When we meet new people, and they ask us to tell them about ourselves, we tell them stories. And the Bible invites us to bring our own story to its story. It compels us to understand our story in the light of the great story of God's dealings with the world."[18] What might pastoral theology, done in this vein, look like? Longman offers us an intriguing glimpse of the possibilities in *Bold Purpose* (co-authored with Dan Allender).[19]

This book tells a fictional story set in modern America. The story interweaves the multiple "quest stories" of its characters: quests for power, relationships, work, money, pleasure, wisdom, spirituality, and immortality.

Chapters of these quest stories alternate with exposition of Ecclesiastes, which is used to deconstruct the quests. As the realistic fiction dialogues with Ecclesiastes, reconstruction of life-meaning takes place as biblical theology enters the conversation, radically rewriting the characters' quests in terms of God's story.

In several of Longman's writings, the flower of biblical theology has budded, and the first-fruits are emerging.

I owe him a considerable personal debt. In the fall of 1992, as part of my seminary coursework, he kindly facilitated an elective study for me, entitled, "Literary Approaches to Biblical Interpretation." As I worked my way through the assigned reading, I had a light bulb moment. "What if," I mused, "Christian ministry tried to unleash the liberating power of the *Exodus* narrative, by fusing that story with the lives of parishioners?"

Back then, I was an Old Testament major. When I later switched to New Testament studies, I had another light bulb moment: The New Testament unleashes the liberating power of the Exodus narrative *by using the plotline and imagery of Exodus as the "grammar" of the story of Jesus* and by fusing Jesus' Exodus-narrative with the lives of the first-century disciples.

---

17. Longman, *Reading the Bible*, 32–33.
18. Ibid., 34.
19. See Allender and Longman, *Bold Purpose*.

From such seeds, this book grew. I view my book as a contribution to *"biblical theology 4.0"*—namely, the sustained investigation of how to fuse our personal narratives with the meta-narrative of scripture.

## Epilogue

I have traced the evolution of Westminster's biblical theology into a pastorally-oriented narrative theology. The seed planted by Vos, watered by Clowney, fertilized by Longman, has started to bear fruit. Time will tell if the harvest is thirty-fold, sixty-fold, or a hundred-fold (Mark 4:8).

Looking back, a lot has changed at Westminster since 1992, when I first stepped onto the venerable campus. Most of my professors from the nineties are no longer on faculty. Some, like J. Alan Groves, have fought the good fight, run the race (2 Tim 4:7).[20] Others now teach elsewhere. In that sense, my communal story has been lost. Like the spores of a dandelion, our personal stories have wafted on the wind to various locations. In fresh soils, the seed takes root anew. "Our God is the author of new seasons. He is the giver of new seeds, new roots, and new fruit. He causes fruits and flowers to grow where weeds and thorns once were. He is the God of the new harvest."[21]

\* \* \* \* \*

This may be the final chapter of my book, but it was actually the first chapter to be drafted. Since writing the first draft, I have learned that the story of Westminster's "biblical theology" intersects the much bigger story of *the Western recovery of narrative wisdom*, the emergence (starting in the sixties) of narrative theology—a story I briefly alluded to in chapter 6.

I have come to see the emergence of narrative theology as a plotline of ascent, in which the "protagonist"—i.e., narrative theology—strives to reach maturity, to fulfill its potential. A potential which I do not think it has reached.

Maturity can, of course, be defined in many ways. Since I owe so much to Christopher Booker, I will use his definition. (I will give him a hall pass for his gender stereotyping.) Booker sees personal maturity as attaining a fusion of ideal "masculine" and "feminine" traits.[22] Using this characterization, maturity would fuse traits such as rationality, independence/strength, with traits such as intuition and empathy.

Regardless of the limits of such a definition, it can serve as a metaphor of the task of narrative theology. To reach its full potential, narrative theology must consolidate the following traits. (One might also say: a narrative theologian must cultivate these traits.)

1. Independence/Strength: Narrative theology should unapologetically cultivate its own *narrative categories of thinking*. Some might respond, "Well, Duh!" as if this

---

20. Al's untimely death was an incalculable loss to the seminary. For a sense of his legacy, see Enns et al., *Eyes to See, Ears to Hear*.

21. Tripp, *Lost in the Middle*, 131.

22. Booker, *Seven Basic Plots*, 268.

injunction is unnecessary. But (in my judgment) narrative theologians have been captive to modern western philosophical and theological categories, which have hindered the maturation of a robust narrative theology. (Please note: I am *not* advocating that we *negate* traditional beliefs. Rather, I am expressing a hunch that sustained reflection on Scripture and life, through the lens of narrative categories, may yield insights not provided by more traditional approaches.)

2. Rationality: Traditional theologians speak of doing "systematic theology." Narrative theologians also need an orderly, systematic description of their discipline. How about a "*systematic narratology*"? For example, making explicit genres and phases of plots (not so easy a task as you might think), making explicit the ways in which people use stories to shape their lives, making explicit the subtle relationship between story and life. And so on.

3. Intuition: True wisdom is always internalized, so it is available "at one's fingertips." An effective narrative theologian will have story seeping through their veins. He/she will intuitively grasp the dynamics of story and storytelling.

4. Empathy: An effective narrative theologian will be able to accurately discern individual, communal, and cultural scripts. She/he will, through experience or imagination, know how it feels to live inside a particular story. This empathy will guide the quest for wisdom into how the healing balm of the gospel narrative can restore the fractured narratives of our lives.

*****

When I picked up my pen to write (it now seems so long ago), I envisaged a better book than the one you have in your hands. Doubtless, many of you readers are thinking, "If only he had talked about XYZ instead!" Certainly, more—much more—wisdom is needed, for narrative theology to fulfill its rich potential. *The powerful play goes on, and you may contribute a verse.*

# Bibliography

Abbott, H. Porter. *The Cambridge Introduction to Narrative.* Cambridge: Cambridge University Press, 2002.
Adams, James Truslow. *The Epic of America.* Piscataway, NJ: Transaction, 2012.
Adams, Jay E. *Sense Appeal in the Sermons of Charles Haddon Spurgeon.* Vol. 1 of *Studies in Preaching.* Nutley, NJ: Presbyterian & Reformed, 1976.
Allender, Dan B. *To Be Told: Know Your Story, Shape Your Life.* Colorado Springs, CO: Waterbrook, 2005.
Allender, Dan B., and Tremper Longman III. *Bold Love.* Colorado Springs, CO: NavPress, 1992.
———. *Bold Purpose: Exchanging Counterfeit Happiness for the Real Meaning of Life.* Wheaton, IL: Tyndale House, 1998.
Alon, Nahi, and Haim Omer. "Demonic and Tragic Narratives in Psychotherapy." In *Healing Plots: The Narrative Basis of Psychotherapy,* edited by Amia Lieblich et al., 29–47. Washington, DC: American Psychological Association, 2004.
Amit, Yairah. *Reading Biblical Narrative: Literary Criticism and the Hebrew Bible.* Minneapolis: Fortress, 2001.
Aristotle. *Poetics.* Edited and translated by Stephen Halliwell. Loeb Classical Library 199. Cambridge, MA: Harvard University Press, 1995.
Baldwin, T. W. *Shakespere's* [sic] *Five-Act Structure.* Urbana: University of Illinois Press, 1947.
Balthasar, Hans Urs von. *Prolegomena.* Vol. 1 of *Theodrama: Theological Dramatic Theory.* Translated by Graham Harrison. San Francisco: Ignatius, 1988.
Balzer, Paula. *Writing & Selling Your Memoir.* Cincinnati: Writer's Digest, 2011.
Bamberg, Michael, et al. "Introduction to the Volume." In *Selves and Identities in Narrative and Discourse,* edited by Michael Bamberg et al., 1–8. Studies in Narrative 9. Amsterdam: John Benjamins, 2007.
Bartholomew, Craig G., and Michael W. Goheen. *The True Story of the Whole World: Finding Your Place in the Biblical Drama.* Grand Rapids: Faith Alive Christian Resources, 2009.
Bartholomew, Craig G., and Robby Holt. "Prayer in/and the Drama of Redemption in Luke." In *Reading Luke: Interpretation, Reflection, Formation,* edited by Craig G. Bartholomew et al., 350–75. Scripture and Hermeneutics 6. Grand Rapids: Zondervan, 2005.
Barzun, Jacques. *From Dawn to Decadence.* New York: Perenniel, 2001.
Base, Graeme. "*The Lord of the Rings* by J.R.R. Tolkien." In *The Book That Changed My Life,* edited by Roxanne J. Coady and Joy Johannessen, 18–19. New York: Gotham, 2006.
Bauckham, Richard. *Bible and Mission: Christian Witness in a Postmodern World.* Grand Rapids: Baker Academic, 2003.
Bausch, William J. *Storytelling: Imagination and Faith.* Mystic, CT: Twenty-Third, 1984.
Beasley-Murray, George R. *John.* 2nd ed. Word Biblical Commentary 36. Nashville: Thomas Nelson, 1999.
Beeching, M. "Name." In *The Illustrated Bible Dictionary,* vol. 2, 1050–53. Leicester, UK: InterVarsity, 1980.
Beker, J. Christiaan. *Paul the Apostle: The Triumph of God in Life and Thought.* Philadelphia: Fortress, 1980.

## Bibliography

Bengel, J. A. *Gnomon of the New Testament*. Translated by James Bryce. 7th ed. Vol. 4. Edinburgh: T&T Clark, 1877.

Bennett, Alan. *The History Boys*. New York: Faber & Faber, 2004.

Berg, Elizabeth. "*The Catcher in the Rye* by J.D. Salinger." In *The Book That Changed My Life*, edited by Roxanne J. Coady and Joy Johannessen, 23–25. New York: Gotham, 2006.

Berger, Peter L., and Thomas Luckmann. *The Social Construction of Reality: A Treatise in the Sociology of Knowledge*. New York: Anchor, 1967.

Berlin, Isaiah. *The Roots of Romanticism*. 2nd ed. Princeton: Princeton University Press, 2013.

Bettelheim, Bruno. *The Uses of Enchantment: The Meaning and Importance of Fairy Tales*. New York: Alfred A. Knopf, 1976.

Bevis, Beth. "January 6 Feast of the Epiphany." In *God With Us: Rediscovering the Meaning of Christmas*, edited by Greg Pennoyer and Gregory Wolfe, 165–68. Brewster, MA: Paraclete, 2007.

———. "Living the Church Year: An Invitation." In *God With Us: Rediscovering the Meaning of Christmas*, edited by Greg Pennoyer and Gregory Wolfe, 11–14. Brewster, MA: Paraclete, 2007.

Bilezikian, Gilbert B. *The Liberated Gospel: A Comparison of the Gospel of Mark and Greek Tragedy*. Eugene, OR: Wipf & Stock, 2010.

Blake, William. "Jerusalem." http://www.poetry-archive.com/b/jerusalem.html.

Bloom, Allan. *The Closing of the American Mind*. New York: Simon & Schuster, 1987.

Bonz, Marianne Palmer. *The Past as Legacy: Luke-Acts and Ancient Epic*. Minneapolis: Fortress, 2000.

Booker, Christopher. *The Seven Basic Plots: Why We Tell Stories*. London: Continuum, 2004.

Boring, M. Eugene. *Mark: A Commentary*. New Testament Library. Louisville, KY: Westminster John Knox, 2006.

Bowker, J. W. "'Merkabah' Visions and the Visions of Paul." *Journal of Semitic Studies* 16/2 (Autumn 1971) 157–73.

Bremond, Claude. *Logique du Récit*. Paris: Éditions du Seuil, 1973.

Brooks, Peter. *Reading for the Plot: Design and Intention in Narrative*. New York: Alfred A. Knopf, 1984.

Brother Christopher. "*The Seven Storey Mountain* by Thomas Merton." In *The Book That Changed My Life*, edited by Roxanne J. Coady and Joy Johannessen, 47–48. New York: Gotham, 2006.

Bruce, F. F. *The Epistles to the Colossians, to Philemon, and to the Ephesians*. New International Commentary on the New Testament. Grand Rapids: Eerdmans, 1984.

Brueggemann, Walter. *Cadences of Home: Preaching among Exiles*. Louisville, KY: Westminster John Knox, 1997.

———. *Texts Under Negotiation: The Bible and Postmodern Imagination*. Minneapolis: Fortress, 1993.

Bruner, Jerome. *Acts of Meaning*. Cambridge: Harvard University Press, 1990.

Buechner, Frederick. *Telling the Truth: The Gospel as Tragedy, Comedy, and Fairy Tale*. New York: Harper & Row, 1977.

Burridge, Richard A. *Four Gospels, One Jesus? A Symbolic Reading*. 2nd ed. Grand Rapids: Eerdmans, 2005.

Buttrick, David. *Homiletic: Moves and Structures*. Philadelphia: Fortress, 1987.

———. "Story and Symbol, The Stuff of Preaching." In *What's the Shape of Narrative Preaching?*, edited by Mike Graves and David J. Schlafer, 99–113. St. Louis: Chalice, 2008.

Caird, G. B. *The Revelation of St. John the Divine*. Harper's New Testament Commentaries. New York: Harper & Row, 1966.

Campbell, Joseph. *The Hero With A Thousand Faces*. New York: Bollingen Foundation, 1949.

Carr, David. "Narrative and the Real World: An Argument for Continuity." *History and Theory* 25/2 (May 1986) 117–31.

Carson, D. A., and Douglas J. Moo. *An Introduction to the New Testament*. 2nd ed. Grand Rapids: Zondervan, 2005.

Cheever, Benjamin. "*The Denial of Death* by Ernest Becker." In *The Book That Changed My Life*, edited by Roxanne J. Coady and Joy Johannessen, 37–38. New York: Gotham, 2006.

Chesterton, G. K. *Orthodoxy*. San Francisco: Ignatius, 1908.

Chilton, Bruce. *Redeeming Time: The Wisdom of Ancient Jewish and Christian Festal Calendars*. Peabody, MA: Hendrickson, 2002.

Clowney, Edmund P. "Living Art: Christian Experience and the Arts." In *God and Culture: Essays in Honor of Carl F.H. Henry*, edited by D. A. Carson and John D. Woodbridge, 235–53. Grand Rapids: Eerdmans, 1993.

———. *The Unfolding Mystery: Discovering Christ in the Old Testament*. Phillipsburg, NJ: Presbyterian & Reformed, 1988.

Coady, Roxanne J., and Joy Johannessen, eds. *The Book That Changed My Life*. New York: Gotham, 2006.

Cobley, Paul. *Narrative*. The New Critical Idiom. London: Routledge, 2001.

Coles, Robert. *The Call of Stories: Teaching and the Moral Imagination*. Boston: Houghton Mifflin, 1989.

Collins, Billy. "*The Yearling* by Marjorie Kinnan Rawlings and *Lolita* by Vladimir Nabokov." In *The Book That Changed My Life*, edited by Roxanne J. Coady and Joy Johannessen, 51–52. New York: Gotham, 2006.

Conn, Harvie M. Foreword to *Practical Theology and the Ministry of the Church, 1952-1984: Essays in Honor of Edmund P. Clowney*, edited by Harvie M. Conn, ix–xiv. Phillipsburg, NJ: Presbyterian & Reformed, 1990.

Corrigan, Maureen "*David Copperfield* by Charles Dickens." In *The Book That Changed My Life*, edited by Roxanne J. Coady and Joy Johannessen, 59–61. New York: Gotham, 2006.

Coupland, Douglas. *Generation X*. New York: St. Martin's, 1991.

Cremeens, Carlton. "Walker Percy, The Man and the Novelist: An Interview." *The Southern Review* 4 (Apr. 1968) 271–90.

Crites, Stephen. "The Narrative Quality of Experience." In *Why Narrative? Readings in Narrative Theology*, edited by Stanley Hauerwas and L. Gregory Jones, 65–88. Grand Rapids: Eerdmans, 1989.

———. "Storytime: Recollecting the Past and Projecting the Future." In *Narrative Psychology: The Storied Nature of Human Conduct*, edited by Theodore R. Sarbin, 152–73. New York: Praeger, 1986.

Crossley, Michele L. "Sense of Place and its Import for Life Transitions: The Case of HIV-Positive Individuals." In *Turns in the Road: Narrative Studies of Lives in Transition*, edited by Dan P. McAdams et al., 279–94. Washington, DC: American Psychological Association, 2001.

Cullmann, Oscar. *Christ and Time: The Primitive Christian Conception of Time and History*. Translated by Floyd V. Filson. London: SCM, 1951.

Derrida, Jaques. *Of Grammatology*. Translated by Gayatri Chakravorty Spivak. Baltimore: Johns Hopkins University Press, 1997.

deSilva, David A. *The Hope of Glory: Honor Discourse and New Testament Interpretation*. Collegeville, MN: Liturgical, 1998.

DiCamillo, Kate. *The Tale of Despereaux*. Cambridge, MA: Candlewick, 2003.

Dillard, Raymond B., and Tremper Longman III. *An Introduction to the Old Testament*. Grand Rapids: Zondervan, 1994.

Drew, Charles D. *A Journey Worth Taking: Finding Your Purpose in This World*. Phillipsburg, NJ: Presbyterian & Reformed, 2007.

Eire, Carlos. "*The Imitation of Christ* by Thomas à Kempis." In *The Book That Changed My Life*, edited by Roxanne J. Coady and Joy Johannessen, 72–74. New York: Gotham, 2006.

Ellis, Elizabeth. *From Plot to Narrative: A Step-by-Step Process of Story Creation and Enhancement*. Little Rock, AR: Parkhurst Brothers, 2012.

Emlet, Michael R. *CrossTalk: Where Life & Scripture Meet*. Greensboro, NC: New Growth, 2009.

Enns, Peter, et al., eds. *Eyes to See, Ears to Hear: Essays in Memory of J. Alan Groves*. Phillipsburg, NJ: Presbyterian & Reformed, 2010.

Ernst, Karl J. *The Art of Pastoral Counseling: A Study of the Epistle to Philemon*. Grand Rapids: Zondervan, 1940.

Eslinger, Richard L. "Narrative and Imagery." In *Intersections: Post-Critical Studies in Preaching*, edited by Richard L. Eslinger, 65–87. Grand Rapids: Eerdmans, 1994.

Evans, Craig A. "Jesus & The Continuing Exile of Israel." In *Jesus & The Restoration of Israel*, edited by Carey C. Newman, 77–100. Downers Grove, IL: InterVarsity, 1999.

Everett, Daniel L. *Don't Sleep, There are Snakes*. New York: Pantheon, 2008.

Fackre, Gabriel. "Narrative Theology: An Overview." *Interpretation: A Journal of Bible and Theology* 37/4 (Oct. 1983) 340–52.

Fairstein, Linda. "*The Adventures of Sherlock Holmes* by Arthur Conan Doyle." In *The Book That Changed My Life*, edited by Roxanne J. Coady and Joy Johannessen, 75–77. New York: Gotham, 2006.

Fasulo, Alessandra. "Theories of Self in Psychotherapeutic Narratives." In *Selves and Identities in Narrative and Discourse*, edited by Michael Bamberg et al., 325–50. Studies in Narrative 9. Amsterdam: John Benjamins, 2007.

Fertig, Judith. "The Healing Power of Story: How Telling Our Truths Can Set Us Free." *Natural Awakenings* (Dallas Metroplex edition, June 2014) 18–20.

Foer, Franklin. *How Soccer Explains the World: An Unlikely Theory of Globalization*. New York: Harper Perennial, 2005.

Foley Center for the Study of Lives. "The Life Story Interview." http://www.sesp.northwestern.edu/foley/instruments/interview.

Ford, David F. "System, Story, Performance: A Proposal about the Role of Narrative in Christian Systematic Theology." In *Why Narrative? Readings in Narrative Theology*, edited by Stanley Hauerwas and L. Gregory Jones, 191–215. Grand Rapids: Eerdmans, 1989.

Frame, John M. *The Doctrine of the Knowledge of God*. Phillipsburg, NJ: Presbyterian & Reformed, 1987.

Freedom Writers with Erin Gruwell. *The Freedom Writers Diary: How a Teacher and 150 Teens used Writing to Change Themselves and the World Around Them*. New York: Broadway, 1999.

Friedman, Norman. *Form and Meaning in Fiction*. Athens: University of Georgia Press, 1975.

Frye, Northrop. *Anatomy of Criticism: Four Essays*. Princeton: Princeton University Press, 1971.

———. *The Great Code: The Bible and Literature*. New York: Harcourt Brace Jovanovich, 1981.

Fukuyama, Francis. *The End of History and The Last Man*. New York: Free Press, 1992.

Gabler, Neal. *Life: The Movie: How Entertainment Conquered Reality*. New York: Alfred A. Knopf, 1998.

Gaffin, Richard B. Jr. *Resurrection and Redemption: A Study in Paul's Soteriology*. Phillipsburg, NJ: Presbyterian & Reformed, 1987.

Gnass, George E., ed. *Ignatius of Loyola: The Spiritual Exercises and Selected Works*. The Classics of Western Spirituality. Mahwah, NJ: Paulist, 1991.

Gombis, Timothy G. *The Drama of Ephesians: Participating in the Triumph of God*. Downers Grove, IL: InterVarsity, 2010.

Gordon, Cynthia. "Repetition and Identity Experiment: One Child's Use of Repetition as a Resource for 'Trying On' Maternal Identities." In *Selves and Identities in Narrative and Discourse*, edited by Michael Bamberg et al., 133–57. Studies in Narrative 9. Amsterdam: John Benjamins, 2007.

Green, Douglas. "Ezra-Nehemiah." In *A Complete Literary Guide to the Bible*, edited by Leland Ryken and Tremper Longman III, 206–15. Grand Rapids: Zondervan, 1993.

Guroian, Vigen. *Tending the Heart of Virtue: How Classic Stories Awaken a Child's Moral Imagination*. New York: Oxford University Press, 1998.

Halberstam, David. *The Best and the Brightest*. New York: Ballantine, 1993.

Harned, David Baily. *Images for Self-Recognition: The Christian as Player, Sufferer, and Vandal*. New York: Seabury, 1977.

Hauerwas, Stanley, and David Burrell. "From System to Story: An Alternative Pattern for Rationality in Ethics." In *Why Narrative? Readings in Narrative Theology*, edited by Stanley Hauerwas and L. Gregory Jones, 158–90. Grand Rapids: Eerdmans, 1989.

Hauerwas, Stanley, and L. Gregory Jones, eds. *Why Narrative? Readings in Narrative Theology*. Grand Rapids: Eerdmans, 1989.

Hays, Richard B. *The Moral Vision of the New Testament: A Contemporary Introduction to New Testament Ethics*. New York: HarperCollins, 1996.

Herder, Gottfried. *Shakespeare*. Translated by Gregory Moore. Princeton: Princeton University Press, 2008.

Hibbs, Thomas S. *Shows About Nothing: Nihilism in Popular Culture*. Waco, TX: Baylor University Press, 2012.

Hoffman, Alice. "*The Catcher in the Rye* by J.D. Salinger." In *The Book That Changed My Life*, edited by Roxanne J. Coady and Joy Johannessen, 84–85. New York: Gotham, 2006.

Holstein, James A., and Jaber F. Gubrium. *The Self We Live By: Narrative Identity in a Postmodern World*. Oxford: Oxford University Press, 2000.

Hooker, Morna D. *Endings: Invitations to Discipleship*. Peabody, MA: Hendrickson, 2003.

Horne, Milton P. *Proverbs-Ecclesiastes*. Smyth & Helwys Bible Commentary. Macon, GA, 2003.

Hoskyns, Edwyn Clement, and Francis Noel Davey. *The Fourth Gospel*. 2nd ed. London: Faber & Faber, 1947.

Howard-Brook, Wes, and Anthony Gwyther. *Unveiling Empire: Reading Revelation Then and Now.* Maryknoll, NJ: Orbis, 1999.

Hudson, Don. "Come, Bring your Story." *Mars Hill Review* 1 (1994) 73–88.

Hunsberger, George R. "Proposals for a Missional Hermeneutic: Mapping a Conversation." *Missiology: An International Review* 39/3 (July 2011) 309–21.

Hunter, James Davison. *To Change the World: The Irony, Tragedy, and Possibility of Christianity in the Late Modern World.* Oxford: Oxford University Press, 2010.

Huston, Matt, et al. "Insights: Past Meets Present." *Psychology Today* 49/3 (May-June 2016) 9–21.

Isaacs, Marie E. *Sacred Space: An Approach to the Theology of the Epistle to the Hebrews.* Journal for the Study of the New Testament Supplement 73. Sheffield, UK: Journal for the Study of the Old Testament, 1992.

Jacques, Brian. *A Redwall Winter's Tale.* Illustrated by Christopher Denise. New York: Philomel, 2001.

Jenson, Robert W. "How The World Lost Its Story." *First Things* 36 (Oct. 1992) 19–24.

Johnston, Robert K. *Reel Spirituality: Theology and Film in Dialogue.* 2nd ed. Engaging Culture. Grand Rapids: Baker Academic, 2006.

Jones, Morwenna. "How Cambridge University almost killed me." http://www.theguardian.com/education/2014/oct/06/cambridge-university-student-depression-eating-disorders.

Junger, Sebastian. "*Bury My Heart at Wounded Knee* by Dee Brown." In *The Book That Changed My Life,* edited by Roxanne J. Coady and Joy Johannessen, 86–87. New York: Gotham, 2006.

Kamps, Louisa. "The Story That Can Change Your Life." *Good Housekeeping* (July 2008) 119–25.

Kearney, Richard. *On Stories.* Thinking in Action. London: Routledge, 2002.

Keen, Ernest. "Paranoia and Cataclysmic Narratives." In *Narrative Psychology: The Storied Nature of Human Conduct,* edited by Theodore R. Sarbin, 174–90. New York: Praeger, 1986.

Kennedy, X. J., and Dana Gioia. *Literature: An Introduction to Fiction, Poetry, and Drama.* 2nd ed. New York: Longman, 2000.

Kidder, Tracy. "*Collected Stories* by Ernest Hemmingway." In *The Book That Changed My Life,* edited by Roxanne J. Coady and Joy Johannessen, 91–92. New York: Gotham, 2006.

Kimball, Dan. *The Emerging Church: Vintage Christianity for New Generations.* Grand Rapids: Zondervan, 2003.

Kirk, J. R. Daniel. *Unlocking Romans: Resurrection and the Justification of God.* Grand Rapids: Eerdmans, 2008.

Köstenberger, Andreas J. *A Theology of John's Gospel and Letters.* Grand Rapids: Zondervan, 2009.

Kurson, Robert. "*The Denial of Death* by Ernest Becker." In *The Book That Changed My Life,* edited by Roxanne J. Coady and Joy Johannessen, 93–94. New York: Gotham, 2006.

La Shell, John K. "Imagination and Idol: A Puritan Tension." *Westminster Theological Journal* 49/2 (Fall 1987) 305–34.

Lakoff, George, and Mark Johnson. *Metaphors We Live By.* 2nd rev. ed. Chicago: Chicago University Press, 2003.

Lamb, Charles. *The Essays of Elia and the Last Essays of Elia.* The World's Classics 2. London: Oxford University Press, 1951.

Lamott, Anne. "*The Only Dance There Is* by Ram Dass." In *The Book That Changed My Life,* edited by Roxanne J. Coady and Joy Johannessen, 99–101. New York: Gotham, 2006.

Leitch, Thomas M. *What Stories Are: Narrative Theory and Interpretation.* University Park: Pennsylvania State University Press, 1986.

Lewis, C. S. *An Experiment in Criticism.* Cambridge: Cambridge University Press, 1961.

Lewis, Robert. *La Crianza de un Caballero Moderno.* Translated by Raquel Monsalve. Colorado Springs, CO: Focus on the Family, 2009.

Long, Thomas G. "Out of the Loop." In *What's the Shape of Narrative Preaching?*, edited by Mike Graves and David J. Schlafer, 115–30. St. Louis: Chalice, 2008.

Long, V. Philips. *The Art of Biblical History.* Foundations of Contemporary Interpretation 5. Grand Rapids: Zondervan, 1994.

Longman, Tremper III. *The Book of Ecclesiastes.* New International Commentary on the Old Testament. Grand Rapids: Eerdmans, 1998.

———. *Literary Approaches to Biblical Interpretation.* Foundations of Contemporary Interpretation 3. Grand Rapids: Zondervan, 1987.

———. *Reading the Bible with Heart and Mind*. Colorado Springs, CO: NavPress, 1997.

Longman, Tremper III, and Daniel G. Reid. *God is a Warrior*. Studies in Old Testament Biblical Theology. Grand Rapids: Zondervan, 1995.

Lonsdale, David. "Ignatian Spirituality." In *The New Westminster Dictionary of Christian Spirituality*, edited by Philip Sheldrake, 354–56. Louisville, KY: Westminster John Knox, 2005.

Lucie-Smith, Alexander. *Narrative Theology and Moral Theology: The Infinite Horizon*. Burlington, VT: Ashgate, 2007.

Luis Borges, Jorge. "The Gospel According to Mark." Translated by Norman Thomas di Giovanni. In *Literature: An Introduction to Fiction, Poetry, and Drama*, by X. J. Kennedy and Dana Gioia, 2nd ed., 167–71. New York: Longman, 2000.

Lyotard, Jean-François. *The Postmodern Condition: A Report on Knowledge*. Translated by Geoff Bennington and Brian Massumi. Theory and History of Literature 10. Minneapolis: University of Minnesota Press, 1984.

MacIntyre, Alasdair. "Epistemological Crises, Dramatic Narrative, and the Philosophy of Science." In *Why Narrative? Readings in Narrative Theology*, edited by Stanley Hauerwas and L. Gregory Jones, 138–57. Grand Rapids: Eerdmans, 1989.

———. "The Virtues, the Unity of a Human Life, and the Concept of a Tradition." In *Why Narrative? Readings in Narrative Theology*, edited by Stanley Hauerwas and L. Gregory Jones, 89–110. Grand Rapids: Eerdmans, 1989.

Malina, Bruce J., and John J. Pilch. *Social-Science Commentary on the Book of Revelation*. Minneapolis: Fortress, 2000.

McAdams, Dan P. "Personal Narratives and the Life Story." In *Handbook of Personality: Theory and Research*, 3rd ed., edited by Oliver P. John et al., 242–58. New York: Guilford, 2008.

———. *The Redemptive Self: Stories Americans Live By*. Oxford: Oxford University Press, 2006.

McAdams, Dan P., and Regina L. Logan. "Creative Work, Love, and the Dialectic in Selected Life Stories of Academics." In *Identity and Story: Creating Self in Narrative*, edited by Dan P. McAdams et al., 89–107. Washington, DC: American Psychological Association, 2006.

McCain, John. "*For Whom the Bell Tolls* by Ernest Hemingway." In *The Book That Changed My Life*, edited by Roxanne J. Coady and Joy Johannessen, 109–11. New York: Gotham, 2006.

McCartney, Dan. *James*. Baker Exegetical Commentary on the New Testament. Grand Rapids, 2009.

McCartney, Dan, and Charles Clayton. *Let the Reader Understand: A Guide to Interpreting and Applying the Bible*. 2nd ed. Phillipsburg, NJ: Presbyterian & Reformed, 2002.

McGrath, Alister E. *What Was God Doing on the Cross?* Eugene, OR: Wipf & Stock, 2002.

McKee, Robert. *Story: Substance, Structure, and the Principles of Screenwriting*. New York: HarperCollins, 1997.

McLaren, Brian D. *A Generous Orthodoxy*. Grand Rapids: Zondervan, 2004.

McLeod, John. "The Significance of Narrative and Storytelling in Postpsychological Counseling and Therapy." In *Healing Plots: The Narrative Basis of Psychotherapy*, edited by Amia Lieblich et al., 11–27. Washington, DC: American Psychological Association, 2004.

Meek, Esther Lightcap. *Loving to Know: Introducing Covenant Epistemology*. Eugene, OR: Cascade, 2011.

Middleton, J. Richard, and Brian J. Walsh. *Truth Is Stranger Than It Used to Be: Biblical Faith in a Postmodern Age*. Downers Grove, IL: InterVarsity, 1995.

Miller, Donald. *A Million Miles in a Thousand Years: What I Learned While Editing My Life*. Nashville: Thomas Nelson, 2009.

Miller, Paul E. *A Praying Life: Connecting with God in a Distracting World*. Colorado Springs, CO: NavPress, 2009.

Moore, Robert L. "Theory and Discoveries." http://www.robertmoore-phd.com.

Morray-Jones, C. R. A. "Paradise Revisited (2 Cor 12:1–12): The Jewish Mystical Background of Paul's Apostolate Part 2: Paul's Heavenly Ascent and its Significance." *Harvard Theological Review* 86/3 (1993) 265–92.

Morrison, Matt. *Key Concepts in Creative Writing*. Palgrave Key Concepts. Basingstoke, UK: Palgrave MacMillan, 2010.

Murray, Kevin. "The Construction of Identity in the Narratives of Romance and Comedy." In *Texts of Identity*, edited by John Shotter and Kenneth J. Gergen, 176–205. Inquiries in Social Construction 2. London: Sage, 1989.

———. "Literary Pathfinding: The Work of Popular Life Constructors." In *Narrative Psychology: The Storied Nature of Human Conduct*, edited by Theodore R. Sarbin, 276–92. New York: Praeger, 1986.

Newman, Carey C. "Acts." In *A Complete Literary Guide to the Bible*, edited by Leland Ryken and Tremper Longman III, 436–44. Grand Rapids: Zondervan, 1993.

Neyrey, Jerome H. "The Symbolic World of Luke-Acts." In *The Social World of Luke-Acts: Models for Interpretation*, edited by Jerome H. Neyrey, 271–304. Peabody, MA: Hendrickson, 1991.

Niebuhr, H. Richard. "The Story of our Life." In *Why Narrative? Readings in Narrative Theology*, edited by Stanley Hauerwas and L. Gregory Jones, 21–44. Grand Rapids: Eerdmans, 1989.

Novak, Michael. *Ascent of the Mountain, Flight of the Dove*. New York: Harper & Row, 1971.

———. *The Rise of the Unmeltable Ethnics*. New York: MacMillan, 1971.

Novelli, Michael. *Shaped by the Story: Helping Students Encounter God in a New Way*. Grand Rapids: Zondervan, 2008.

Nussbaum, Martha C. *Upheavals of Thought: The Intelligence of Emotions*. Cambridge: Cambridge University Press, 2003.

O'Dwyer, Cáit. *Imagining One's Future: A Projective Approach to Christian Maturity*. Rome: Editrice Pontificia Università Gregoriana, 2000.

Old, Hughes Oliphant. *The Age of the Reformation*. Vol. 4 of *The Reading and Preaching of the Scriptures in the Worship of the Christian Church*. Grand Rapids: Eerdmans, 2002.

Olin, John C., ed. *The Autobiography of St. Ignatius Loyola*. Translated by Joseph F. O'Callaghan. New York: Harper & Row, 1974.

Owen, Wilfrid. "Strange Meeting." In *The Poems of Wilfrid Owen*, 95–96. Ware, UK: Wordsworth Editions, 2002.

Pennoyer, Greg, and Gregory Wolfe, eds. *God With Us: Rediscovering the Meaning of Christmas*. Brewster, MA: Paraclete, 2007.

Pépin, Jacques. "*The Myth of Sisyphus* by Albert Camus." In *The Book That Changed My Life*, edited by Roxanne J. Coady and Joy Johannessen, 132–36. New York: Gotham, 2006.

Perry, Anne. "*The Man Who Was Thursday* by G.K. Chesterton." In *The Book That Changed My Life*, edited by Roxanne J. Coady and Joy Johannessen, 137–39. New York: Gotham, 2006.

Peterson, Eugene H. *Eat This Book: A Conversation in the Art of Spiritual Reading*. Grand Rapids: Eerdmans, 2006.

———. Introduction to *Stories for the Christian Year*, edited by Eugene H. Peterson, vii–ix. New York: Collier, 1994.

———, ed. *Stories for the Christian Year*. New York: Collier, 1994.

Plato. *Republic*. Edited and translated by Chris Emlyn-Jones and William Preddy. Loeb Classical Library 276. Cambridge, MA: Harvard University Press, 2013.

Powlison, David. "Illustrative Counseling." *Journal of Biblical Counseling* 16/2 (Winter 1998) 49–53.

———. *Speaking the Truth in Love: Counseling in Community*. Greensboro, NC: New Growth, 2005.

Poythress, Vern S. *Symphonic Theology: The Validity of Multiple Perspectives in Theology*. Grand Rapids: Zondervan, 1987.

Pratt, Richard L. Jr. *He Gave Us Stories: The Bible Student's Guide to Interpreting Old Testament Narratives*. Phillipsburg, NJ: Presbyterian & Reformed, 1993.

Propp, V. *Morphology of the Folktale*. Translated by Lawrence Scott. Bloomington: Indiana University Research Center in Anthropology, Folklore, and Linguistics, 1968.

Rainer, Tristine. *Your Life as Story: Discovering the "New Autobiography" and Writing Memoir as Literature*. New York: Jeremy P. Tarcher, 1997.

Reid, D. G. "Principalities and Powers." In *Dictionary of Paul and his Letters*, edited by Gerald F. Hawthorne et al., 746–52. Downers Grove, IL: InterVarsity, 1993.

Rhoads, David, et al. *Mark as Story: An Introduction to the Narrative of a Gospel*. 3rd ed. Minneapolis: Fortress, 2012.

Richardson, Don. *Peace Child*. 3rd ed. Glendale, CA: G/L Publications, 1976.

Robinson, John A., and Linda Hawpe. "Narrative Thinking as a Heuristic Process." In *Narrative Psychology: The Storied Nature of Human Conduct*, edited by Theodore R. Sarbin, 111–25. New York: Praeger, 1986.

Rookmaaker, H. R. *Modern Art and the Death of a Culture*. Downers Grove, IL: InterVarsity, 1970.

Rosenblatt, Louise M. *Literature as Exploration*. New York: Appleton-Century, 1938.

Rossi, Philip J. "Narrative, Worship, and Ethics: Empowering Images of the Shape of Christian Moral Life." *Journal of Religious Ethics* 7/2 (1979) 239–48.

Ryken, Leland. *Windows to the World: Literature in Christian Perspective*. Eugene, OR: Wipf & Stock, 2000.

Ryken, Leland, and Tremper Longman III, eds. *A Complete Literary Guide to the Bible*. Grand Rapids: Zondervan, 1993.

Sandars, N. K., ed. and trans. *The Epic of Gilgamesh*. Rev. ed. Penguin Classics. London, 1960.

Sarbin, Theodore R. "The Narrative as a Root Metaphor for Psychology." In *Narrative Psychology: The Storied Nature of Human Conduct*, edited by Theodore R. Sarbin, 3–21. New York: Praeger, 1986.

———, ed. *Narrative Psychology: The Storied Nature of Human Conduct*. New York: Praeger, 1986.

SARK. "*I Know Why the Caged Bird Sings*, by Maya Angelou." In *The Book That Changed My Life*, edited by Roxanne J. Coady and Joy Johannessen, 149–50. New York: Gotham, 2006.

Schaeffer, Frank. *Crazy for God: How I Grew Up as One of the Elect, Helped Found the Religious Right, and Lived to Take All (or Almost All) of It Back*. New York: Carroll & Graf, 2007.

Scheibe, Karl E. "Self-Narratives and Adventure." In *Narrative Psychology: The Storied Nature of Human Conduct*, edited by Theodore R. Sarbin, 129–51. New York: Praeger, 1986.

Schmemann, Alexander. *For the Life of the World: Sacraments and Orthodoxy*. 2nd ed. Crestwood, NY: St Vladimir's Seminary, 2004.

Schmidt, Victoria Lynn. *45 Master Characters*. Cincinnati: Writer's Digest, 2001.

Schweitzer, Albert. *The Mysticism of Paul the Apostle*. Translated by William Montgomery. Baltimore: Johns Hopkins University Press, 1998.

Scobie, Charles H. H. "A Canonical Approach to Interpreting Luke: The Journey Motif as a Hermeneutical Key." In *Reading Luke: Interpretation, Reflection, Formation*, edited by Craig G. Bartholomew et al., 327–49. Scripture and Hermeneutics 6. Grand Rapids: Zondervan, 2005.

Scott, J. Julius Jr. *Jewish Backgrounds of the New Testament*. Grand Rapids: Baker, 1995.

Scott, J. M. "The Triumph of God in 2 Cor 2.14: Additional Evidence of Merkabah Mysticism in Paul." *New Testament Studies* 42 (1996) 260–81.

Scott, Ridley, dir. *Gladiator*. Universal City, CA: DreamWorks, 2000.

Shakespeare, William. *The Complete Works of William Shakespeare*. Edited by Arthur Henry Bullen. Reprint, New York: Barnes & Noble, 1994.

Shaw, Luci. "Epiphany." In *Stories for the Christian Year*, edited by Eugene H. Peterson, 40–48. New York: Collier, 1994.

Shelley, Percy Bysshe. "Ozymandias." https://www.poets.org/poetsorg/poem/ozymandias.

Siegel, Bernie S. "*The Human Comedy* by William Saroyan." In *The Book That Changed My Life*, edited by Roxanne J. Coady and Joy Johannessen, 154–56. New York: Gotham, 2006.

Singer, Jefferson A. "Living in the Amber Cloud: A Life Story Analysis of a Heroin Addict." In *Turns in the Road: Narrative Studies of Lives in Transition*, edited by Dan P. McAdams et al., 253–77. Washington, DC: American Psychological Association, 2001.

Slade, Carol. "Comments & Questions." In *Don Quixote*, by Miguel de Cervantes, translated by Tobias Smollett, with introduction and notes by Carol Slade, 897–900. Barnes & Noble Classics. New York, 2004.

Smith, Adrian T. "The Fifth Gospel." In *Eyes to See, Ears to Hear: Essays in Memory of J. Alan Groves*, edited by Peter Enns et al., 77–91. Phillipsburg, NJ: Presbyterian & Reformed, 2010.

———. *The Representation of Speech Events in Chariton's "Callirhoe" and the Acts of the Apostles*. Linguistic Biblical Studies 10. Leiden: Brill, 2014.

Snyder, Blake. *Save the Cat! The Last Book on Screenwriting You'll Ever Need*. Studio City, CA: Michael Wiese Production, 2005.

Steele, Robert S. "Deconstructing Histories: Toward a Systematic Criticism of Psychological Narratives." In *Narrative Psychology: The Storied Nature of Human Conduct*, edited by Theodore R. Sarbin, 256–75. New York: Praeger, 1986.

Stoddard, Alexandra. "*Letters to a Young Poet* by Rainer Maria Rilke." In *The Book That Changed My Life*, edited by Roxanne J. Coady and Joy Johannessen, 165–67. New York: Gotham, 2006.

Stott, John. *The Contemporary Christian: Applying God's Word to Today's World*. Downers Grove, IL: InterVarsity, 1992.

Strom, Mark. *Reframing Paul: Conversations in Grace and Community*. Downers Grove, IL: InterVarsity, 2000.

———. *The Symphony of Scripture: Making Sense of the Bible's Many Themes*. Phillipsburg, NJ: Presbyterian & Reformed, 1990.

Stroup, George W. *The Promise of Narrative Theology: Recovering the Gospel in the Church*. Eugene, OR: Wipf & Stock, 1997.

Sutton-Smith, Brian. "Children's Fiction Making." In *Narrative Psychology: The Storied Nature of Human Conduct*, edited by Theodore R. Sarbin, 67–90. New York: Praeger, 1986.

Swartley, Willard M. *Israel's Scripture Traditions and the Synoptic Gospels: Story Shaping Story*. Peabody, MA: Hendrickson, 1994.

Sykes, S. W. "Story and Eucharist." *Interpretation: A Journal of Bible and Theology* 37/4 (Oct. 1983) 365–76.

Tannehill, Robert C. "The Disciples in Mark: The Function of a Narrative Role." *Journal of Religion* 57 (1977) 386–405.

Taylor, Daniel. *The Healing Power of Stories: Creating Yourself Through the Stories of Your Life*. New York: Doubleday, 1996.

Thomas, Susan Gregory, et al. "Rewrite Your Life." *Psychology Today* 49/3 (May-June 2016) 50–59.

Tidball, Derek. *The Social Context of the New Testament*. Grand Rapids: Zondervan, 1984.

Tilley, Allen. *An Introduction to Plot in the Modes of Experience*. Jacksonville, FL: Stone Snake, 2009.

———. *Plot Snakes and the Dynamics of Narrative Experience*. Gainesville, FL: University of Florida Press, 1992.

Tilley, Terence W. *Story Theology*. Collegeville, MN: Liturgical, 1990.

Tobias, Ronald B. *20 Master Plots (And How to Build Them)*. Cincinnati: Writer's Digest, 1993.

Toffler, Alvin. *The Third Wave*. New York: Bantam, 1980.

Tolkien, J. R. R. *The Two Towers: Being the Second Part of The Lord of the Rings*. Boston: Houghton Mifflin, 1999.

Tölölyan, Khachig. "Narrative Culture and the Motivation of the Terrorist." In *Texts of Identity*, edited by John Shotter and Kenneth J. Gergen, 99–118. Inquiries in Social Construction 2. London: Sage, 1989.

Tomkins, Silvan S. "Script Theory." In *The Emergence of Personality*, edited by Joel Aronoff et al., 147–216. New York: Springer, 1987.

Tripp, Paul David. *Lost in the Middle: Midlife and the Grace of God*. Wapwallopen, PA: Shepherd, 2004.

Turner, Victor. "Social Dramas and Stories about Them." *Critical Inquiry* 7/1 (Autumn 1980) 141–68.

Underhill, Evelyn. *Worship*. New York: Harper & Row, 1936.

Virgil. *Aeneid*. Translated by Stanley Lombardo. Indianapolis: Hackett, 2005.

Vos, Geerhardus. *Biblical Theology: Old and New Testaments*. 1948. Reprint, Edinburgh: Banner of Truth Trust, 1975.

———. *The Pauline Eschatology*. 1930. Reprint, Phillipsburg, NJ: Presbyterian & Reformed, 1994.

Walbert, Kate. "*Charlotte's Web* by E.B. White." In *The Book That Changed My Life*, edited by Roxanne J. Coady and Joy Johannessen, 173–4. New York: Gotham, 2006.

Waltke, Bruce K., with Charles Yu. *An Old Testament Theology: An Exegetical, Canonical, and Thematic Approach*. Grand Rapids: Zondervan, 2007.

Whitman, Walt. "O Me! O Life!" In *Leaves of Grass*, 215. Philadelphia: David McKay, 1891–1892.

Wilcock, Michael. *The Message of Revelation*. The Bible Speaks Today. Downers Grove, IL: InterVarsity, 1984.

Wilkens, Steve and Mark L. Sanford. *Hidden Worldviews: Eight Cultural Stories that Shape our Lives*. Downers Grove, IL: InterVarsity, 2009.

Winkler, Matthew. "What Makes a Hero?" http://ed.ted.com/lessons/what-makes-a-hero-matthew-winkler#review.

Wood, James. *How Fiction Works*. New York: Farrar, Straus, and Giroux, 2008.

Wright, N. T. *The Climax of the Covenant: Christ and the Law in Pauline Theology*. Minneapolis: Fortress, 1992.

———. *What Saint Paul Really Said*. Grand Rapids: Eerdmans, 1997.

Wyatt, Frederick. "The Narrative in Psychoanalysis: Psychoanalytic Notes on Storytelling, Listening, and Interpreting." In *Narrative Psychology: The Storied Nature of Human Conduct*, edited by Theodore R. Sarbin, 193–210. New York: Praeger, 1986.

Young, Katherine. "Narrative Embodiments: Enclaves of the Self in the Realm of Medicine." In *Texts of Identity*, edited by John Shotter and Kenneth J. Gergen, 152–65. Inquiries in Social Construction 2. London: Sage, 1989.

Zak, Paul J. "Empathy, Neurochemistry, and the Dramatic Arc." https://futureofstorytelling.org/video/empathy-neurochemistry-and-the-dramatic-arc.

www.ingramcontent.com/pod-product-compliance
Lightning Source LLC
Chambersburg PA
CBHW080934300426
44115CB00017B/2813